BEFORE SCARLETT

Girlhood Writings of Margaret Mitchell

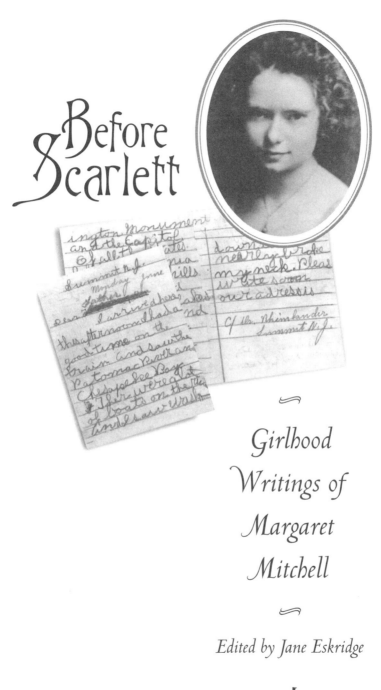

Before Scarlett

Girlhood
Writings of
Margaret
Mitchell

Edited by Jane Eskridge

Hill Street Press **d** Athens, Georgia

A HILL STREET PRESS BOOK

Published in the United States of America by
Hill Street Press LLC   191 East Broad Street, Suite 209   Athens, Georgia 30601-2848 USA
706-613-7200   info@hillstreetpress.com   hillstreetpress.com

"The Little Pioneers," "Forest and Foothills," and "Two Little Folk," by Margaret Mitchell copyright ©2000 The Trust Company Bank, as Executor Under the Will of Stephens Mitchell. Printed by permission of G.W.T.W. Literary Rights, Inc., with the assistance of the Hargrett Rare Book and Manuscript Library, University of Georgia Libraries.
Foreword copyright ©2000 by Mary Rose Taylor.
Preface, Introduction, section introductions, photographic reproductions of Margaret Mitchell's writings, and all other writings by Margaret Mitchell not specified above copyright ©2000 by Jane Eskridge.
A portion of "Hugh Warren, A Spy for the Union" was originally published as "Through the Eyes of Youth: A Civil War Story," edited by Jane Powers Weldon, in the *Atlanta Historical Journal.* Reprinted by permission of G.W.T.W. Literary Rights, Inc.

Photograph on page 7, courtesy of the Atlanta History Center. ✍ All other photographs, courtesy of G.W.T.W Literary Rights, Inc. and the Hargrett Rare Book and Manuscript Library, University of Georgia Libraries.

All rights reserved.
Text and cover design by Anne Richmond Boston.
Printed in the United States of America.

Library of Congress Cataloging-in-Publication Data

Mitchell, Margaret, 1900-1949
     Before Scarlett : girlhood writings of Margaret Mitchell
        p.   cm.
     ISBN 1-892514-62-1 (alk. paper)
     1. Children's writings, American I. Title.
     PS3525.I972 .B44 2000
     813'.52—dc21   00-023513

ISBN# 1-892514-62-1
10   9   8   7   6   5   4   3   2   1
First printing

Contents

～

Foreword

⌐∽

We at the Margaret Mitchell House and Museum believe that teachers live on the side of angels. When you read this exquisitely edited collection of Margaret Mitchell's girlhood writings, you will probably agree. Jane Eskridge, who discovered these writings with her friend Wailes Thomas in moldering boxes in a basement of a family house in Atlanta, and then seamlessly wove them together in this book, is a middle school teacher in Greensboro, North Carolina. From the moment of her discovery, the teacher in Jane understood the value of this collection, not in dollars and cents but rather as a window into the creative mind of a young Southern girl who would one day write *Gone With the Wind*, the world's most beloved novel.

As her brother Stephens described it, Margaret was writing almost from the time she could hold a pencil. Inspiration surrounded her. Many a Sunday afternoon, she would gather with relatives on the veranda of her Jackson Hill home listening with rapt attention to the stories of her ancestors who had been fighting in wars since the early Irish Rebellions. Sitting on the lap of her Grandfather Mitchell, she moved her fingers through the groove in his forehead, carved out by minié balls during the Civil War. Always the tomboy, she rode ponies with her "boon companions" from the Confederate Veterans Home and played military games along the banks of Confederate trenches that ran through her backyard.

Steeped in the Southern tradition of storytelling, as well as the children's pulp fiction of the time, Margaret's earliest stories reveal a remarkable gift for well-developed beginnings, middles, and endings—an achievement for a writer of any age. Initially, her subjects were her animals. (Margaret had cats, ducks, and a pony.) Quickly she progressed to fairy tales and then on to adventure stories set in exotic locations. Often she placed her friends and family, even herself, in her stories.

By the time she is twelve, Margaret is writing about loftier subjects. In the story that Jane has titled "Hugh Warren, A Spy for the Union," Margaret portrays the moral dilemma facing a father who learns that his son is a spy for the enemy. In her teenage years, Margaret selects New York and San Francisco as locales for her plots, and she imports a character from France. At fifteen, she sets a play in Japan, creating a lead role for herself in a play about the Ku Klux Klan, and writes an essay about relations between the United States and Mexico in the days leading up to World War I.

Throughout this book we learn about Margaret's personal thoughts which she records in intimate detail in her journals. Like many teenage girls, she complains that her mother doesn't understand her: "[Mother] thinks I have no ambition I suppose—but I have," she writes. "Perhaps it's very small but it's there alright." And with the astute analysis that characterizes her later work, she describes a new girl at school: "She looks like a girl with hard, common sense. Also, I'll wager she likes the out-of-doors, reading, writing, and acting." Her ability, for which she would later become so renown, to develop a character through descriptive detail is revealed in a journal entry of 1916. Reflecting on the boys of summer at

Wrightsville Beach, North Carolina, she writes: "I never think of the ocean, but that I see him—6 ft. of hard, bronze muscle, in his bathing suit, standing with folded arms, staring out over the water. . . . He was one man I feared, and yet, liked. It was the pure brute strength of that man that I feared, and the same brute strength that fascinated me."

During her high school years, under the guidance of her English teacher, Eva Paisley, Margaret saw her short stories published in the school yearbook. "Little Sister," the story of a young American girl in Mexico, who witnesses the murder of her parents and hears the cries of her older sister being raped by bandits, was published in her junior year. In her senior year, Margaret published "Sergeant Terry," a story in which she ponders the fate of women whose men are off at war. It was a foreshadowing of the young writer's own fate. She would become engaged and lose her fiancé to World War I before the year was over.

Like other art forms, literature is closely intertwined with the history and politics that shape the artist's perspective, and so it is with Margaret Mitchell. While we cannot know the extent of the conversations that took place within the Mitchell household, we do know that Margaret's parents were actively involved in the affairs of their day.

When Leo Frank, a Jew, was accused of murdering young Mary Phagan in an Atlanta pencil factory, Margaret's father, a lawyer, wrote a brief in his defense. After Frank was convicted and before he was lynched by a group of vigilantes, Eugene Mitchell, then president of the Georgia Bar Association, wrote a letter to the Atlanta newspapers calling for an appeal of his conviction. This was a time as haunting for Jews in Atlanta as the 1906 race riots were for blacks.

Equally tenacious in pursuit of her own convictions was Margaret's mother May Belle. A staunch Irish Catholic, May Belle was incensed when Georgia politician Tom Watson campaigned across Georgia, espousing views that were anti-Semitic, anti-black, and anti-Catholic. At a time when women still had not achieved the right to vote, she co-founded the Catholic Layman's Association, a men's organization, to combat religious prejudice. She also was a leader in the Woman's Suffrage Movement.

Perhaps these early events of Margaret's childhood and her parents' strong influence explain her interest, seen often in this collection, both in the broad sweep of human conflict and her favoring of heroines over heroes in her girlhood stories—to say nothing of her ability, so in evidence in her famous historical novel, to portray characters possessed of the kind of strength and passion she saw in her own parents.

This collection of newly discovered writings and archival material is remarkable in that it marks the evolution of a Southern woman writer in the early part of the twentieth century, a world vastly different from the one we know today in terms of race, gender, and religious tolerance. As a complement to Mitchell's best-known work, it provides Mitchell scholars and enthusiasts with the rare opportunity to see her development as a writer. It is my hope that the discovery and publication of these girlhood writings helps to preserve Mitchell's legacy and introduces new generations to the imagination and craft of her writing.

MARY ROSE TAYLOR
Executive Director
Margaret Mitchell House and Museum
Atlanta, Georgia

Preface

❦

I magine you are in Atlanta in mid-August during one of the hottest weeks of the summer. It is only eleven in the morning, but already you are feeling the oppressive heat and humidity. The attic fan is blowing but is useless in providing any relief. There is a portrait of Margaret Mitchell in the dining room, a pencil sketch of the author in the hallway, and a much-published photograph of Mitchell and her cat placed prominently on the table across the room. For the past five days, you have been going through closets and drawers, trying to sort a sixty-year accumulation of things in the old house. You are on your fifth glass of iced tea and wondering if you can justify taking a break. Behind you are five large cardboard boxes labeled "Family," "Buenos Aires," "Portraits," "Ikebana," and "Margaret Mitchell." The "Margaret Mitchell" box contains newspaper clippings and memorial issues of the *Atlanta Journal Magazine.*

You veto the idea of taking a break and plunge into the first of five boxes that have been brought up from the basement. The box is filthy and partially crushed. You keep an eye out for dead roaches as you pull out the first item, a mildewed black shoe. Next comes stained lace that has been wrapped around a piece of cardboard, and then comes dried-up tubes of paint. You next retrieve some ten or so small white envelopes. Opening one, you read the name "May Belle" as the signature on a letter. The name does not ring a bell, so you put the letters aside to try to discover later which family member this might be. Then you find what looks like an address book. It is dark green, about six-by-four inches in size. On the inside front cover you see written in a child's hand:

![handwritten inscription reading "Margaret Mitchell 1149 Peachtree Atlanta, Ga. Jan 1, 1913"]

Turning to the first page, you see "The Green Snake," "Big Bob of the Sierras," and "Just a Greaser." Skimming through the book, you realize that these are story titles. You scream with excitement.

By the time the box is empty, you have two 1910 letters from Margaret to her father from Summit, New Jersey; four handmade books (written between 1912 and 1913) containing the story "Forest and Foothills," one untitled shipwreck story, one untitled Civil War story and the beginning chapters of another; two copybooks (circa 1913) containing a poem and the stories "The Green Snake," "Big Bob of the Sierras," "The Greaser," "Old Brindle," "The Silver Match Box," "Steve of the X-B," and an untitled story about Native Americans; a play about Japan and an essay, "If Roosevelt Had Been President," (both written in 1916); and eight journal entries (written between 1915 and 1916) describing everyday happenings. You learn the letters you had first taken from the box turn out to be from Margaret Mitchell's mother, May Belle Stephens Mitchell.

↩

This is how Wailes Thomas and I discovered the stories and journal entries written by the young Margaret Mitchell which are part of the collection in this volume. To understand how they happened to be in the basement of Wailes's house, a brief explanation of the family connection is needed.

Wailes's aunt, Margueryte Reynolds Sharp, was married to Glascock Reynolds, a noted portrait painter of the 1940s and 1950s. Stephens Mitchell, Margaret Mitchell's only sibling, was Glascock's brother-in-law. After the death of her second husband, Wailes's aunt came to live with his mother. The box containing Mitchell's childhood writings was one of five boxes used to store some of the books from the library of Joseph S. Reynolds, Glascock Reynolds's and Carrie Lou Mitchell's father.

In editing the material for this collection, I corrected spelling and standardized capitalization. Some minor changes in punctuation, as in the treatment of dialogue, have been made to avoid misreading. Very occasionally, verb tenses have been changed to agree with surrounding material for the sake of clarity. Brackets denote missing or interpolated material. When pages or words are known or can be assumed to be missing, this is noted.

The young author rarely erased or rewrote anything in her stories. They are all first drafts. Margaret wrote in a copybook, "Born writers make their characters real, living people, while the 'made' writers have merely stuffed figures who dance when the strings are pulled . . .

That's how I know that I'm a 'made' writer." There are many who would disagree with this assessment of her writing, even in these early examples.

Margaret Mitchell Marsh requested that her unpublished writings be destroyed upon her death. We feel fortunate that this material survived and that we didn't toss out that dilapidated cardboard box before checking the contents. Besides being fun to read, these treasures from Mitchell's childhood give new insight into the development of her talents as a gifted writer and storyteller.

Introduction

⤳

Margaret Munnerlyn Mitchell was born in Atlanta on November 8, 1900. Her parents, May Belle and Eugene Muse Mitchell, were part of the "old guard" of the city. Relatives on the Mitchell side of the family had resided in the Atlanta area for five generations, many distinguishing themselves as civic leaders, politicians, and soldiers. Margaret's mother's family traced their Catholic heritage in the South to the seventeenth century and, more directly, from Phillip Fitzgerald and John Stephens who came from Ireland in successive generations.

As an infant, circa 1901

The Mitchells lived at 179 Jackson Street. The family's sprawling two-storied Victorian house consisted of twelve rooms and was painted red with yellow trim. It boasted a deep porch covered with honeysuckle vines where Margaret loved to sit and read. The house was down the street from Maybelle's mother, Annie Stephens, and next door to Ruth and David Crockett, May Belle's sister and brother-in-law. Both May Belle and Eugene Mitchell came from very large families which provided Margaret and her brother Stephens with twenty or more aunts and uncles. Quite a few of these relatives also resided in this genteel, well-to-do neighborhood.

Tomboyish Margaret climbing a tree, possibly at the Mitchell's Jackson Hill home

The Crockett cousins, Stephens and David, were constant playmates of Margaret and her brother, who was five years older than Margaret. There was a vacant lot nearby where the Crocketts, Mitchells, and other neighborhood children spent their playtime building forts on long-forgotten Confederate breastworks or playing generals in an old pavilion tent commandeered for just that purpose. They flew kites, skated, played baseball and football, and had glorious mudball fights. In *Margaret Mitchell and Her People*, brother Stephens commented, "I remember Margaret in several of these engagements, crouching behind the big girders and passing mudballs to the larger boys in front." The Mitchells had a Texas pony that both children learned to ride almost as soon as they could sit in the saddle. Stephens summed up the essence of these carefree days when he wrote that he and Margaret spent their safe and secure childhoods agonizing over how to spend their nickel allowances, having lemonade parties on the lawn, going to school, and obeying their parents.

Margaret enjoyed being a tomboy. She had a bad scare at about age three when her dress caught fire after she got too close to an open grate. Luckily she was not hurt, but May Belle Mitchell dressed her in boy's clothes from then until she entered grade school. Margaret's blonde hair was tucked under a cap and her new appearance earned her the nickname "Jimmy" after a cartoon character in the newspaper.

Summertime vacations found the Mitchells en route to the mountains or the beach. Perhaps the most-anticipated vacation for the children was when their parents left them with great-aunts Mamie and Sadie Fitzgerald at their mother's family homeplace in Clayton County, Georgia. Great-aunt Sadie had lost a beau during the Civil War and was known as the beauty of the family. Neither she nor her sister Mamie ever married.

Stephens remembered these days fondly. He has written that he and his sister ran barefoot, played, rode the farm's old mules, gathered fruit from the orchards, and tried their hands at picking cotton. Margaret endured the painful scratches and finger-pricks caused by cotton-picking so she could earn extra spending money. Every night the children fetched cool spring water from a well to wash their grimy feet.

In 1906, Eugene Mitchell and his family were caught up in the race riots that broke out in Atlanta. Over a five-day period beginning on September 22, at least ten blacks and two whites were killed. Rumors were rampant. White rioters threatened the city and Atlanta was put under martial law. At the height of the tension, the Mitchells's neighbor John Slaton went up and down Jackson Street warning the men to secure their homes and arm themselves. All Eugene Mitchell found was an ax and an old waterkey until five-year-old Margaret suggested using Mr. Daley's sword. He added the sword to his weaponry and kept watch through the night.

Stephens said that his sister learned to read before she went to school and that she made up stories even before she learned to write. Her first stories were written in books she made by hand, but Margaret soon began to use store-bought memorandum books that could hold up to three of her stories.

Margaret was enrolled for first grade at Forrest Avenue School in Atlanta and, at age six, decided that there was absolutely no rhyme or reason for learning arithmetic. She later recounted that her mother's reaction to this decision was quick and to the point. May Belle Mitchell put Margaret into the family buggy and headed out toward Jonesboro, twenty miles south of Atlanta, showing her all the destroyed houses along the road. She called the blackened chimneys "Sherman's sentinels." She told Margaret that wealthy people had once lived in the houses and, though some had been destroyed by Sherman, others had decayed because the owners lacked backbone. The gist of the warning that she imparted was that Margaret would need an education to fall back on when hard times hit. Margaret listened to her mother's words, but never did become proficient at math.

May Belle kept a tight rein on the children and believed the old adage "spare the rod and spoil the child." Corporal punishment in the Mitchell household was accomplished with the use of May Belle's size three slipper or a hairbrush, whichever was handy. Stephens said that his mother would take Margaret upstairs to spank her when she was unresponsive and shy with people. Mrs. Mitchell considered this rude and believed "rudeness ranks with sins which cry to heaven for vengeance." Other attempts were made to turn Margaret into a young lady of grace and manners. She learned deportment from the Hudson sisters and dancing from a Professor Segadlo.

By 1912 the Mitchell family moved into a Colonial Revival mansion on Atlanta's fashionable Peachtree Street. Margaret had two special places to read and write her stories in the new locale: a ring of privet hedge in the backyard that kept her safe from prying eyes, and her bedroom which served as her sanctuary when she was indoors.

With brother Stephens off at school and her old gang of cousins and chums left behind, Margaret was soon forming a new set of friends. Her best friend was Courtenay Ross who lived in the nearby neighborhood of Ansley Park. Other friends in the new neighborhood were Elizabeth and Eugenia Buchanan, Sue and Harlan Bucknell, William Coburn, Dick and Bob Goodhart, Erskine Jarnagin, Leila and Wallace Kirkpatrick, Bill Lawson, Lucille Little, Dorothy McCullough, William Patterson, and Maude Powers. Many of the journal entries in this volume were written about these new friends. Although the Peachtree house has long since been demolished, many of the sites on Sixteenth and Seventeenth streets and Peachtree Circle remain as they appeared in one of Margaret's journal entries in this collection.

She wrote and produced numerous plays that were performed by her new circle of friends. The girls formed a sewing club, and Margaret and Courtenay joined a boys' baseball team where Margaret became a star player. Courtenay Ross told of a club called the "Dirty Three," or "D. T." for short, that teamed the two girls with another friend, Henry Angel. Margaret went so far as to send an announcement of one of their meetings to the newspaper.

Saturday nights would find the neighborhood gang at one or another's house telling ghost stories. Childhood friend Dewitt Alexander wrote to Margaret in 1937, "It has

Margaret gathering grapes as a young teenager

been many years since you used to tell those hair-raising ghost stories to us kids, every Saturday night in the basement. Many the time after they were over, I would take the middle of the street and run from Peachtree to Prado in less time than it takes to write about it." Margaret responded, "I, too, remember the ghost stories we used to tell. I always thought I especially excelled in 'Who's Got My Golden Arm?'"

William Coburn wrote Margaret in 1945 reminding her how Bob Goodhart and Jimmy Boykin had enticed him to fire a shotgun in the middle of the street and how they all used to play "pop the whip" in front of the Christian Science Church on Peachtree Street.

Margaret attended Tenth Street School and Woodberry School before entering the Washington Seminary for girls in 1914. Bill Cantrell used to walk her home from Tenth Street School and carry her books. At the Seminary Margaret spent more time on her activities and social life than she did on studying, but managed an *A* or two in English and history. Margaret headed one of the Seminary's literary societies and was recognized as a class leader during her senior year when she was chosen to be a member of the Senior Round Table, an honorary society. She was literary editor of the yearbook, acted in drama club productions, and continued to write. Two of her stories were printed in *Facts and Fancies*, the Seminary yearbook. She credited Eva Paisley, her English teacher, with encouraging her to improve her writing skills. She completed a fourteen-chapter, four-hundred-page manuscript called *The Big Four*, which, according to Margaret E. Baugh, Mitchell's secretary in later years, dealt with "the rivalry of some schoolgirls over the editorship of a school publication."

Martha Angley was an Atlanta high school student who wrote a class essay about Mitchell before the publication of *Gone With the Wind*. In a letter to Angley, Mitchell wrote, "Senior Class night at the Seminary and I was there on the front row of the study hall in my old desk. I recall that in other days I occupied this desk, not through any desire of my own, but because Miss Emma decreed it. She said it was tempting Providence to seat me somewhere where she could not keep an eye on me." In describing what she wore to school she wrote to Angley, "I wore middy blouses or Buster Brown suits and braids and hair ribbons up to graduation and also skated to school every morning."

A tragic event happened on May 21, 1917, during Margaret's junior year. A fire swept through a part of Atlanta which included her old Jackson Street neighborhood, destroying all businesses and residences in its path. Gone were the houses owned by her grandmother and the one in which Margaret herself had grown up. The girls were attending a junior-senior reception at Washington Seminary on the afternoon of the fire, but Margaret later joined her mother at the Municipal Auditorium to assist survivors. Margaret's job, according to Mitchell biographer Darden Pyron, was "matching lost goods to missing owners."

When the United States joined the war in 1917, life suddenly became a whirlwind of activity for the Seminary girls. Margaret and Court were soon caught up in the entertainment of the boys at Camp Gordon and Fort McPherson. Neither lacked for beaus. It was at one of these parties that Margaret met her future husband, Berrien Upshaw; however, it was another young officer who truly caught her fancy. He was twenty-two-year-old U.S. Army Lieutenant Clifford Henry, a wealthy and socially prominent New Yorker who had gone to school with the Roosevelt children. Although Margaret was just seventeen, the two fell in love during the two months that Clifford was a bayonet instructor at Camp Gordon. Just before being shipped overseas in July, Clifford presented Margaret with an old family ring, signifying their engagement. This was not looked upon with favor by Eugene Mitchell, but May Belle assured her husband that love at seventeen was not usually of the lasting variety. Margaret's fiancé was killed in October of 1918 in France. Theodore Roosevelt wrote Clifford Henry's eulogy, and Margaret would honor Clifford's memory by sending his mother flowers every year on the anniversary of his death.

With the single exception of a short one-act play, this volume contains all of Margaret Mitchell's surviving unpublished childhood writings, including the twenty-one recently discovered ones and three pieces from the Margaret Mitchell Marsh Collection at the Hargrett Rare Book and Manuscript Library of the University of Georgia Libraries. A story published previously as a fragment is here joined with newly discovered material preceding it, and two complete previously published stories are included.

This collection of Margaret Mitchell's childhood writings spans the period from 1907 to 1918. A mere eight years later, she would begin writing *Gone With the Wind*.

Margaret in roller skates in front of the Mitchell's Peachtree Street house, circa 1915

Part One

Beginnings

〜

"MARGARET IS CRYING ABOUT HER CATS. Have [Mitchell family servant] Old John or someone go and get them and then lock them up, otherwise her trip is spoiled." Margaret's mother wrote this to Margaret's father from Summit, New Jersey, in the summer of 1910. May Belle Mitchell and Margaret were spending several weeks taking the "milk cure" at the American Hygienic Institute there. May Belle took the "milk cure" seriously and believed that drinking fresh cow's milk had helped prevent the family from getting tuberculosis. During the same trip, Margaret wrote a letter filled with descriptions of all the animals on the place. Young Margaret loved animals.

The family had numerous pets when they lived on Jackson Street. They usually had a collie dog and it was always named "Colonel" after Teddy Roosevelt. The Mitchells were never without an assortment of cats.

May Belle Mitchell with Margaret and Stephens, circa 1904

There were several cat stories Stephens enjoyed telling. In one, Margaret taught a cat named Lowpatia to stand up and salute by putting her paw next to her ear. Cantaloupe was used as a reward. Another time Margaret accidentally hit a kitten in the head with a baseball, causing the kitten to have one green eye and one blue eye for the rest of its days. Stephens has recounted how he and his sister used to put kittens in a basket attached to a rope and pull them up to a treehouse they had built in the backyard. In the move from Jackson to Peachtree, Margaret was the one in charge of getting Rameses the cat to the new house. This involved changing streetcars, during which she proceeded to lose the cat. With the help of a kind policeman and other spectators, the cat was recovered, and both pet and owner reached their new home without further mishap.

Besides the cats and dogs in the Mitchell household, there were two ducks named Mr. and Mrs. Drake, a cow, some turtles, a pony belonging to Stephens, and a couple of baby alligators.

Margaret's love of ponies is evident in her western and adventure stories.

Margaret, circa 1902

She learned to ride at a very early age and often roamed the countryside around Atlanta for hours at a time. In later years, she told of riding her pony with elderly Confederate veterans and learning a cuss word or two from them. The Mitchell children eventually outgrew their pony. Bucephalus, their new mount, was a much larger, but less sure-footed horse named after Alexander the Great's famous steed. When she was eleven, Margaret injured her leg in a bad fall from Bucephalus. This was shortly before the move to Peachtree Street so the family sold the horse. Even though Margaret would ride again, she never owned another horse.

In this section are two letters written by Margaret from Summit, New Jersey, to her father, and Margaret's earliest surviving story, written when she was about seven. The spelling in the letters is the author's.

LETTER TO
Eugene Muse Mitchell, Atlanta, Ga.
1910

Dear Father,

I arrived here this afternoon. I had a good time on the train and saw the Potomac River and Chesapeke Bay.

Ther were a lot of boats on the river and I saw Washington Monument and the Capitol.

Of all the states I liked Virginia the best. It had hills hollows and woods and lakes and creeks and level ground. It is a pretty place on top of a hill. I ran down it and nearly broke my neck. Pleas write soon. Our address is.

C/Dr. Rhimlander

Summit, N.J.

LETTER TO
Eugene Muse Mitchell, Atlanta, Ga.
JUNE 20, 1910

Sumet, N.J.
June 20, 1910

My dear Father,

I am glad you enjoyed my letter. I have a lot of dogs
to play with. There are three dogs here. There is a very large dog.
Then there is a yellow cur dog and fox terrier. There are all sorts of
birds, Robins, BlueJays, Sparrows, Blue birds, Red birds, Crows, and
Whipourwills. There are a lot of squirrels. There is a hole in the
roof of a cottage, and I saw a squirrels go into it. And the flowers.
There are so many I do not even stop to pick them. There are three
cherry trees. Plase write soon. Tell me how Ram and Riffle and the
kittens are. Ask Bertha if she gave the dog to John. Please ask
Florence and Lola Noyes to write to me. I am well and Mother is
too. I have gained two and a half pounds and Mother has gained
five ponds and is looking so much better. Ask Aunt Ruth to write
to me. Please come and take us to New York. I am very lonesome.
Ask Grandma to. It is very hot. There are two cats.

With love to all,
Margaret Mitchell

"Two Little Folk"

To my cousins
David and Stephens Crockett

TWO LITTLE PEOPLE

Two little people live in my back yard. One is named Tommy and the other, Sarah. Tommy is the boldest and the bravest. Each morning he gets up and salutes Sarah saying, "Come, Sarah, the sun has been up an hour; you are very sleepy, my dear."

Sarah rubs her eyes. They go together and get breakfast. Sarah is lazy and lets Tommy do the work. She does not even cook his food, but eats it raw.

Every day they have a singing lesson. This is what they sing, "Quack, quack, quack," for Tommy and Sarah are two ducks.

The End

Part Two

The Mitchell house on Peachtree Street

Fairy Tales

DURING THEIR ELEMENTARY SCHOOL DAYS at Tenth Street School, Margaret and her friend Edgarda Horton wrote "Nickel and Dime Novels and Fairy Tales." They made sure that each was the other's heroine or villainess. In one of Edgarda's stories, the enchantress Margaret used all her magical powers to make herself beautiful. Margaret, in turn, made Edgarda the evil lady of the court in her fairy tale entitled "The Green Snake." The story was found in a copybook dated January 1, 1913, making Margaret twelve when she wrote it.

Two children's books belonging to Margaret were found in the boxes containing the new manuscripts. One was *The Story of King Arthur* by Edward Brooks and the other was *Submarine Boys' Trial Trip* by Victor G. Durham—both are typical of children's reading tastes at the time.

In a letter written to Margaret Mitchell years later, Edgarda reminisced about their novels and how seriously they had taken these writing efforts. Their obsession with these stories sometimes got them into trouble in class. In Mrs. Thrasher's seventh grade class, a note from Edgarda to Margaret was intercepted by their teacher. The note began, "Margaret my darling Dave has my book and I am scared to death." Mrs. Thrasher wasn't as upset over the passing of the note as she was over Edgarda calling Dave Collins her "darling." Both girls learned the importance of commas from this episode. The note, with correctly placed commas, would read, "Margaret my darling, Dave has my book . . ."

Another friend from those days, John Knox, said that Margaret used to get mad at him because he tried to dip her pigtails in the inkwell. He said that Margaret and Edgarda were continuously writing their stories at recess while the rest of their class were playing. Bill Lawson recalled that Edgarda was very serious, but could faint quite professionally when called upon to do so in the course of their many play productions.

In his book, *Southern Daughter*, Darden Pyron writes that Margaret probably wrote "The Knight and the Lady" when she was eight or nine years old.

Knighthood

"THE KNIGHT AND THE LADY"

In a valley between high mountains, there lived a beautiful lady. She was so beautiful that everyone loved her. She was very rich, also.

Up in the mountains there lived a wild, rough knight. He loved the lady, but she did not love him. This made him angry. He called his men together and said, "Tomorrow we take the lady's lands," and they agreed.

Near the lady there lived a good, but poor, knight. He overheard the plot and hid in the bushes.

The wild knight came up to them and said, "You will not marry me, so I will marry you."

The good knight stepped out of the bushes and asked the other to fight him. Both knights drew their swords and rushed together. The good knight hit the bad one such a blow that he was killed. The lady fell in love with her rescuer and they were married.

"The Green Snake"

Once in a far off country there lived a prince named Wendell. He was very much in love with the Princess Lowdie, the daughter of the King of Noland, and she returned his love.

In Prince Wendell's father's court there was a court lady by the name of Lady Garda of Mugwump. She loved Wendell, but he did not love her at all. This angered her greatly and she was determined to have her revenge.

On a high mountain, a good way from the city, lived an old witch. The Lady Garda decided to visit her.

It was a long journey, but the revenge in her heart made Garda strong! At last she arrived at the witch's cave.

The ugly witch was stirring a pot of simmering bull frogs and crooning to herself when the lady arrived. "What do you want?" she mumbled.

Garda told her her story and finished by begging the witch to give her something that would make Wendell love her and would make Princess Lowdie hate him.

The witch promised and went into her cave. Soon she returned with two bottles. "This!" she said, as she laid one bottle in Garda's hand, "is the love potion, and this," she gave her another bottle, "is the hate potion. Take care and do not mix them!"

Garda thanked her and started home, but the witch stopped her. "You haven't paid me yet," she said.

Garda threw her a diamond necklace.

The old woman laughed contemptuously. "I don't want your necklace," she said. "I only want a promise."

Garda stopped. "What shall I promise?" she questioned, curiously.

"Only this," said the witch, "that if you do not succeed, I can change you into a charming green snake."

The lady shuddered, but she thought, "My plans will not fail," and she said aloud, "I promise."

The sorceress laughed in a hollow tone. "Begone," she said.

Garda hastened home. When she arrived at the palace, all the other ladies told her that Prince Wendell was to marry Princess Lowdie the next day.

Garda clenched her teeth. "I'll not be foiled," she cried. She took a bottle of wine and three glasses and went to the room where the lovers were. This opened into a beautiful garden. Wendell and Lowdie were sitting on the steps.

Garda hastily poured out three glasses of wine. Then she poured in one glass the powder of hate, and in the other two, the powder of love. She bowed to the two and said, "I humbly ask the favor of being allowed to drink to your health."

"Certainly, fair lady," smiled Wendell, "and we will drink with you."

This was exactly what Garda wanted and she handed a glass to each, but in her excitement, she mixed the glasses and by mistake took the hate powder herself! She did not discover her mistake and raised her glass to her lips. "To your health!" she cried, joyfully, and took a large drink.

Wendell and Lowdie drank, also, and immediately loved each

other more than ever. As for Garda, the last seen of her was a long, green snake that crawled into the bushes with a soft hiss.

Part Three

Margaret and her first cousins David and Stephens Crockett, circa 1910

Kinfolk and Playmates

MARGARET'S EARLIEST STORIES ARE EASILY

dated because she collected them into little handmade books. The

covers were made of cardboard and the pages were taken from tablets

and folded in half so that the lines were vertical rather than hori-

zontal. In the first books, she drew pencil lines across the page. Later

she omitted this step. She decorated the covers and included in some

of them dedication and title pages.

The one book cover still in existence, from "Forest and Foothills," has a hand-printed title on the front and a dedication on the inside back. Margaret wrote on the dedication page, "copyright 1912 by Urchin Publishing Co.," making her eleven when that story was written. The first page of the tablet-paper book is the title page. The story begins on the back of this title page.

Margaret started out using her cousins and friends as the characters of her stories and herself as the heroine. In "The Little Pioneers" and "When We Were Shipwrecked," cousins Stephens and David Crockett and friends Eugene and Willie Noyes were her cohorts in the exciting adventures she penned. The story "Forest and Foothills" was dedicated to her best friend, Florence Noyes, Eugene's and Willie's sister. Margaret liked to be the only heroine and so Florence does not appear in the two stories with her brothers. Bob Goodhart, seen in "Forest and Foothills," was also a neighborhood friend.

In his biography of Mitchell, Finis Farr writes that Margaret sometimes changed the titles of her stories. According to Farr,

Margaret and her first cousins David and Stephens Crockett playing baseball, possibly at the Mitchell's Jackson Hill home, circa 1910

"When We Were Shipwrecked" was renamed "When You and I Were Cast Away." One of the stories in the collection could be the middle section of the story to which Farr refers. Margaret's handmade books were flimsily constructed and often fell apart, which accounts for sections of the same story being found in different collections. Although the title page and beginning chapters are missing, the shipwreck adventure story in this section appears under the title "When We Were Shipwrecked."

"The Little Pioneers," part of the collection of the Hargrett Library, is another of Margaret's earliest stories and is also missing pages. Darden Pyron has suggested that Margaret was nine when she wrote it. The same neighborhood characters appear in both stories, indicating that Margaret wrote "The Little Pioneers" and "When We Were Shipwrecked" while the family lived on Jackson Street.

"The Little Pioneers"

M. Mitchell

I

"Hold on Margaret, hold on. Don't you wait on a fellow?" The speaker, a red face boy on a wiry little pony was urging it to its utmost speed in order to catch up with a girl who was galloping in front of him.

At last she pulled up. "What is it, Will?" she asked.

"Come back to the fort, quick," he answered.

"Anything wrong?" she inquired anxiously.

"Yep, Father says he thinks that there's going to be an Indian uprising, so he doesn't want you to go very far away from the fort. He says to come quickly," finished up the boy breathlessly. Both turned their ponies round and started in the direction from which the boy had come.

As they neared the fort, two other boys, smaller than the first, hailed them. "Have you seen Eugene?"

"No, can't you find him?" answered Margaret.

"No, and everybody is looking for him," replied the younger, as she rode on.

Margaret and Willie continued on towards the fort. The fort was a long row of log cabins surrounded by a large stockade with two large gates. A handsome man in a captain's uniform helped Margaret to the ground.

"Well, little lady," he cried, "Willie found you, did he?" His face grew grave, "Have you seen Eugene?"

"No," replied Margaret, "no, Uncle Dave, I haven't seen him since yesterday evening. Is he missing?"

"Yes, and I'll have to tell Lieutenant Noyes about it," began the young officer, when an orderly ran up and saluted.

"Scout Johnson just returned with important news, sir," he said.

"All right," and Captain Crockett ran off without another word.

Margaret Mitchell was his niece and a visitor from the East. Captain Crockett's two boys, David and Stephens, were her cousins. Lieutenant Noyes had two sons, also. Eugene, the eldest who had been strangely missing, and Willie, a year younger.

As Captain Crockett disappeared, David and Stephens rode up. "Have you heard the news?" yelled David as he rode by.

"No," answered Margaret.

"Johnson just told me that that tribe of Apaches has had a council and were on the war path," he cried as he swung to the ground, "and that they might attack us tonight. And what's more, Eugene is gone, and everyone thinks that he's been captured." This was startling to the girl from the East and she ran to tell Willie of it.

In the night she was wakened by shrieks and yells mingled with shouts of defiance from the garrison. Quickly slipping on her clothes she hurried out, only to start back at the scene which lay before her. Many men lay, either wounded or dead, on the ground, while the air was thick with smoke and shots whistled through the air. As the sun arose, all could be plainly seen; the band of Apaches were in the usual way, galloping around the fort, and firing. Every little while one, bolder than the rest, would clammer over the stockade, only to be shot or beaten back by the brave defenders, whose ranks were steadily thinning out.

[*The last pages of the manuscript are missing. Margaret's handmade books were put together in such a way that it was very easy for a page to come loose or fall out. The title page and the first page were probably connected to the missing pages that contained the ending. There could have been a second folded page between the very last page that also fell out.*]

"When We Were Shipwrecked"

[*The title page and the beginning are missing.*]

Their two sons, David and Stephens, aged respectively nine and eight, were Margaret's cousins. Among their many friends were Eugene and Willie Noyes, sons of Mr. and Mrs. Noyes. They were good friends, and often where one was found, all were found.

But that day, unaware of any danger, they were playing happily at the game of "Indians and Cowboys." Having slipped their father's and mother's pistols (for all of them carried guns, pistols, and ammunition, as they were going on a hunting trip) they were at the height of the game when a grinding, crashing noise was heard. Then a sudden shock threw them all on the cabin floor. The shock had knocked down two or three pistol belts with a good many rounds of cartridges in them. Hardly knowing what she was doing, Margaret grasped these, and followed by the rest, ran on deck.

There was a scene of mass confusion. Many people were shouting, "We are going to drown," or "The ship is sinking," but all were rushing for the boats! Before the children gathered their senses, many of the boats had put off. They saw only one small lifeboat left, in which two sailors were tumbling boxes and many other things into, not knowing whether they were provisions or not.

"Here, you kids, get in here," said one of the men. The children obeyed quickly and the sailors lowered the boat.

Soon the fog closed around them so that they lost sight of the sinking vessel. The two men took up the oars and began to pull away. No one spoke for some time, 'til the practical Eugene, who was twelve years old, asked one of the sailors if they were near any land.

"Not if I know it," answered the sailor shortly.

"Ump," said the other, "much you know about it. Now if this ornery fog would lift up."

Nothing else was said 'til about two hours later. Willie, with the natural appetite of an eleven year old boy, declared himself hungry. The largest sailor got out a tin of crackers and divided them. "You'd better save them," he warned. "They're all you get." He also opened the keg of water and they all took a drink. The men stopped rowing, and went to sleep as darkness drew on, as did the children.

Early in the morning, they were wakened with a shout of, "Land, I see land!" Getting up they saw Margaret pointing to a dark spot on the horizon.

"Bless me, but it is!" exclaimed the smallest sailor. They started rowing, but they seemed to get nowhere.

"May I inquire," asked Eugene sarcastically of Margaret, "what you have in your hand?"

She turned red and held up three pistol butts. They all laughed. David and Stephens held up three pistol butts. "I found one on the floor," explained David, "and I held on to the others since yesterday!" It seemed to them a year.

"Why, I've got papa's pistol!" said Eugene, Willie, and Margaret together.

"If we get to land, we can shoot things," cried Stephens.

"Yes, *if,*" said the sailor. But now they were so close to the land, they could see a shelf around it, on which the sea was breaking furiously.

"Well, mate, we'll try it," said the largest sailor. "Hold tight, kids," and away they went. The boat was half way through the breakers when it suddenly struck a rock. Both sailors, not holding on, were thrown over the stern. Fortunately by this time, the boat was through the breakers and into calm water, before David shouted, "They're gone!" It was true, there was nothing to be done, they were gone! Slowly, the boat came up on the beach, when a few yards away, a large wave overturned the boat and threw them all, and the provisions, on the beach. All had a dim recollection of being tossed, bumped, and thrown on the shore. Then Margaret, for one, knew no more.

When she opened her eyes, she heard a sound of weeping. Sitting up, she saw David sitting on the boat, crying as if he were half killed. "What's the matter, Dave?" she asked weakly, and, "What happened?"

The boy jumped at the sound of her voice. "Thank goodness you're not dead. I thought you were dead, you lay so still. Don't you remember, the boat turned over?"

"Oh yes, I remember!" she replied. "Were the provisions lost?"

"I don't think so," he answered.

"David, there are some boxes on the beach! Where are Eugene, Willie, and Stephens?"

"Over there, behind the sand hill. I'm afraid they're dead."

"Quick, we'll see," said the girl, getting up. With David's help she then dragged out to where another body lay. She directed David to roll Eugene across a log, which he did. She employed herself in executing "the first aid to the injured" on Willie and Stephens.

Just then David said, "I wish you'd come hear what Eugene is saying."

In spite of their serious condition, Margaret could not keep from laughing. Eugene was muttering, "I never thought they'd make biscuits out of me, but they're rolling the rolling pin over me for sure!" David laughed, too.

In an hour all were sitting upon the beach in the sun, weak, but thankful that they had not been drowned. "But where is the boat?" asked Willie, after thanking the others for saving him. Stephens looked up and down the beach.

[*Pages are missing, but clues from the rest of the story suggest that they find a treasure cave with two skeletons, have a run-in with a leopard, and that Willie is captured by islanders. The story resumes with Willie in captivity.*]

He fell asleep. When he awoke, he found that his limbs were stiff from being tied so long. It was a gloomy prospect for poor Willie, for he had expected to be rescued during the night.

One of the native women came out of a hut and looked at Willie for a long time, evidently admiring his white skin. One man, evidently the chief, gave an order in a language that Willie had never heard before, but he was overjoyed to see her fill a large gourd with a mixture of food, for he was hungry. The chief watched at first, and then walked away. Then he was fed by the other woman, from the gourd, and he thought, dismayed, "I bet she's thinking which I'm better for, dinner or supper?" This, however, did not happen and he remained securely tied to the tree for the rest of the day. As it may be supposed, he was filled with pain and was exceedingly stiff, so that he hardly cared what happened.

That night there was excitement among the tribe and the captive was horrified to see many of the natives point first to him and then to the fire, which confirmed his suspicions. "I'm a goner, in the morning," he groaned, which was true, "but what were Margaret, Eugene, David, and Stephens doing?"

Early in the morning they had started out, a determined working party, bent on saving their comrade if it were possible. All the while Willie was captive, they searched the island. Tired and hungry as they were, the march was kept steadily on, until David declared that they were in the vicinity where their hapless companion was captured. "I'm sure it is," he declared. "Yes, look, yonder is the fire. Oh quick, into the bushes! I heard someone coming!" All scurried into the bushes and were safely hidden, except Margaret, whose foot caught on a root and made her stumble.

When she arose she saw a native girl, somewhat larger than she, gazing at her in astonishment. Quick as a flash, however, the native drew out a long, dangerous-looking knife, and ran toward Margaret. She thought to herself, "Gracious, if she gets me with that knife, I'm a goner." As the native lifted the knife to strike, Margaret's hand shot out and gripped it in mid-air.

Then there was a struggle, the civilized muscle against the trained, savage muscle.

By this time the boys had returned and all asked, "Need any help?"

"No!" gasped Margaret, who was struggling bravely, "I can beat her!" It was some ways from the native village so they were not afraid of being discovered.

Twice Eugene started to help his friend, but between gasps, she sternly told him to stop. There were pauses, in which the quick, labored breathing of the two combatants was heard. Slowly, but surely, Margaret felt her strength leaving her, but was too proud to call for aid. The fight would have ended in tragedy for her, had she not made a quick move. Dropping one of her adversary's wrists, she quickly landed a blow with her fist in the face of the native and took a step backward. Then she renewed her onslaught and with a quick jerk, sent the weapon spinning from the black girl's hand.

For a moment they stood glaring at each other; then they grappled and finally rolled over on the ground. Margaret was on the bottom when the two stopped rolling, and was in danger. She, however, was able to give her opponent so hard a blow under the chin, that the young native lay back senseless for a time. Margaret leaped up.

"Gee, that was a peach of an uppercut!" said Eugene in admiration. "But what shall we do with her?" he added slowly.

"Tie her up with something," suggested David, which was carried out.

"Say, I didn't think you could wrestle and box like that," said Eugene. "I thought that she would kill you for sure with that knife!"

"She would have killed me if I hadn't socked her between the eyes," said Margaret, white-faced and leaning against a tree.

"Let's find Willie, quick," pleaded Stephens.

As it grew dark, they crawled toward the village. Eugene could scarcely keep from laughing as he perceived Willie tied to a tree, looking very gloomy, and he would have betrayed their hiding place if Margaret's indignant, and not overly clean hand, was [not] clasped over his mouth. "Now, for punishment, you and David must untie him," she declared calmly. He demurred, but she replied that such things did not agree with her health or Stephens's either, so that he was obliged to do it whether he wanted to or not, so he agreed.

Finally all grew quiet and Eugene and David shook hands with their companions and crawled cautiously toward the spot where Willie was secured. Unfortunately, David stumbled over a sleeping native.

[*Pages are missing but probably relate to Eugene's and David's capture by the islanders who have Willie.*]

which her comrades were in, and what was worse, a large native sat by the fire to keep guard.

"Now, Stephens, you take this pistol and when I croak like a frog, you fire it off; then you foot it to camp and get in the cave," she directed grimly.

"But—but—but—where are *you* going?" asked Stephens.

"To try to get the boys loose. Scoot, and don't bungle. Can you find the cave?"

"I guess so," said Stephens, "good-bye," and he disappeared in the underbrush.

Margaret waited some time and then, looking every step, she advanced. On she went, creeping behind the tree where Willie was tied. In a moment, he was awake.

"I knew you'd come," he whispered.

"Yes, I came," she answered. "Do you think you can walk?"

"Not a step," he responded. "I'm so stiff that I can hardly move."

"You've got to move," she said in desperation. "I'll cut you loose and you get in the bushes and rub yourself. That Negro's back is turned. When you hear a pistol shot, make for the cave," and with a deft slash, she cut the thongs.

Willie managed to creep into the bushes, while Margaret slipped into his place. The guard turned and looked at her, but the tree was in a shadow, so that he did not see that the boy was gone. The fire made him drowsy for his head sank lower and lower, 'til at last, when Margaret stepped out of the shadow, he did not start up. Just as she had freed the other boys, the native opened his eyes and stretched himself. Margaret whispered, "When you hear a shot, run for the cave," and slipping into the bushes, gave an excellent imitation of a frog.

Instantly, there was a pistol shot and all children ran. The natives poured from the huts, and seeing the captives gone, ran in the direction of the pistol shot. Stephens, however, climbed into a tree and shivered as he saw the natives pass beneath him.

He remained in hiding for some time; then he slipped down. It was in the darkest part of the night, which comes before dawn, and he had no sense of direction. After he had wandered aimlessly for some time, he was astonished to hear a voice say, "Is that you, Stephens?" in a low tone.

"You bet it is," he cried in delight. "Is everybody safe?"

"All except Margaret," replied the voice sorrowfully, and Eugene thrust his head from a bush. "I thought that she was with you!"

"No, I have not seen her," said Stephens anxiously. "She started with us when we started running, but when I looked around, she was gone!"

"Well, let's get to camp," said another voice. "I'm hungry!" which, of course, came from Willie. By good luck, Eugene knew the way back to the glade and soon they arrived at camp. All threw themselves down on the grass to try to sleep a little.

The sun had been up some time when they awoke. Willie started a conversation by saying, with a woeful face, "Golly, but I'm hungry."

"Well, if you are, go fishing. It's your time. Don't shoot or you'll have those imps on us," directed Eugene.

Willie started off and soon came back with a good-sized fish! Eugene made a fire with his burning glass and as they ate the fish, they discussed what to do about their lost comrade. Willie, waxing eloquent after his third piece of fish, made a speech. "Friends, Romans, countrymen, our good friend is departed."

"Cheerful and encouraging," muttered Eugene.

Willie eyed him. "Don't interrupt," he said. "Without the help of our noble Margaret, they would have made hash out of us all."

"How nice," said David sarcastically.

"Don't interrupt," said the speaker. "Without her help, we would have perished long ago. I appeal to your honor, gentlemen; we should avenge her death."

"Death? Say, Willie, you are about as cheerful as a rainy day!" said a familiar voice.

"Margaret!" all shouted in joy.

"It's me," said she, with scarce regard for grammar as she clambered down from a tree.

"How long have you been here?" was the general question.

"Oh, I arrived here long before you did, but had to come down when I heard Willie giving my funeral oration."

After she had eaten, affairs were discussed. Margaret dispatched Willie and Stephens to bring back as many gourds as they could find, David to go fishing, and Eugene to go hunting. As David left, Margaret whispered to him, "See if the lifeboat is still there on the beach."

While they were gone, she built up the fire, but not too high, and took the leopard skin. With her knife, she cut off the paws, and then with some trouble, cut the skin in half. Then along the sides of each piece, she pierced holes. She found a very slender vine and ran it through the holes in both pieces, thereby lacing them together. Finally, she slipped this on and tied the vine over her shoulders. She was very proud of her skirt, which reached below her knees.

"Now," she thought, "I will make me some slippers." This was more difficult, but she employed the same method that she had used in making the skirt, and soon had a substantial pair of Indian moccasins. Wishing to decorate herself more, she went into the treasure cave and selected a gold chain of strange workmanship, for she had overcome her horror of the two skeletons, and put the chain around her neck.

"I must look funny," she thought, "moccasins, bare legs, leopard skin skirt, and cloth jacket or shirtwaist, with a gold chain on my neck. I wonder who left all this treasure here? Perhaps pirates," and for some time she thought on this subject.

An ear-splitting yell greeted her as she came from the cave. Willie, on seeing her attire, laughed so much that he rolled on the ground. Willie and Stephens obtained a large supply of gourds and also some bananas. Margaret immediately filled the gourds with water and carried them into the cave. Willie was puzzled.

"Well, you see, if those black fellows come after us, we can get in the cave," explained the girl.

David came back. "The boat's safe," he whispered. "I found the oars and stuck them in the sand." He also had several fish, which Willie looked hungrily at. Eugene had luck also, and brought in several birds and a male animal like a rabbit.

Margaret told of her idea of an attack, and that they had better lay up provisions for the "siege." All approved of this and part of the fire was transferred into a cave branching from the treasure cave. Watches were arranged. Stephens was to go first, as he was the smallest. Willie's watch was at midnight.

No one was surprised when he woke them, calmly saying that he was sure the natives were attacking them. "I heard noises, saw the bushes moving, and saw someone's head from the bushes," he added.

"Everyone get to the cave," ordered Eugene, "and get your pistol ready." All crawled cautiously towards the cave and once within this shelter, Margaret turned and fired into the bushes. War-splitting yells greeted this volley and a number of black bodies charged toward the entrance to the cave.

"Shoot!" yelled Margaret fiercely. There was a volley of five shots fired, and the natives drew back, but not for long. They assailed the entrance again, only to be driven back by the brave defenders, with some loss of life.

"When the morning comes, they will see us and throw their spears at us! Then it will be 'good-bye,'" said Willie gloomily.

"I have an idea," cried Stephens.

"Wonderful," muttered Eugene.

"Why not take those big stones in the back of the cave and block up the entrance?" questioned Stephens. All approved of this and with some trouble, dragged the stones to the entrance and blocked it. Nothing happened until morning and all were glad Margaret had stocked the cave with provisions and water. The fire filled the cave with smoke until David discovered a crack through which it might pass. They were able to cook one of the fish over the flames and all, especially Willie, felt better.

"I wonder how long we'll stay here. Maybe we'll starve," said the cheerful Willie.

"Help, come quick!" came the call from Margaret. All ran to the entrance. "They are going to attack again," she said in excitement. "You had better lie down behind the rocks and load your pistols."

And they did attack! It seemed strange that five American children should be holding this cave against the natives, who outnumbered them ten to one, but that did not hold them back when a party attacked them with spears and they "made every shot tell," as Willie expressed it. "But we can't hold out forever," explained this young pessimist. "I'm very thirsty and haven't but eight more charges." The ammunition was indeed, alarmingly low, and when a compilation was held, it was found that only fifteen cartridges among them all, were left.

After eating a little, all went back to guarding the mouth of the cave. When Willie, incautiously, peered forth from behind his rock, he was greeted with a volley of spears from various bushes. No one looked out for some time after this.

As night drew on, the natives made another attack and the last of the bullets were fired. "Not another charge left! What shall we do?" gasped Margaret.

"I know what!" said Stephens.

"What?" said all.

"This!" he said, drawing a package from his blouse. On opening it, they discovered thirty or more rounds of ammunition. All cheered Stephens and he explained that he had found them on the beach during the night.

While Eugene was guarding, David thinking earnestly, and Willie dreaming of chicken salad and ice cream, Stephens and Margaret explored the cave. After following its many twistings and curvings, both felt a draught blowing on them. Hastening on, they discovered an opening large enough for both of them to creep through. Both were wild with joy and raced back to tell the news.

Margaret's plan was to fill the boat with water and provisions and sail off, in hopes that some ship would pick them up. "It's going to be risky, but there's more chance of us getting out alive, than if we stay here," she argued.

"Maybe so," said Eugene doubtfully, "but if we're not picked up?"

"We'll have to turn up our toes, then," said the girl briskly.

All agreed to take the boat and Eugene slipped out to find its location. Soon he came back, and reported that the boat looked as if it were going to float off on the next big tide. All the provisions and water were put in the boat, as Margaret suggested to Willie (for they were the last to leave the cave) that they had better take the treasure with them.

"But there's not time," said Willie. "See, they are going to attack again. I'm going!"

"I'll make time," she muttered, setting her teeth and darting back. Into the treasure cave she ran, seized the first two things which met her eye, the bag of jewels and an old native shield. As she grasped these, she heard the triumphant yells of the savages. Quick as a flash she darted back down the passage, gaining more speed at each moment; however, she stumbled and the skin bag fell from her hand, and the majority of the stones were lost. There was no time to pick them up, so on she sped until she found the rest of the children in the boat.

"Give her a push, when you jump, Margaret," said Eugene. This was done and with the help of a large wave, the boat was shoved off. Luckily the tide carried them through a channel in the reef or all would have been lost.

When the sun rose, it shone on a strange scene. Eugene sat at the bow of the boat sleeping, with his pistol in his hand. Margaret sat at the stern, looking strangely savage in her skin dress and native shield. In the middle lay David, Stephens, and Willie. David and Stephens were sleeping the sleep of the just, but the latter was dreaming for he muttered, "I'll take two ice cream sodas, please."

Margaret was the first to awaken. She wondered if all had been a bad dream, but knew this was not so, for she held in her hands the remnants of the skin bag. Eagerly she opened it, but found comparatively few—to what had been the original number of—stones.

There was no land in sight, only a blue expanse of water. Soon the others awoke and all felt gloomy. The stock of bananas was not large, nor was the water supply, but half rations were served. Had it not been for the big shield, all would have fared badly from the heat, but by huddling under this, they were able to keep off some of the blistering rays.

Suddenly, David sprang up. "There's a steamboat!" he yelled in glee, dancing up and down, in danger of falling.

"Fire your pistol," cried Eugene.

One after another, they fired, and were delighted to see the steam-boat turn toward them. On coming nearer, they perceived a boat putting off. In ten minutes, all were taken safe on the deck, surrounded by many people, who looked at these large, sun-tanned, healthy-looking children in wonder.

[*The end of the story is missing.*]

"Forest and Foothills"

·

Julia Weston waited where Sam had left her—alone, she thought, in the great woods. She leaned up against a tree, nearby, thinking. Suddenly, some one caught her hands. Another hand was placed over her mouth. She felt a rope being tied around her wrists; a handkerchief was over her eyes. She was picked up and carried off for some distance, gently, she thought. She was set down, the rope and handkerchief taken off. Opening her eyes she saw before her eyes—Paul Matherson with a smile on his lips. She gave a cry and fainted away.

"Paul, Paul," said Parry, rushing in breathlessly. "That skunk, Sam Laria, is at the clearing."

[*Pages are missing.*]

"Ah! Ha!" cried Paul Matherson, as he quickly passed the ropes around Sam's body, "I have you now in my *power!*"

"Where is Julia?" said Sam Laria quickly, though he was uneasy.

"Never mind, you'll see soon," laughed Paul.

"Don't you dare touch her," said Sam writhing around.

"Stop that wiggling or I'll knock you senseless."

[*Pages are missing.*]

"Take him back to camp," said Paul.

"Not I," Frank said, "I'm tired."

"Then he'll stay here!"

There was a rustle in the bushes and out came Julia. "Oh, please don't hurt him, please! Please! He is hurt," she said. "Please take him back where I can tie him up," she pleaded. Paul's heart softened.

"Let's see if he's alive first," he said.

Julia ran forward and laid her ear to Sam's heart. "Yes," she said, "he lives."

Sam's brown eyes opened. "Julia," he murmured and tried to stand. Julia took his hand and assisted him to rise. Malone took his other hand. When he was on his feet, they put his arms about their necks and walked slowly along. Sam's strength gave out as he came to camp and he fell. Julia, excited and tired, fainted and fell on Sam, clasping him in her arms.

"Here's a fix," said Paul, as he brought his crude cot out of the cabin and laid Sam on it. "What are Julia and I to sleep on?"

"Yo! Ho!" He yawned. "One o'clock. I am going to sleep."

He leaned over Julia and touched her. "S'cuse me, but here is a cot."

Thanking him she spread her cloak out on the cot and went to sleep. The men moved their knapsacks and went off to dreamland. Paul lay on the other end.

As the campfire was dying down, silently a band of Indians appeared, four men going to each sleeper. They did not notice Sam, whose cot was small and behind a bush.

The chief surveyed the camp with a grim smile, folded his arms, and gave some orders. The unsuspecting sleepers were captured, but not without a struggle. Paul, who was a light sleeper, leaped up and seizing his pistol, fired at one of the braves holding him. He fell, shot through the heart. Paul was seized and tied. All were captured, excepting Sam, who, wakened by the shot, saw what was going on and "lay low."

The prisoners' hands were tied; they were made to walk on. Two braves rounded up the horses, but Paul's bronco, who was a wild little mustang, broke away and ran off. They did not notice it. Sam heard them ride off in the distance. He got out of bed the best he could. He heard the trot of a horse; Paul's little mustang came galloping up. Sam caught his bridle with his good hand; he tightened the girth of the saddle and climbed on its back, taking his pistol, a canteen, and a little food.

[*Pages are missing.*]

The man opened his eyes and said faintly, "Where, where am I?"

"You're safe," assured Bob Goodhart. "What happened?"

"I am Sam Laria," said he and he told them the story.

"Please, send some troops after them," he added, "for their lives depend on it." Sam now had strength to stand.

"It shall be done," said the officer in command.

"Will you go, too?" asked Goodhart.

"Yes," responded Laria, "that girl's my sweetheart and I will save her."

Twenty-five troopers mounted their horses, giving Sam a fresh one. They started off.

Meantime the captives had been put on horses and were taken off. Their hands were tied, except for Julia. The men, being good riders, sitting on tight, rode for hours, it seemed to them. At last at dark, the band stopped. The captives were made to get off the horses. A fire was made. Matherson, Parry, Dickson, and Malone were tied fast to four trees. The chief took Julia roughly by the arm and pushed her into his large teepee, which was the only one which had been brought.

Then folding his arms, he said, "Ma-gi-hack-a-tai-ce?" Julia was frightened. She did not know Apache. The chief gave a grunt.

A young Indian stepped in. He spoke to the chief in guttural grunts; they both went out. Julia peeped out. There was the Indian sitting in front of the wigwam. She sighed and lay down to try to sleep.

It seemed only a short while when she woke, finding the chief beckoning to her. She came out and looked around. To her surprise she saw Matherson, Parry, Malone, and Dickson—the latter three were yet tied to trees, but Matherson was loose and struggling with the savage that had been her guard. She saw a flash of steel. Paul had succeeded in getting the Indian's knife.

The chief said something to the Apache warrior, which caused him to smile a grim smirk. He stopped, sighting two savages who sprang behind Paul and secured him tightly. Julia was given something to eat, and was made to get on a horse. The others were also put on horses.

At twelve o'clock, they came to the village. The squaws came running out to meet them. The men were tied to large posts driven in the ground and were let alone by the Indians, excepting at times, a squaw would flourish a knife very near them.

"Say, Dick," asked Paul in a low tone, "can you get loose?"

"No," said Malone, "but I'd give a lot to be loose, with a pistol."

"Look here," said Matherson, "I've got a pistol!"

"Where?" asked Malone eagerly.

"Here in my pants pocket, but hush," he said.

"Do you know what they are going to do with us?" said Malone.

"Yes," said Paul grimly, "we are going to be tortured tomorrow night."

"What's that?" asked Parry and Dickson.

"We are going to be tortured tomorrow night," said Paul calmly.

Parry muttered, "No, they won't. I'll kill myself first."

"So say we all!" said the rest.

"But how?" asked Frank Dickson.

"Paul's got a pistol," said Malone.

"Look here, now, old fellow," he went on, "if you get loose and those red devils are on me, put a bullet straight through me, understand?"

"And me."

"And me!" said the others.

"All right," said Paul sadly. "Of course, you know how much I hate to do it. Of course, it will be better for you." Here, he almost broke down. "God knows, and I hope he will forgive me all my sins."

"Old fellow, you haven't been bad," said Malone.

"Oh, you don't know me," said Paul. "I'm worse than you think."

The Indian chief approached, so they stopped talking. Evidently, the chief was angry. Tom Parry, who understood a little Apache, heard him say, "The paleface dogs were on my hunting ground. They are desecrated. They must die!" Then Tom was led out between two lines of young braves, while wood was laid all around the feet of the others.

The chief then roughly pulled Julia from her tent and tried to take her in his arms. The girl fought bravely, but was, of course, overpowered. Paul Matherson struggled to free himself that he might go to her help. At last he broke loose from his captors. He struck the chief a blow that made him drop the girl.

Another Indian came up behind him and hit him a resounding blow on his head. He dropped like a log. With a triumphant shout, the Indians closed in.

But hark! There comes a galloping of horses' hooves, twenty-five troopers with Sam Laria at their head. The Indians stood their ground, but were soon pushed back. Sam rode over to the fallen Julia and lifted her to his horse.

The Indians were soon beaten. The troopers dismounted and untied the prisoners, but Tom Parry was never heard of again. Some say he untied himself and got away and is still living in the forest. But others say that he was killed by Indians and carried off.

As Bob Goodhart untied Paul Matherson, a wounded brave raised up on his elbow. Seeing a pistol near, he seized it, aimed at Matherson, and fired. The bullet struck home. The man reeled and would have fallen, but Captain Goodhart caught him and laid him on the grass.

Matherson's wound was looked at, for there was a surgeon among the company. He shook his head gravely. "It's no use. One of the arteries is severed. He may live an hour, but I doubt it. If he has anything to say, you'd better make him say it now," and he walked off.

"Sam! Sam!" said Julia. "He tried to save me. Go and tell him that I forgive him and that you do, too. He was brave."

"But he's my worst enemy, Julia. If it were not for him, I would have been a rich man," argued Sam.

"What! You never told me about it. What was it?"

"My father was a rich man; he left me a fortune. Matherson was the cashier of the bank. I placed a great deal of trust in him, but he made off with a good deal of money. I worked pretty hard to pay off my creditors. Then I came West and met up with him out here, at the place I worked. I loved you. So did he. I was going to have him arrested, but he skipped with Malone, Parry, and Dickson. I and the sheriff chased him for a good way, then the sheriff gave up the chase. I still hunted him. He knew this and captured me, and you, too. But how did you get out there?" he asked her.

"The stagecoach was held up. Why they captured me, I don't see, but I was carried a good way. At last, I escaped and met you in the clearing. You told me to wait there 'til you could find some water. I was taken prisoner again. You know the rest, but I wonder if Mr. Matherson will give up that money?"

"Beg pardon, sir," said a trooper, "but that man that is wounded, wants to see you and Miss Weston."

"All right, I'm coming," said Sam.

Matherson had been made as comfortable as they could make him. As Sam and Julia came up he raised upon his arm. "Sam Laria," he said, "I wanted to tell you before I go. That money I stole from you"—Here he sank back on the ground again. Julia quickly dashed some water in his face, and slipped her arm underneath his head. He went on, "is in that hollow tree," he gasped, "by the camp where we was captured—down by the brook, understand?"

"Yes, I do," said Laria breathlessly.

"It's all there." He began again, "Laria, I am a scoundrel, I know, but will you shake hands and say you forgive me?" Sam looked at Julia. She nodded.

"Yes," he said, taking the dying man's hand, "you've been pretty bad, Matherson, but I forgive you."

"Thanks," muttered the other, "can—you—get the boys?"

"Parry's not here. Don't know where he went," said Sam. "Send for Dick and Frank! Quick!"

Malone and Dickson were quickly sent for. They both immediately dropped beside him.

"How do you feel, old fellow?" asked Malone tenderly.

"I'm going to die soon boys;" he said, "that's why I sent for you. Boys, shake hands with Sam now—before I go." This was done.

"Julia—Miss Weston—could—could you give me—one—kiss, just one?" Julia looked at Sam. He nodded "yes." She leaned and

Girlhood Writings of Margaret Mitchell

kissed him on the forehead. He smiled faintly and murmured, "Good-bye," and fell back.

The surgeon leaned over him. "It's all up with him, poor fellow," he said. Instantly, all heads were bared and bowed. Dickson, though he was a large, strong man, broke down. Julia fainted. Malone was nearly as broken as his friend, and tears were in the eyes of Laria.

An hour later all were assembled under the shade of a large tree. Matherson was lowered into the grave prepared for it, while Captain Goodhart read the burial services from a small book that one of the men carried. A crude cross was put on the grave to show where he lay.

They started for the fort the next morning. On the way they stopped by the eventful camp, and Malone showed him where the money was hidden. When they reached the fort, Sam said, "Julia, after all this delay and trouble, can't you say 'yes' and be mine forever?"

She blushed, but did not lower her eyes as she answered softly, "Yes."

He drew something from his pocket. "Julia," he remarked, "I got this before I started to hunt for poor Matherson. I didn't lose it, either. There." He slipped a beautiful ring on Julia's finger and kissing her hand as he did so.

"Dear, it's a beauty," Julia said, blushing.

"Won't you get married tomorrow? There's a Justice of the Peace around here."

"I'm willing," responded Julia.

The next day, they came from out of the Justice's office, no longer lovers, but man and wife. There had been no wedding supper, no flowers, or bridesmaids, but they were just as happy—maybe happier.

"Sam," said Julia, five years later, when she looked at the child on the floor.

"Yes dear," he answered, looking up from his paper.

"There's something I'll never forget," she said.

"What's that, lovely?"

"I'll never forget Paul Matherson's lonely grave away out on the plains, will you?"

"I should say not," he answered, "but now I think we're all happy. Frank and Dick are in our business and are very happy, or at least, I think they are happy. If only we knew where Tom Parry was. He may be out at his comrade's grave now."

"Yes, dear," Julia answered, "I think we are all happy, but I won't ever forget our adventure in the forest and foothills."

The End   *Finis*

Part Four

Margaret poses in a studio portrait, circa 1911

Civil War Tales

⌒

MARGARET MITCHELL BEST DESCRIBED HER

Southern heritage and knowledge of Civil War lore in a letter writ-

ten in 1936 to Julia Collier Harris, a friend of her mother's and a

newspaper journalist. She wrote:

As to how I got started on Civil War material, I suppose I

started in my cradle. Father is an authority on Atlanta and

Georgia history of that period and Mother knew about as

much as he did. I heard so much when I was little about the fighting and the hard times after the war that I firmly believed Mother and Father had been through it all instead of being born long afterward. In fact, I was about ten years old before I learned the war hadn't ended shortly before I was born. Mother used to sing me to sleep with those doleful tunes of the Sixties.

She goes on to describe hearing her relatives recount their own experiences during the war.

On Sunday afternoons when we went calling on the older generation of relatives, those who had been active in the Sixties, I sat on the bony knees of veterans and the fat slippery laps of great-aunts and heard them talk about the times when Little Alex was visiting them and how much fried chicken Father Ryan could put away and how nice thick wrapping paper felt when put between the skin and the corset in the cold days during the blockade when woolen goods were so scarce. And how Grandpa Mitchell walked nearly fifty miles after the Battle of Sharpsburg with his skull cracked in two places from a bullet. They didn't talk of these happenings as history nor as remarkable events but just as part of their lives and not especially epic parts. And they gradually became a part of my life.

When Margaret was seven or eight, Eugene Mitchell took the family to Sharpsburg, Maryland, to see where her grandfather had received those cracks in his skull at Antietam.

Atlanta itself had numerous reminders of the war. The children played on the old Confederate breastworks that ran through the back corner of the vacant lot on Jackson Street. They found minié balls and were captivated by visits to the Atlanta Cyclorama, a 358-feet-long painting-in-the-round depicting the Battle of Atlanta. Stephens and Margaret both had vivid recollections of Atlanta's Confederate Day parades in which surviving veterans solemnly marched every April. In a 1936 letter to Donald Adams, who reviewed *Gone With the Wind* for *The New York Times*, Mitchell wrote, "I cut my teeth on that Johnston-Sherman running fight, dug bullets out of the old breastworks when I was little, climbed the steep side of Kennesaw Mountain where the guns were pulled up by hand (and it's hard climbing even when you aren't dragging cannon!). And went out at low water to see in the shallows of the river the Federal cannon lost in a brave attempt to cross the ford in the face of the Confederate rifles." It is not surprising that among the surviving childhood stories, two are set against the backdrop of the Civil War.

In the early 1980s, Darden Pyron attributed a manuscript at the Atlanta History Center to the young Margaret Mitchell based on the work's similarities to Mitchell stories found in the Hargrett Library. Jane Powers Weldon edited the manuscript, which she published in the *Atlanta Historical Journal* under the title "Through the Eyes of a Youth: A Civil War Story." The discovery of the first three chapters of this story confirms the attribution to Mitchell.

On one of the newly discovered pages Mitchell had written "237 pages are in this book. This story was begun on January 16, 1913." Sixty-seven pages are missing between the conclusion of the newly discovered first chapters and where the story picks up again in "Through the Eyes of a Youth." As Weldon suggests in her introduction to the story, a mouse may have chewed through parts of the handmade book, thus missing or illegible words are noted by the use of brackets. The previously published fragment has been edited in the same manner as the recently discovered material and both are printed here.

A similar second story about the Civil War was found in the new collection. Both stories were written on tablet paper folded to make a booklet like those containing the stories "The Little Pioneers," "When We Were Shipwrecked," and "Forest and Foothills." It is very likely that this second story was also written by Margaret in 1913 as a companion piece to the one found in the AHC archives.

Since the title pages of both stories are missing, I have taken the liberty of entitling the stories "Hugh Warren, A Spy for the Union" and "Dan Morrison, A Spy for the Confederacy."

"Hugh Warren, A Spy for the Union"

[*The title page and four pages of the first chapter are missing.*
Following is the beginning of page five.]

half convinced, Mrs. Warren turned to her fire and began to prepare the supper. It was late in the night when John woke up, white-faced and weary.

"Oh, Betty, it was so dark! Never mind, we'll have our little man with us before tomorrow night." His surmise was not correct, for the next night he sadly took an old family Bible out of the wagon and wrote under the names of John and Elizabeth Warren—

Hugh Warren—8 years
Son of John and Elizabeth Warren
Lost on July 30, 1849

CHAPTER II

"Tom?"

"Yes, dear?"

"What is that?"

"What?"

"Why, don't you see that thing moving right in front?"

"Yes, I see it now! I'll drive over there and find out what it is," and Tom Haverhill turned his horse's head around.

"Why, Mother, it's a boy," said Haverhill, as the old "prairie schooner" was stopped beside a figure which was seated on the ground.

Sturdily built, with a mop of brown, curly hair, his blue eyes looked steadily into Tom Haverhill's brown ones, but the man saw a mute appeal behind this gaze. He leaped down. "Are you lost, boy?"

"Yes," answered the boy, rising with difficulty.

"Where are your father and mother?" questioned Mrs. Haverhill.

"I don't know, ma'am," said the stranger. "I started out to walk about and I got lost, but I believe we were camping in that direction," and he pointed to the setting sun. "I'd be greatly obliged, ma'am," he added timidly, "if you'd give me something to eat. I'm awfully hungry."

"Of course, I will," said Mrs. Haverhill, climbing into the back of the wagon and taking out several articles. "I guess, Tom," she added to her husband, "this spot will do just as good as any to camp on." He nodded and unhitched the horses.

In the meantime, the little girl advanced boldly up to the boy and inquired, "What's your name?"

"Hugh Warren," answered he, "and what's yours?"

"Marion Haverhill," she replied, and in a few minutes they were talking as if they had been lifetime friends.

"What is your name, child?" questioned Mrs. Haverhill.

"Hugh Warren," replied the one addressed, hungrily eyeing the food that she was preparing.

Tom Haverhill noticed this. "Hungry, eh?" he inquired. Hugh nodded. "When did you have your last meal?"

"Day before yesterday," Hugh answered in a matter-of-fact tone. "What—what? Day before yesterday?" Tom Haverhill laid his hand on Hugh's shoulders. "Boy, you're brave. You've got more grit than a lot of men I know!"

After Hugh had eaten and drunk his fill, he told his story. He had wandered off a good way and had mistaken his way. He had found a spring, but nothing to eat. He'd given up hope of ever being found when Mrs. Haverhill had seen him.

"Well, Hugh," said Tom Haverhill, "you just sleep well tonight, like nothing had ever happened. We'll go back and find your father and mother for you."

"Oh, sir," cried Hugh in gratitude, "I can't hardly thank you. I—"

"Never mind thanking me," interrupted Haverhill. "You tell me where 'bout you think you were camping."

The boy looked thoughtful, "I am almost sure it was there," and he pointed to the West, which was now faintly tinged with pink, but was rapidly growing dark.

"All right, don't worry, we'll find them, wherever they are," said Haverhill, disappearing into the wagon.

Hugh also climbed into the wagon and lay down, but it wasn't until shortly before dawn that he dozed off to sleep.

CHAPTER III

"Hey there, stranger, don't you go no farther." It was at noon the following day and Hugh had just announced in delight that the land looked familiar to him, and that he was sure they were near where the

Warrens had camped, when a man on horseback rode over a high ridge of mountains and shouted these words at them.

Behind him, hidden by a big cloud of dust, came a party of people

[*Pages are missing.*]

Chapter VII

He was horrorstruck at the loss of [his] precious weapon, but noiselessly he drew his sword, determined to defend himself till the last. The Confederate threw the door open and stepped back as Hugh leaped out, sword drawn, and then began a furious battle. The Confederate was a good swordsman, as Hugh soon discovered, and once his sword had struck Hugh's chest but had hit the dispatches and glanced off. Neither spoke. There was no time for words as round and round the room they went, striking and parrying thrusts. Hugh was bleeding from several wounds but he had not struck his adversary once. At last Hugh's sword glided under the other weapon and struck the Confederate full in the chest. Hugh stepped back, his sword in a defensive position.

There was no more use for it, however, as the Confederate took a step forward and then fell on the floor and lay still.

The sun, setting, sent its rays filtering through the window on the face of the man who lay on the floor. For some moments Hugh gazed at the pale face, and then with a cry of pain, he dropped on his knees beside the fallen Confederate. It was his old friend and schoolmate Bob Oswald!

CHAPTER VIII

As Hugh knelt beside Bob, all the hatred which two years of war had embedded in his heart vanished, and Bob was not a foe, but a dear friend. Hugh unbuttoned his friend's coat, fanned him with his hat, rubbed his hands, and did all he could to restore him to consciousness, and finally had the satisfaction of seeing him open his eyes.

"Why, Hugh," he exclaimed in weak tones after gazing around, "then it *was* you all the time. Old fellow you've done me now."

Hugh, who had forgotten all thoughts of escape and danger, clasped the wounded man's hand. "Oh Bob, I didn't know it was you or I—"

"Hugh," the Confederate interrupted, "are you aware of your danger?"

"*My* danger?" Hugh exclaimed.

"Your danger, yes, you have papers—don't interrupt—but you have," he said seeing that the Federal was about to speak. "I came to look for a Confederate that was said to be hiding in this neighborhood and there's a squad a soldiers with me. I left them at a house down the road eating, but I told them to come here. So there's no escape for you, for there are sentries all around here and you are bound to be caught. Your camp is ———," and he told Hugh in which direction his camp lay.

"But, Bob," cried Hugh in astonishment, "why are you telling me this? When you go back you'll be shot for letting me, carrying dispatches, escape."

"Because, Hugh, I could not keep you from escaping if I wanted to with this wound in my chest." He was silent for a minute, then he spoke abruptly, "Take off that uniform of yours."

Hugh stared at this former roommate in astonishment. Was his mind wandering? "Take off my uniform?" he repeated, astounded.

"Yes, and be quick too," replied the other sharply, "and take off mine too. Put your uniform on me and you put on mine. Don't ask any questions, and be quick." Hugh did as he was directed, wondering. It was a matter of a few minutes to exchange clothes and soon Hugh stood in a gray Confederate captain's uniform while Bob lay on the floor, his hand pressed over his chest, in a blue Federal lieutenant's uniform.

"Now old fellow," begged Hugh, "tell me what you mean?"

"It's this way, Hugh," answered Bob. "You are sure to be captured and then you would be shot, and [in that] uniform of mine you can get through safely," he ended with a gasp.

"But you, Bob," cried the Federal, "what will you do?"

"Hugh," said the Confederate solemnly, "you know as well as I do that I'm dying."

"Bob, it's not so! It's not so," exclaimed Hugh passionately as he bent over his old friend whose face was deathly white.

"Hugh,—hurry—they'll be here—soon," almost whispered Bob brokenly. Hugh paid no heed.

"Oh! Bob, and to think that it was I who hurt you," he cried remorsefully.

"Fortunes—of war," gasped the other, his eyes closing. "Goo— goo—good-bye."

"Oh! Bob, isn't there any thing that I can do for you?" As if in answer the Confederate sighed [weakly] and ceased to breathe. The hand which Hugh held slipped from Hugh's clasp and fell to the floor. Hugh rose to his feet and staggered against the wall, his arm over his eyes.

Then, from the yard came the sound of horses, the clank of spurs, and the sound of voices. Hugh straightened [up], squared his shoulders, and pulled the gray hat low over his face, and started down the stairs. It was lucky for Hugh that he and Bob had been nearly of the same stature and the downstairs hall was dark. As he came down the steps a dozen or more gray coats entered the front door.

"Did you get him, Captain?" asked a corporal.

"Yes, upstairs," said Hugh in a voice which he tried to steady, and trying to imitate Bob's voice, "file up, men," he added. The men obeyed the order and filed up the stairs. Their horses were standing outside and Hugh leaped on the first he saw and rode off at top speed.

CHAPTER IX

"Oh! Hugh, you are not hurt much, are you? Tell me, quick!"

"Well, Tom, if you don't call a saber cut on the head and a ball through the leg very bad, I don't know what you call bad. Of course it could be worse."

"I suppose that you'll go home, Hugh. I'm certainly glad that you, that you are not hurt worse."

This was two months after Hugh had escaped through the Confederate lines. There was no difficulty in getting through them as he wore his gray uniform. But there was difficulty in getting into his own camp. Hugh had been wounded on the preceding day and lay in the hospital with Tom Lacy sitting beside him. He and a good many others were put on the next train and soon Hugh arrived at home. He was taken to a hospital and then he sent word to Mrs. Haverhill. Within an hour's time that worthy lady's carriage stood outside of the hospital and Hugh was carried and [laid on] one of the seats. Then the carriage was driven home carefully. Arriving in front of the house, Hugh was carried inside by two colored servants and laid on a bed upstairs.

"You poor, *poor* boy," cried Marion as Mrs. Haverhill and she hurried about to make Hugh more comfortable. "Is your head hurt badly?"

Hugh smiled, "The surgeon said that if my head hadn't have been as thick as a wall, I might have been serious hurt."

That night, as he lay propped up on pillows with the light of the fire shining on his face, Hugh thought of his friends in camp. "Well, Hugh," exclaimed Marion running in a moment later, "you were always a good shot, but could you shoot better than the rest of the boys?"

"I wish that I didn't know how to shoot at all," cried he.

"Why?" questioned she.

For an answer he said, "Do you remember Dick Dalton?"

"Yes," Marion smiled, "he went to college with you."

"Well," said Hugh, "I'll make the story short. One night we camped acrossed the river from the Rebs, [only they did not know it] as we were in the woods. We were going to make a night attack and so we all crawled up to the top of a small hill on the riverbank. It was a bright moonlight night. Right on the [other] side of the river was a Rebel sentry. I was the nearest to the major who was leading, so he said, "Shoot the Reb, Warren, but don't miss." Just as I got out my pistol the sentry stopped and took off his hat and ran his hand through his hair. His figure was familiar and even across the river I could see his face and it was Dick. I stopped with my pistol raised. The major got mad and told me to shoot, and I shot." Hugh gazed intently at the fire. "Yes, I shot him," he continued. "We were crossing the bridge when he raised up and fired his gun. In a minute all the Rebels were up and ready and we were beaten back. I wish I knew whether he was dead or not. I feel like a murderer." Both were silent for a while.

Then Marion spoke, "Hugh, I know something." She smiled.

"What?" questioned he.

Marion gave a rippling laugh. "You are in love," she said.

He gave a startled exclamation. "How did you guess?" he cried.

Marion laughed again. "There you confessed it," she said. "Well, I knew it by the way you talk and the way you act. Her name must be Edith."

"Marion," interrupted Hugh, "You are a [   ]

"She must be named Edith," continued she, "because when I came and told you that Edith was here, and asked how you were, you grew very red and confused and said 'Edith Allerton?' and said 'no, Edith Johnson.'"

"You have good eyes," laughed Hugh.

"I have all the evidence," said Marion, "and there's nothing to do but confess."

"All right, I'll confess," replied he, "but it's a long story."

"Go on," she urged, and so Hugh began.

"It was last month," he said, "when we were down in Virginia, that

I was riding along a pretty road; I was taking four messages to Major Andrews and was coming back. As I was in no hurry I let the horse walk and was enjoying the scenery when someone called, 'Oh please stop.' I pulled out my pistol and ordered them to come forward. No one showed up, but the voice said, 'Oh! Please come here. I'm right around the bend in the road.' I came, but very slowly, expecting to be shot. However when I rode slowly around the bend I found the prettiest girl I had ever seen. She was sitting in a buggy, but one of the wheels was off. She laughed when she saw my pistol. I asked her what had happened and she replied that one wheel had come off and while yet deliberating, a band of our foragers came up and took the horse, leaving her to get home, which she said was two miles off. When she heard me she thought that it might be a neighbor who would give her a ride to her house. She was sorry at having stopped me, but that it was a mistake; then she got out and started up the road, but she had not gone a dozen steps before I jumped off and ran after her. I said that I would take her if she wouldn't mind riding behind me. She accepted with thanks and I helped her on behind. Marion, by this time I was so in love with her that I could scarcely drive. It was love on first sight in my case. I introduced myself and she said that her name was Edith Allerton. That ride was the pleasantest ride I ever had in my life. In a short while we stopped before a large, white house with pillars in front. I helped her down and she asked me to come into the house. As I was in no hurry to get back to camp, I went inside the house. It certainly was furnished beautifully. She said, 'Please wait until I get off my hat,' and she went into the next room. I looked at several of the pictures then suddenly I heard a noise behind me. On looking around I saw a half dozen Rebels with guns on a level with my head. I tried to get my pistol, but the Rebel captain was too quick for me and I found myself gazing down the muzzle of his revolver. 'Put up your hands, Yank,' he ordered. I obeyed. 'Take off his belt, Jake,' he said to another man who immediately relieved me of my sword and pistol. I felt like committing murder for once in my life. 'Now, Yank,' said the captain, 'you behave and we aint a-goin' to hurt you, but I won't answer for your life if you try to get away.' I was marched into a room at the end of a hall, and put inside of it, and a sentry was put at the door. There were no windows and so there was no escape. I suppose it was a store room."

Hugh paused a moment and Marion eagerly inquired, "How did you get away?"

"Well," continued Hugh, "I had been in there about two hours when there was a big commotion in the house and then an old colored man ran into the room and [   ] to a cupboard ⌊in⌋ the cor[ner] of the room and took out a bottle and looked at it but it was empty. I asked him what was the matter and he said Edith's mother was very sick and that there was no medicine in the house. You know, Marion, I always carry a few different kinds of medicine in my saddle bags. I told the Negro about them and I [   ] [   ]d that they were all [   ]d, and perhaps they might help her. He said that he would tell Miss Edith about it and then he went out and then the house became quieter. In another hour I heard someone talking outside and then Edith came. She didn't say a word but she pulled a pistol out of her dress and handed it to me. I took it and started to speak but she put her hand to her lips and [   ] me a note. I caught her hand and kissed it. She turned very red and grabbed a bottle off the table and ran out. I looked at the note; it said, 'You will have to forgive me for what I did but my father made me do it. Your medicines saved my mother's life. The door is not locked and so you can get out. Shoot the guard if necessary. Your horse is where you left it. I am everlastingly indebted to you. Edith Allerton.' And so," concluded Hugh, "I burst the door open and hit the sentry on the head before he could shoot me and then ran out of the house; my horse was on the outside, where I had left him. I got on and got back to [   ] as quickly as I could."

[*Pages are missing*]

this locket since the night Mr. and Mrs. Haverhill adopted me. Mother gave it to me." He suddenly changed the subject. "Look here, Tom, how are we to arrange this business?" Tom replied that he had the plans already laid out, when a little boy about nine years old came in sig [   ] on coming [   ] Tom asked the boy if he knew how far off the Confederate camp was. The child looked at him somewhat curiously but answered that it was over the hill and he pointed towards the left. Tom and Hugh thanked him and went the way he directed. It was a little [   ] away from the camp that they ha[l]ted.

"Now," said Tom, "I'll tell you what to do. Do you see that tree?" He pointed to a large tree near by with thick foliage. Hugh nodded. "Well," said Tom, "you meet me there tomorrow morning at about twelve o'clock. If nothing happens I'll be there. You got some grub in your knapsack and you got a canteen of water, so you are all provided for. Stay around anywhere tonight but don't get caught and, Hugh," he added [   ] his hand in his coat. "[   ] get back, or something [   ] give this to Marion [   ] "this" was a small, though rather bulky letter. "Good-bye," and he was gone.

Hugh tramped for some ways in the woods and then sat down to rest; for the rest of the day and the night he stayed there. Then at about 11 o'clock the following morning he retraced his steps to the tree. By looking at his [   ] he found that he [   ] an hour early.

Then suddenly he felt a sudden desire to climb the tree. Catching the lowest limbs, he swung himself up, and from thence he climbed to the top of the tree. It was a splendid view. Hugh was startled, however, at the nearness to the Confederate camp. He was just preparing to descend, when he heard voices below him. He stopped [   ] he heard a gruff [   ] say, "Your beat is from this tree to that rock."

And then another voice responded, "Yes sir!" and then there was a sound of tramping feet and Hugh saw a squad of men marching toward the camp. His heart seemed to stand still. "They've posted a sentry [   ] here and Tom [   ]nt know it; when he comes back, he'll be arrested. If I get down most likely I'll be arrested for I can't give an account of myself. What shall I do?" From his position he could see the sentry pacing back and forward. He could shoot the man easily, but the shot would arouse [   ] camp. There was nothing to do but to[   ] At last Hugh saw Tom hurrying along. Hugh cautiously crawled down to the lowest limb he dared. The sentry reached the tree and turned to pace to the rock; just then Tom stepped out of the bushes and looked for Hugh, but did not see the Confederate. Hugh climbed down the tree [   ]dly, "Give me [   ] of the papers; hurry, there's a sentry." Tom saw the sentry and hastily handed Hugh several papers folded together. "Run," he said, and just then he heard the sentry yell "Halt there!" but both started running. "Halt or I fire!" cried the Confederate. Hugh dropped the papers, and as he turned to pick them up the sentry fired [   ] felt as if a hot knife been run along his chest, but he regained his feet and dashed off before the sentry came up. The Confederate rushed off to the camp firing his pistol as he ran.

Hugh did not know what had become of Tom. To avoid dropping the papers again he t[   ]st them into his [   ] as he did so his hand came in contact with something warm and sticky. It was blood. On the front of his coat there was a small red spot which was growing larger. He felt weak from pain and loss of blood, but he kept steadily on. Hardly knowing where he was going he stumbled up the driveway of a large house. An old Negro man was standing on the porch, as Hugh came up. Hugh leaned [   ] a tree and beckon [   ] the Negro, who came up.

"Law's a mercy massa! What de matter?"

"I—I—I'm hurt," gasped Hugh, now not able to stand. The old man sprang forward and slipped his arm under Hugh's shoulders and began shouting, "Miss 'Lisbeth! Oh Miss 'Lisbeth! Step 'har a second."

A sweet-faced woman ran [   ]t on the porch [   ] the matter, "Toby?"

"[   ] here soldier hurt [   ]," answered Toby.

"Oh! Bring him in the house," cried she, opening the door wider, and Hugh, assisted by the Negro, was brought into the house and laid on a sofa. Hugh's head seemed to swim and the floor reeled and he fell backward. "He has fainted," said the woman quietly. "Get me some warm water."

Old Toby hurried out and return [   ] some warm water and some cloths. "He must be shot in the chest, m'am," said Toby, "'cause deres blood on the front of his coat."

"I guess so, Toby," she answered. "You can go now, for I don't guess I'll need you," and Toby made his exit.

As [   ] woman opened his coat her eyes [   ] the locket suspended from his neck.

"That locket," she whispered, "that locket." She caught it in her hands and opened it. She gave a startled exclamation and took Hugh by the arm and shook him. "Where did you get this locket?" she cried, "Where did you get it?" but there was no response. Quickly taking the pan [of] [wa]ter she sprinkle [   ] over his face and shook him again. Under this vigorous treatment, Hugh gained half-sensibility. "This locket," cried the woman as he partly opened his eyes, "where did you get it?"

"Locket?" gasped Hugh. "My mother—gave—it to me."

"Where is she now?" [   ] woman.

"[   ]" gasped Hugh, "dead [   ] killed—them."

"My boy," cried she.

"Oh!" groaned Hugh setting his teeth, "My chest," and he fainted again.

"Oh, my boy," she cried, "you thought me dead and I thought you dead, too!"

In joy Mrs. Warren (for it was she) started to unbutton his coat. [   ] ther, when s [   ] her hand on [   ] pieces of paper. They came unfolded. There to her horrified eyes were several well-drawn maps which she knew were maps of the fortifications and of the neighboring camp. She dropped them as if they [had] burnt her hands. "Spy," she gasped. "Spy!" She whispered again, "But he is my son and hurt," and so taking no further notice of the maps she went on dressing his chest.

She had just finished bandaging Hugh's chest when there was a tramp of feet and in walked Mr. Warren in a Confederate colonel's uniform. [   ]

"Why Betty," h [   ] "What's this?" [   ]

"Oh, John, it's Hugh; it is my son," cried Mrs. Warren.

"What?" roared Mr. Warren.

Mrs. Warren explained all. "Oh, John and it really is," she cried tearfully.

"Betty and what is this?" "This" was the maps that lay on the table.

"Oh!" gasped Mrs. Warren.

"He had them in his coat, didn't he?" demanded her husband coldly.

[   ] assented in an almost inaudible tone.

"Then," Hugh's father's face was ashy gray and his mouth in a grim line, "then Hugh, our son, is a traitor, a spy!"

"Oh, John, you wouldn't think of giving him up, would you?" cried his wife.

Mr. Warren did not answer. His heart was the conflicting battlefield of love and duty [   ] love conquered. [   ] "No," he said slowly, "Betty, I wouldn't."

"Then, John, what shall we do with him?"

He was just about to answer when two Confederate officers walked into the room. The one in front gave a cry of surprise as his eyes fell on Hugh. "The same fellow, isn't it Sam?" he cried to the other [   ]e responded.

With a great effort Mr. Warren questioned, "What are you talking about?"

Instantly both were at attention. "Your pardon, Colonel," said one politely, "for coming in so abruptly, but the general says to report at

once. Two spies have just escaped. I shouldn't wonder if this isn't one,"
he [   ] again at Hugh w[   ] all unconscious[dram? a back   ]

"How do you know?" questioned Mrs. Warren.

"Because m'am," said one, "we were coming along after a battle
and we picked this fellow up. He escaped that night and"—he
stopped. "Look there," he cried. "There are the [   ] that were stolen.
We've caught [the] spy!"

CHAPTER XII

There was a long silence and then Mrs. Warren gave a cry, "No! No,
you must not arrest him."

"Madam," said the one addressed as Sam, "we arrest this man on
charge of being a spy."

Just then Hugh [   ] his eyes. He overheard the last part [   ] sentence "We arrest this man on charge as a spy."

There was nothing for the unhappy parents to do. Several other
soldiers tramped in and assisted Hugh to his feet. He looked around
in a dazed [   ]. Who was [this] white-faced woman [   ] Who was
that man with clenched fists? And how did all these soldiers get there?

Assisted by two soldiers he was brought into camp, before the general. He was charged with being a spy. The fact that he wore [a] gray
uniform [   ] fied that, and [   ] officers identified him. Hugh answered
their questions dazedly admitting that he was a Yankee, but denying
that he had been to the camp. It was no use however for he *was* a spy.

He was sentenced to be shot [at] sunrise; a [   ]ce which he took
[   ]g. A heavy [   ] was placed [   ] the one-roomed cabin where he
was put. When darkness came on, a lamp was placed on the table and

a soldier placed some food on the table beside it. Hugh, however, paid no attention. He was lying on a cot in one corner, with his arm over his face, [   ] appearances [   ] But he was n [   ] he was thinking of the morrow. [   ] trying to recall to his memory when and where he had seen those two faces, the white-faced woman and the man with the clenched fist. Finally he gave it up, his mind being far from clear.

It was a very dark night [   ]d see that through [   ] door. As he [   ]king there came the [   ] a rifle then another and another. Then a trampling of horses and shouts and yells. He sprang up, just in time to see the sentry fall across the doorway, dead. With a cry he stepped over the body and out of the cabin. There was no one to hinder him. A riderless horse trotted up. With some difficulty Hugh mounted [   ] was raging fur [   ] let the horse tak[   ] course, hardly [   ] where he we[   ] The animal turned to the right coming out into a road. Hugh had hardly turned him around when another person on horseback caught his rein, "Stop," cried a voice, which made Hugh jump.

"What do you want?" he said. [   ] this Hugh [   ]oked the voice [   ]d, this is Tom, [   ]?"

"Yes," said the speaker who *was* Tom. "Oh! Hugh, are you hurt?"

"Yes," said Hugh whose horse was alongside of Tom's.

"Bad?"

"Not very. Did you [get] the maps safely?"

"Yes, did you?"

"No, they were taken [from] me while I was [   ] land."

"Hugh, come [   ] I know you're hurt. We've licked these Rebels fair and square," cried Tom.

"Lead on, Tom," said Hugh wearily leaning over the front of the saddle worn out. Tom took the bridle rein and led Hugh's horse off. As he [   ] e enemy were [   ] and had retreated [   ] it was many [   ] before he left the [   ]

CHAPTER XIII

It was a warm summer day in 1864, and the army of the Federals was again passing through Virginia. The troops were tired and so was the general. He was looking for a suitable spot for headquarters and he has sent a [   ] head for this [   ] purpose. T [   ] had reported [   ] was a large house several miles on which would do admirably. The general laughed, "I don't guess the people who live there will thank you for picking their house."

He turned to a young man on his left, "You ride ahead and announce our coming, colonel."

"Yes sir," said the colonel w [   ] was Hugh Warren [   ] e spurred his [   ] n. As he drew [   ] e house some [   ] ed familiar to him. As he drew up before the house, a little girl of about 8 years, who was playing near by, gave a shriek and ran into the house shouting, "Mamma, sister! Here's another damned Yank!"

Hugh could not suppress a smile [   ] but he knocked [   ] door. It was [   ] tly opened by [   ] woman of ab [   ] They both gazed at each other. "*You!*" cried she in astonishment.

"*You,*" cried Hugh equally astonished. It was Edith Allerton.

Then she spoke again in a cold tone. "What do you want, sir?"

Hugh drew himself up and said stiffly, "I regret to cause you any inconvenience, but the [   ] e has chosen this [   ] as his headquarters," then he bowed [   ]ed off and mounted his horse. Then he rode back to the general and reported.

It was not long before the general and his staff were installed in the Allertons' home. Hugh and Tom were on his staff.

It was in the late afternoon and the two [   ] sitting in the [   ] talking over the [   ] a small head [   ] cautiously [   ] through the [   ] a pair of blue eyes surveyed them with interest. "Won't you come in?" said Hugh presently.

The curtains parted and the same child that he had seen in the morning came in. "Yes, I'll come in," she answered, "'cause I can't go outside, 'cause of the soldiers." She moved closer and gazed in- [   ] at Hugh's head. "[   ] the matter?" he [   ] he child's face [   ] earnest as she [   ] question.

[*Pages 174-237 are missing.*]

"Dan Morrison, A Spy for the Confederacy"

[*The first chapter and part of the second are missing.*]

held a gun at a threatening attitude.

"Well?" asked Dan coolly.

"Where are you going? Who are you?" asked the sentinel.

"Oh, that's what you want, is it?" laughed Dan. "Well, here's my pass," and he gave the soldier a pass the general had given him.

The sentry looked at it suspiciously, but handed it back saying, "All right, I guess you can pass." Dan laughed and rode on.

That night he slept in the open with Banyard's saddle for a pillow. He did not mind as he was an old campaigner and used to out-of-doors living. So far he had seen no Yankees, but he had heard from a Negro that the Northern Army lay straight in front of him, but by a wide detour he could escape it. He determined to do this, but on his way back he passed through the Yankee camp.

CHAPTER III

"Man outside that says he must see you, sir. Shall I bring him in?" asked an orderly.

"Yes," responded the general absently. The orderly returned with Dan Morrison behind him. Dan saluted and handed the general the dispatch. The general read it over, then looked up.

"When did you start?" he asked.

"I started yesterday at five o'clock. It is now five o'clock. I brought it in thirteen hours," said Dan.

"You are well mounted?"

"Yes, I don't believe there's a better horse in the state," said Dan proudly. The general called an orderly.

"See that this man's horse has forage and that Lieutenant Morrison has something to eat, too. Report here tomorrow at eight o'clock, Morrison."

"Yes, sir." Dan saluted and followed the soldier. Food was scarce in the Confederate camp, but he was given what they had.

The next morning at eight, Dan reported to the general.

"Here," said the commander, General Stuart. "Be very careful of it for a good deal depends on it; but I know you will, so there is no use taking precautions."

"I will do my duty the best I can," Dan promised earnestly. Dan inquired, as he left, as to the position of the Northern fort. He was told that it was about twenty-five miles away. Dan rode slowly as there was no use tiring his horse.

The next day he was near the Yankee fortifications so he dismounted, put on a suit of rough clothes that he had with him; then he turned Banyard loose in a clearing, knowing the horse would come at his call.

Dan had brought some money with him so he went to a farm house and knocked on the door. A pleasant woman opened the door, but on seeing him, shut it quickly. "You need not come here," she said, "for the Yankees have taken everything I've got. Thank goodness, both of my boys are out fighting the Yanks. What do you want to know? And who are you?"

"I am a Confederate scout, ma'am. I tell you this because I know you'll not betray me!"

"Of course I won't," said the woman, opening the door. "What do you want?"

"Could you sell me some kind of drink?" asked Dan. "I want to get into the camp."

"Well, there's not an orange or lemon on the place," answered the woman, "but I've got a little gin buried in the woods. I'll get it for you."

"I'll pay you well for it," replied Dan, as she hurried off. Soon she returned with the liquor.

"I mixed it with some sweet herbs and a little molasses," she explained.

"How much must I pay you?" asked Dan.

"Well, as times are hard, I must ask you two dollars for it," she replied. Dan paid the required amount and, after thanking the woman, went in the direction of the camp.

Dan sold a good deal of his liquor to a Negro regiment that was working on some fortifications, but in reality, he was taking notes of all he saw—positions of guns, etc. The Negro soldiers did not take much notice of him so he moved unhindered from one part of the camp to the other.

As it grew late he started to leave the camp, but it was hard work. At last he managed to slip away unseen. Once in the shelter of the woods, the disguise was removed for a gray uniform. "I wonder if any suspected me?" he thought. "It would seem rather strange for a man to be selling things. Anyway, I'm safe for the time." His horse was found eating nearby, so he took the saddle from where he had hidden it, buckled it on his steed's back, and mounted. He made a wide detour for he was very anxious.

He had ridden until sunset when, on crossing a small bridge, the barrel of a rifle showed through the bushes and a stern voice exclaimed, "Halt! Who goes there?"

Dan took no chances for he had seen a blue uniform in the thicket. He clasped his spurs to the horse's side, but not before a Yankee in full uniform barred his path and asked again, "Who goes there?"

"I do," said Dan with grim humor, placing his hand on his pistol. "Let me pass, my man!"

"Not much!" said the sentry, never changing his position. "Who are you? And what are you doing in a Rebel uniform? You're a spy! That's what you are! I arrest you in—"

"No you don't!" muttered Dan savagely, covering the sentry with his pistol before the startled Yankee could raise his gun. "You don't arrest anyone. Hand me that gun, quick now!" Very reluctantly the bluecoat gave Dan the weapon, which he flung into the bushes. "Now your pistol, and don't you make a sound or, well, it won't be good for you!" This was also done. "Now you run, scoot, quick—" The Yankee turned and ran, but only into the bushes where, without Dan's knowledge, he recovered his weapon.

Dan had put spurs to his mount and was going down the road at a lively pace, when he heard some bullets over his head. Instinctively, he bent lower in the saddle, but not quick enough. The sentry sent a well-aimed shot, which plowed its way deep in the fugitive's shoulder. The pain was intense, but Dan set his teeth, turned in his saddle, took aim, and fired. In spite of the pain he gave a low, mirthless laugh of satisfaction at seeing the unfortunate sentinel throw up his arm and go down in a heap.

It grew dark, but Dan urged his mount faster and faster, thereby putting a greater distance between himself and his enemies. He rode 'til his horse, jaded and weary, stopped in front of a log cabin. Weak and faint from loss of blood, Dan could scarcely keep his saddle. "I'll risk it," he muttered, slowly climbing from the saddle. He stumbled up to the door and knocked. There was no response. He turned the knob; the door came slowly open on its rusty hinges, and Dan walked in. It was empty and there was nothing but several old pans and a pile of grass in the corner. "There must be a well or spring near. I have got to have some water," thought he. "Banyard can't go any farther; neither can I. I suppose we'll spend the night here."

He removed his horse's saddle and led him to a shelter of leaves and tied him. Then he hunted for the spring. One was found and after some trouble, he removed his coat and washed his wound. He made a pad of his handkerchief and placed it on his shoulder, and then pulled his coat over it. Going back to the cabin, he loaded his pistol as a precaution and lay down on the grass.

All night he tossed feverishly and awoke in the morning feeling very sick and with an intense pain in his shoulder. He managed to saddle Banyard and to climb onto his back. He felt to see if the dispatch was in its place; it was. Every jolt sent another pain through the wounded arm until Dan thought that he couldn't stand it a moment longer.

[*The bottom of the page is cut off.*]

The guard showed no signs of moving. "General Stuart's head-quarters is nothin' to you," he remarked, shifting on the other leg.

"Where did you find me?" asked Dan, trying to keep from being angry.

"Well," said the Confederate, "I see'd a horse coming down the road and as it's my duty to stop everybody, I yelled to you to stop. You was laying over the pommel of your saddle when I stopped your horse. You had fainted, so I dashed some water in your face, and then you woke up. But, look here, give account of yourself," explained the sentry in a sing-song tone.

"I am Lieutenant Colonel Morrison, of the cavalry. I have dispatches for the general," answered Dan. "Let me pass."

"I will not let you pass," said the sentinel easily. "It's a good story you made up, but you can't fool me!" as he chewed a bit of grass.

Dan was in a dilemma, while the wounded shoulder grew more painful each moment. He gave a cry of joy as he saw two cavalry officers riding by. He called to them and they turned and rode toward him. "It's Dan!" exclaimed one joyfully. "What are you doing here?"

"At present, I am under arrest," laughed Dan, though the laugh was forced. "I can't identify myself. Will one of you do it for me?"

The guard, finding his mistake, begged Dan's

[*The bottom of the page is cut off.*]

went immediately to the general's tent, trying to walk as if he were not hurt, but it was hard work. The orderly lifted the tent flap and Dan walked in. After the first greetings, he handed the general the dispatch. As the general read it, Dan found it hard to maintain his position of "Attention."

When the general looked up, it did not take his sharp eyes long to discover where the tell-tale blood was beginning to show. "You're wounded, Morrison," he said quietly. "Sit down; hope it's not too bad."

"No!" said Dan, flushing, "only a scratch, sir."

"Well, I hope it is. Do you suppose that you could draw a map of the fortifications?" Dan was a fair draftsman and so he had drawn this.

[*The bottom of the page is cut off.*]

Yankee sentry fired at me."

"Morrison," commanded the general, "go to the surgeon and have your arm attended to. We couldn't afford to lose a fellow like you!"

"Thank you, sir," said Dan smiling faintly, lifting the tent flap and saluting, "I will, sir." He walked out of the tent and fell, only to be caught by the surgeon who had come to report to the general.

[*The bottom of the page is cut off.*]

thought as much," said he, summoning four men to carry Dan to an empty house which served as a hospital.

CHAPTER IV

This was Dan Morrison's first "scouting expedition," as he termed it. His shoulder had taken some time to heal but long before it was well,

Dan was up in saddle again. In the Battle of Chancellorsville, the Seven Days Battle, Fredericksburg, and many others Dan fought

[*Pages are missing.*]

Many of the bluecoats knew the "handsome young fellow that rides a black horse well" for Dan had taken the responsibility of a spy. Many times Dan had carried dispatches through the Northern lines, but oftener in a blue uniform. He had boldly entered the Federal camps and taken note of many things that the general had needed. Dan was almost fearless. He knew well enough that there was a reward on him, four hundred dollars, living or dead! Yet fearlessly, he continued his duty. It was in the darkest part of the war in 1865, when Dixie was fighting, fighting on the courage of her valiant sons. The brave Stuart had been killed and so had Stonewall Jackson, yet the South was still fighting. It was the first of April when Dan volunteered to carry an important message to a commander of a division of cavalry, a good way off.

Dan knew that this was the last scouting expedition that he would make. "For," he remarked, "we might hold back Grant up here, but Sherman's too strong for us down South." He, like the majority of Confederates, wore a ragged uniform and was hungry most of the time. His love for the Confederacy was unusually high and his

[*The bottom of the page is cut off.*]

He was two days in making the trip and as he was returning the precious dispatch to his inner pocket, he discovered a dozen or more

Federal soldiers, halted in the road. Dan pulled up quickly; there was no time to turn back. Quickly slipping from Banyard's back he gave the steed a blow with his hand, which set the horse galloping at a quick pace. He slipped into the bushes. All the Federals gave chase of the fleeing horse, which gave Dan the chance to plunge into the woods near the swamp.

For two days Dan remained in the swamp living on berries and a few yams, which he obtained from a Negro woman. On the third day he emerged from his hiding place, intending to borrow a horse at a neighboring farm if it were possible.

Cautiously, he approached a farm, only to draw back softly as he perceived a number of bluecoats within. He was not to get off so easily for the captain shouted, "There goes that Rebel! After him, men!"

"You'll never get me, Mr. Yank!" muttered Dan, as he broke through a screen of bushes. It was plain that the pursuers were gaining on him, for he was tired. With the last of his strength, he ran up a driveway toward a large mansion. He knocked hurriedly with the knocker. A young girl of about fourteen years threw open the door.

"Lieutenant Morrison!" she exclaimed.

"Janise!" he gasped, "I am pursued! Can you hide me?"

"Hide you? You don't mean—?"

"Yes, I carry a dispatch. If I'm caught—"

"Of course, I'll hide you," said the girl quickly. "Come, get in here," and she opened a secret panel in the wall and shoved him in, closing it after him.

She was the daughter of a rich man before the war and was well acquainted with Dan.

Quickly she settled herself in a chair and began knitting. She had not long to wait, for the door burst open and a dozen or more Federals swarmed into the room.

"May I ask," said Janise, her voice as cold as steel, "what is the meaning of this intrusion?"

The commanding officer raised his hat. "A man we are looking for is in this house. I regret, Madam, but I must search the building."

"Certainly, search all you wish," answered Janise in a colder tone.

The officer gave some orders and the men tramped away. "Believe me, ma'am," said the bluecoat more respectfully, "I mean no intrusion, but our man was seen to come here."

"You are mistaken," said Janise rising and drawing herself to her full height. "No one has come here." There was a long silence. The soldiers tramped in.

"I searched everywhere, sir," said the corporal. "No sign!" The officer arose.

"File out, men," he ordered and with a low bow, left the room. Janise heard him say to the big corporal, "Put a guard around the house; our man's inside."

"Dan," she whispered through the wall, "you can't escape! They've surrounded the house."

Chapter V

Inside the panel it was not dark for a tiny window, which was hidden by vines from the outside, lighted up the small space. It was not large but roomy enough for the tired Confederate spy to half sit and half lie on the floor. He listened breathlessly to the conversation and sighed in relief, as he heard the order, "File out." He lay back only to start up again as he heard the girl whisper this warning to him.

"What shall I do, Dan?" she asked softly.

"Is your mother here?" whispered Dan.

"No," said Janice, "she's gone to see Mrs. Johnston, who is sick. Dan, I guess you have to stay in there until those Yanks leave."

"But Janise, the risk is too great," protested Dan, "especially to you!"

"Risk! Sir, I am a Southerner!" she retorted. This convinced Dan and he lay still for some time. Cautiously, she handed him a canteen filled with water and a pone of cornbread. On looking out, she saw that the bluecoats surrounded the house and seemed to be waiting for Dan to come out.

Through the night and all the next day, Dan remained in the hiding place. "If you see a chance for me to get out, please let me know, Janise," whispered he, when she passed him some provisions.

"Certainly," she replied. On the second day of Dan's stay, Janise opened the panel. "Quickly, now's your chance," she said. "A trooper rode up and told them something. Anyway, they are gone."

"Janise, I can't ever thank you for what you have done for me," said Dan earnestly.

"You are welcome to all I can do," she answered. "You had better hurry now."

After thanking her again, Dan slipped out of one of the back windows. His aim was to make for the swamp again and throw off his pursuers.

During the night Dan slept in a deserted cabin and arose early in the morning. He had walked until midday in the bushes beside the road without being seen when, on passing a farm, he incautiously stepped into the road. Not quick enough did he discover his error, for he heard a cry of surprise, and turning saw a Federal soldier.

[*Pages are missing.*]

fell exhausted over the rough pine table, with the sound like the roaring of the sea in his ear, through which he faintly heard a voice say, "Get up, Reb, I guess I've got you this time."

There was something familiar about the voice, which caused Dan to stagger to his feet. There, with pistol drawn, stood a Federal soldier in a captain's uniform.

"Get up, Reb," ordered he impatiently. The cornered spy turned and looked at his captor.

"Herbut!" he cried.

"Dan," exclaimed the other in astonishment, his pistol slipping to its case. And for a moment the war was forgotten as the two shook hands.

Then the Federal straightened, and a look of pain crossed his face. "Dan—I!"

"Have to arrest me," said the Confederate quietly. "I hate to claim it, but remember our promise to help each other out of any danger?" he said in a quieter tone.

The Federal placed his hand over his face. "I know it, Dan—," he broke off suddenly. "Do you carry papers? Dispatches?"

"Why do you ask?" questioned the Confederate, whose face was pale.

"Look here, old fellow, I'll make a proposition," said the bluecoat facing his captive. "Give me your papers or dispatches, and I'll let you go."

Dan drew himself to his full height. "Never!" he cried. "Never! I swore to guard those papers with my life and I will." He quickly drew his pistol and pointed at the Yankee. Herbut, however, did not make any resistance.

"Yes, Dan," he said, in a quiet voice, "shoot and shoot your friend. It will be better for me, for then I can escape dishonor and keep from breaking my word."

The weapon clattered to the floor and the Confederate gave a groan and sank into a chair, covering his face with his hands. There was a long pause. Finally, the Confederate arose. "You are right, Herbut," he said, his face pale but his voice resolute. "You are right. All is fair in love and war. I'll break my promise. I surrender," but as he said this, he clutched the edge of the table.

[*Pages are missing.*]

for I saw them only a short while before you saw me. No doubt they are following now."

The Federal, however, leaned against the door, lost in thought for a moment. Then he turned and walked up and down the room. Finally, he faced his prisoner. "Dan," he said slowly, "a man's honor is his best thing, but his word is better. Old fellow, if I helped to capture you, I'd never forgive myself, not if I lived to be a hundred. Whether I lose my honor or not, I won't break my word. Take my horse, Dan; it's near the road. Get on him and ride as hard as you ever rode!"

"What!" exclaimed Dan, starting up. "You—really?"

"Yes, Dan, I mean it," replied the bluecoat, his face turned in the other direction. "Take your pistol; you may need it, but go quickly!"

The Confederate seized his hand and said in a tone of intense gratitude, "Herbut Carey, you're a man, and a mighty good one, even if you do fight on the wrong side. I can't ever repay you. You have saved my life. If I ever find a chance to save yours, I'll do it, at any risk. Good-bye," and picking up the pistol, he started toward the door.

"Yes, sir, you've had better luck than we. I'm glad you caught him." This voice startled both men. On looking around, they saw the big corporal, looking through the window. Behind him several blue-coats were seen moving about.

Dan's face went pale and Herbut's jaw dropped as the corporal said this. The latter recovered first. "Yes," he said briskly, "I've got him. Bring the men around." As the corporal disappeared, the Yankee caught his friend's hand. "If there's any earthly way to save you, Dan, I'll find it. But this is not my fault," he whispered quietly.

"No," answered Dan coolly, "it's not your fault. It's the fortune of war, and there's no way out of it. Good-bye." He squared his shoulders as the men filed in, and took his place among them.

The squad marched Dan for some distance down the road, till the camp was reached. He was escorted to the headquarters and cross-examined. "I am Lieutenant Colonel Morrison. I was captured by Captain Carey," he said calmly, in answer to the questions of the commanding officer.

"Do you carry dispatches?" was the next question.

"Yes," responded Dan.

"Give them to me!" Dan took out the paper, but before anyone could interfere, he had torn them into small bits.

The officer sat quietly for a moment and then said, "You know the penalty?" Dan nodded. "I regret it, but you must pay it at sunset tomorrow."

Dan nodded again, "I took the risk," he said.

"Corporal! Place Lieutenant Colonel Morrison under heavy guard until tomorrow afternoon," ordered the officer. Dan was marched to a small hut nearby, and placed within. He saw, with a glance, that it was impossible to escape as here was a guard at the door and one at the window. There was nothing to do but to think, which Dan did. Plan after plan raced unchecked through his head, but he could come to no conclusion. "Well, I'm glad I saved the dispatches. It was the only way," he thought in satisfaction. He thought of his mother and father and his face grew paler, and the lines about his mouth grew tight. His father—"I think you'd be proud of your son," he muttered to himself. "I've served Dixie to my best ability and it's not my fault or Herbut's, God bless him, that I'm caught," and he placed his head in his hands and uttered as earnest a prayer as he had ever prayed.

His guard was changed and food was given him, and a heavier guard was placed around the hut. "They must think I'm rather strong if they place such a heavy guard around me," Dan thought. "Dan Morrison, you're a clumsy fellow to get captured like this. Well, I guess I've got to die sometime, why not now?"

Through the night and all the next day, Dan was kept in the hut. Strange to tell, but the prisoner did not feel frightened at the prospect of the approaching death, for a sudden calm seemed to have fallen on him. He was to die, and hundreds of thousands of other men were dying, for Dixie.

When, in the late afternoon, the firing squad came to the cabin, he took a place in their midst without any outward sign of alarm. He was conducted to a spot in the woods behind the camp and placed against a tree, while his hands and feet were secured. As the lieutenant of the squad approached with a bandage to cover Dan's eyes, he shook his head. "No sir, I prefer to die gazing at your guns than with my eyes bandaged," he declared firmly.

The officer drew his sword and turned to the group of Federals. "Present Arms!" he ordered in an expressionless tone. It was done. "Take Aim," and Dan saw twelve rifles aimed at him. With a murmured prayer, Dan thought all was over, when a galloping was heard.

"Halt there! Stop!" ordered someone in an authoritative tone. The rider, in a blue uniform and covered with dust, swung quickly to the ground and ran towards the lieutenant.

"Read this quick!" he said.

"Ground Arms, men," ordered the officer, sheathing his sword.

Dan had not seen the rider, for his thoughts were far away. He was aroused by a sound of cheering and someone saying in hoarse tones, as he cut Dan loose, "Thank God, I was in time!"

"Why—why it's you Herbut," cried Dan, as he gazed into the Federal's pale face.

"Yes, Dan, it's I. I said if there was any earthly way to save you, I would find it," cried the Yankee, seizing his friend's hand.

"But Herbut, how did you save me?" questioned the Confederate, looking at the group of Yankees who were laughing and talking excitedly. "You know that I'm so thankful that I'm alive. You must know that I can never tell you how much I owe you! But how did you do it?" exclaimed Dan in gratitude.

"It's bad news for you, but good for us. Anyway, it has saved your life. General Lee surrendered the Army of Northern Virginia at Appomattox Court House today. Never mind, Dan!" for the Confederate's head sank into his hands. "Never mind, it saved you!"

The End

Part Five

A double exposure taken in Margaret's teenage years

Copybooks

~

BETWEEN AGES TWELVE AND THIRTEEN, Margaret stopped writing her stories in small books she fashioned herself. She switched to using four-by-six-inch memorandum books that could be readily purchased in five-and-ten cent stores. Stephens Mitchell recalled that Margaret filled so many of these copybooks that his mother resorted to storing them in inexpensive white enamel breadboxes. Gradually, as more and more breadboxes were filled, May

Belle Mitchell moved them to the basement for safekeeping.

We found two of these books, one with a cover and the other with its cover missing. The stories in the copybook with a cover were "The Green Snake," "Old Brindle," "Big Bob of the Sierras," and "The Greaser." ("Old Brindle" was unfinished. The part that was written took up four pages in the copybook but Margaret had saved about nine pages to complete it.) The copybook was dated January 1, 1913.

As in her earlier stories, we recognize that certain characters were based on her real-life neighbors; for example, in "Old Brindle," Flo and Willie were clearly based on her friends, the Noyeses. The female character in "Big Bob of the Sierras" was another friend and neighbor, Leila Kirkpatrick. Bill Lawson and the Goodhart brothers, Robert and Dick, were part of the gang who lived on Peachtree Street and they also appear in the

Margaret at the family house on Peachtree Street, September 6, 1914

story. There is a minor reference to another neighbor, Sue Bucknell, as well. This cowboy story was probably inspired by Margaret's predilection for such book series as Edward Stratemeyer's *Rover Boys*. In the story, Margaret refers to the Piedmont Hotel in Atlanta, a swanky hotel built in 1903. It was located on Peachtree Street where the Equitable Building is today.

The stories in the copybook with the missing cover were "The Silver Match Box," "Steve of the X-B," and an untitled story which appears here as "The Arrow Brave and the Deer Maiden." The first pages of the last story are missing, but this could easily have been the actual title as Margaret used the phrase at the end of her story. Similarly, the phrase "forest and foothills" appears in the final line of the story with that name.

Margaret also used her copybooks to jot down ideas, words, and settings for future stories. Farr records a list of twenty-nine locations that she had copied in the back of another one of these copybooks of the same period which included such real and mythical places as Africa, Alaska, China, Egypt, Hades, Mexico, Paris, Russia, South America, and Turkey. Some of the keywords she wrote as reminders were *Crook, Civil War, Smugglers, Shipwreck,* "*Society,*" and *Sepoy Rebellion.* In the copybook from 1913, Margaret had written another title for a new story, "King of the Cannibal Isle."

A nickel novel of the worst description!
To the parties concerned in this story: Please forgive me for what I write.

"Big Bob of the Sierras"

CHAPTER I

It was twilight in the Sierras, the tops of the mountains were just losing the ruddy glow of sunset, and the dark shadows were falling. A narrow trail ran through the pass to the town of Buckhorn, twenty miles distant. In a clump of trees stood a log cabin with a thin wisp of smoke curling from its chimney. It was a large cabin with three rooms. Inside a young girl was fixing supper. She was evidently excited, for when a pounding of hooves sounded outside, she ran to the door and clapped her hands.

The rider leaped off his horse. He was a tall, handsome young fellow of some twenty years. He tethered his horse to a bush and went up to her. "Have you heard the news?" he cried breathlessly. "I've ridden all the way from Buckhorn to tell you."

"No," cried the girl. "No, what is it, Dick?"

Dick paused, "You know William Patterson, don't you?"

A flush mounted her cheeks, but she answered, "Certainly, what of him?"

"A lot," grunted Dick, sinking on to a bench. "Look here, Leila, I'll explain it to you. You know that Robert hasn't been here today?"

Leila nodded. "I wondered where he was," she said.

Dick continued, "Well, down in Buckhorn a greaser got plugged and Bob happened to be there. Then, being sheriff, Patterson came in. He asked who had done it and Hudson Moore said that Bob Goodhart did it."

"Did he?" cried Leila, wide-eyed in horror.

"'Course he didn't," replied Dick, "but Patterson believed it and besides, all the boys said Bob did it. Then Patterson started to put him in jail and—"

"What did Bob do?" questioned Leila.

"What did the old fellow do?" grinned Dick. "In a second he had 'em covered with his guns and then he skipped. I was at the door and I held them back 'til he rode off."

"What did Will—I mean Patterson say?" asked his audience.

"Well," said Dick scowling, "Patterson swore like a blue streak and then he called Bob several things that I'd have shot him for." He stopped and looked thoughtful. "Do you know, there's more between those two men than you think. Five years ago, when Bob was in Nevada, he had trouble with that man over a gold mine. Patterson hates Bob and Bob hates Patterson and for two cents, Bob would fill that sheriff full of lead." At this, Leila gave a little cry of horror. Dick looked at her sharply. "Say," he questioned slowly, "do you love that fellow?"

She nodded, "Yes," without hesitation.

Dick groaned, "Leila, I'm only your half-brother, but I'll give you some advice. Will Patterson may be all right to you, but he's an enemy of mine and Bob's and he was one of Dad's."

"Listen," interrupted she. Then from the direction of the town came a man on horseback. One look told Leila who it was. It was

Will Patterson. A frown crossed Dick Goodhart's face and his hand slipped to his belt where his pistol was. The girl caught his hand. "Don't Dick, for my sake, don't!" she cried, and Dick stopped. William rode up the trail and disappeared among the trees on the mountain.

"Where's he bound?" breathed Leila Kirkpatrick of Dick.

"After Bob," answered he.

"Where's Bob?"

"Up at William Lawson's cabin in the mountains. Patterson is hunting him, and—by jingo," he broke off and made a leap for his horse.

"Where are you going?" cried his half-sister.

"I'm going to warn Robert," he cried back. "Lock the door and don't get scared tonight," and he, too, disappeared up the mountainside.

She stood a moment, undecided, while her thoughts ran fast. She loved William, and if Robert or Dick caught sight of him, they would not hesitate to shoot him. "But they must not," she cried. "I'll go and warn William!" She hurried to the stable and quickly saddled the one pony that was there, and then she dashed up the mountain at full speed.

CHAPTER 2

William Patterson's heart was full of anger as he rode up the mountain. He was angry for one reason—that Goodhart had escaped him. He was angry for another reason—that Robert was Leila's half-brother. If he killed Robert, there would be nothing more between Leila and himself. Still, as sheriff, he had his duty and it was to capture Robert. He had long suspected Robert of being responsible for the many robberies in the neighborhood.

He was now on his way to William Lawson's cabin. Lawson was an individual about whom little was known. It was a well known fact that Bob spent most of his time at his cabin, and so William decided to seek him there. The trail divided a few miles farther on. Both trails went in the same direction and both led by Lawson's cabin, only one was somewhat longer than the other. William Patterson, busily engaged in his thoughts, paid no attention as to the trail that his steed took, and consequently the animal took the longer path.

Dick Goodhart rode up the trail a few minutes later. He took the short trail and soon arrived at the cabin. The moon was just rising and the little cabin looked strangely weird and mysterious. A small light from a candle showed through the window. Dick leaped down and led his horse into the bushes and tied him. Then he opened the door and walked in. Before he could cover himself, he was gazing into two pistols. "Say, this is a nice reception to give your brother, Bob," he grunted, sinking into a chair. The two men replaced their pistols when they saw who it was.

Robert was a blue-eyed, light-haired young man of about twenty-five years, while William was his opposite, being dark-eyed, dark-haired, and small. "What news?" questioned Robert.

"Lots," replied his brother. "Patterson is up here hunting you. Everyone believes that you plugged the greaser or they say you did at least. If you are caught—"

"I'd be lynched!" answered Robert conclusively.

"When will he be here?" put in William Lawson.

"He'll be here in about five minutes," answered Dick.

"Then you'd better skip, Bob," advised William.

Robert had been doing some quick thinking. "Will Lawson, will you stand by me?" he questioned.

"To the last bullet," replied William.

"And you, Dick?"

"Ditto."

"Then listen," Robert went on in a hurried voice, "I'm not skipping. That red-eyed coyote of a sheriff won't catch me. *Let's catch him!*"

CHAPTER 3

"I'm on," cried Dick.

"And I," said William.

"Then," responded Robert, "I'll lie on the bench outside, pretend to be asleep, and, Dick, you and William get behind that big rock over there in front. When he starts to catch me one of you rope him. If he fights give him a lick on the head, savvy?"

"Yes," they both nodded and both ran out behind the rock. Robert stretched out on the bench in the moonlight. He had not long to wait, as a few minutes later, Patterson rode up.

He dismounted and started for the cabin, when his eyes fell on Robert, seemingly asleep. He drew nearer. Yes, it was the man that he was hunting. Cautiously, William removed Robert's pistol. Then the "sleeper" awoke.

"Hands up, Goodhart," ordered Patterson crisply. Up went Robert's hands. Just then a lasso came hurling through the air. It fell over the sheriff's arms, pinning them to his sides, but William did not give up. He fought and struggled manfully until Dick, true to his orders, raised his pistol and hit William several hard blows on the head. William ceased struggling.

"Don't hit him again," cried Bob anxiously, as Dick raised his pistol again. "Don't kill him!"

Dick looked frightened at what he had done. "What are we going to do with him?" he asked. "When he comes around, he'll be as bad as ever," as he rubbed his shin where he had been kicked.

"Tie him, of course," said Robert. "Lend a hand, now, and tote him in." The unconscious sheriff was toted and duly deposited on one of the bunks. "Turn him over," ordered Robert, "and tie his hands. No need to tie his feet." All this was done; then Dick stretched out on the floor, and Robert and William Lawson sat down by the fire.

CHAPTER 4

It was a good many hours later when William Patterson opened his eyes. Robert and William Lawson were conversing in low tones, while Dick lay on the floor snoring lustily. William glanced at a clock on the table. It was two o'clock. "Gee whiz," he thought, "then I've been here since six." Then he became conscious of the fact that his hands were tied, and also that his head ached badly. Just then Robert arose. Instinctively, William closed his eyes. Robert leaned over him and caught his arm and shook him, but Patterson lay like a log.

"Oh, Will," called Robert, "come over here."

Then William Patterson heard the trampling of feet and Dick say anxiously, "Bob, do you suppose I've—I've killed him?"

His brother grunted. "Wouldn't matter if you did," he said.

Dick shot a quick, startled glance at him. "Bob," he murmured, "how changed you are! I—I never saw you look that way before. What are you going to do with him? For heaven's sake, don't harm him and for Leila's sake, too."

Robert grunted again. "Never mind what I'm going to do," he said. Then he pointed to a canteen of water. "Bring that here," he ordered. Dick obeyed. Robert dashed a good quantity in William's face; then he waited for results. Soon William opened his eyes and gazed blankly about him. "How do you feel?" inquired Robert sarcastically.

"My head feels like it was split open," answered his captive politely.

"S'pose you wonder what I'm going to do?" questioned Robert, straddling a chair in front of him.

William rose to his feet. "Yes," he assented.

Goodhart turned to Lawson and Dick. "You all go to sleep. I and Mr. Patterson are going to talk business," and the two moved away. "Well," continued he, "I guess you know that I've been down on you since you did me out of that gold mine up in Nevada."

"It was mine," interrupted Patterson.

"Twasn't!"

"Twas!"

The two glared at each other. "We won't dispute the point," commented Robert, "but I'm going to ask you some questions. Are you going to answer them or will I have to make you?"

This was too much for William's temper. "Nothing on the face of the earth can make me talk if I don't want to!" he declared.

Goodhart, unheeding this outburst, "First," he said, "*what do you know about me?*"

"I know that you and Will Lawson are responsible for the stage that was held up at Devil's Gulch and the one at Bear's Pass and plenty of others. Is that enough?" shot out the sheriff.

William Lawson leaped up. "Shoot him, Bob," he cried. "He knows too much!"

Robert waved him back. "I know what I'm doing," he said. Then he turned to William. "You answered that correctly, my boy," he said sarcastically. "Now listen here. You know the story well enough, but I'll still tell it to you. When we were up in Nevada, I met a girl." William Patterson stiffened visibly. "I met a girl," continued Robert, "and a nice one with blue eyes. I told her that I loved her and she said she liked me, um——" he broke off. "I guess you liked her, too, eh?"

"Not a bit!" cried Patterson hastily.

"Well, *I* did," went on Goodhart. "She said that her father was going East the next morning, and for me to come over there that night. I asked where she was going, but she said she'd tell me that when I came. I started out that night and when I was going by a lonely spot, I was captured by five men, and you, Will Patterson, you were one! I know you had on a mask, but I'd know your voice anywhere. Then I was taken off a good way and tied to a tree. It was in the middle of the day when I got loose, and she was gone. No one knew where. She had given a note to a man for me, but you had got it by saying your name was Bob Goodhart, and I never knew where the girl was," he concluded. Then he spoke again, his voice husky, "You skunk! Where's that girl? Where is she? You know and you've got to tell me!"

William Patterson glanced at his enemy. Then he shuddered. He could not help it. Robert's eyes were narrowed until they were like slits, his teeth were clenched and his breath came through them in a gasp. His hand grasped the butt of his pistol and his whole form quivered. William retreated in fear, step by step, backward toward the wall, and Robert following stealthily as a cat. Finally, the sheriff backed up against the wall. Goodhart drew his pistol and pressed it against William's belt. "What in the devil do you want?" cried William, summoning up his courage.

"I give you five to tell me where that girl is. Are you going to tell?" answered Robert.

"Not a syllable," responded the sheriff firmly.

"One," counted Robert, "two, three, four—"

Dick leaped forward. "Bob, what *are* you doing?" he cried, catching his brother's arm.

Robert turned like a tiger. "Tie that loco steer to the bunk!" he yelled to William Lawson. Before he could make any resistance, Dick's arms were tied behind him and then Lawson skillfully tied him to the beam of the bunk. Robert gazed at his brother awhile; then he replaced his pistol.

"I give you 'til the morning," he said grimly, turning to Patterson, "'til six and it's three now. Now you lie down flat," he commanded. As William did so, he tied the sheriff's feet. "Six, remember!" he said and lay down on the bunk while William Lawson climbed into the upper bunk. Then all was quiet.

CHAPTER 5

"Hist," called Dick softly. It was two hours later. "Are you asleep, Patterson?"

"No," came the answer from William softly.

"I've gotten one hand loose," said Dick. A thrill of hope filled the captured sheriff's breast. He had rubbed all the skin off his wrists trying to free himself. Dick continued, "I'll cut you loose, too, if I get away." No other words were spoken and a few minutes later the ropes fell from Dick. Like a flash he straightened, pulled out his knife and slashed at the rope around Patterson's wrists, then at his ankles. William fell to rubbing his wrists, but Dick glanced at Robert anxiously. There was no need to fear him as he was sleeping soundly. Dick seized a pistol lying on the table and thrust it into the sheriff's hands. "Hurry," he whispered. "Bob may wake up any minute."

William Patterson arose and hurried, as quickly as he could, out the door. He had not disappeared before Robert leaped up, his hand on his pistol. Dick shrank into a corner. William Lawson leaped down from his bunk. "Who untied that darned sheriff?" roared Bob in a fury.

"I did," said Dick courageously. Robert fired twice in Dick's direction, but the bullets went wild, one striking Lawson and making him drop to the floor. Without waiting to see the results of his shots, Robert rushed out. Dick, sadly shaking his head, lifted Lawson on to the bunk.

Some while later a shadow darkened the room. Dick turned and there stood Leila. Her dress was torn in many places from coming in contact with briars. Her hair was hanging over her shoulders and her face was haggard with anxiety and worry. When half way up the mountain her horse had shied, flinging her senseless to the ground, where she lay several hours. Then she had made her way slowly to Lawson's cabin.

"Oh Dick," she cried. "Where—" Dick pointed out of the door; then came the sound of shots, one after another. Leila shuddered, but ran out of the door, leaving Dick behind.

CHAPTER 6

When Bob dashed from the house he snatched up a coil of rope that lay on the bench. He saw William Patterson sink behind a rock and take aim at him. Quick as a flash, he threw himself on the ground, and the bullet whizzed harmlessly over his head. As he sprang up, he saw the sheriff disappearing behind a large boulder; nevertheless he fired, but to no effect. The sheriff was running around the bend in the mountain, which led to a steep slope that ended at the bottom with a turbulent stream. A savage joy filled Bob's heart. "He's only got five more shots! Then there's the slope—and . . ." he did not finish his thought.

Patterson stopped and sank behind a rock; he could go no further. Robert Goodhart shut off one avenue of escape, the steep precipice another, while the mountainsides were like high walls on the other two sides. William gripped his weapon. "Well," he muttered, "at least I'll die with my boots on!"

Robert Goodhart was well hidden by a large boulder. Robert was doing some thinking. Suddenly, he thrust both hands above the rock and was rewarded by two shots from the cornered sheriff. Robert chuckled and fired twice. He could afford to fire at random as he had a whole belt of ammunition. By thrusting his head out at various times, he made William fire the remaining three shots. Then Robert leaped up and with drawn pistol, rushed over to the rock behind which Patterson had taken refuge. There stood William, his back against the mountainside and his hunting knife in his hand.

Bob stopped short, his weapon leveled. Patterson's eyes flashed. "You coward," he yelled.

"Why so?" said Bob calmly. "You must admit that I have the drop on you, Patterson!"

"Yes, you have!" blazed forth the sheriff, "and *now* you're going to shoot me. Kill a defenseless man! You skunk!"

Silently, Goodhart tossed his weapon to the ground and pulled out his own knife. "Come on," he said.

CHAPTER 7

The struggle was brief as the sheriff was weakened by the events of the previous night. The knives were soon dropped to the ground, and the battle taken up with naked fists. Finally, Bob landed a blow on William's jaw that sent him to the ground. Robert turned him over. In the sheriff's back pocket was a pair of handcuffs. Stopping only long enough to brush the blood from a cut on his forehead and from his cheek, he pinioned Patterson's hands behind him with the handcuffs. Then he tied his rope around his captive's legs. Next he went through every pocket, but not finding the object of his search, he leaned over and picked up William and carried him to the edge of the precipice.

"Here's where I even up my scores with you!" he cried savagely. But then, as he laid him down, there was a sound of footsteps. Leila, panting and breathless with eyes dilated with horror, rushed up and flung herself between her half-brother and his captive.

"Bob, what are you doing?" she cried.

"Out of my way!" yelled he.

"What are you going to do?" she questioned in a frightened way.

"Pitch this devil over!" he roared.

"What's he done?"

"A lot!"

"Why should you murder him?"

"That's my business!" Robert paused for an instant. "Get out of my way or I'll make you!"

"Bob! Bob!" entreated Leila, "for my sake, for the love I bear for you, spare him!"

"Why?" demanded Bob, suddenly gazing at her curiously.

"Because—because I love him!" Leila did not pause. "Bob, you've loved someone." Bob gave a choking cry and pressed his hands over his face. "For her sake, don't!"

Bob looked around like a drunken man; then whipping out his knife, he cut the ropes. He turned the sheriff over and reached into William's back pocket and soon produced a small key, with which he unlocked the handcuffs. As he straightened up, Leila's arms stole around his neck. "Dear old boy," she whispered brokenly, "you'll never regret this." Bob said nothing but drew his hand across his eyes.

Leila gave a cry of joy as William opened his eyes and looked around. Bob did not look at his enemy but walked over and picked up his revolver. Then he returned to where the two were standing. Leaning over, he picked up the handcuffs, which he placed in William's hand. Then he took the revolver and gave it to William, too.

"What's this for?" said William rather weakly still.

For answer, Bob held out both his hands. He spoke only a few words, but they carried a world of meaning. "Handcuff me!" The sheriff understood.

CHAPTER 8

A look of pity came over his face. "What do you mean?" he said quietly. Bob's hands slid to his sides, and he bowed his head.

"You've got the pistol. You've evidence that I was going to murder you. Then you know I held up that stage last month, and you can give me a few feet of rope and a tree, easily," he paused. "Shoot me now, Patterson; I've nothing to live for!"

With one stride, the sheriff stood beside him and his hand rested on Bob's shoulder. "Goodhart," he said earnestly, "I would not arrest you for the world!"

A curious look came across Bob's face. He stiffened. "You mean—"

"I mean to give you a new start," said William quietly. Goodhart grasped his hands.

"Patterson," he murmured, "I'll not try to thank you, for it would be too big a job, but I'm going to make the most of this start!"

Leila, who had not spoken so far, gave vent to a fervent exclamation, "Thank God!"

"Thank God!" echoed both men.

Then they all started for the cabin. Dick met them at the door. "Bob, it was a mighty close shave for Will Lawson," he said.

"What do you mean?" cried Bob.

"You shot at me," answered Dick, "but you hit poor William."

"Dick! Dick!" Bob choked, "he isn't dead?"

Dick laughed. "Of course not; just nipped Will's head. He got up and rode off just a minute ago. Now tell me what's happened?"

Bob looked at William and William looked at Bob. "Nothing," replied Bob.

CHAPTER 9

That day, Bob returned to Buckhorn with the sheriff, who soon found witnesses to clear him of the accusal of shooting the Mexican. As Bob turned to look out of the window, William Patterson drew from his pocket a much soiled letter, which he pressed into Goodhart's hand. Bob gazed at it. It was addressed in a small, feminine hand, "To Robert Goodhart." The sight of it made his heart jump. 'Round he whirled to Patterson. "You rascal," he said in tones that belied his words, "I guess you'll have to excuse me!"

"Oh! Go ahead!" said William, going out and closing the door behind him.

Bob did "go ahead." He tore open the letter and read the contents, which were as follows:

Dearest Bob,

I do not understand why you did not come last night, but I guess you had a good reason.

We are going to Atlanta, Georgia. Please come to see me soon. I'll always be waiting for you!

Lovingly,

Mary Lee S.

Bob sighed in rapturous delight. "She won't wait much longer!" he thought, as he ran out of the building and leaped on his horse.

That night, as he walked out of his room, suitcases in hand, he encountered Dick similarly burdened.

"Hello," cried Bob, "where are you going?"

Dick drew up and saluted with a mock military air. "Atlanta, Georgia, sir, to see Miss Sue Bucknell."

"Come on," said Bob, "I'm going, too."

CHAPTER 10

Two weeks later Leila received this telegram:

Atlanta, Georgia
Piedmont Hotel

Just married. Congratulate me! Wife and I start home tomorrow!
Bob

Leila sent this reply:

Greetings! We are married, too!
Leila and William

The End

"The Arrow Brave and the Deer Maiden"

[*The title page is missing.*]

Long ago before the white man came, the Arrow tribe and the Deer tribe were at war. Every prisoner who was captured was made to run the gauntlet, was burned to death, or killed in another way. In spite of the hate one tribe bore the other, there were two who loved one another—Long Feather, a Deer girl, and Blue Mountain, an Arrow warrior. It was their custom to meet each other on certain nights at an agreed place. Led by a rejected suitor of Long Feather, a large party of the Deer warriors followed the girl to her meeting place. On seeing that her lover was an Arrow warrior, they fell upon Blue Mountain. He fought bravely with his back against a rock, but was outnumbered and slain. Before he died, however, he struck his sweetheart on the head with his tomahawk and killed her. As Long Feather's father bent over the two, he caught sight of an arrow tattooed on the warrior's chest. He turned to his braves and announced that any Deer girl that loved an Arrow warrior ever after this should die, and her lover, too.

Time passed. The white man came. The country, once wild, was now mostly settled. The descendants of the Deer tribe lived in houses of sun-dried brick called pueblo. They were not civilized. Nothing could tame them, and they still clung to their old ways, legends, and beliefs.

Not far away from the pueblos was the camp of a surveying party.

Among them was a young Carlyle graduate. It is true he was not a full-blooded Indian for his father had been a white man. His name was Jack Donelson. The surveyors were eating their evening meal when a voice hailed them. A dignified-looking Indian warrior limped up to the camp. He was middle-aged and pleasant-looking, for an Indian. He at once made his way to Donelson.

"What's the matter?" questioned Jack.

In broken English the Indian answered that he had stepped on a rattlesnake and had been bitten in the foot, could Jack help him? Of course Donelson could. There was no remedy for snake bites in the camp, but that did not appall him. Pulling the ramrod from his gun, he thrust it into the fire. He pulled off the Indian's moccasin, and when the iron was red hot, he applied it to the injured foot. It was a crude method, but it was a good one. In spite of the intense pain, not a sound passed the redskin's lips.

When his foot was tied up, the Indian arose and put out his hand. "Thank. Leaping Deer will not forget," and he limped off.

"That's a brave man," said Jack, as he returned to his meal.

The next morning Jack set out to take notes on a certain piece of ground, and he would not return until the next day. As the day grew hotter, Jack grew thirsty and made his way to a nearby stream. As he advanced toward the water, something caught his foot. It was an Indian trap used to catch animals. Jack fell heavily. His head struck a rock and then all went blank.

When he opened his eyes, he felt that his face was wet. Next he felt a pain in his leg and a more intense one in his arm. He looked up. An Indian girl was sitting beside him, pouring water on his face. He smiled weakly, "I think my arm is broken," he said.

To his astonishment, she replied in good English, "I think so."

In spite of the pain Jack asked, "How do you speak such good English?"

"I went to school in the city," she answered. "Get up; I'll help you." It was a painful task, but Jack was Indian enough to make no sound. His arm was broken, he was sure, and his ankle badly sprained. With her help he advanced toward the Indian village.

The first man Jack saw was Leaping Deer, the Indian he had seen the day before. Leaping Deer was the uncle of the girl who had assisted him who, by the way, was named Sun Bird.

The Indian welcomed Jack to his pueblo, inviting him to stay until cured. Jack consented and sent word to his friends of his accident. Sun Bird, to his utmost surprise, announced that she could set bones and proceeded to set Jack's arm.

Fever set in, and it was sometime before Jack was up again. Still he lingered. One day he announced to Sun Bird that he loved her and would not go away without her. She looked at him frankly and replied that, though she loved him, she would never leave the village.

Jack talked with Leaping Deer. The Indian replied that he would soon be old and that he would be glad for the two, Jack and Sun Bird, to marry and live with him. Jack was delighted. The Indian in his nature was stronger than the white, and he felt a longing to live as his ancestors had lived.

One day Leaping Deer brought a bundle, which he handed to Jack. It was a full Indian costume. Jack retired to the privacy of the pueblo and soon came out in the costume. But that his skin was fairer and his hair short, he would have been mistaken for a full-blooded Indian. Sun Bird, with a cry of delight, leaped over to him and taking a string of beads from her neck, she placed them on him. As she did so, the Mexican jacket that he wore was blown back by the wind. On his bare chest was tattooed an arrow! He was an Arrow warrior and she was a Deer girl. At this, she shrank back in horror.

"What's up?" cried Jack. For answer, she pulled his sleeveless jacket over his chest.

"Are you an Arrow brave?" she cried.

"My mother was of that tribe," he replied. "What of it?" She told him of the old legend of Blue Mountain and Long Feather and of the unwritten Indian law.

"Don't you worry," he said. "They'll never know."

"It will be seen," she answered. Then she took a large shell necklace from her throat and put around his neck, so that it hid the hated mark completely.

"It would not matter if it were discovered," he said contemptuously. "These are civilized times."

"Don't believe that," cried Sun Bird. "We are never civilized. If you are discovered, you would be tortured or—" She stopped as a young Indian came in and beckoned to Jack, who followed him out.

The Indian wished to wrestle with Jack, who nothing loath, accepted the challenge. The two antagonists faced each other in deerskin leggings and moccasins. Jack was slightly out of practice, but he had no fear of being defeated. The two faced each other and then circled round to try to get hold. Finally, they clinched. The Indian's hand caught in the necklace around Jack's neck. It broke and fell to the ground, but Jack did not notice. By a skillful trip, the Deer brave sent Jack to the ground. But Jack, not to be caught, leaped up and sprang on the Indian.

A large crowd of Indians had assembled and were watching the match with interest. Again the Indian tripped Jack, who fell, and his adversary on top of him. The Indian seized Jack by the shoulder and held him down. As Jack looked up into the Indian's face he saw the look of triumph change to one of hate. The brave gave a yell and the crowd drew nearer. On Jack's chest was a perfectly tattooed arrow!

"An Arrow brave! An Arrow warrior!" ran from mouth to mouth. With an effort Jack rolled his opponent off and sprang to his feet. He did not try to escape for he knew that he was helpless. With a warrior's calmness, he folded his arms and called coolly, "Silence!" and every tongue was stilled. "Warriors of the Deer tribe," said Jack, and the spirit of his mother's people filled him, "my father was a white man, but my mother was an Arrow squaw. I, too, am an Arrow warrior! I am not ashamed of it! I have spoken!"

At this short speech the tribe went wild. Hatchets, guns, and tomahawks were brandished. Jack, seeing a chance of escape, made an effort to pass through the ring of warriors, but he was caught by two Indians. He struggled but was overpowered and thrown to the ground. A knife was raised, but an authoritative voice said, "Stop! Is a brave to die this way? No, there is a better way!"

There was a commotion and Sun Bird was brought forward. The chief ordered her to be locked in one of the pueblos until later. Then the tribe was formed into two lines, and every man, woman, or child bore some weapon. Like a flash the meaning of this burst on Jack. It was an old Indian custom. The prisoner was made to run through these lines twice and every man struck him with his weapon. If the prisoner was unconscious after passing through the second time, he was safe until the next day. Then his fate was decided.

Jack stiffened and threw back his shoulders. He would bear himself like a warrior and show no sign of fear! He rushed toward the two lines. As he passed them, every person struck him a hard blow. Hardly conscious from this treatment, he turned and rushed down the line again. Just before he reached the end of the line, he was hit in the head with a club. He reeled, tried vainly to recover his feet, but fell to the ground only conscious of a dull pain, and then all went blank.

When he opened his eyes, he was first conscious that he was badly cut and bruised; next, that he was lashed tightly to a thick post; and third, that an Indian sat in front of him with a rifle across his knee. He gave a sigh. At that moment, the Indian with whom he had wrestled came up to him. In taunting tones he addressed him, calling him a squaw. Jack looked past him with calm indifference. This enraged the brave. Out came his knife, and he drew it across Jack's chest. It was a painful cut, but Jack clenched his teeth and made no sound.

"What will the squaw do when he feels the flames or the scalper's knife?" cried the brave. When Jack made no answer, he turned and walked off.

All through the afternoon Jack was subjected to the taunts and sneers of the tribe, who told him to wait for the morning. Jack was sick and hungry, and above all things, very thirsty, but he gave no sign of it.

At last, night came and all retired into the pueblos, except the man on guard. Jack had dropped off to sleep, but he awoke. Why, he knew not. The moon was shining brightly. Suddenly, a figure darted from a pueblo and a rifle butt descended on the head of the guard, who collapsed in a heap. A flask of water was lifted to Jack's lips. It was Leaping Deer who had come to his rescue. In a few minutes Jack was freed by the sharp knife of Leaping Deer. He was so stiff that he could scarcely walk and as he moved, the cut in his chest began bleeding again. He did not notice it.

He clasped the Indian's hand and murmured his thanks. "Sun Bird?" he questioned. The Indian pointed to a pueblo. Jack slipped to the door. There was no one inside, but a door leading into another room was bolted. Jack lifted the bar. "Sun Bird," he called softly.

"Jack!" came the joyful whisper.

"Come," he said, and they walked out.

Leaping Deer beckoned to them; he held two horses by the bridles. "Get on," he said, and Jack and Sun Bird mounted. Leaping Deer clasped Jack's hand for the last time. Then the Arrow Brave and the Deer Maiden rode away together.

The End

"The Silver Match Box"

A tale of New York and San Francisco

Characters:

Hugh Travis—a lieutenant in the army

Marion Owens—the girl engaged to Hugh

Jack Hays—Hugh's friend

Jules Arsen—a French spy

soldiers, cab drivers, thugs, etc.

Time: Present

Place: New York

CHAPTER I

The door of the commandant's office opened and a young lieutenant stepped out with a puzzled expression on his face. In his hand were several small, thin papers. "To New York," he murmured, "and a first lieutenant commission if I bring them safely. What a cinch! I must call on Marion and tell her," and off he hurried. He was saved this trouble, however, for as he turned a corner, he nearly bumped into a pretty young lady, who was evidently shopping.

"Good morning, Hugh," she greeted demurely.

"Marion," he greeted joyfully. "This is lucky! I was just going up to your house. I've something to tell you; come on in the soda fountain."

They both were soon seated at a table, drinking a Coca-Cola. "Now first," said Hugh, "I'm to leave San Francisco tonight for New York!"

"You are?" cried she. "I'm leaving for New York, too, tonight!" Neither noticed a rather small-looking man seated at a table next to them.

Hugh lowered his voice, "I ought not to tell you," he said, "but I will. I'm taking some papers to an officer in New York. If I bring them safely, I'll be a first lieutenant."

"But what papers?" she inquired. The foreigner bent closer.

"Maps of some fort on the Pacific coast, disappearing guns, and so forth. Anyhow, they are pretty valuable." It would have puzzled them both to have seen the look of exultation which crossed the foreigner's face.

"That's fine!" said the girl. "Well, good-bye."

"I'll see you on the train," he said. "By the way, who is going with you?"

"Only my maid," she answered rising. "Good-bye."

"Good-bye," he answered. Just then someone pulled his sleeve. On turning, he saw the foreigner standing beside him. "What the devil does he want?" thought Hugh.

"Monsieur," the man was undoubtedly French, "Monsieur, I would speak to you, if it were no trouble."

Much astonished by such a request from a stranger, Hugh replied, "Oh! Certainly, no trouble at all. Sit down." Both sat down.

"First," said the little Frenchman, "you will pardon me for my boldness. I'm Jules Arsen from France."

"Lieutenant Hugh Travis, at your service," said Hugh, wondering what was coming next.

"We will come to business," said the Frenchman. "I am in this country for the interests of France. I hear that you carry papers, eh? Government papers?"

"Damn!" ejaculated Hugh.

"Mon Dieu," cried the foreigner, laughing. Then he lowered his voice, "Monsieur Travis, I will give you three thousand dollars for those papers."

Hugh rose from the table, his eyes flashing. "You dog of a spy!" he said in low tones. "Did you think I would sell my country's plans for a little money?"

"But I will give you more money!" cried Arsen. Hugh, with an exclamation of disgust, walked out.

"Mon Dieu!" ejaculated the spy. "I must have the papers!" He turned to a little newsboy. "I'll give you a quarter to follow that man," he pointed to Hugh, "for awhile and see what he does or says!" The boy, glad to earn the money, raced off after Hugh's departing figure.

The spy walked up and down impatiently. In a half an hour the boy returned. "The gent must a been cussin'," he said in reply to Arsen's eager questions. "Then he got out some tiny little papers and put 'em in a little silver match box. Then he got in a car and went off."

"Here's your money," said the spy, handing the boy a quarter. Then he made his way to the ticket office.

"When do trains leave for New York?" he inquired of the ticket seller.

"One leaves in two hours," was the reply, "and one leaves tonight."

"Give me a ticket," ordered Arsen, "to New York. I'm going this evening. I've got to beat Travis," he added to himself.

CHAPTER 2

It was a few days later when the San Francisco train pulled up in New York. It was nearly dark when Hugh Travis assisted Marion Owens off the train.

"Good gracious, Hugh," cried Marion, "I'm starved."

"Same here," responded her escort. "I say, let's get some supper before we go to the hotel. I don't have to report to the commandant until tomorrow."

"All right," she replied. Then turning to her maid, she gave orders to the maid to go to the hotel, for she had reserved rooms. Hugh hailed a cab, and as he did so, he saw three men watching him intently. As he assisted Marion into the taxi, he saw the three men climb into an automobile and follow them. "Marion," said he, after informing the driver where to go, "what is your business in New York?"

She laughed. "Oh, business," she replied. "I and Mother own some property here and our lawyer told us that someone was disputing our claim. Mother was sick, and Father was terribly busy, so I came."

"Marion," said Hugh, "will you do something for me?"

"Of course," she answered.

He pulled out a little silver match box. "Hide this then."

"What is it?" questioned she.

"Those plans. They are very valuable. I feel sure that I am being watched."

"Well, you are the most foolish thing I ever saw, Hugh Travis," she cried, but nevertheless, she slipped the precious box underneath her hat.

"There," said Hugh, "I feel better!" Soon they were seated in a restaurant enjoying a good supper. "Oh," cried Hugh, suddenly, "I forgot. I promised to call up Jack Hays, a friend of mine, as soon as I got here. Will you excuse me?"

She nodded and he made his way towards the telephone booth, and soon was talking to Jack. "Jack," he said, after telling where he was, "Jack, I'm being watched. Just as I looked out, I saw three men watching me. You know I have valuable papers."

"Come over to my house tonight, after you take Miss Owens home. By the way, are you engaged to her?"

Hugh turned red, but answered, "Yes," and then, "Good-bye." As he left the telephone, he saw the three men seated at a table not far from his table. They were well-dressed, but they had the appearance of thugs. Finally the meal was finished and Marion and Hugh arose to go. Then the three men arose, too.

Hugh called a taxicab and told the driver where to go. After going for the best part of an hour, Hugh looked out. They were in the slums of New York. Hugh was about to tell the driver to stop, when the machine came to an abrupt halt. Hugh leaped out and so did Marion. They were in the worst part of the town and they were in front of a saloon.

"The tire's busted," said the driver.

"Well, what in hell induced you to bring us here," growled Hugh, who was really angry. He did not notice when another machine drew up and three men leaped out. "I guess we'll have to walk," said Hugh to Marion. At that moment the men closed about them. Each carried a little automatic pistol.

"Please walk in that door," said one of them, pointing to the saloon.

"What does this mean?" exclaimed Hugh, while Marion shrank back aghast.

"Don't make a fuss or there'll be trouble," advised a man. "Just you walk into that door." There was no help for it, so in they went.

There were several men leaning against a bar, but they took no notice of the party. Into the next room they went. There was a trap door in the floor. One of the men lifted it. "Get down," he said, and Marion and Hugh went down the ladder. It was a large, bare room that met their gaze, and it was badly lighted with gas. A man sat on a stool in the corner, reading a paper. Hugh gasped in surprise. It was Jules Arsen, the French spy!

CHAPTER 3

"See here, Arsen," demanded Hugh, "what does this mean?"

The Frenchman smiled, "Have patience, Monsieur. You shall know soon enough."

"I want to know now," growled Hugh angrily. "This is an outrage."

"I want those—" the spy stopped and turned to the three men. "Go upstairs," he ordered, "but guard the door." They obeyed. "I want those papers," hissed the spy. "I'll have them, too!"

"You don't say so," said Hugh calmly.

"See here, Monsieur," said the little Frenchman, "I give you five thousand dollars for them. If you refuse, I'll take them anyway."

Hugh's temper had been rising, and now it had reached the boiling point, "You—you spy! You dog! I would not sell my country to save you from—" Marion gripped his arm. The spy, enraged, sprang toward him.

"Spy, eh? Dog? I'll show you!" His hand sought his pocket, and he brought out a little automatic pistol, which he pointed at Hugh. Marion felt Hugh's muscles grow taut beneath his sleeves, but there was not a tremor in his voice that denoted fear.

"You can put that pistol down, Jules Arsen," he said, "for I know you don't have the nerve to shoot me!"

This was the truth and Arsen felt a thrill of admiration for this intrepid youth. "I'll have you searched," he said. A pang of fear rushed through Hugh's heart. "You have them in a small silver match box," stated Arsen.

"Have I?" questioned Hugh, concealing his surprise with difficulty.

"Certainly," was the spy's reply. "I must search you and the young lady. Here!" The men entered. "Search them!" ordered the Frenchman.

Marion passed her hand over her forehead, as if to brush back a stray hair, and then passed her hand over her mouth. This movement went unnoticed. Then suddenly, she fell prone on the floor.

"The lady has fainted," said Arsen, "I'll search her!"

CHAPTER 4

A half an hour later Hugh grinned gleefully into Jules Arsen's face. A thorough search had not brought the silver match box to light. To tell the truth, Hugh wondered where Marion had hidden the box, for she had been searched, too. The spy gave a grunt and proceeded to pinion Hugh's hands behind him with a pair of handcuffs. Then he tied his prisoner's feet with a rope, turned the gas off, and went out.

Then Hugh heard a sound of spluttering and Marion said, in low, but plaintive tones, "That box was awfully dirty, Hugh!"

"You're a cutter, Marion," said Hugh abruptly. Then they fell to talking over the strange situation in which they were. Marion admitted that she was frightened, and Hugh did not feel comfortable.

"If I don't turn up, Jack Hays will hunt for us," he told her and this cheered her a little. At last both fell asleep.

It was late in the morning, though they did not know it, when Arsen and two of his cohorts climbed in. The spy held a package in his hand. The gas was lighted and Hugh could see determination in every feature of Arsen's face. He unwrapped the package. It contained a bottle with a poison label on it. The spy held it up so that Hugh might read the name. It was carbolic acid.

"Well?" said Hugh.

"You don't believe it's carbolic acid, do you?" questioned Arsen testily.

"No," said Hugh, "frankly, I don't." Arsen turned the bottle so that a few drops of the liquid were left on the stopper. He then leaned over and pressed it on Hugh's hand. The young lieutenant felt as if a lighted match had been held against his hand.

"Extremely sorry to burn you, but you must be convinced!" mocked the little Frenchman.

"I'm convinced," grunted Hugh, rubbing his hand on his coat. The spy went over to one corner of the room and picked up a large bottle, and Hugh heard him pour the carbolic acid into it.

"What in the dickens *is* he up to?" thought Hugh. Arsen called in one of the men and had him fix the bottle to the ceiling. Then a string was tied to the stopper.

"Get up!" ordered Arsen to Hugh.

"I'm comfortable where I am," responded Hugh. The veneer of politeness vanished from the spy's face, and he let drive a savage kick at the young lieutenant.

"Get up, you dog! I'm master here and I expect to be obeyed!"

"Stop that, you brute!" cried Hugh, smarting from the blow, while Marion glared daggers at the rascally Frenchman.

"If I were loose, I'd pulverize you, I would," grunted Hugh, rising. Arsen caught him by the shoulders and pushed him up against the wall.

"Jim," he ordered to one of his men, "keep this fellow covered while I tie him."

Here Marion stepped forward. "This is an outrage," she cried. "I demand to be set free at once!"

"Demand what you please. It will do you no good, Mademoiselle. I have you and this fellow, and I intend to keep you," was the reply she received.

In obedience to Arsen's orders, Jim leveled his pistol at Hugh, who feeling crushed and downhearted, submitted to being tied. To his astonishment, one of his hands was left free. His other hand, however, was secured tightly, as were his feet. Then he was placed neatly under the suspended bottle of carbolic acid. While Hugh was puzzling over this new move, he noticed that Marion had been tied hand and foot, and placed under the bottle.

"See here, Arsen!" grunted Hugh, "I admit that you have the drop on me, that you *could* kill me, and all that, but can't we make a compromise?"

"My only compromise is those plans," replied the spy, "and I'll have them, too!" he added viciously.

"Not while I live!" Hugh said with firmness.

"Perhaps not, but after your death," replied Arsen, in such a cool, calm manner that Hugh winced. "Hold up your hand!" came the order. As there was no use resisting, Hugh raised his hand. The man slipped a cord around his wrist. The cord was fastened to the stopper of the bottle. Then the whole devilish plot dawned on him. If he lowered his hand, the string would pull out the cork and then the contents would fall on Marion.

"Good God!" he blurted out in horror.

"Am I not a smart man?" mocked Arsen.

"You're the devil, himself!" was Hugh's answer.

CHAPTER 5

Five minutes later Arsen left the room. Hugh turned to Marion. "Great heavens! We'll have to give up the papers!" he said.

"But think of their value!"

"But think what will happen to you, if I lower my arm!"

"Don't lower it!"

"But Marion, I'll have to soon. I'm tired."

"Then lower it."

"Marion, don't take it so coolly! I'd rather give them up than have a hair on your head hurt."

"A fine soldier you are, Hugh Travis. If you tell, I'll never speak to you, and I'll break our engagement, so there!" Before Hugh could reply, Arsen entered. He coolly searched Hugh's pockets until he found a box of cigarettes. He proceeded to light one and then leaned back in his chair.

"Getting tired?" he inquired.

Now, to tell the truth, Hugh felt as if needles and pins were being stuck in his arm, and he knew that it would be impossible to keep his arm erect much longer, but he answered, carelessly, "Oh, no." A few more minutes passed and Hugh's endurance was beginning to give way under the strain. The spy noted this with satisfaction. Then there was a commotion up above them. Out came Arsen's pistol.

"If anyone comes to help you," he stated, "I'll kill you!" At this moment the trap door was lifted and the well known Jack Hays, Hugh's friend, appeared. Neither Hugh nor Marion knew what happened next, but they had a happy memory of several policemen and volleys of pistol shots. Hugh heard the Frenchman yell, "I keep my word!" Then there was a sharp retort. Hugh felt an intense pain and knew he had been shot. Unable to stand any longer, he fell to the floor, his last conscious thought becoming, "I've killed Marion. I've pulled out the cork."

CHAPTER 6

When he next opened his eyes, he was lying on a bed in a hospital, with Marion sitting on one side of him and Jack on the other. He could scarcely believe his eyes. He thought that he was dreaming, but when he moved, a sharp pain told him that it was no dream.

"Aren't you hurt?" he managed to articulate.

Marion laughed. "My dear boy," she said, "there was no carbolic acid in that bottle! It was just water. I only got a wetting!"

Hugh was mystified, but he turned to Jack. "How did you find us?" he questioned.

"When you did not turn up, I got anxious and went to the police station. Just then, a man came in and said that another man had captured a young lady and a soldier, and had taken them, by force, into a certain saloon. He thought the police should look into the matter. I paid him to show us the saloon, and then we rescued you. Miss Owens had the match box up her sleeve, so it was safe. In fact, we're all safe, except you, and *you'll* be safe and sound inside of two weeks! Arsen's safe, too. He's in jail."

"And it's the best place for him!" sighed Hugh in relief.

The End

"Old Brindle"

I n the little town of Enterprise and in the region around, Marjory had gained the name of "tom-boy-girl." She deserved it, too, for she could beat any child, boy or girl, of her size. She could do anything a boy could do.

One day the town was filled with excitement. The "Squire" Jones's house had been robbed! The "Squire" was the richest man in town and was looked upon with awe by the children. All the old family silver had been stolen and tied up in a tablecloth. Besides, Mrs. Jones's jewelry had been stolen. There was a two hundred-dollar reward out for the thieves and also for the stolen goods!

After talking on this subject all the morning Marjory Jones and her gang adjourned to Mrs. Jones's backyard. It was a hot day and so they all sat down under a tree. Finally, Marjory spoke up, "Willie, what do you want more than anything right now?"

Willie grinned and scratched his head. "I guess five gallons of ice cream would do me," he replied.

Marjory questioned all the other children as to what they wanted and Frances wanted a diamond ring. Amy wanted a collie puppy. Flo thought that an air rifle suited her. Jimmy wanted a pair of skates and Will a bicycle.

"What do you want?" questioned Flo of Marjory.

"Oh, I couldn't get mine," cried the tomboy. "I want that Texas pony over at the stock yards."

Will suggested a game of "I'll spy" and soon all were engaged in playing this game.

[*The story was unfinished.*]

Part Six

Drama Club photo from the Washington Seminary yearbook, Facts and Fancies, *1917
(Margaret, third from left)*

Plays

〜

THE MITCHELL FAMILY HOUSE ON PEACHTREE

Street was perfect for staging plays. The front hall, sitting room,

and music room could be opened up to provide a seventy-foot ex-

panse for the productions of the would-be thespians. The neigh-

borhood children and friends spent many happy hours making sets,

sewing costumes, setting up chairs, and selling tickets. Some of the

titles of these endeavors include *The Cow Puncher, The Fall of Ralph the*

Rover, In My Harem, Bayou Royale, The Regular Hero, The Exile, Mexico, and *Phil Kelly, Detective.*

Lucille Little remembered performing some of the productions in Erskine Jarnagin's backyard in which "we drew straws to determine whose turn it was *this* time to make the noble leap off the six-foot-high cliff and be seduced, usually as I recall, by one Margaret Mitchell in the role of the Little Colonel . . ."

In a letter to Bill Lawson, Margaret sent some old photographs in the hopes that the images

> might bring back pleasant memories of the days when we and twenty or thirty of our playmates were the terrors of Peachtree and 17th Streets. I believe the photograph showing you with the cap pistol in hand, with David and Stephens Crockett and Dick Goodhart as Indian and cowboys, was taken during a rehearsal of *Custer's Last Stand.* I am sure the faded one of you with arms folded, wearing gray pants with a black military side stripe, was after our successful performance of some Civil War and Reconstruction drama which I wrote . . .

The most notorious of the productions at the Mitchell residence was an adaptation of Thomas Dixon's *The Traitor: A Story of the Fall of the Invisible Empire.* Margaret and her friends had seen D. W. Griffith's movie *The Birth of a Nation* during its Atlanta run in 1915 and wanted to create a similar epic. The film, controversial today because of its racism, was hailed in its time as a breakthrough in the making of motion pictures. It was the first feature-length film and moviegoers were enthralled by the magnitude of the production. Two of Dixon's books, *The Leopard's Spots* and *The Clansman*, were used as the basis for the film. Wanting to emulate the famous director, Margaret adapted *The Traitor* for her play.

In her response to a 1936 letter from Dixon, Mitchell confessed that she had written a play based on his book.

Jan 1, 1916

When I was eleven years old I decided that I would dramatize your book *The Traitor*—and dramatize it I did, in six acts. I played the part of Steve because none of the little boys in the neighborhood would lower themselves to play a part where they had to "kiss any little ol' girl." The clansmen were recruited from the small-fry of the neighborhood, their ages ranging from five to eight. They

As Steve Foyle in her play
The Traitor

were dressed in shirts of their fathers, with the shirt tails bobbed off. I had my troubles with the clansmen as, after Act 2, they went on strike, demanding a ten cent wage instead of a five cent one. Then, too, just as I was about to be hanged, two of the clansmen had to go to the bathroom, necessitating a dreadful stage wait which made the audience scream with delight, but which mortified me intensely. My mother was out of town at the time. On her return, she and my father, a lawyer, gave me a long lecture on infringement of copy-rights. They gave me such a lecture that for years afterward I expected Mr. Thomas Dixon to sue me for a million dollars, and I have had a great respect for copy-rights ever since then.

(Actually Margaret had recently turned fifteen when her group performed *The Traitor.*)

After the production of *The Traitor,* Margaret recorded in a journal entry of January I, 1916, some of her trials and tribulations as the writer, star, producer, and director of the piece.

Two of Margaret's plays survive today. The first part of her play set in Japan is missing, therefore we cannot be sure of the identities of the American women who find themselves stranded in Japan. We do learn that they are welcomed and take part in a birthday celebration for Hann Sann, the fairest maiden in Japan. The play, which appears here under the title *The Birthday Celebration of Hann Sann,* was written on stationery dated March 22, 1916. The later second play, *(Seen) Scene at a Soiree,* now archived at the Hargrett Library, has Margaret and two of her friends, Courtenay Ross and Dorothy McCullough, deciding which characters each will be in their upcoming play, what they will wear, and what locale they will choose as the setting for the play. Underneath this seemingly innocuous theme, the author uses plays on words and innuendoes to suggest that the Shero (heroine) of the upcoming play is not quite virtuous.

JOURNAL ENTRY
January 1, 1916

Now, since it's all over, I'll start at the beginning. I got the idea when I was coming home from E.'s party with Bill L. We wanted a play. *The Birth of a Nation* was in town and we wanted something like it, therefore, we thought of *The Traitor*.

The next day, I worked hard—and got the outline. We settled a few details and then I began writing. I changed the ending a lot and I changed a good many names. I had in mind a girl or boy for each character and I wrote accordingly. Then came the "Dorothy difficulty."

I had written the part of "Kitty" for Maude Powers and "Hal" for Dot, but Dot wanted "Kitty." Well, I had no objections, but others did. Some of the cast—especially the boys—said they'd drop out if she took "Kitty." I worried over it a week. Then we had a showdown. It was quite thrilling for I had to be spokesman. The up shot was that she dropped out entirely and Florence took "Hal."

Then there were the parts. Of course, I could have let the people copy them, themselves, but there were changes to be made, so I wrote 52 big pages of parts—it nearly finished me, too.

Monday morning, we started. Neither Courtenay nor George turned up and I had the deuce of a time getting Eugenia to take the part of "Jully Anne," the colored girl. That first rehearsal was frightful. Bill L. acted as silly as I knew he would, and nothing seemed to go right.

Next day, no Court, George, or Eugenia—in wild despair, I tore my hair!

Thursday, we had the full cast and we certainly worked. It was the hardest work I ever did. Leila and Flo would always giggle when I was trying to get over a love scene with Maude, and the two Bills insisted on dueling all the time.

Then came the fuss! We will pass gently over it. It is very painful, I assure you.—Sufficient to say, I never wanted to bruise my knuckles on anybody's face more than I did on Bill L.'s that day!

Bill wouldn't do the prologue and I knew we'd flubbed it. Friday came. We got the tickets and sold some—not enough tho—and got the programs.

Heavens above, but I was worried!

Saturday, George didn't show up and George alone, did not know his part. If I had known how to swear, I would have cussed like a blue streak that day. Slave-driving would be easy—dead easy compared to bossing that cast. I did swear some and shocked them somewhat, I'll wager.

We got in a dress rehearsal Sat. afternoon and it was puke— showed up our bad points something fierce. I could leave. Thank the Lord, I didn't. The cast left at six and I didn't get off my boy's wig and trousers for two blessed hours!

I sewed on red epaulets and white crosses for clan costumes. I was about frantic for I had no clan suit. I tore madly around and got a new nightgown, a skirt to a white crepe dress, and a red circle and hastily converted them into a costume.

The two Bills arrived and we got the chairs together. Then the rest of the cast arrived. Court was a beaut. She looked exactly like "Gus"

in *The Birth of a Nation*—her face was a gingerbread brown, a bandana handkerchief was around her head. The big blue norfolk and white sports trousers gave her an evilly disreputable look.

[*This entry ends abruptly, probably indicating that pages, perhaps describing the performance itself, are missing.*]

The Birthday Celebration of Hann Sann

[*The first pages of the play are missing.*]

(*Enter* Messenger.)

Messenger. I have come to appraise your ladyship that His Majesty and wife are on the way to attend your festival and will be here immediately, so prepare to welcome him. The Emperor!

(*All stand*)

Chaya. Whatever shall we do?

(*Enter* Emperor.)

Long live the Emperor!

(*All bow to the floor as the music begins*) Japanese National Anthem

Emperor. I thank you most loyal subjects for this touching expression of your love and admiration—but do not let me delay the festivities. Where are the dancers? Come, let them begin.

(*Japanese dances*)

I - 2 - 3

Emperor. Most excellent—But do I not see strange guests. Who are the maidens there?

Hann San They, your Majesty, are some Americans who chanced to pass this way and whom we have persuaded to stay for our party. May I present them?

(They bow very deeply)

Emperor. I bid you a hearty welcome. May your stay be long and happy in our land!

Miss Keromall. Alas, your Majesty, our stay must be brief—within one short hour, we must all sail for America.

(All) "In Praise of America"

Emperor. Quite right to praise America, but we must not forget the purpose of our assembly this evening. It is Yim Kum, the birthday of one of Japan's fairest maidens, and I am sure we all wish her great happiness! In token of this love and respect, we present this basket of flowers to our much loved Hann San. Let us have more music!

Margaret at her desk at Washington Seminary

Seminary

MARGARET ATTENDED THE PRIVATE WASHINGTON

Seminary for girls in Atlanta from 1914–18. The white-columned

mansion which housed the school is no longer standing. It was de-

molished several years after the 1953 merger of the Washington

Seminary and the Westminster Schools.

Margaret's highest academic achievements were in English and

history, but mathematics continued to elude her throughout her

Washington Seminary

schooling. She later wrote, "They had to dynamite that worthy institution to get me out of geometry." She was a chatterbox and frequently had to be brought to task for inattentiveness. Margaret also did her share of passing notes.

Biographers have differing views of Margaret's popularity among her classmates. The question of popularity probably stemmed from the fact that she was not asked to join a sorority and that she held none of the top class offices. The latter point may be explained by the fact that in boarding schools, the boarders tend to garner the highest offices over the day students. Courtenay Ross asserts that both Margaret and she were well liked by their peers. According to Ross, "It soon became apparent that neither of us would become beauty queens, so we teamed up as bona fide school politicians."

Margaret demonstrated her leadership capabilities as well as her sociability by participating in a variety of activities and clubs during her days at the Seminary. As a founding member and officer of the Dramatic Club, Margaret played Bottom in *A Midsummer Night's Dream*, Gobbo in *The Merchant of Venice*, the Mikado in *The Japanese Girl*, and the roommate in her own *The Class President*, a play about class snobs in a Northeastern college. Courtenay Ross, Erskine Jarnagin, and Lucille Little were also part of the eleven-member cast of this play. In an interview with Darden Pyron, Elinor Hillyer said that Margaret was perfectly cast as Bottom because she was such a ham. Mitchell told Virginia McConnell in a 1936 interview for the Seminary's student magazine that she and her classmates "studied *A Midsummer Night's Dream* too, and when we enacted it, I was always the donkey because I had a donkey's head; not this one, but one of cardboard." Lucille Little remembered "the classic pageants in which Courtenay Ross and MM as Launcelot Gobbo and pal stole the show even from the cool and stately May Queen (hooray!)."

The class of 1918 produced a gala Senior Circus featuring such attractions as the Famous Wild Woman, a Hula-Hula tent, and the Golden Tornado.

Perhaps the most satisfying achievement for Margaret was being the literary editor of *Facts and Fancies,* the Washington Seminary yearbook. "How I politicked to be editor. I so wanted a story of mine to be published in the annual," she confessed in the McConnell interview. The two literary clubs at the school were the Washington Literary Society and the Alice Chandler Society. The societies debated each other and competed for prestige and new members. Anne Hart from the Alice Chandler Society won the literary editorship during Margaret's junior year, but Margaret gratefully accepted the job her senior year, 1918. She served as secretary

Margaret (far left) and school friends, circa 1914

Members of the Senior Round Table, 1918
(Margaret, second from right)

and later president of the Washington Literary Society. Margaret was one of five members of an honorary society of class leaders called the Senior Round Table.

The following section contains journal entries from Margaret's days at the Seminary. In the entry for January 7, 1915, Margaret is upset over failing math and her mother's response that she might have to go back to public school. She is full of self-pity and lists her own shortcomings as well as her mother's, and makes a resolution to do better the remainder of the school year. The most appealing part of this diary entry is her stated desire to become famous, which she accomplished far beyond her childhood dreams.

In the entries for March 26, 1915, and April 27, 1915, we catch a glimpse of the ups and downs in the friendship between Courtenay and Margaret, who were best friends all through school. The entry for February 2, 1916, gives a thumbsketch appraisal of Lucille Little's arrival at Washington Seminary.

Journal Entry

January 7, 1915

They don't understand me! This is the cry of every boy and girl when there's a dilemma or a scrape. Mother doesn't understand me. Mother never shows her feelings, hardly ever. She brought me up that way, too. I hate public shows of emotion—crying, anger, love, loud laughing, great joy or sorrow. I don't like these in public, but I don't mind them in the privacy of your home.

I love Mother and I suppose she loves me, but I might be her ward for all she says or does to me, and so I generally keep my mouth shut.

She never asks anything for love's sake. It's nothing for her. She yells "duty" at me all the time. I don't look it, but I do want some show of something except anger and mirth. Pride. That's sarcasm, for I don't suppose there's anything about me to be proud of. I'm not pretty, that's certain. I'm lazy. I can't study. I can't do mathematics. I guess my morals are mighty low and I don't give a damn for anything that happens.

Mother doesn't often give people 2 chances—and I'm not the person to beg. I would like to put my head in Mother's lap and say "I'm sorry, give me more chances and I'll try hard," but I won't. I'd just about rather cut off my hand than say it. I failed in my mathematics and Mother says I may have to go back to public school. But I won't go. *That's all.* I feel like I want to cry, but I'll be durned if I do.

I know I'm as smart as the other girls, but the trouble is that I am lazy. I never learned to study. I mean real study—unless something happens or someone makes me—I will flunk the year and there is not doubt to the matter. I am one of the people who never do anything well unless they are made to do it. I'm human.

I want to be famous in some way—a speaker, artist, writer, soldier, fighter, stateswoman, or anything nearly. If I were a boy, I would try for West Point, if I could make it, or well I'd be a *prize fighter*—anything for the thrills. I think there is a piece in the Bible that says "knock and it shall be opened unto you—ask and thou shalt receive." Of course, I'm sensible enough to know that I've got to try as well as ask and I have tried, *in my way*, to do my best, and heaven knows that I have asked enough to be the smartest person on earth— *only I'm not.* Quite a difference.

Well, here's to one more try for 1915. I know I flunked every midyear exam and I would not care if it were not for Mother. Father can't worry me—Mother can for she makes me mad and when I'm mad I'm as stubborn as a mule. She thinks I have no ambition I suppose—but I have. Perhaps it's very small but it's there all right.

When I go back to school I *will* work hard and heaven help me, make 1915 the best year I ever had.

Journal Entry

March 26, 1915

We were to have a test in spelling today but that Court and Evod and I were going to the matinee today, I really believe was the cause that we didn't have it. Miss Sharp's mighty white to us.

Well we went to the Forsythe and the bill was pretty good, but when coming out, I handed Court my party bag and my handkerchief to hold, while I put on my coat. I then took my party bag back, but forgot to take my handkerchief.

While we were eating and drinking, Court held up my handkerchief. Well, it wasn't clean and besides, it had a big blue stain on it. The place was rather comfortably filled up and I didn't care to have everybody view my handkerchief, so I grabbed it! Well, I got most of it, but Court held one corner. We both pulled savagely.

"You shouldn't snatch things like that," she said angrily.

"It's mine," I commented, "give it here!" I gave a vicious jerk.

"You lent it to me," she said, her eyes narrowing. My eyes narrowed, too, I suspect.

"Indeed? I have no recollection of doing such a thing!" Another pull.

"Let go and I'll give it to you!"

"You all are *so* foolish," broke in Evod. "Give me this handkerchief."

Neither Court nor I said a word, but we kept twisting. "It's mine," I said coolly.

"Yes, but don't you grab it," retorted Court, equally as cool. And so we twisted and talked until my hand hurt frightfully.

"You two are *so* foolish," said Evod. "Give me the old handkerchief."

Well, we agreed to this and we were going to settle the matter when we got home. We went downtown and did some shopping, but I did not do much talking. I was busy trying to keep from exploding. Gee, I was hot.

We got on the car and Court said, "Two of my hunches are coming true. Do you know what they are?"

Did I know? Well, I should say I did, but I said, "No." Then I turned around and said, "Yes." Louise L'Engle was on the car and Evod told her the case.

"Look here, Margaret, let's postpone the fighting until after a certain affair," said Court, and she looked at me searchingly.

"All right," I replied.

"That's a go!" We shook hands.

"Was she speaking of the play?" whispered L'Engle.

"Sure," I said.

Well, we got home and I had decided how to fix the matter. I got a pair of scissors and told Court to take her end of the blamed old handkerchief. She did and I took my end. Just then we looked each other in the eye and I saw that she was glad I had found a peaceable way of settling matters. I cut the cloth amid the murmuring of Evod about our foolishness.

"I know what I'm going to do with this," said Court, holding up her scrap while her eyes shown.

"Put it in your 'memory' book?"

"No!"

"Well then, I know." It seemed as if all my hard feeling had gone when I cut the cloth.

We walked to her house together. "Aren't we foolish?" I said. She assented. "It's a pity we're both so stubborn, but I wasn't going to give in to you, and you weren't going to give in to me." We talked some time longer, then we shook hands.

"This isn't going to hurt us," said Court, "It's going to get us closer together."

Well, I agreed with her, but it's a pity we're so much alike for each is too stubborn to give in to the other and some day—my gracious! I'll kill Court or she'll kill me, and neither will give in.

"Verily, verily. What fools these mortals be."

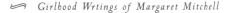

Journal Entry

April 27, 1915

Miss Sharp has played Court & me a square game up until the last three days. We can't help losing our books, we can't help not having our notebooks ready when she didn't tell us to have them on that particular day, and so she says we get "zero." It's not square and it's not fair either. Then she wouldn't let Court sit next to me in English, but that didn't worry me for we made crazy signals all through [   ].

Miss Sharp is thinking of giving up the play until next year. Miss Sharp is all right. At least she's been all right up until this time and I'm not going to blame her for being unfair.

Court had to play Mary E. Patterson all over again. It was raging hot and she had the sun in her eyes. They played some time and then they stopped for a rest and both were hopping mad. I went to see if there was any water in the cooler and then Court walked up behind me.

"I'm mad." There was an audible gulp. "I'm mad. It's not fair!" I took a glance out of the corner of my eye. Court's face was as red as a brick bat, and the corners of her mouth were twitching. I had expected something like this, for playing tennis in the boiling sun is not a pleasant pastime. I said nothing.

"It's not fair. She gave me the heavy racquet. I had the sun in my eyes! Oh, I'm mad!" She gulped again. I did not need to be told that she was mad and when she sat down on the swing, I got a cup full of water and handed it to her. She was trying to stop crying. She wasn't crying hard—just a little. She took the water and then Jessie Mae came loping along.

"For heaven's sake, buck up," I whispered. "Here comes Jessie Mae." She did "buck-up" a little for Mary came up then. By the light in Court's eyes, I think that she would have enjoyed scalping Mary immensely. Jessie Mae also gave Court some water which seemed to peeve Mary muchly. She stalked haughtily off.

At this moment, I saw Miss Martin coming. Court was starting to cry again when I said, "Stop quickly, Court. Do you want Miss Martin to see you crying?"

Evidently Court didn't for she jumped up and yelled, "Tell Miss Martin not to come here," and bolted for the tennis court. But she came back when Miss Martin called her, and after getting Mary, they played another set. This time they came off the field arm in arm, Mary being ahead.

Court came home with me—tired and hot and bewailing the fact that she had cried. She said Mary would beat her tomorrow and I said she wouldn't. We lolled on the swing for a little while. Then she went home.

Well, here's hoping she beats when she plays tomorrow.

Journal Entry

February 2, 1916

We have two new girls in the neighborhood, Lucille and Georgia Little. I met Lucille at school. I had noticed a new girl sitting in the Junior section. She looked about my age and it peeved me to think she would be a grade ahead of me.

Then it slowly filtered into my cranium that perhaps this was the new girl, who had moved on to 17th.

Court and I called her over at recess and found that I was right.

She's built something on Leila's style and looks something like Squele—tall, thin, rather nervous, brown hair and eyes, and a dark complexion. Also, northern accent!

She looks like a girl with hard, common sense. Also, I'll wager she likes the out-of-doors, reading, writing, and acting. If so, we'll be pretty good friends.

I know she is a dreamer, tho whether a practical one or not is yet to be found out.

But she'll never be a storm center!

Part Eight

With Courtenay Ross and an unknown man at Wrightsville Beach, North Carolina

Boys

~

AS THEY GREW INTO THEIR TEENAGE YEARS, Margaret and her classmates at Washington Seminary entered that common phase of adolescence in which they discovered that boys are creatures to be viewed as something more than mere playmates. She relates the giddiness and awkwardness of adolescence in the following untitled poem from one of her circa-1913 copybooks.

Over the treetops fly the bird,
While in the forest, his song is heard
Under the trees, sweet Dorothy talks
Round the glade, William Patterson wildly stalks.
The bird lights in the tree and screeches—
While down below, William peels some peaches.
Bill Lawson comes in to hear his Dot,
Say she loves William an awful lot.
In comes Robert with a gun
Just see Bill and William run!
Bob sits down beside his Dot,
Saying he loves her, an awful lot.
Enter Dick upon the scene
And with jealously, turns quite green.
Going up behind his Bob
Calling him, an awful slob—
Up jumps Robert, wild with rage,
Seizing Dick, he tears a page.
Dick 'course, objects to this,
But Dorothy settles it with a kiss.
In come Bill and William, too,
They want some of this, you knew.
Dorothy gives them each a smack,
Finishing off with a hand on the back.
As for the bird, he flew away.
And wasn't seen for many a day.

Margaret and her friends formed a sewing club, but it is doubtful they ever threaded a needle. It was more likely just an excuse to meet and, perhaps, to exclude boys. The club was mainly a neighborhood group and at one time or another the members, in addition to Margaret, included Elizabeth and Eugenia Buchanan, Sue Bucknell, Erskine Jarnagin, Leila Kirkpatrick, Jean Lambdin, Lucille Little, Dorothy McCullough, Maude Powers, Courtenay Ross, and Constance Wells. In a journal entry for December 17, 1915, Margaret describes a fight with neighborhood boys that occurred after a meeting of the club at the home of the Bucknells, or Bucks for short. In an earlier entry, she shows how silly some teenage girls can be on the subject of boys.

Margaret and Courtenay spent two weeks at Wrightsville Beach, North Carolina, in June of 1916. They stayed at the Seashore Hotel and Steel Pier, where the Blockade Runner Hotel is today. The hotel

With Courtenay Ross, circa 1916

had a huge veranda fifteen feet wide and eight hundred feet long that encircled the main building, and the girls may have spent many a lazy afternoon there after their time on the beach. The Steel Pier was built in 1910 and was the first of its kind on the South Atlantic coast. It extended seven hundred feet into the ocean and had a two-story pavilion and observation deck. Further down the beach was the Lumina, a pavilion lit during the summer season with hundreds of electric lights. Dancing at the Lumina, enjoying the vaudeville acts at the theater in the Casino, watching the yacht racing, and meeting boys made Wrightsville Beach a haven for the two fifteen-year-olds from Atlanta. On June 30, 1916, Margaret wrote a journal entry on hotel stationery describing the men and boys she had met at Wrightsville Beach.

Margaret's previously published story *Lost Laysen* was written during this same summer from July to August. Debra Freer, who edited the story for publication, noted that several titles for other stories were found in the composition book containing "Lost Laysen." One was "Man Who Never had a Chance." In her diary entry about Wrightsville Beach which follows, Margaret describes a fellow named Ridgely as "a man who'd never had a chance." It is possible that she planned to use his sad tale in one of her stories.

Journal Entry

January 23 Saturday Night, 1915

I'm as ashamed as I can be, but I could not help it. I saw red today and for the first time in I don't know how long.

It was up at the McCulloughs' and Margaret was making up some foolish things about Bill and me. Dorothy is wild over the subject of William and so she popped up and said, "They're crazy about each other."

"We're not," I said, getting a little hot.

Then Margaret smoothed matters down and began talking about the sweater that he used to wear. "Do you remember that little 'turned-up' hat he wore?" she questioned, giggling.

"Well I ought to," I said. "He used to leave it up at my house regularly."

"So he could come back?"

"Oh, you hush up!" I said, grinning.

And then Dorothy (confound it) broke in, "He used to go down to see Margaret *every* afternoon!"

Well, what if he did? "Well," I said, drawling, "seems to me, Dorothy, that you were down at my house pretty regular, yourself," I couldn't help saying. *That* about floored her.

"Well, I'm not a boy!" she said.

"I think he's real cute," broke in M. W., determined not to have a fuss. "I like him!"

"So does Margaret," declared Dorothy, "but it's a one-sided affair. She's *wild* over him and he doesn't give a snap of his fingers for her!" She emphasized this by snapping her fingers.

And right then, I got hot. Holy smoke! But I was mad! I don't know or care what I said, but I hope *I swore like 60!*

"Aw, look at her getting mad!"

My dear friend was getting a little uneasy. "Yes, I guess I am mad," I spit out, "when you deliberately say that I run after any boy. There's no boy worth running after. And what's more, I don't give a snap of my fingers for any boy!"

"You say a woman's better than a man?" she questioned, trying to change the subject.

"Yes, I do," I yelled, "and you better not say I run after any boy, Dorothy McCullough!" Then I began to cool, for I never stay hot long, "and if I do run, I'm not the only one! It's a pity that a certain boy can run away faster than you can run after him!"

Then I left. I'll bet I felt madder than Court did last night. I'd just like to choke Dorothy McCullough or to pummel her 'til there wasn't anything left of her. But, honest to goodness, I think I'll reserve her for something worse.

Journal Entry

December 17, 1915

Yesterday the club met at the Bucks and, as usual, the boys were on hand to "pester" us. When I went home, Dick and Bill Coburn were waiting behind the hedge. They walked a little way with me and then went back to waylay the other girls—as I didn't make a good victim.

I came home, got off my coat, and got a book. Then I heard some noise outside and I ran out. Constance Wells was defiantly crossing the street with those two imps walking solemnly behind her. I called out and she ran into my yard. They followed. I offered to walk home with her and we started.

Soon they began to grab at our dresses and hands, which peeved me greatly. I hate to have a boy put his hand on me in that way. Well, we just got to 17th street when Coburn made a frantic dash, caught poor Constance, bent her back and kissed her! I could have choked his life out of him! I let drive, all from the shoulders, that got him amidships and there the fight began.

Oh! But it was glorious! The air was just frosty enough to let us run well. We sprinted for dear life and when they caught up, we'd stop and fight them off. Glory be, Con gave Bill a solid kick on the shin. That made Coburn disappear for awhile.

In front of D. McCullough's, we had the biggest fight of all, and hang it all! I got rattled and pushed too hard—this by Coburn who caught my hand again. Then we ran again, Dick in front, Bill behind and Con and I fighting every step.

We got to 16th and turned down. I called a truce and asked Bill what the object of all this was. He replied, very sweetly, that it was kisses! Well, I brought the truce to a happy close and off we went—panting, half gasping, half giggling.

Constance was some little fighter. We fought back to back and then we got to Constance's house.

She tore madly up the embankment yelling, "Open up the door," at the top of her voice. I yelled good night to her and turned around, pushing up my middy sleeves that would just come down. It was a significant action, so they gave up as nice as they could be. "Now, aren't you ashamed?" I cried scathingly, still on the defensive.

"No!" they chortled gleefully and then we started for home, talking as nice as you please.

Squele and Florence came along. The boys started to assault them, but we crowded together and looked so war-like, that they contented themselves with insulting remarks.

Squele went up Peachtree, but I walked home with Florence. We had some trouble going there, too, and I got one arm ripped up on some roses on the Goodharts' fence. Florence ran up her steps with Bill in hot pursuit. With a backhand swing, fair Flossie decked him.

"May we escort you home?" they sneered when she had gone.

"No," I said, but they did.

Journal Entry

June 30, 1916

SEASHORE HOTEL AND STEEL PIER

Out of Wrightsville at last, with a mighty big pain in my heart, too. I can't define the pain—I haven't tried to. I've only been at the beach for two weeks—short weeks, but chock full of interest. I guess life up here has been divided into two parts—before the "epizoat" and after. That "epizoat" taught me many things I had not known before, and it has impressed an indelible mark on my memory that I would give a lot to erase.

Noble and Charles Weathers—both mighty good fellows, who I liked an awful lot, each in my own way for they were certainly different boys. I do believe that I did get under Noble's skin and see the real man despite all his foolishness. He was a good fellow and a gentleman, which is as great a compliment as I can give a man. As for Charles, I liked him in a far different way from Noble. Noble always reminded me of a knight in silver armor, riding through a sunny valley, but Charles was much more serious. He was a dependable fellow with a sense of humor, and I can say the same of him as I did of Noble—both mighty good comrades.

Then there was Leopold Spriegler, the "little Austrian." I did like that fellow for all his peculiarities. He was foreign and I'll forgive him some things for that. He was a good seaside friend, that's all—an interesting companion to be on the beach with or to walk with. Though sensitive and fickle, he was a pretty good sort for he was a kind-hearted, good-natured fellow, even though he did have a good opinion of himself.

Next comes Rhodes Perdue. He was just plain boy—a little better than average, but at 16—that awful age when a boy fancies himself Lord of Creation, and scarcely condescends to notice a girl under 18—but he was a good arguer, well up on current events—a reader, good-humored, and the children liked him. Would there were more Rhodes at 16 and less of the other kind!

Enter the "bulldog man"—Mr. Barrack. I only knew him for two hours, but I liked him better than some people I've known for years. He was 26, but he had the maturity of a man of 35 or 40 and he wasn't ashamed to spend two hours talking with a pair of 15-year-old girls, when he could have found far pleasanter things to do. He was one of the most interesting men I ever met, and I wish our acquaintance could have been longer. He was kind and the sort of fellow you felt that you could tell your troubles to and be sure of sympathy— not pity, but the true sympathy of a friend. Though I only knew him a few minutes, (comparatively) I would have trusted him to the utmost. He was a man who had seen much of the dirty side of life, but his face showed that he thought only of the clean side. May I meet him again for he is certainly a man I'd like for a friend.

Then there was Ridgely. He's one fellow I feel sorry for. He's not my "class" certainly, but I liked him. That fellow has had a hard time since he was a kid, and I'm afraid there's been a big sorrow in his life. Physically, he is a splendid specimen, but his brains haven't kept pace with his brawn—not that he was stupid or ignorant, but a man who'd never had a chance. He always reminded me of the man in the novel, who loves the girl, loses her to the hero, and is finally killed. When I think of him, I'll never forget the choking catch in his voice, when he spoke of the little fifteen-year-old girl he married and the little 4-year-old boy. I'm glad I met you, Ridgely, for you gave me many pleasant minutes and made me thankful for many things. Good luck to you, wherever you may be!

In my memories of the beach, one man stands out predominantly—Fritz Hausen. I never think of the ocean, but that I see him—6 ft. of hard, bronze muscle, in his bathing suit, standing with folded arms, staring out over the water. Hausen was a boy in many respects and more particularly—his pride in his strength. It was not an offensive pride—only a natural one. He was one man I feared, and yet, liked. It was the pure brute strength of that man that I feared, and the same brute strength that fascinated me.

He really did not realize how strong he was and he sometimes hurt people unawares. He had a very primitive sense of humor, though he laughed seldom, only a quick splash of teeth or a little chuckle. He had a lot of devil in him—too much to suit me—and he was not to be denied anything he wanted. There was worlds of good in him, and every child up and down the beach loved him. He was a strange person to talk to, for you never knew whether he approved or disapproved of what you were saying. He only fixed his blue eyes on you and watched with an expressionless face. He was a true soldier of fortune all right, having been a boxer, sailor, on the stage, wrestler, and heaven knows how many other things! Yes, Hausen stands out strongly in my memory of Wrightsville. I'll never forget that straight browed, big muscled, clean-cut man!

It seems a year since I was at the beach!

A review of the beach
June 30, 1916

Part Nine

"Little Sister" as it appeared in Margaret's high school yearbook, 1917

Mexico

THE MEXICAN REVOLUTION WAS HEADLINE

news in the United States in the 1910s. Mexico's government under-

went several military coups and figures such as Venustantio

Carranza, Porfirio Diaz, General Victoriano Huerta, Francisco

Madero, Francisco "Pancho" Villa, and Emiliano Zapata became

household names in the U.S.

In the earliest of Margaret Mitchell's three Mexican stories,

Visiting her brother Stephens in Musella, Georgia, October 8, 1917

"Steve of the X-B," the main character was a Texan who joined the rebels in Mexico. The politics of Mexico was not a major theme of the story, but the country provided a place of escape for the unhappy lover after he feels that his love has been rejected. Margaret must have imagined this escape as romantic and glamorous as having a character join the French Foreign Legion.

The name Juan Mardo is used for a minor character in "Steve of the X-B" and again for the villain in *Lost Laysen*. Mendoya was one of the major characters and the revolutionaries Zapata and Carranza are mentioned in "The Greaser," written in January, 1913. In the story the heroine is kidnaped by Mexican rebels. Ironically, it is Mendoya who courageously achieves her rescue. Margaret's sympathetic portrayal of the Mexican leader goes against the ethnic slur of the title.

The essay "If Roosevelt had been President" was written in late March, 1916, after Pancho Villa led a raid into the border town of Columbus, New Mexico, killing sixteen people. The reference to the German U-boats concerned the sinking of a French channel sweeper with two Americans on board. President Woodrow Wilson threatened to abandon all ties with Germany which, in turn, pledged no further destruction of neutral ships. For years many Americans had believed that Germany and Japan were secretly planning an invasion of the U.S. through Mexico. In early 1917, British intelligence, having previously broken a German code, revealed a plot proposing that Mexico ally with Germany and Japan if the United States entered World War I. In her book *The Zimmermann Telegram*, Barbara Tuchman emphasizes the hostile feelings of most Americans of Margaret's childhood era toward Mexicans and what had begun to be called the "yellow peril."

The two literary clubs at Washington Seminary debated whether the U.S. should annex Mexico, which probably further stimulated Margaret's interest in Mexico and Mexico's relations with the United States.

In her junior year, Margaret submitted a story titled "Little Sister" for inclusion in the Washington Seminary's yearbook, *Facts and Fancies*. It is the story of a young girl who witnesses the brutal killing of her mother and father and who hears the cries of her older sister's rape. It was not originally chosen by the literary editor to be included, but Eva Paisley, the yearbook advisor and Margaret's English teacher, overrode this decision and "Little Sister" appeared in the annual in 1917.

"Steve of the X·B"

Cast:

Mr. Johnson—a rancher
Mrs. Johnson—his wife
Steve Stuart—the foreman
Nell Donelson—the schoolteacher
Juan Mardo—cowboy
Joe Hunter—cowboy
Rattlesnake Pete—cowboy
Red Smith—cowboy
Bill Bradford—cattle thief
Danny Mains—cattle thief
Al Williams—cattle thief
cowboys, cattle thieves, sheriff, Mexicans

Scene: In Texas

CHAPTER I

It was nearly night, and the dark shadows were falling. The road was deserted, except for two figures. One a man, and the other, a horse—the man, young and erect. From his dress he was evidently a cowboy. His sombrero was pushed back on his forehead, and he was whistling in a carefree manner. In his eye was the fearless, "devil-may-care" expression which is found in nearly every cowboy. Somehow he did not seem like the general run of cowpunchers, but he seemed to look more educated and intelligent. The horse was a large black beast, evidently very strong. I have said that he looked carefree. To tell the truth, he was carefree. He was the foreman of the X-B (X bar B) ranch and a trusted employee of Mr. Johnson, the owner of the ranch. He had been into town, some thirty miles distant, to arrange a shipment of cattle with another rancher and had, by shrewd bargaining, netted several hundred dollars' profit on the deal.

As he rounded a curve in the road, at a swinging lope, he pulled up in surprise. The stagecoach, which ran through the mountains weekly, was standing in front of him. The driver was frowning in perplexity, but when he saw the cowboy he gave a yell of joy.

"Come 'ere, Steve!" he bellowed. Steve came.

"What's the matter?" he inquired.

"Axle's broken. Nothing for this lady to get to old man Johnson's ranch in. Will you take her?"

Steve did not answer the question. He was gazing at the girl inside the stage, who in turn, was regarding him with a good deal of curiosity. She was rather pretty, Steve thought, with her blue eyes and golden curls. She flashed a dazzling smile at him.

"Good evening," she greeted sweetly. All the carelessness vanished, and he became a confused boy. He snatched off his hat.

"Good mornin'! I mean evenin', ma'am."

The driver interrupted. "Will you take her?" he questioned.

"'Course," replied Steve, recovering somewhat. "What are you going to do?"

The driver looked around, "There's money inside. I can't leave it. You send someone from the ranch to fix the stage, when you get there," he said.

The girl stepped out. "Thank you for offering to take me. May I ask your name?"

Steve, twisting his hat wildly, looked helplessly at the driver, who answered, "Oh, he's Steve Stuart, foreman at Mr. Johnson's ranch."

"I'm Nell Donelson," she said, "and if you will help me up behind you, we can start."

CHAPTER 2

Steve never forgot that ride. Recovering from his confusion, he soon learned that she was coming West for her health. She was going to teach school and live at Mr. Johnson's. By the time they arrived at the ranch, Steve realized that he was in love—desperately, with the golden-haired girl.

He removed his horse's saddle and bridle and turned him loose in the corral. Then he went to the bunkhouse. As he entered, ear- splitting yells greeted him.

"Who was the girl?" yelled one cowboy, who went by the name of Rattlesnake Pete.

"What girl?" replied Steve innocently.

"The girl you brought," yelled the chorus.

"Now what are you talking about?" said Steve, grinning tantalizingly. In an instant all was in an uproar. The cowpunchers sailed into Steve, and there was an all-around scrimmage with Steve at the bottom.

"Let up, fellows!" he managed to gasp. "I'll tell you all about her."
Joe Hunter yanked him to his feet.

"What do you want to know?" inquired Steve, with an air of injured dignity.

"Who is she?" "What's she come for?" "What's she going to do?"
were some of the questions hurled at him.

"She's Miss Nell Donelson and she's goin' to teach in the school
out here," replied Steve, "and now, I'm going to flop on to my bunk."
Suiting the action to the words, he sank down on one of the numerous bunks.

When the school was started, there was no lack of pupils for it.
The children from miles around attended, and a good many of the
cowpunchers would present themselves, shyly, on their holidays. Nell
Donelson had hosts of admirers among the cowboys, and she was
never lacking in escorts.

One night, Joe Hunter entered the bunkhouse. He was wearing an
ill-fitting black suit. His neck was encased in a high collar, which
seemed to choke him. He held a large bunch of wild flowers in his
hand. "Boys," he announced, "I'm a-going to propose to Miss Nell."

All the cowpunchers set up a yell, but they bade him good luck,
and set to work to wait for his return. In a hour's time, he returned.

"Did she blush?" "What'd she say?" "Were you scared?" were
some of the questions hurled at him.

"Boys," he said, "she never batted an eye, but—um," he chuckled.
Nor could any coaxing make him tell what happened.

That was only the beginning. Every cowpuncher, except Steve
Stuart, was shyly paying court to the schoolteacher. Steve held himself aloof. He loved her, there was no use to deny that, but some-

how—well, he thought that he would bide his time.

In the meantime, the cattle rustlers were getting bolder. Ten steers had been lost the week before. As foreman, it was his duty to see that the cattle were safely guarded.

One morning the sheriff rode up and presented Steve with a bit of pasteboard on which was printed:

$1,000 REWARD
FOR THE CAPTURE OF
DANNY MAINS, BILL
BRADFORD, AND AL
WILLIAMS—CATTLE THIEVES
A.C. SANFORD
SHERIFF

"Thanks," said Steve. "I'll take this one. I know all three of those coyotes or I used to know 'em. They were pretty tough."

Shortly after this he was out on the range with the rest of the cowpunchers, watching the cattle. He had ridden up. "There's some cattle missing," reported Red Smith.

"How many?"

"Fifteen."

"Strayed?"

"I guess so."

Steve looked around. There were the tracks of the cattle. "'Round them up," he said and rode off.

He followed the tracks for some distance. They were leading into a clump of trees from which some smoke was rising. "Whew!" he thought, "suppose I should get all those rustlers at once!" The vision of $1,000 rose up before his eyes, but that did not prevent his being cautious. He had met up with Danny Mains, Al Williams, and Bob Bradford a few times in the course of his young life, and so he was sure of recognizing them.

He dismounted, tied his horse to a tree, and pulled out his pistol. Very cautiously, he advanced. Two men were sitting by a fire with their backs to him. A good many cattle, bearing the X-B brand, were standing or lying about. "Al Williams and Bill Bradford," gasped Steve, "what luck!" then, "Hands up!" he yelled. In a semi-civilized country this order is seldom disobeyed. The rustlers leaped up, but seeing that they were caught, elevated their hands.

"Why, it's Steve Stuart!" cried Al Williams, a man with the face of a hardened criminal. "Hello, Steve."

"Hello," responded Steve coolly. "You've got a nice bunch of cattle there," he added meaningfully. Bradford coughed apologetically. "You need not make like you are innocent for I'm going to get one thousand for you two. I only wish Mr. Mains would show up!" Steve laughed; he was sure of his ground.

"Your wish has come true," said a calm voice. Before Steve could turn, he felt a pistol pushed against his neck. "Don't look around, but drop that gun," came the order. As Steve was not a fool, he obeyed. As the weapon hit the ground, Steve was covered by the pistols of the other two rustlers. In less time than he could think, Steve found himself tied to a tree while Williams and Bradford were shaking hands with Danny Mains, to whom they owed their freedom.

Mains was a young man of twenty-four, perhaps, with very good-looking features. The only thing that marred his face was a scar on his cheek. "Oh let up, boys, you needn't thank me," he said. "Let's see if this skunk has any money with him."

Steve was searched; only a few dollars and a piece of crumpled paper was brought to light. Danny Mains straightened it out. It was the notice of the reward offered for the three rustlers. Mains laughed bitterly, "What to do with Stuart?" he questioned. "We can't let him go."

"I should say not," spoke up Al Williams. "Plug him full of holes, I say." The other rustler nodded.

"Who'll do the job?" questioned Danny Mains.

Bill Bradford pulled out a pack of greasy cards. "The one who gets the first ace," he said and started dealing the cards.

A multitude of thoughts rushed through Steve's mind. He was not afraid to die, but he wanted to live. Life had never before seemed so sweet, and especially now that Nell had come into his life. Bill Bradford kept on dealing the cards. Danny had the first ace—an ace of hearts. Steve wondered why he noticed this. Mains advanced, took a pin from his shirt and pinned the card on Steve's chest, above his heart. "I'll bet I can knock the spots out of that ace," he declared.

"I'll bet two bucks you can't," declared Al Williams.

"Done," said Danny, taking out his pistol and getting some yards away from Steve. Steve thought that his last moment had come when he saw the pistol raised.

"Fire when I say three!" said Al Williams. Mains nodded.

"One," commenced Al, "two." Before "three" left his lips, there was a pistol shot. Steve thought he had been shot, but he felt no pain. Danny Mains was lying on the ground with a dark red stain across his shirt, moaning and writhing. Before the other two rustlers could gather their wits together, there was a trampling of hooves and a voice shouted, "Get 'em boys. Kill 'em."

There was a second shot and Al Williams collapsed on the ground. Bill Bradford made a flying leap for his horse, but the relentless "crack" brought him to the ground.

Steve, raised from the depths of despair to the height of joy, looked to see some of the cowpunchers ride up, but no one came. Nell Donelson, the schoolteacher, rode up with a pistol in her hand. She dismounted and quickly untied Steve. He shook his head vigorously. "You certainly saved me, Miss Nell," he said fervently.

"Are—are they dead?" she questioned in horror.

"I hope so," said Steve heartlessly. "Miss Nell, won't you stay here while I go get some of the boys?" She nodded and Steve mounted one of the horses and rode off to find the cowboys.

CHAPTER 3

To Steve, the days that followed this exciting adventure were happy ones. To Nell, they were happy ones, too. Nearly every day that he could have from his work, he was at her side. He went riding with her, took her hunting, was her escort to any of the dances in the neighborhood, and, as Mrs. Johnson expressed it, "was jes' Nell's slave." He was her slave in fact. He loved her more than he could tell.

One afternoon, on a holiday from work, Steve went riding with Nell. They went farther than they had ever been before, finally stopping at a spring for a drink. She sat down on a large rock. Suddenly he burst out, "Miss Nell, I guess you know by now; I love you."

Nell's heart jumped. If she had ever loved any man, it was Steve, but as many women are, she was a good deal of a coquette and a flirt.

She answered banteringly, "Oh, really?"

Steve was taken back. "Yes'm, really. Miss Nell, I love you so—"

"Oh, Steve, you know you don't," she cried.

Steve grew exasperated. "Yes, I do. Don't you like me at all?"

Nell tilted back her head and gave vent to a laugh. "Oh, you cow-puncher!" she cried.

"Miss Nell," pleaded Steve, "I do love you. I've never loved anyone before."

She laughed again and shook her head at him. A pang shot through Steve's heart. He had been mistaken. She had never loved him. Feeling sadder than he ever remembered feeling before, he sprang on his horse. "Let's be going, Miss Nell," he said in expressionless tones. Frightened at what she had done, Nell mounted.

All the long ride, neither spoke a word. When the ranch was reached, Steve sought out Rattlesnake Pete. "Pete," he said sadly, "will you give a note to Miss Nell for me?" Pete nodded, surprised. Steve pulled out a pencil and procuring a piece of paper, he wrote a note to Nell Donelson. "Don't give it to her until I'm gone," he said.

"Gone?" repeated Pete. "Where are you goin'?"

"I'll join the rebels and fight. I don't care whether I'm killed or not, but I hope I'm shot soon, the sooner the better." At his hopeless tone, Pete understood.

"Steve," he said, "do you mean she don't love you?"

"I don't care whether she does or not," cried Steve defiantly. He made a bundle of the few belongings that he possessed and strapped them on his horse's back, behind his saddle. "Tell the boys good-bye for me," he said, as he wrung Pete's hand. He sprang into his saddle. At the top of a ridge of ground, he stopped for a moment, then rode from the hill and disappeared.

Pete gave a sigh. "It's funny how a fellow like Steve will get all broke-up over an affair like that!" As he walked toward Mrs. Johnson's house to deliver Steve's message, he thought of the number of times that he had seen Steve face death without flinching. Pete shook his head. He was a hardened cowboy and he would not understand how a man of Steve's "grit," who could face death fearlessly, could be broken up over this affair.

Mrs. Johnson looked at him curiously when he asked for Nell. Outside of Steve, Pete was about the only cowboy who did not pay court to Nell. Pete sat down on the porch. Mrs. Johnson came back. "Miss Nell says that she has a headache and can't see anyone," she said.

"I've got a message for her," said Pete. Mrs. Johnson was dubious, but she returned to say that Nell would be down in a few minutes. It was late in the afternoon, but when Nell came down to the porch, Pete saw that her eyes were red from crying.

"Have you a message for me, sir?" she questioned in strangely altered tones.

"Yes'm." Pete pulled out Steve's letter and placed it in her hand.

"Thank you," she said. "Don't go," she added, seeing that he was going to go. "I want to speak to you afterwards." Pete sat down. She opened the note and sat down. Suddenly she started up, a cry on her lips and her face like marble. "Oh God, help me!" she cried.

Pete sprang up. "You aint goin' to faint, are you, Miss Nell?" he cried in anxiety.

"No, no, I'll not faint." She laughed a little hysterically and continued reading Steve's note. It was not long and was as follows:

Dear Miss Nell,
I hoped that you loved me, but I guess
that I was wrong. I've never loved any woman
except you and I'd rather die than live without
you. I wish I was dead now, but I'm not dead,
so I'm going across the border into Mexico and
join the rebels. I'm just waiting for a bullet to
take me away, for I don't want life without you.
But if you ever need me, I'll be ready to
help you.
May this not be good-bye forever, but
so long!
Steve

Nell gave a gasp and collapsed into a chair. Pete took matters into
his own hands. "Now, Miss Nell," he said, "you've caused more mis-
ery than you can think. I love Steve like a brother, and it hurt me
worsen I can tell, to see him so broken up, what—"

But Nell could stand no more. "Oh, Pete, don't! I shall go mad if
you say another word!" She paused. "Pete, I deserve all that's coming
to me and more, too! I loved Steve—" Then she leaped up and ran
into the house, leaving Pete gazing after her, sadly shaking his head.

CHAPTER 4

So the months passed on and Nell continued her teaching. One of
the neighboring ranchers had given a barbeque and a dance, and Nell
attended it. A Mexican, by the name of Juan Mardo, had insisted on

escorting her home. He was a dark, handsome young fellow, whose dashing ways had won the heart of many a dark-eyed Señorita.

When Mrs. Johnson came home an hour later, she found Nell lying on her bed, crying. By degrees she learned Nell's tale. "He asked me to marry him," explained Nell between sobs. "Of course, I said no. He just glared at me and said, 'Miss Nell, you shall regret this day.' He—he looked just like a snake and he said he'd always loved me, but now he was going to have his revenge. I—I took out my pistol and told him to go. He did. I came home by myself. Oh, Mrs. Johnson, he's going to do me harm some way. I know it!"

When Nell said that she knew the Mexican would do her harm, she spoke correctly. Juan Mardo, smarting with disappointment, was now bent on ruining Miss Nell's good name.

From time to time, Nell would catch scraps of conversations about herself, which she knew were untrue. More than one time, she noticed that crowds of people gazed after her with sneering smiles. This was not pleasant to her.

One day Pete picked up one of Nell's combs, which she had dropped while riding. He took it to the ranch house. Mrs. Johnson was busy making bread when he arrived. "Take it upstairs, Pete; she's in her room."

Pete ascended the stairs and knocked on the door. There was no answer, so he pushed the door open. Nell was lying across the bed, fast asleep. "I'll jest lay this on the table," thought Pete, as he tip-toed across the room. On the table was a piece of paper. Pete knew that he should not have looked at it, but he opened it, nevertheless. It was the note from Steve. Pete's eyes fell on these lines, "but if you ever need me, I'll be ready to help you." Pete put the paper down, feeling very conscience-stricken. Then an idea came to him. "If ever Miss Nell needed help, it's now."

That night Pete obtained a leave of absence from Mr. Johnson, on the plea of important business. He set off, not towards the town, but in the direction of the Rio Grande, the boundary line of Texas and Mexico. Pete had not heard from Steve, personally, since he had seen him last, but in indirect ways, he had heard much of him. Steve had joined the rebels and was now a captain. His recklessness in battles won much admiration from the men he commanded, and hatred from those he fought. He seemed to have no regard for his own life and he led his men to victory many times. Pete pondered over these things as he rode along. He knew where the rebels were encamped and he hoped to find Steve there. He crossed the river and, by hard riding, reached the rebel camp by morning.

Pete made inquiries about Steve. A tall, dark Mexican gave him this reply, "El Capitán Stuart? Si, Si, the Federals capture him last night. Si!" Pete was horrified. He knew the hatred that many of the Federals bore Steve, and he would not vouch for his friend's life.

He continued his inquiries. Steve had been captured by a small detachment, while out riding. "Where was this detachment?" "Who commanded it?" Pete pressed these questions eagerly. The rebels did not know for certain, but thought that the detachment was camped outside a certain village, some twenty miles down the road. Pete thanked them and remounted.

His horse was jaded and he saw, at a glance, that it was not equal to twenty miles under the broiling sun. There was no other mount to be had, so Pete set out at a jog trot, urging his steed on at intervals. The pony was a good one and he did his best, but it was nearly nightfall when Pete neared the village the Mexicans had spoken of.

As he dismounted, his horse staggered, sank to his knees, and rolled over. "Plum played out," muttered Pete. "If those greasers have killed Steve—" Within a clump of trees, a campfire twinkled merrily.

Pete, with pistol drawn, advanced cautiously. About twenty Federals were grouped about the fire. Pete gave a sigh of relief for there, close by the fire, lay Steve, tied hand and foot. The guns were stacked in a pile on one side of the fire, while the soldiers sat on the other side. Pete gazed at his friend. He saw that Steve's teeth were tightly clenched, as if to keep back a cry of pain. His bare wrists where the cords were tied were bleeding, and in spots, little splotches of blood showed through his shirt. Pete was puzzled. "He aint been shot I know, but what's the matter?" He took another glance at the ropes around Steve and saw that they were made of freshly cut leather thongs. Then Pete understood. Perhaps you may know that these thongs, if subjected to heat, will shrink. When he was captured, Steve had been tied tightly with them. He had lain in the hot sun, doubtless, and therefore the thongs had shrunk.

Pete did not know what to do. Just at this time one Federal, in passing Steve, let drive a vicious kick at the prisoner. This brutality settled Pete; out of the bushes he stepped, a pistol in each hand.

"Up with yer damn paws, yer dirty greasers!" he yelled, advancing. As among their few virtues, prudence is enumerated, the Mexicans obeyed. "Now one of you, cut El Capitán Stuart loose. You—" he said, pointing to one. The fellow obeyed. "Can you walk, Steve?" questioned Pete anxiously.

"No," replied Steve indifferently, "I can't."

Pete moved closer. "Can you move your arms?"

"Yes."

"Then take this gun and keep the greasers covered."

Steve took the pistol and did as directed. Pete replaced his second pistol, and leaning over he gave a heave, and lifted Steve on to his shoulder. This was no little feat, as Steve was not a light weight. Pete, staggering under his burden, made his way toward the Mexican horse. Steve fired his pistol, and a soldier, who had endeavored to obtain his gun, dropped to the ground.

The horse reached, Pete assisted Steve to mount. "Go on, Steve," he cried. "I'll follow," and Steve rode off. Pete, with a pistol in one hand, gave a flying leap. He landed in the saddle without as much as touching the stirrups, then dashed off after Steve. Volleys of shots followed them, but they were soon out of range.

CHAPTER 5

That night Steve and Pete sat at a table in a saloon near the border. Pete studied Steve. How changed he was! The joking, laughing boy was gone, and in his place, a firm, determined man, accustomed to the grim horrors of war. Steve called for a drink. Pete did the same. Steve ordered a second. "See here, Steve," postulated Pete, "you didn't use to drink like that!"

"I drink to forget," was Steve's listless reply.

Then Pete got down to business. He told of the delivery of Steve's letter, then the treachery of Juan Mardo. "She needs help, she does," he finished up.

Steve lit a cigarette and puffed it reflectively. "I played square with her and she did me dirty," he commented.

"But you like her," shot in Pete.

"I did." There was a pause.

"Then, Steve old pal, you've got to plug that Mexican. I don't know how it feels to be in love, but, oh well, look here, she likes you a lot, she does."

Steve did not brighten, but he held out his hand.

Pete grasped it. "Pard, you'll come?"

Steve's jaw set in a manner peculiar to him. "I'll come," was his reply.

CHAPTER 6

Nell's room was all in confusion. The trunk was opened and Nell was packing her clothes in it. Mrs. Johnson stood by the door. "Nell, I'm sorry to see you go," she said.

Nell did not look up. "I'm sorry to leave you, Mrs. Johnson," she said.

Two days previously, Pete had returned from his "important business" to discover that Nell was to leave the ranch at the end of the week.

Nell slammed down the lid of the trunk, snapped the lock, and then walked downstairs and out on the porch. "Pete," she called. Pete, in the act of mounting his pony, stopped and walked over to where she stood.

"Yes'm?" There was a questioning note in his voice.

"Saddle my horse, Pete. I want to make a long ride before I go this afternoon, and after you fix the pony, I've got something to tell you," said Nell.

Pete hurried off and soon returned leading Nell's horse by the reins. Nell mounted. Then she put her hand in her pocket and drew out a letter, which she handed to Pete. "Pete," she said sadly, "I'm trusting you to give this to Steve the next time you see him. It will explain all!" She struck her horse with her squirt, and galloped off. Her reins dropped loosely from her hand and she let the pony make his own direction.

CHAPTER 7

Steve rode along carelessly, not caring which way his horse went; however, he pulled up by the spring where he had proposed to Nell, that his horse might drink. As he looked around he gave a bitter laugh. How much had happened since he and Nell had stood there! His reverie was broken by the sound of a horse's hooves. He started, looked around, and then gave a cry of surprise. The Mexican, Juan Mardo, was riding toward him. Steve wheeled his horse and rode up to him.

"Mornin'," he hailed.

"The Señor Stuart," cried the Mexican in surprise.

"Yep, that's me." Steve moved closer. "See here, Mardo, I've business with you."

"Business?" The surprise was genuine.

"Yes, business." Steve slipped his hand to his pistol. "Why did you tell those lies about Miss Donelson?"

The Mexican went white, but he hastily controlled himself. "You are mistaken, Señor. I have told no lies!"

"You liar!"

Quick as a flash Juan Mardo sought his pistol, but not quick enough, for Steve already had him covered. Reluctantly, he raised his hands. "Did you do it? Tell the truth or I'll shoot."

Evidently, the Mexican believed Steve. "Yes," he said arrogantly, "I did."

"Then I'm going to kill you!" Steve spoke as if he were speaking of a refractory puppy.

"And be hung for it," sneered Mardo.

"Yes, it would be tough to hang for a fellow like you!" remarked Steve with cutting emphasis. He paused. "Then," he said "we'll have what's called a duel, in the East. You ride up on that knoll and I'll ride to the spring. When I say 'three,' fire—savvy?"

Mardo nodded. At least this was better than being shot down while you held up your hands. Steve backed his horse slowly. Suddenly, the horse stumbled, and the pistol that Steve held fell to the ground. He leaped down, intent on picking it up. He did so and as he straightened up, Juan Mardo raised his own pistol and fired.

Steve staggered back against his horse, clutching the saddle for support. He looked round in a dazed fashion, one hand pressed to his chest, where a dark red splotch was rapidly growing larger. Then he heard the taunting, triumphant laugh of the Mexican.

A light of rage blazed into his eyes. The Mexican rode up closer to observe the effect of his shot. "You devil!" roared Steve, steadying himself. Then up came his pistol. There was a sharp report. For an instant, the Mexican sat erect in his saddle and then he collapsed. Steve's aim had been unerring. Juan Mardo had been shot through the head. His horse plunged wildly and then dashed off, dragging his rider, whose foot had caught in the stirrup, over the rough ground.

Steve gave a groan and staggered toward the spring. Then he collapsed on the ground and passed into merciful oblivion.

CHAPTER 8

As Nell rode close to the spring, with surprise, she saw a horse grazing nearby. She was about to return to the ranch when curiosity prompted her to have another look at the animal. A look of surprise flitted over her face. "Well I'm a jack rabbit, but that's Steve's pony." She whirled her horse around, intent on returning to the ranch without meeting Steve, when something on the ground caught her attention.

"It—it looks like blood!" she cried falteringly. Then she dismounted and advanced toward the spring. Within a foot of the bubbling water lay Steve. Nell recognized him though she only saw his back. With an effort she turned him over and gave a gasp of horror. The front of Steve's shirt was covered with blood. Nell gave a bitter cry, "Oh, he's dead!" and sank on her knees. Not until that instant did she fully realize how much she loved Steve. "No, I don't believe he's dead," she cried, laying her hand on his wrist. "I must get back to the ranch. If I leave him, he might die. I must try to get him on the horse," she pondered.

She slipped one arm under his shoulder and tried to lift him, but to no avail. She had not dreamed that he was so heavy. She arose in desperation and brought her horse close up, then she put all her strength in lifting him. She was successful this time and was able to half pull and half lift Steve until she had laid him across the saddle; then she mounted behind him.

"It's about the worst position he could be in," she thought, as she started her horse, "but what can I do?"

Shortly afterward, she arrived at the ranch with her burden. Steve was taken into the ranch house and Mrs. Johnson dispatched a cowboy for a doctor.

The doctor arrived in half an hour and went into the room alone. Nell waited on the outside. There were no thoughts of returning home now; all her thoughts were in the room with the doctor.

After what seemed to Nell an age, the physician came from the room, looking very grave.

"Has he a chance?" Nell spoke calmly.

"One in a million," replied the doctor bluntly. All the world seemed to whirl around to Nell, but she controlled herself.

"One in a million," she murmured. "Thank heavens, there is one!"

CHAPTER 9

During the weeks that followed, Nell was ever staunchly by Steve's side. Not that he knew her, however, for while conscious, he mostly talked deliriously of the rebels that he had commanded or of cattle round-ups. These were anxious days for Nell. Steve hovered between life and death, but slowly, he began to win the fight for his life.

"That was the closest shave there ever was," remarked the doctor. "It's a miracle how he's getting well."

One morning Steve opened his eyes to perfect sanity. He looked around. "Where was he?" A woman was arranging something in one corner of the room. She turned. Steve peered out at her from

[*Pages are missing. The book that contained this story, as well as two others, was missing the cover, the first few pages, and the last few pages.*]

"The Greaser"

Characters:

Kit Carhart—a border rancher
Bob Jennings—her foreman
Manuel Mendoya—a Mexican
Squint-Eye—a cowboy
Pedro—a Mexican soldier

CHAPTER I

Kit Carhart walked out of the house reflexively, swinging a light, plaited raw-hide squirt in her hand. "Guess I'd better ride out on the range and see how the cattle are getting along," she thought, as she stepped out on to the porch. The morning sun was shining brightly, and she pulled her gray felt hat lower over her eyes. A small, very vicious-looking cow pony was munching the scattered tufts of grass that grew at the foot of the porch steps. She walked up to him and caught the bridle reins, which were trailing along the ground. She stroked his neck while her eyes musingly swept the horizon.

Instantly, she became alert and her hands tightened on the reins. From a clump of small scrubs, which grew about a spring, there rose a large cloud of dust. Kit frowned. What did this mean? It was not mealtime, so there was no excuse for the cowpunchers leaving the range. Kit tossed the reins over her pony's head, and then placing one foot on her broad stirrup, she swung lightly to her saddle. The pony reared, as was his want, but quickly came back to his four feet when he felt the prick of Kit's spurs on his sides.

"Up, Dare-Devil," she said, leaning forward. "Giddy-up," and like a shot, the pony was off. Straight for the water hole he headed, which not being over a half mile away, was soon reached. Kit's brows were clouded with anger by this time. What right had the cowpunchers to leave the cattle unguarded? Mexican cattle thieves could easily drive them off, or worse, a stampede might occur. She dismounted and threw the reins over Dare-Devil's head, and pushing aside the bushes, she walked angrily forward, her corduroy riding skirt swishing back and forth with each step. Then she stopped with a little cry of anger and horror.

Underneath the boughs of a large tree sat a man on a horse, his hands tied behind him, and his dark face mask-like and expressionless.

"Want to say yer prayers?" jeered a weather-beaten cowboy, as Kit approached.

"I want a cigarette." The captive's voice was perfectly cool. There were about a dozen cowboys, and all gave a jeering laugh. That is, all save one—a tall, sunburned fellow who seemed to be the foreman. He whipped out a box of cigarettes and riding up to his prisoner's side, he placed one between the man's lips. It was at this moment that Kit noticed with horror that a rope was tied about the prisoner's neck and more over, that the rope was tied tightly to the limb above. The cowpunchers intended to lynch this man!

"Stop!" Kit sprang forward just as one of her cowboys was lifting a whip to strike the prisoner's horse. All gave startled gasps. Kit sprang forward and caught the bridle of the prisoner's horse, and it was then that she saw that he was a Mexican.

"Bob Jennings," she turned on the young foreman, who peered vainly, trying to sink through the ground, "what's the meaning of this?"

To be precise, the Mexican was the calmest of the crowd. He sat on his horse, coolly smoking the cigarette, his swarthy face set grimly. It was not Jennings that answered Kit, but the weather-beaten fellow who had asked the Mexican if he wanted to pray—a fellow who rejoiced in the name of Squint-Eye.

"Miss Kit," he pulled off his sombrero, "the greaser was so careless as to ride off on Pete's horse this morning and forget to bring it back. We was aiming to decorate this tree with him."

Kit listened scornfully to this virtuous version of the story. Then she turned like a tiger on Bob Jennings, who by the way, having found it impossible to sink through the ground, had evidently decided to appear indifferent, but was making a poor job of the matter. For more than one reason, the young foreman was uneasy. "And you were going to stand by and see this man hung? You, the foreman!" Kit spit out her words with such vehemence, that Bob Jennings looked all the more uneasy. The Mexican began to evidence some interest in the affair, for a look of admiration crept into his dark eyes as Kit's gray ones flashed fire.

"No, m'am."

Another puncher interrupted, "Bob didn't want to, but we made him come!" For some reasons of her own, Kit was not half so angry after this explanation.

"Well," she ordered, "take the rope off him and untie him and let him go!"

"Look here, Miss Kit," broke in Squint-Eye coolly, "this fellow's a horse thief. Besides, he's only a *greaser*, and we're going to hang him whatever you say, eh boys?" The boys, omitting Bob, made loud affirmative rejoinders.

Kit's hand went up to her throat and from that point, it quickly stole under her khaki shirtwaist, and came out holding a formidable little blue-steel pistol. Each puncher made an instinctive grab for his pistol, but each thought better of it and raised his hands. Old man Carhart had been the best and coolest shot on the range. It was rumored that his daughter was not far behind his record, and at any rate, no one wanted to try her.

"Squint-Eye," her voice was very pleasant, "drop your gun." Squint-Eye did, but with no good grace. "Now, get down." The puncher dismounted. "Now, go get every fellow's gun and lay it down beside yours. I'll give them back to you in a little while." Scowling blackly, Squint-Eye did as he was bidden. The ground inside the arc of horses began to assume the appearance of an armory.

"Now, Squint-Eye, cut this man loose." Squint-Eye gave a gasp of protest, but with a dispassionate gesture of her pistol, Kit gave him to understand that her orders were to be obeyed. The Mexican, being freed, gave Squint-Eye a coolly personal stare, which nearly drove that cowboy frantic, and began to flick the ashes off the end of his cigarette.

"I want you men to know that I will not tolerate any lawless act on this ranch, and any fellow who doesn't like it can go." Kit knew her cowboys well. She knew that each one separately would give up his life to save hers. She had grown up with most of these men, and she knew that they would not leave the ranch.

She smiled a singularly boyish smile. "Now you fellows run along and play with the cows," she laughed, and greatly to their surprise, the cowpunchers laughed with her.

They slowly rode out of the clump of bushes, and then with loud yells, they tore off at break-neck speed toward the cattle. Only one man remained—Bob Jennings, the foreman. "Miss Kit, I'm sorry this happened, and I don't like to leave you with this fellow." There was more than a common anxiety in his voice.

"Run along, Bob." Her voice had a tender note in it that did not escape the Mexican. "I'm safe." Bob reluctantly turned his pony around and rode off.

As soon as he was out of sight, all trace of indifference left the Mexican's face. He slid down from his horse and cast away his cigarette. "Señorita," his voice shook with emotion that he could not control, "you save my life!" He took hold of the end of her riding skirt and pressed it to his lips.

"Stop!" she cried and pulled her horse backward.

"You save me," he repeated, his dark eyes glowing with gratitude.

"Of course," replied Kit tersely, "I don't want murder done on my ranch. Did you steal Pete's pony?"

"No, No!" he protested glibly, "I only borrow it, and would bring it back tomorrow or the next day, but they catch me—they say they lynch me—Ah, Señorita," he drew himself up proudly, "I do not mind dying." His eyes flashed. "I have faced death many times—they would hang me—I want to die a soldier's death."

Somewhat interested in the man, Kit studied him carefully. He was tall and dark, with a graceful bearing. His face was dark, and Kit gave a little sigh as she recalled Squint-Eye's words, "He's only a greaser."

"A soldier's death?" she exclaimed scornfully, "A horse thief's death would suit you better."

He smiled bitterly, "I am what the vaquero said, 'Only a greaser.'"

Kit started as the Mexican voiced her thoughts.

"You, a soldier?"

"Si, Si," his white teeth flashed in a winning smile.

"Carranza?" she questioned.

"Zapata!" he answered.

"Zapata!" Kit literally spit the word out. The name called to mind night raids, robberies, hold-ups, murders, and numberless other depredations, committed by Zapata's men. The name was a watch word to all the ranchers on the border.

For a short space of time, both were silent. The Mexican never moved his gaze from Kit's face, and his eyes glowed with something more than common admiration. Then Kit smiled. "You can go if you want to, Señor—Señor—What *is* your name?"

"Manuel Mendoya, at your service, Señorita."

"All right, Manuel. You can go now, but stay clear of my cowboys." She stretched out her hand to him. To her surprise, instead of shaking it, the Mexican pressed it to his lips.

"My life is yours, Señorita." Then he turned, and picking up his hat, he walked down the path and disappeared.

Kit's lip curled scornfully, "Zapata? Oh, he's just a greaser."

CHAPTER 2

Bob Jennings ran his hands through his hair in pure joy. His heart was beating fast, so fast that it startled him. His lips were still tingling with the memory of Kit's lips. He cast his eyes over the moon-lit prairie and wondered inwardly if anyone on earth could be as happy as he was. Kit had just left him; had ridden away on Dare-Devil towards the ranch. Bob knew that he would always remember this night as one of the happiest of his life.

Then suddenly, off to his right in the direction of the ranch, came a spurt of fire and the sound of a pistol shot. Bob started violently. He knew the sound of *that* pistol only too well. It was Kit's little revolver. Then came another spurt of fire and another retort. Then came two cries. One of a man in pain, the other, of a woman crying for help.

Bob sprang to where his horse was calmly munching the grass. One bound and he was on the animal's back and had stuck the horse with his spurs. He could see clearly for the moon was high up in the heavens. He saw a band of horsemen, perhaps a dozen, riding with all speed toward the Rio Grande, the Mexican border. Bob groaned, "Oh! Damn those greasers! They've got her. They're taking her to Mexico." He spurred forward, his pony convulsively jumping each time the steel spurs struck his sides.

Two of the Mexicans dropped behind the rest of the band and advanced toward Bob. "Now, what in the devil are they going to do?" thought Bob, his hand going towards his belt. He was not quick enough, however, for there was a crack of a rifle and Bob felt his horse stagger under him. Out came his own pistol, but as he raised it, there was another retort. Bob lurched forward, his left hand going to his right shoulder. At this moment, the horse fell to the ground and with him, fell Bob. He half raised on his elbow, tried to extricate himself from beneath the horse, but failing, he fell back. He heard the faint sound of the laughter of the two Mexicans, and then he closed his eyes and lay still.

CHAPTER 3

It was not one of Kit's cowboys who rode up five minutes later. It was a Mexican who came upon Bob lying beside his dead horse, his pallid face upturned to the clear sky. The stranger dismounted, and unstrapping a canteen from his saddle, he knelt down beside Bob. He made a quick examination of the cowboy. "Not dead." Then he poured some water over Bob. It was some minutes before Bob, face contorted with pain, sat up, and passed his hands over his face in a dazed manner.

"Where have they gone?" questioned the Mexican, roughly shaking the cowboy. Bob looked at him in a dull, uncomprehending way, as if wondering what all this meant. One corner of the Mexican's mouth curled in a sneer, and then he brought his open hand down on Bob's cheek with no little force. This blow seemed effective, for as Bob sank back to the ground, he raised one hand in protest and the words, "Cut it, you bully," fell with difficulty from his lips.

"Where have they gone?" demanded the Mexican, giving him another shake. Then with a sudden rush of memory, Bob remembered everything.

"Over the border," he cried, struggling to a sitting posture. "Oh, heavens! Zapata's devils have taken Kit over the border!" He attempted to rise, forgetful of the weight of his horse on him, but the Mexican did not wait. He sprang to his horse and mounted like a flash. He rode off in the direction of the river, leaving Bob prostrate beneath his dead horse.

CHAPTER 4

"One of you fellows, bring me a drink of water, quickly!" Kit's voice rang out imperatively in the small cave. One of the Mexicans lazily uncrossed his legs and carelessly removed a cigarette from between his lips.

"And if I give you water, will you give me kiss, Señorita?" Kit's eyes flashed fire.

"Oh!" she gritted out, "You damned greaser! If I weren't tied—I would—I'd—"

"You would not do one thing," replied the Mexican, but he looked to see if the knots were as tight as ever. "No kiss, no water," and he settled himself comfortably. The other Mexicans laughed. Kit clenched her teeth tightly and gave a desperate tug at the rope that tied her hands.

The cave, in which she was now captive, was a small one and dimly lighted by two lamps. The place was full of smoke as each of the eleven Mexicans were puffing at cigarettes. Kit's throat was very dry, and it was this reason that prompted her to demand some water. Her hair was down, her skirt was ripped, her face and arms were scratched and bruised, and altogether she bore the appearance of having been roughly handled. "I want some water, I tell you, and I want it quickly!" Kit raised her chin higher.

"Then I can kiss you?" The man rose.

"No," almost yelled Kit.

"Oh well, then, I get kiss and you no get water at all." He advanced toward her, casting away his cigarette as he came.

What would have happened will never be known, as at this moment there was a sharp retort, and Kit's insulting captor fell to the floor, writhed a moment, turned over on his back, and lay still. To Kit's horror, she saw an ever-widening red blotch appear on the Mexican's shirt.

The other men fell back to the wall while murmurs of "El Capitán!" rose from all sides. Kit's eyes traveled from the motionless form on the floor to the newcomer.

"Manuel Mendoya!" she ejaculated.

The Mexican sneered, "Who else?" and then turned to the other men. "Who ordered you to take this girl?" he questioned in Spanish.

"Colonel Jaunana, sir," replied one man saluting.

"How long are you to keep her here?"

"'Til the colonel comes, sir," was the reply.

Mendoya turned and walked over to Kit. "Ah, most beautiful one," he declared, making a mocking bow, "we are all your humble servants." At this a snicker of laughter arose from the rest of the men. Mendoya leaned over and deliberately pushed the hair away from Kit's cheek. "A scratch upon your pretty cheek? I will kiss it and make it well!" He leaned over and pressed his lips to her cheek. For a moment Kit was speechless with rage.

"Oh! You ungrateful dog!" she finally blurted out. "You—you—and I saved your wretched life! Oh! I wish to heaven I had let them hang you." She stopped suddenly, for there was a queer look in Mendoya's eyes. He turned away.

"You can all lie down and sleep," he said, "but you, Pedro," pointing to one man, "will keep guard." The men saluted and Pedro took his rifle and sat down. Mendoya spread a blanket on the floor and then lay down. Kit expected the others to follow his example, but only five lay down, leaving the other five whispering together.

Time passed. Kit dozed and woke and dozed again. The dull gleam of the lantern, the thick smoke, the whispering men, and the dead man lying at her feet, all helped to make things assume a nightmarish manner. At last, one by one, the men dropped off to sleep until there was no one awake but Kit and the guard. No sound came except the regular breathing of the sleepers and the puffing of the cigarette of the guard. Behind her back, Kit struggled with the ropes that tied her hands, but to no avail. She leaned back against the post in despair. She remembered that Bob might be dead, for she had heard the shots and the triumphant laughter of her captors. With Bob dead, she would have nothing to live for. Lower and lower her spirits sank, until she could look forward to nothing but death—or worse.

She was aroused from her reverie by the sound of someone moving. Mendoya arose and going over to the sitting guard he addressed a question to him in a whisper, and as he did so, Kit saw his hand go to his belt and he drew out a heavy pistol. Like a flash, he raised it and brought it down with great force on the head of the guard. Without a sound Pedro crumpled up in a heap on the floor. Mendoya gave the fallen guard a vicious kick, and then pulled out his knife and advanced toward her. Kit's heart beat like a trip-hammer. Either Mendoya intended to kill her or to set her free. Evidently the latter was his intention, for he cut the ropes from around her hands, and then sinking on one knee, he quickly severed the ropes from about her ankles. Her wrists were raw and bleeding, but in her joy and thankfulness at being free, she did not notice them. Mendoya did, however, and Kit had never before seen such a look of rage on any man's face before, as he saw the marks left by the ropes. In a thrice, he had his handkerchief out and had it tied about one wrist. Then a sudden rush of feeling overwhelmed Kit. How she had misjudged this man! He was going to save her! There was no time for meditations, for her rescuer thrust one of his pistols into her hand. Then he turned and bestowed a hard kick on the senseless Pedro. At this piece of brutality, Kit felt an unutterable longing to shoot this man, her rescuer. He caught her hand in a vise-like grip.

"This way, Señorita," and started for the entrance of the cave. At this moment, a sound of trampling horses was heard from without, and several of the men sat up. Caught between two fires, Kit was suddenly paralyzed. She could only gaze imploringly at Mendoya. In his eyes she saw a great flame of fear leap up, fear, not for himself, but for the girl with him. He knew his countrymen—his own men especially, and he knew the small amount of mercy Kit would be likely to get in their hands.

"Stop! Stop!" cried one of the men in the back of the cave and whipping up his gun he took aim and fired. Kit saw a thin red line appear on Mendoya's forehead, and then a large party of men entered the mouth of the cave. Simultaneously, there came two retorts, one after the other, and the cave was left in total darkness. Mendoya had shot the lights out! What occurred next was no more than a dream to Kit. Mendoya yelled, "Get behind me, Kit." In this time of peril, she did not notice the familiar use of her first name.

She stood behind him, her left hand grasping his velvet jacket in order not to lose him, and with her right hand she was fighting with her revolver. The cave resounded with cries of pain and yells of rage. It was filled with smoke and dust, and Kit's mouth, nose, and eyes were filled with both. Her breath came in choking sobs, but she swung her pistol in a half circle about her. It fared ill to the men who came within her reach. There were no lights. The cave was filled with men, and no one knew whom he was fighting. Clinging to Mendoya, Kit was dragged, step by step, to the cave's mouth. Mendoya fought silently, but Kit could feel the muscles in his shoulders leap.

There were many shots fired, but Kit was not hit. Then, simultaneously, there came three shots at once. Mendoya gave a stilled cry, which in the din was not heard. Kit felt him stagger, but only for an instant, for with renewed vigor he struggled for the opening.

It was reached at last and Kit rushed to where the horses were standing, leaving Mendoya fighting back the men at the entrance. There he stood, finely silhouetted in the moonlight, making a splendid mark for the Mexicans within the cave. They took advantage of this opportunity and blazed away at him.

"Stampede the horses," came to Kit, and she obeyed, catching the bridle of a horse. She rode swiftly among the others, and only a few seconds elapsed before the animals were scattered. Kit turned, and in the moonlight she saw Mendoya rushing toward her.

"Quick! Quick!" she screamed, as he drew nearer. "Mount!" With a volley of bullets following him, Mendoya made a flying leap and landed in the saddle without touching the stirrups. What happened next, Kit never knew, but she knew someone had her bridle reins and that the horses were running neck and neck while the "Yip!" "Younce!" of bullets were heard over her head. They were soon out of range.

The furious pace did not abate a jot, and Kit soon began to recover. Manuel Mendoya, lying low in the saddle, almost on his horse's neck, held her reins in his hands. In his other hand he held his own reins and his long Mexican spurs were relentlessly digging into the horse's sides, which were already covered with blood. In a flash, all Kit's hatred for the brute in this man returned. "Stop!" she cried, hardly knowing whether she meant to abate this pace or to stop spurring the horse, but to both meanings he was deaf.

In five more minutes, the Rio Grande was reached. As it was summer, the river was scarcely larger than a creek and it was only a matter of a few minutes to pass it. Not a word had been spoken since Kit had cried out for a stop, but Mendoya swayed to and fro with each leap of his horse. The furious pace was beginning to tell on the horses as the waterhole of Kit's ranch appeared. Kit's horse stumbled several times before this place was reached. Kit dully wondered why Mendoya went to this place instead of going to the ranch, but she made no objections, and they rode up to open space above the spring.

The Mexican dismounted, and walking to the side of Kit's horse, he held his hand to assist her to dismount. She placed her left hand in his and her right on his shoulder, and leaped to the ground. As she did, her hand slid down his chest beneath his velvet jacket, and she encountered something wet and sticky.

She pushed him back against her horse, and in spite of his violent protests, she pulled aside his jacket.   (continued in the red templeton book)

[*The preceding part of the story was in the copybook dated January 1, 1913.
The red templeton book referred to in the final note was not with the
material we found.*]

"If Roosevelt Had Been President"

President Wilson has received much adverse criticism on his "watchful waiting" policy in Mexico and his conduct in the "U-Boat Controversy."

Even our own Theodore has added his voice to the many who have blamed Wilson. But if Roosevelt himself had been elected President would the country have fared any better when "my policies" were consistently carried out?

When Wilson first took a hand in Mexican affairs the yellow shadow of Japan was looming upon the Pacific coast, and Japanese as well as German money and power were stirring up strife in an endeavor to gain a foot hold in Mexico and thereby drawing us into a war. Wilson did not save us entirely from this, for the raid on Columbus was a direct defiance to the United States and it was necessary to send troops into Mexico. But Wilson put off the day of reckoning until we were better prepared. In course of our preparations, it was found that our navy was all but useless in war because we had no colliers or lighters. Our submarines were of an almost obsolete type and incapable of performing the work required of them. Our few airplanes were badly manned and in charge of men who did not know their business. We were nearly defenseless.

Considering the "U-Boat Controversy," how could we have fought Germany without transports or submarines, with anarchy on our borders, and without a trained army?

Wilson's diplomacy has kept us out of war for a year and he has given us time to prepare. For a war with real preparedness is better than a war undertaken with politics and speeches.

"Little Sister"

Peggy lay in the sand behind some mesquite bushes, hugging her father's big rifle to her breast and watching Alvarado's men move about in the house. Since the late hours of the night before she had lain there and though now the early Mexican sun was burning her blue eyes and blistering the little arms that so tightly held the big gun, no thought of changing her position had entered her mind.

The little freckled face was tear-streaked and dirty, but set as stone, and grim lines, so alien to the childish mouth, had been drawn there by hours of unrelaxed vigilance. But the blue eyes were not wet now. She had cried—in the night—a million years before.

She had been in the kitchen spreading sandwiches for Bob, Big Sister's intended, when Alvarado and his bandits arrived, and the trampling of hoofs, the noise, the loud voices had brought her to the door of the living room just in time to see the coolly smiling Mexican leader shoot down her father. Mother had screamed, thrown herself beside him, only to receive Alvarado's second bullet.

Peggy, wide-eyed with horror, stood on the threshold, her eyes taking in the dusty, picturesque leader, the reckless, jeering men who filled the room, father, mother and last of all, Big Sister. Big Sister, pretty and sweet, the embodiment of every grace and virtue in ten-year-old Peggy's eyes, overcome with terror, was crouched, half fainting, in the corner, shielded by Bob's defiant shoulders. At a sign from their leader two of the men in the circle took careful aim and fired. Alvarado's eyes blazed with exultation as he strode forward towards the defenseless girl.

No one had seen Peggy's frightened face at the door. No one saw the child who fled when the bandit laid hands on her shrinking sister. Through the hall she rushed, Big Sister's cries ringing in her ears, and stumbled over her father's rifle that leaned against a chair in the kitchen. Clutching the gun, she gained her feet and disappeared into the darkness.

Safe in the mesquite bushes on a bank a little distance from the house, she lay in the sand, sobbing and murmuring over the names of the dear dead. Long she watched the lights in the cottage, saw the raiders moving about in the kitchen satisfying their hunger, shivered and hid her head at Big Sister's screams.

But one by one the lights went out. With ominous suddenness Big Sister's voice was stilled, and the child was left alone in the silence and the dark. Dawn found a hard-faced Peggy with dry eyes still centered on the house and one great resolve—the result of her long night vigil—filling her heart and soul—Alvarado would never lead another raid. The moment he stepped out of the house, she would shoot. That it meant sure death for her, Peggy knew—well knew that she would be riddled with bullets within the minute he fell, but she cared nothing. Her little world had crumbled.

The horses tethered in the cottonwoods behind the house moved restlessly, stamping and neighing softly. On the early morning air was borne the faint, far-off beat of cavalry, but the sounds fell unheeded upon the deaf ears of the child who lay in the mesquite. She was dead to all things save the one thought of vengeance in her heart.

Within the house there was a general stir. Some one had heard the whisper of the wind and, as if by magic, a Mexican appeared, ran across the porch and bent his head to the ground intently a moment, then called excitedly to someone inside. Out in the early morning sunlight hurried the bandit leader, tossing away a cigarette as he came and hastily buckling on his gun belt. At the words of the scout he raised his head, listening anxiously. Crowding behind him came the rest of his unkempt band, stopping short at his upraised hand for silence.

With infinite care Peggy slid the gun up to the level of her eyes and found the man across the sights. Coldly, dispassionately she viewed him, the chill steel of the gun giving her confidence. She must not miss now—she would not miss—and she did not.

Margaret Mitchell, '17

Part Ten

Wahington Seminary yearbook from Margaret's senior year

World War One

⌐

DURING MARGARET'S SEMINARY DAYS, THE United States entered World War I. There was a feeling of exuberance and patriotism as all of Atlanta tried to boost the morale of the soldiers going off to war. Stephens was stationed at Camp Gordon near the city and the Mitchell home became a haven for young servicemen, particularly for those who had been students at Georgia Tech in Atlanta before they enlisted.

"There was a social duty on the young men to go to war and there was a social duty on the young ladies to see that the soldiers had as nice a time as they could," Stephens wrote in his unpublished memoir. "Most of the young officers in the regiments at Fort McPherson were young university students or recent graduates. Margaret could entertain these young men. She had a big house, servants, a car that would hold seven people and, if you crowded enough, quite a few more. She was a good dancer and, just as important, a good conversationalist, and she also had the gift of listening to other people. There was no girl in Atlanta more popular with the young officers."

According to Stephens, there were many parties and dances at the Mitchells's house, the Piedmont Driving Club, and the roof garden of the Capital City Club. He remembered his stateside service as an enchanting time with starlit nights, orchestras playing under the stars, and young people having a good time. They danced to "Poor Butterfly," "The Girl on the Magazine Cover," "Long, Long Trail," "Where Do We Go from Here," and "Over There." May Belle Mitchell encouraged Stephens and Margaret to savor every minute.

At the Washington Seminary, the seniors bought and sold four thousand thrift stamps and, instead of having an elaborate annual, they purchased a five-hundred dollar Liberty Bond to support the war effort. Seminary student Laura Rose wrote in the yearbook's senior class prophecy, "The metronome stopped with a blinding crash and a great battle plane dropped from the sky. Scrambling briskly out over the propellers came none other than Margaret Mitchell. As she threw back her trim aviator's coat, I discovered the child-like Buster Brown collar and the black velveteen dress . . ." Continuing the war theme, the directory for the 1918 annual listed Margaret's appearance as "swaggering." Her hobby was given as "aviators," her pet aversion as "civilians," her favorite expression as "curses," and her highest ambition as her desire "to send them away with a smile!"

It is no wonder that Margaret's writing efforts now dwelt on the subject of the war. In the course of the research for his 1965 biography of Mitchell, Finis Farr had access to material now lost. From a short story that was never completed Farr quotes, "God, it couldn't be true! Yet there the crumpled telegram lay on the floor under the poor bed with its too thin coverings. The shabby room was bitter cold—the carpetless floor was cold as she knelt down to retrieve the telegram and smooth it out in the dull hope that she had misread. But the words were unchanging—'The War Department regrets to report the death in action of Private William Souther.'"

In "Sergeant Terry," Margaret once again turns to the fate of the women who wonder if their loved ones are alive or dead. This was the literary selection for the Washington Seminary's yearbook, *Facts and Fancies*, for Margaret's senior year.

"Sergeant Terry"

ergeant Terry McGovern clung with one hand to the strap of the camp-bound street car, a hot stuffy car, crowded with soldiers, while with the other hand he graphically illustrated the story with which he was entertaining all within sound of his voice. Roars of appreciative laughter rewarded his efforts and cries of "Tell another, Terry!" further encouraged him, for Sergeant McGovern's repertoire of jokes was undoubtedly the best in the camp.

In the streets the newsboys were bawling the latest extra, and as the car stopped for passengers, the insistent shrilling rose above the din of the soldiers. "Hospital ship, *Monaco*, torpedoed! Hundreds lost! Extra! Extra!"

But the news barely raised a comment in the car. "A fellow died one way or another. It didn't matter how so long as he died" was Sergeant Terry's idea of the matter.

In response to the conductor's "Up to the front, please!" there stumbled forward a slim girl in a worn serge dress, her soft eyes staring wide and dazed from under a drooping hat brim. Beside the sergeant she stopped, looking unseeingly through him. In the seat across the aisle were two soldiers, one a tall man who lay back dozing with his hat over his eyes, the other, a Little Italian whose animated jabber had begun at the conclusion of Terry's jokes. But when his glance, flashing upward, took in the white-faced girl standing beside him he was upon his feet in an instant. With a mechanical

"Thank you" she sunk into the proffered seat pulling from under her arm a newspaper which she opened with shaking fingers. The two-inch headline seemed to leap up at her shouting "Hundreds Lost!"

Frantically her eyes scanned the column racing from the paragraph that told of the sinking of the *Monaco*, and the subsequent death of three hundred soldiers invalided home, to the second paragraph announcing that the death list would be printed later.

Only two short paragraphs, the utmost expansion of an official dispatch, but her imagination clothed each word of the terse phraseology with a picture. Her brain conjured up the darkened ship filled with helpless wounded hastening homeward; then the shock, the mad panic of the men trapped to die in the dark; the few over-crowded life boats shelled by the submarine that had risen to view its work.

With a half-choked gasp, her hand went to her throat, and Terry, who had been waiting for an opening, thought it only proper to lean over and inquire respectfully, "Maybe ye have a fellow on the *Monaco*, Miss?"

She nodded, the constriction in her throat barring utterance, and the warm heart of Terry ached, for somewhere back in New York, a girl had cried when he had left, and here before him was a shabby little figure who had a "fellow" on the *Monaco*, as careless and lovable a boy as ever misunderstood but won the heart of a woman. How happy they had been, as seated in the red firelight on that last night, they had planned all the details of the "wee sweet bungalow" that was to have been theirs when her man returned from the war. How anxiously happy she had been, when, two months before, news had come that he would be invalided home with a shoulder that would never again carry a heavy army pack.

And all her dreams had come to this. She sobbed softly as she thought of the gay chintz curtains and the canary bird. Terry, trying to comfort her in clumsy man fashion ventured to pat her shoulder. The newspaper slid from her fingers and rustled unnoticed to her feet. The soldier sitting beside her, rousing himself, bent to pick it up and through scalding tears, she wistfully thought how much like her soldier's hair was this man's curly mop.

Terry looked away, hoping none of his comrades were noticing what a fool he was making of himself. Outside he saw the arc lights flickering in the gray winter twilight just as they had flickered in a quiet street in New York, when he had patted a little hand and told a pair of blue eyes that "some day, it would all come out the right way." No doubt the soldier who went down on the *Monaco* had told the same thing to the girl who now sat crying softly. Terry's jaw set suddenly as the mental picture of his own girl scanning the death list rose before his eyes. Suppose—

But his gaze suddenly lowered as a gasp, a happy incredulous gasp, and a joyous bit of profanity struck his ears. The shy girl in the drooping hat was unashamedly holding the hands of the big soldier beside her, holding them as if she doubted her eyes and feared he would vanish. The soldier looked into her eyes with a tender grin and Terry heard him say that he was going to "kiss away every blessed tear she had cried."

What a load rolled from the stalwart shoulders of Sergeant McGovern! His spirits soared! Feeling himself so privileged, he listened to the low, broken explanations of how the curly-haired soldier had not been on the *Monaco* at all but had been sent home hastily on the ship just before it, and had not written because there had been no opportunity.

The soldiers grinned and nudged each other as they saw Terry's faraway beaming smile but they did not know that he, too, was seeing a "wee sweet bungalow" with gay chintz curtains and a canary bird that sang all day.

Margaret Mitchell, '18

Margaret in front of the Mitchell family house on Peachtree Street, circa 1917

Sources

~

ARCHIVES

Atlanta History Center Library Archives.

Margaret Mitchell Marsh Collection. Hargrett Rare Book and Manuscript Library, University of Georgia.

Special Collections Department, Robert W. Woodruff Library, Emory University.

BOOKS AND JOURNALS

Edwards, Anne. *Road To Tara.* New Haven and New York: Ticknor and Fields, 1983.

Farr, Finis. *Margaret Mitchell of Atlanta.* New York: William Morrow, 1965.

Freer, Debra. *Lost Laysen.* New York: Scribner, 1996.

Garrett, Franklin M. *Atlanta and Environs,* Vol. 2. Athens, Georgia: University of Georgia Press, 1969.

———. *Yesterday's Atlanta,* Miami, Florida: E. A. Seemann, 1977.

Gwinn, Yolande. *I Remember Margaret Mitchell.* Lakemont, Georgia: Copple House Books, 1987.

Hall, Lewis Philip. *Land of the Golden River: Historical Events and Stories of Southeastern North Carolina and the Lower Cape Fear.* Wilmington, North Carolina: The Wilmington Press Publishers, 1975.

Harwell, Richard. *Margaret Mitchell's "Gone With the Wind Letters, 1936–1949.* New York: Macmillan and London: Collier Macmillan Publishers, 1976.

Mitchells, Stephens. "Margaret Mitchell and Her People." *Atlanta Historical Bulletin* 9, no. 34 (May 1950).

———. Unpublished memoirs. Margaret Mitchell Marsh Collection, Hargrett Rare Book and Manuscript Library, University of Georgia.

Peacock, Jane Bonner. *A Dynamo Going to Waste: Letters to Allen Edee 1919 - 1921.* Atlanta: Peachtree Publishers, 1985.

Pyron, Darden Asbury. *Southern Daughter: The Life of Margaret Mitchell.* New York: Oxford University Press, 1991.

Russell, Anne. *Wilmington: A Pictorial History,* Virginia Beach, Virginia: Donning Company, 1981.

Shavin, Norman and Shartar, Martin. *The Million Dollar Legends: Margaret Mitchell and "Gone With the Wind."* Atlanta: Capricorn, 1974.

Tuchman, Barbara W. *The Zimmermann Telegram.* New York: Ballantine Books, 1979.

Walker, Marianne. *Margaret Mitchell and John Marsh: The Love Story Behind "Gone With the Wind."* Atlanta: Peachtree Publishers, 1993.

Washington Seminary. *Facts and Fancies,* Atlanta, Georgia: annuals 1916, 1917, 1918.

Weldon, Jane Powers, editor. "Through the Eyes of Youth: A Civil War Story," *Atlanta Historical Journal* 29, no. 4 (winter 1985 - 1986): 47 - 59.

NEWSPAPERS

Atlanta Journal Magazine, 18 December 1949, memorial issue.

Atlanta Journal Magazine, 16 May 1954.

Atlanta Journal, 15 March 1949.

Atlanta Weekly, 1 May 1983.

Atlanta Weekly, 22 June 1986, anniversary issue.

Acknowledgments

~

There are many people I wish to thank for their contributions toward making this book a reality. I am very grateful to the executors of the Margaret Mitchell Estate, Eugene and Joseph Mitchell, for graciously granting permission to publish these childhood writings and to their attorneys, Paul Anderson and Thomas Hal Clarke, for their help and good advice. Thanks also to Jane Powers Weldon.

Mary Rose Taylor provided invaluable help from the beginning. I wish to thank her for including Wailes Thomas and me in the Margaret Mitchell House "family," for writing the foreword to this book, and especially for her efforts in saving the house where Margaret Mitchell Marsh wrote *Gone With the Wind*.

I am indebted to the staff and volunteers of the Hargrett Rare Book and Manuscript Library of the University of Georgia Libraries, the Atlanta History Center, and the Special Collections Department of the Robert W. Woodruff Library at Emory University. A very special thanks goes to Mary Ellen Brooks, director of the Hargrett Library, who was a valuable guide through the maze of Margaret Mitchell Marsh papers. Barbara Rowe, curator of the New Hanover Museum in Wilmington, North Carolina, helped me in my research of the Seashore Hotel and Steel Pier at Wrightsville Beach, for which I am also grateful.

To my publisher, Thomas Payton, and my editor, Patrick Allen, I can honestly say this has been such fun. I'm sure no editor, author, or writer has had more nurturing or been treated more professionally than I have and for this I am in your debt. Anne Richmond Boston deserves credit and many thanks for creating just the right appearance for the book.

I wish to thank Marianne Walker, author of *The Love Story Behind "Gone With the Wind,"* for being my telephone pal. She was always ready with a sympathetic ear, answered every question (no matter how trivial), and offered much-needed encouragement.

To the administration and staff of Aycock Middle School in Greensboro, North Carolina, I want to express my gratitude for their taking over some of my responsibilities while I worked on the book and for their continued friendship. I must single out Brenda Dukes, who served as my grammar expert, for extra thanks.

I am thankful that I knew Elizabeth Scott Thomas and Margueryte Reynolds Sharp and that they saved every newspaper clipping, historical bulletin, and magazine article written about Margaret Mitchell and, of course, the short stories and journal entries she wrote as a child. I am indebted to them, too, for all the wonderful family memories they shared.

My love and gratitude go to my mother, Elizabeth Stewart Howie; my sister, Stewart Gordon; my three daughters, Blair Laughter, Porter Young, and Ali Eskridge; my three wonderful grandchildren, Kyle Pfeiffer and Will and Ali Young; my one hundred and three-year-old great-aunt, Blanch Benton; my attorney, Mike Abel; and Linda and Terry Reeves.

My last thank-you is for "my special beau" and partner in this adventure, Wailes Thomas.

⌐

Also by Thomas Harris

BLACK SUNDAY

RED
DRAGON

by

Thomas Harris

G. P. PUTNAM'S SONS   NEW YORK

Frontispiece, "The Red Dragon and the Woman Clothed
with the Sun," by William Blake (1757–1827),
courtesy of The Brooklyn Museum,
gift of William Augustus White.

LIBRARY OF CONGRESS CATALOGING IN PUBLICATION DATA

Harris, Thomas, date.
  Red dragon.

  I. Title.
PS3558.A6558R4   1981   813'.54   81-8674
ISBN 0-399-12442-X   AACR2

PRINTED IN THE UNITED STATES OF AMERICA

One can only see what one observes, and one observes only things which are already in the mind.
—ALPHONSE BERTILLON

. . . For Mercy has a human heart,
Pity a human face,
And Love, the human form divine,
And Peace, the human dress.
             —WILLIAM BLAKE, *Songs of Innocence*
             (The Divine Image)

Cruelty has a Human Heart,
and Jealousy a Human Face,
Terror the Human Form Divine,
and Secrecy the Human Dress.

The Human Dress is forged Iron,
The Human Form a fiery Forge,
The Human Face a Furnace seal'd,
The Human Heart its hungry Gorge.
             —WILLIAM BLAKE, *Songs of Experience*
             (A Divine Image)*

*After Blake's death, this poem was found with prints from the plates
of *Songs of Experience*. It appears only in posthumous editions.

RED DRAGON

CHAPTER 1

WILL GRAHAM sat Crawford down at a picnic table between the house and the ocean and gave him a glass of iced tea.

Jack Crawford looked at the pleasant old house, salt-silvered wood in the clear light. "I should have caught you in Marathon when you got off work," he said. "You don't want to talk about it here."

"I don't want to talk about it anywhere, Jack. You've got to talk about it, so let's have it. Just don't get out any pictures. If you brought pictures, leave them in the briefcase—Molly and Willy will be back soon."

"How much do you know?"

"What was in the Miami *Herald* and the *Times*," Graham said. "Two families killed in their houses a month apart. Birmingham and Atlanta. The circumstances were similar."

"Not similar. The same."

"How many confessions so far?"

"Eighty-six when I called in this afternoon," Crawford said. "Cranks. None of them knew details. He smashes the mirrors and uses the pieces. None of them knew that."

"What else did you keep out of the papers?"

"He's blond, right-handed and really strong, wears a size-eleven shoe. He can tie a bowline. The prints are all smooth gloves."

"You said that in public."

"He's not too comfortable with locks," Crawford said. "Used a glass cutter and a suction cup to get in the house last time. Oh, and his blood's AB positive."

"Somebody hurt him?"

"Not that we know of. We typed him from semen and saliva. He's a secretor." Crawford looked out at the flat sea. "Will, I want to ask you something. You saw this in the papers. The second one was all over the TV. Did you ever think about giving me a call?"

"No."

"Why not?"

"There weren't many details at first on the one in Birmingham. It could have been anything—revenge, a relative."

"But after the second one, you knew what it was."

"Yeah. A psychopath. I didn't call you because I didn't want to. I know who you have already to work on this. You've got the best lab. You'd have Heimlich at Harvard, Bloom at the University of Chicago—"

"And I've got you down here fixing fucking boat motors."

"I don't think I'd be all that useful to you, Jack. I never think about it anymore."

"Really? You caught two. The last two we had, you caught."

"How? By doing the same things you and the rest of them are doing."

"That's not entirely true, Will. It's the way you think."

"I think there's been a lot of bullshit about the way I think."

"You made some jumps you never explained."

"The evidence was there," Graham said.

"Sure. Sure there was. Plenty of it—afterward. Before the collar there was so damn little we couldn't get probable cause to go in."

"You have the people you need, Jack. I don't think I'd be an improvement. I came down here to get away from that."

"I know it. You got hurt last time. Now you look all right."

"I'm all right. It's not getting cut. You've been cut."

"I've been cut, but not like that."

"It's not getting cut. I just decided to stop. I don't think I can explain it."

"If you couldn't look at it anymore, God knows I'd understand that."

"No. You know—having to look. It's always bad, but you get so you can function anyway, as long as they're dead. The hospital, interviews, that's worse. You have to shake it off and keep on thinking. I don't believe I could do it now. I could make myself look, but I'd shut down the thinking."

"These are all dead, Will," Crawford said as kindly as he could.

Jack Crawford heard the rhythm and syntax of his own speech in Graham's voice. He had heard Graham do that before, with other people. Often in intense conversation Graham took on the other person's speech patterns. At first, Crawford had thought he was doing it deliberately, that it was a gimmick to get the back-and-forth rhythm going.

Later Crawford realized that Graham did it involuntarily, that sometimes he tried to stop and couldn't.

Crawford dipped into his jacket pocket with two fingers. He flipped two photographs across the table, face up.

"All dead," he said.

Graham stared at him a moment before picking up the pictures.

They were only snapshots: A woman, followed by three children and a duck, carried picnic items up the bank of a pond. A family stood behind a cake.

After half a minute he put the photographs down again. He pushed them into a stack with his finger and looked far down the beach where the boy hunkered, examining something in the sand. The woman stood watching, hand on her hip, spent waves creaming around her ankles. She leaned inland to swing her wet hair off her shoulders.

Graham, ignoring his guest, watched Molly and the boy for as long as he had looked at the pictures.

Crawford was pleased. He kept the satisfaction out of his face with the same care he had used to choose the site of this conversation. He thought he had Graham. Let it cook.

Three remarkably ugly dogs wandered up and flopped to the ground around the table.

"My God," Crawford said.

"These are probably dogs," Graham explained. "People dump small ones here all the time. I can give away the cute ones. The rest stay around and get to be big ones."

"They're fat enough."

"Molly's a sucker for strays."

"You've got a nice life here, Will. Molly and the boy. How old is he?"

"Eleven."

"Good-looking kid. He's going to be taller than you."

Graham nodded. "His father was. I'm lucky here. I know that."

"I wanted to bring Phyllis down here. Florida. Get a place when I retire, and stop living like a cave fish. She says all her friends are in Arlington."

"I meant to thank her for the books she brought me in the hospital, but I never did. Tell her for me."

"I'll tell her."

Two small bright birds lit on the table, hoping to find jelly. Crawford watched them hop around until they flew away.

"Will, this freak seems to be in phase with the moon. He killed the Jacobis in Birmingham on Saturday night, June 28, full moon. He killed the Leeds family in Atlanta night before last, July 26. That's one day short of a lunar month. So if we're lucky we may have a little over three weeks before he does it again."

"I don't think you want to wait here in the Keys and read about the next one in your Miami *Herald*. Hell, I'm not the pope, I'm not saying what you ought to do, but I want to ask you, do you respect my judgment, Will?"

"Yes."

"I think we have a better chance to get him fast if you help. Hell, Will, saddle up and help us. Go to Atlanta and Birmingham and look, then come on to Washington. Just TDY."

Graham did not reply.

Crawford waited while five waves lapped the beach. Then he got up and slung his suit coat over his shoulder. "Let's talk after dinner."

"Stay and eat."

Crawford shook his head. "I'll come back later. There'll be messages at the Holiday Inn and I'll be a while on the phone. Tell Molly thanks, though."

Crawford's rented car raised thin dust that settled on the bushes beside the shell road.

Graham returned to the table. He was afraid that this was how he would remember the end of Sugarloaf Key—ice melting in two tea glasses and paper napkins fluttering off the redwood table in the breeze and Molly and Willy far down the beach.

➤

Sunset on Sugarloaf, the herons still and the red sun swelling.

Will Graham and Molly Foster Graham sat on a bleached drift log, their faces orange in the sunset, backs in violet shadow. She picked up his hand.

"Crawford stopped by to see me at the shop before he came out here," she said. "He asked directions to the house. I tried to call you. You really ought to answer the phone once in a while. We saw the car when we got home and went around to the beach."

"What else did he ask you?"

"How you are."

"And you said?"

"I said you're fine and he should leave you the hell alone. What does he want you to do?"

"Look at evidence. I'm a forensic specialist, Molly. You've seen my diploma."

"You mended a crack in the ceiling paper with your diploma, I saw that." She straddled the log to face him. "If you missed your other life, what you used to do, I think you'd talk about it. You never do. You're open and calm and easy now . . . I love that."

"We have a good time, don't we?"

Her single styptic blink told him he should have said something better. Before he could fix it, she went on.

"What you did for Crawford was bad for you. He has a lot of other people—the whole damn government I guess—why can't he leave us alone?"

"Didn't Crawford tell you that? He was my supervisor the two times I left the FBI Academy to go back to the field. Those two cases were the only ones like this he ever had, and Jack's been working a long time. Now he's got a new one. This kind of psychopath is very rare. He knows I've had . . . experience."

"Yes, you have," Molly said. His shirt was unbuttoned and she could see the looping scar across his stomach. It was finger width and raised, and it never tanned. It ran down from his left hipbone and turned up to notch his rib cage on the other side.

Dr. Hannibal Lecter did that with a linoleum knife. It happened a year before Molly met Graham, and it very nearly killed him. Dr. Lecter, known in the tabloids as "Hannibal the Cannibal," was the second psychopath Graham had caught.

When he finally got out of the hospital, Graham resigned from the

Federal Bureau of Investigation, left Washington and found a job as a diesel mechanic in the boatyard at Marathon in the Florida Keys. It was a trade he grew up with. He slept in a trailer at the boatyard until Molly and her good ramshackle house on Sugarloaf Key.

Now he straddled the drift log and held both her hands. Her feet burrowed under his.

"All right, Molly. Crawford thinks I have a knack for the monsters. It's like a superstition with him."

"Do you believe it?"

Graham watched three pelicans fly in line across the tidal flats. "Molly, an intelligent psychopath—particularly a sadist—is hard to catch for several reasons. First, there's no traceable motive. So you can't go that way. And most of the time you won't have any help from informants. See, there's a lot more stooling than sleuthing behind most arrests, but in a case like this there won't *be* any informants. *He* may not even know that he's doing it. So you have to take whatever evidence you have and extrapolate. You try to reconstruct his thinking. You try to find patterns."

"And follow him and find him," Molly said. "I'm afraid if you go after this maniac, or whatever he is—I'm afraid he'll do you like the last one did. That's it. That's what scares me."

"He'll never see me or know my name, Molly. The police, they'll have to take him down if they can find him, not me. Crawford just wants another point of view."

She watched the red sun spread over the sea. High cirrus glowed above it.

Graham loved the way she turned her head, artlessly giving him her less perfect profile. He could see the pulse in her throat, and remembered suddenly and completely the taste of salt on her skin. He swallowed and said, "What the hell can I do?"

"What you've already decided. If you stay here and there's more killing, maybe it would sour this place for you. *High Noon* and all that crap. If it's that way, you weren't really asking."

"If I *were* asking, what would you say?"

"Stay here with me. Me. Me. Me. And Willy, I'd drag him in if it would do any good. I'm supposed to dry my eyes and wave my hanky. If things don't go so well, I'll have the satisfaction that you did the right thing. That'll last about as long as taps. Then I can go home and switch one side of the blanket on."

"I'd be at the back of the pack."

"Never in your life. I'm selfish, huh?"

"I don't care."

"Neither do I. It's keen and sweet here. All the things that happen to you before make you know it. Value it, I mean."

He nodded.

"Don't want to lose it either way," she said.

"Nope. We won't, either."

Darkness fell quickly and Jupiter appeared, low in the southwest.

They walked back to the house beside the rising gibbous moon. Far out past the tidal flats, bait fish leaped for their lives.

➤

Crawford came back after dinner. He had taken off his coat and tie and rolled up his sleeves for the casual effect. Molly thought Crawford's thick pale forearms were repulsive. To her he looked like a damnably wise ape. She served him coffee under the porch fan and sat with him while Graham and Willy went out to feed dogs. She said nothing. Moths batted softly at the screens.

"He looks good, Molly," Crawford said. "You both do—skinny and brown."

"Whatever I say, you'll take him anyway, won't you?"

"Yeah. I have to. I have to do it. But I swear to God, Molly, I'll make it as easy on him as I can. He's changed. It's great you got married."

"He's better and better. He doesn't dream so often now. He was really obsessed with the dogs for a while. Now he just takes care of them; he doesn't talk about them all the time. You're his friend, Jack. Why can't you leave him alone?"

"Because it's his bad luck to be the best. Because he doesn't think like other people. Somehow he never got in a rut."

"He thinks you want him to look at evidence."

"I do want him to look at evidence. There's nobody better with evidence. But he has the other thing too. Imagination, projection, whatever. He doesn't like that part of it."

"You wouldn't like it either if you had it. Promise me something,

Jack. Promise me you'll see to it he doesn't get too close. I think it would kill him to have to fight."

"He won't have to fight. I can promise you that."

When Graham finished with the dogs, Molly helped him pack.

CHAPTER 2

WILL GRAHAM drove slowly past the house where the Charles Leeds family had lived and died. The windows were dark. One yard light burned. He parked two blocks away and walked back through the warm night, carrying the Atlanta police detectives' report in a cardboard box.

Graham had insisted on coming alone. Anyone else in the house would distract him—that was the reason he gave Crawford. He had another, private reason: he was not sure how he would act. He didn't want a face aimed at him all the time.

He had been all right at the morgue.

The two-story brick home was set back from the street on a wooded lot. Graham stood under the trees for a long time looking at it. He tried to be still inside. In his mind a silver pendulum swung in darkness. He waited until the pendulum was still.

A few neighbors drove by, looking at the house quickly and looking away. A murder house is ugly to the neighbors, like the face of someone who betrayed them. Only outsiders and children stare.

The shades were up. Graham was glad. That meant no relatives had been inside. Relatives always lower the shades.

He walked around the side of the house, moving carefully, not using his flashlight. He stopped twice to listen. The Atlanta police knew he was here, but the neighbors did not. They would be jumpy. They might shoot.

Looking in a rear window, he could see all the way through to the light in the front yard, past silhouettes of furniture. The scent of Cape

21

jasmine was heavy in the air. A latticed porch ran across most of the back. On the porch door was the seal of the Atlanta police department. Graham removed the seal and went in.

The door from the porch into the kitchen was patched with plywood where the police had taken out the glass. By flashlight he unlocked it with the key the police had given him. He wanted to turn on lights. He wanted to put on his shiny badge and make some official noises to justify himself to the silent house where five people had died. He did none of that. He went into the dark kitchen and sat down at the breakfast table.

Two pilot lights on the kitchen range glowed blue in the dark. He smelled furniture polish and apples.

The thermostat clicked and the air conditioning came on. Graham started at the noise, felt a trickle of fear. He was an old hand at fear. He could manage this one. He simply was afraid, and he could go on anyway.

He could see and hear better afraid; he could not speak as concisely, and fear sometimes made him rude. Here, there was nobody left to speak to, there was nobody to offend anymore.

Madness came into this house through that door into this kitchen, moving on size-eleven feet. Sitting in the dark, he sensed madness like a bloodhound sniffs a shirt.

Graham had studied the detectives' report at Atlanta Homicide for most of the day and early evening. He remembered that the light on the vent hood over the stove had been on when the police arrived. He turned it on now.

Two framed samplers hung on the wall beside the stove. One said "Kissin' don't last, cookin' do." The other was "It's always to the kitchen that our friends best like to come, to hear the heartbeat of the house, take comfort in its hum."

Graham looked at his watch. Eleven-thirty P.M. According to the pathologist, the deaths occurred between eleven P.M. and one A.M.

First there was the entry. He thought about that . . .

The madman slipped the hook on the outside screen door. Stood in the darkness of the porch and took something from his pocket. A suction cup, maybe the base of a pencil sharpener designed to stick to a desktop.

Crouched against the wooden lower half of the kitchen door, the madman raised his head to peer through the glass. He put out his tongue and licked the cup, pressed it to the glass and flicked the lever to make it stick. A small glass cutter was attached to the cup with string so that he could cut a circle.

Tiny squeal of the glass cutter and one solid tap to break the glass. One hand to tap, one hand to hold the suction cup. The glass must not fall. The loose piece of glass is slightly egg-shaped because the string wrapped around the shaft of the suction cup as he cut. A little grating noise as he pulls the piece of glass back outside. He does not care that he leaves AB saliva on the glass.

His hand in the tight glove snakes in through the hole, finds the lock. The door opens silently. He is inside. In the light of the vent hood he can see his body in this strange kitchen. It is pleasantly cool in the house.

Will Graham ate two Di-Gels. The crackle of the cellophane irritated him as he stuffed it in his pocket. He walked through the living room, holding his flashlight well away from him by habit. Though he had studied the floor plan, he made one wrong turn before he found the stairs. They did not creak.

Now he stood in the doorway of the master bedroom. He could see faintly without the flashlight. A digital clock on a nightstand projected the time on the ceiling and an orange night light burned above the baseboard by the bathroom. The coppery smell of blood was strong.

Eyes accustomed to the dark could see well enough. The madman could distinguish Mr. Leeds from his wife. There was enough light for him to cross the room, grab Leeds's hair and cut his throat. What then? Back to the wall switch, a greeting to Mrs. Leeds and then the gunshot that disabled her?

Graham switched on the lights and bloodstains shouted at him from the walls, from the mattress and the floor. The very air had screams smeared on it. He flinched from the noise in this silent room full of dark stains drying.

Graham sat on the floor until his head was quiet. Still, still, be still.

The number and variety of the bloodstains had puzzled Atlanta detectives trying to reconstruct the crime. All the victims were found slain in their beds. This was not consistent with the locations of the stains.

At first they believed Charles Leeds was attacked in his daughter's room and his body dragged to the master bedroom. Close examination of the splash patterns made them reconsider.

The killer's exact movements in the rooms were not yet determined.

Now, with the advantage of the autopsy and lab reports, Will Graham began to see how it had happened.

The intruder cut Charles Leeds's throat as he lay asleep beside his wife, went back to the wall switch and turned on the light—hairs and oil from Mr. Leeds's head were left on the switchplate by a smooth glove. He shot Mrs. Leeds as she was rising, then went toward the children's rooms.

Leeds rose with his cut throat and tried to protect the children, losing great gouts of blood and an unmistakable arterial spray as he tried to fight. He was shoved away, fell and died with his daughter in her room.

One of the two boys was shot in bed. The other boy was also found in bed, but he had dust balls in his hair. Police believed he was dragged out from under his bed to be shot.

When all of them were dead, except possibly Mrs. Leeds, the smashing of mirrors began, the selection of shards, the further attention to Mrs. Leeds.

Graham had full copies of all the autopsy protocols in his box. Here was the one on Mrs. Leeds. The bullet entered to the right of her navel and lodged in her lumbar spine, but she died of strangulation.

The increase in serotonin and free histamine levels in the gunshot wound indicated she had lived at least five minutes after she was shot. The histamine was much higher than the serotonin, so she had not lived more than fifteen minutes. Most of her other injuries were probably, but not conclusively, postmortem.

If the other injuries were postmortem, what was the killer doing in the interval while Mrs. Leeds waited to die? Graham wondered. Struggling with Leeds and killing the others, yes, but that would have taken less than a minute. Smashing the mirrors. But what else?

The Atlanta detectives were thorough. They had measured and photographed exhaustively, had vacuumed and grid-searched and taken the traps from the drains. Still, Graham looked for himself.

From the police photographs and taped outlines on the mattresses, Graham could see where the bodies had been found. The evidence— nitrate traces on bedclothes in the case of the gunshot wounds— indicated that they were found in positions approximating those in which they died.

But the profusion of bloodstains and matted sliding marks on the hall carpet remained unexplained. One detective had theorized that some of the victims tried to crawl away from the killer. Graham did not believe it—clearly the killer moved them after they were dead and then put them back the way they were when he killed them.

What he did with Mrs. Leeds was obvious. But what about the others? He had not disfigured them further, as he did Mrs. Leeds. The children each suffered a single gunshot wound in the head. Charles Leeds bled to death, with aspirated blood contributing. The only additional mark on him was a superficial ligature mark around his chest, believed to be postmortem. What did the killer do with them after they were dead?

From his box Graham took the police photographs, lab reports on the individual blood and organic stains in the room and standard comparison plates of blood-drop trajectories.

He went over the upstairs rooms minutely, trying to match injuries to stains, trying to work backward. He plotted each splash on a measured field sketch of the master bedroom, using the standard comparison plates to estimate the direction and velocity of the bloodfall. In this way he hoped to learn the positions the bodies were in at different times.

Here was a row of three bloodstains slanting up and around a corner of the bedroom wall. Here were three faint stains on the carpet beneath them. The wall above the headboard on Charles Leeds's side of the bed was bloodstained, and there were swipes along the baseboards. Graham's field sketch began to look like a join-the-dots puzzle with no numbers. He stared at it, looked up at the room and back to the sketch until his head ached.

He went into the bathroom and took his last two Bufferin, scooping up water in his hand from the faucet in the sink. He splashed water on his face and dried it with his shirttail. Water spilled on the floor. He had forgotten that the trap was gone from the drain. Otherwise the bathroom was undisturbed, except for the broken mirror and traces of the red fingerprint powder called Dragon's Blood. Toothbrushes, facial cream, razor, were all in place.

The bathroom looked as though a family still used it. Mrs. Leeds's panty hose hung on the towel racks where she had left them to dry. He saw that she cut the leg off a pair when it had a runner so she could match two one-legged pairs, wear them at the same time, and save money. Mrs. Leeds's small, homey economy pierced him; Molly did the same thing.

Graham climbed out a window onto the porch roof and sat on the gritty shingles. He hugged his knees, his damp shirt pressed cold across his back, and snorted the smell of slaughter out of his nose.

The lights of Atlanta rusted the night sky and the stars were hard to see. The night would be clear in the Keys. He could be watching shooting stars with Molly and Willy, listening for the whoosh they solemnly agreed a shooting star must make. The Delta Aquarid meteor shower was at its maximum, and Willy was up for it.

He shivered and snorted again. He did not want to think of Molly now. To do so was tasteless as well as distracting.

Graham had a lot of trouble with taste. Often his thoughts were not tasty. There were no effective partitions in his mind. What he saw and learned touched everything else he knew. Some of the combinations were hard to live with. But he could not anticipate them, could not block and repress. His learned values of decency and propriety tagged along, shocked at his associations, appalled at his dreams; sorry that in the bone arena of his skull there were no forts for what he loved. His associations came at the speed of light. His value judgments were at the pace of a responsive reading. They could never keep up and direct his thinking.

He viewed his own mentality as grotesque but useful, like a chair made of antlers. There was nothing he could do about it.

Graham turned off the lights in the Leeds house and went out through the kitchen. At the far end of the back porch, his flashlight revealed a bicycle and a wicker dog bed. There was a doghouse in the backyard, a dog bowl by the steps.

The evidence indicated the Leedses were surprised in their sleep.

Holding the flashlight between his chin and chest, he wrote a memo: *Jack—where was the dog?*

Graham drove back to his hotel. He had to concentrate on his driving, though there was little traffic at four-thirty A.M. His head still ached and he watched for an all-night pharmacy.

He found one on Peachtree. A slovenly rent-a-cop dozed near the door. A pharmacist in a jacket dingy enough to highlight his dandruff sold Graham Bufferin. The glare in the place was painful. Graham disliked young pharmacists. They had a middle-of-the-litter look about them. They were often smug and he suspected that they were unpleasant at home.

"What else?" the pharmacist said, his fingers poised above the cash register keys. "What else?"

The Atlanta FBI office had booked him into an absurd hotel near the city's new Peachtree Center. It had glass elevators shaped like milkweed pods to let him know he was really in town now.

Graham rode up to his room with two conventioneers wearing name tags with the printed greeting "Hi!" They held to the rail and looked over the lobby as they ascended.

"Looka yonder by the desk—that's Wilma and them just now coming in," the larger one said. "God damn, I'd love to tear off a piece of that."

"Fuck her till her nose bleeds," the other one said.

Fear and rut, and anger at the fear.

"Say, you know why a woman has legs?"

"Why?"

"So she won't leave a trail like a snail."

The elevator doors opened.

"Is this it? This is it," the larger one said. He lurched against the facing as he got off.

"This is the blind leading the blind," the other one said.

Graham put his cardboard box on the dresser in his room. Then he put it in a drawer where he could not see it. He had had enough of the wide-eyed dead. He wanted to call Molly, but it was too early.

A meeting was scheduled for eight A.M. at the Atlanta police headquarters. He'd have little enough to tell them.

He would try to sleep. His mind was a busy rooming house with arguments all around him, and they were fighting somewhere down the hall. He was numb and empty and he drank two fingers of whiskey from his bathroom glass before he lay down. The darkness pressed too closely on him. He turned on the bathroom light and went back to bed. He pretended Molly was in the bathroom brushing her hair.

Lines from the autopsy protocols sounded in his own voice, though he had never read them aloud: ". . . the feces was formed . . . a trace of talcum on the lower right leg. Fracture of the medial orbit wall owing to insertion of mirror shard . . ."

Graham tried to think about the beach at Sugarloaf Key, he tried to hear the waves. He pictured his workbench in his mind and thought about the escapement for the water clock he and Willy were building. He sang "Whiskey River" under his breath and tried to run "Black Mountain Rag" through his head from one end to the other. Molly's music. Doc Watson's guitar part was all right, but he always lost it in the fiddle break. Molly had tried to teach him clog dancing in the backyard and she was bouncing . . . and finally he dozed.

He woke in an hour, rigid and sweating, seeing the other pillow silhouetted against the bathroom light and it was Mrs. Leeds lying beside him bitten and torn, mirrored eyes and blood like the legs of spectacles over her temples and ears. He could not turn his head to face her. Brain screaming like a smoke alarm, he put his hand over there and touched dry cloth.

Having acted, he felt some immediate relief. He rose, his heart pounding, and put on a dry T-shirt. He threw the wet one into the bathtub. He could not move over to the dry side of the bed. Instead he put a towel on the side where he had sweated and lay down on it, propped against the headboard with a stiff drink in his hand. He swallowed a third of it.

He reached for something to think about, anything. The pharmacy where he bought the Bufferin, then; perhaps because it was his only experience all day that was not related to death.

He could remember old drugstores with soda fountains. As a boy, he thought old drugstores had a slightly furtive air. When you went in, you always thought about buying rubbers whether you needed any or not. There were things on the shelves you shouldn't look at too long.

In the pharmacy where he bought the Bufferin, the contraceptives with their illustrated wrappings were in a lucite case on the wall behind the cash register, framed like art.

He preferred the drugstore and sundry of his childhood. Graham was nearly forty and just beginning to feel the tug of the way the world was then; it was a sea anchor streamed behind him in heavy weather.

He thought about Smoot. Old Smoot had been the soda jerk and manager for the pharmacist who owned the local drugstore when Graham was a child. Smoot, who drank on the job, forgot to unroll the awning and the sneakers melted in the window. Smoot forgot to unplug the coffeepot, and the fire department was summoned. Smoot sold ice cream cones to children on credit.

His principal outrage was ordering fifty Kewpie dolls from a detail man while the store owner was on vacation. On his return, the owner fired Smoot for a week. Then they held a Kewpie doll sale. Fifty of the Kewpie dolls were arranged in a semicircle in the front window so that they all stared at whoever was looking in.

They had wide eyes of cornflower blue. It was a striking display and Graham had looked at it for some time. He knew they were only Kewpie dolls, but he could feel the focus of their attention. So many of them looking. A number of people stopped to look at them. Plaster dolls, all with the same silly spit curl, yet their concentrated gaze had made his face tingle.

Graham began to relax a little on the bed. Kewpie dolls staring. He started to take a drink, gasped, and choked it onto his chest. He fumbled for the bedside lamp and fetched his box from the dresser drawer. He took out the autopsy protocols of the three Leeds children and his measured field sketches of the master bedroom and spread them on the bed.

Here were the three bloodstains slanting up the corner, and here were the matching stains on the carpet. Here were the dimensions of the three children. Brother, sister, big brother. Match. Match. Match.

They had been in a row, seated along the wall facing the bed. An audience. A dead audience. And Leeds. Tied around the chest to the headboard. Composed to look as though he were sitting up in bed. Getting the ligature mark, staining the wall above the headboard.

What were they watching? Nothing; they were all dead. But their eyes were open. They were watching a performance starring the madman and the body of Mrs. Leeds, beside Mr. Leeds in the bed. An audience. The crazy could look around at their faces.

Graham wondered if he had lit a candle. The flickering light would simulate expression on their faces. No candle was found. Maybe he would think to do that next time . . .

This first small bond to the killer itched and stung like a leech. Graham bit the sheet, thinking.

Why did you move them again? Why didn't you leave them that way? Graham asked. *There's something you don't want me to know about you. Why, there's something you're ashamed of. Or is it something you can't afford for me to know?*

Did you open their eyes?

Mrs. Leeds was lovely, wasn't she? You turned on the light after you cut his throat so Mrs. Leeds could watch him flop, didn't you? It was maddening to have to wear gloves when you touched her, wasn't it?

There was talcum on her leg.

There was no talcum in the bathroom.

Someone else seemed to speak those two facts in a flat voice.

You took off your gloves, didn't you? The powder came out of a rubber glove as you pulled it off to touch her, DIDN'T IT, YOU SON OF A BITCH? You touched her with your bare hands and then you put the gloves back on and you wiped her down. But while the gloves were off, DID YOU OPEN THEIR EYES?

Jack Crawford answered his telephone on the fifth ring. He had answered the telephone in the night many times and he was not confused.

"Jack, this is Will."

"Yes, Will."

"Is Price still in Latent Prints?"

"Yeah. He doesn't go out much anymore. He's working on the single-print index."

"I think he ought to come to Atlanta."

"Why? You said yourself the guy down here is good."

"He *is* good, but not as good as Price."

"What do you want him to do? Where would he look?"

"Mrs. Leeds's fingernails and toenails. They're painted, it's a slick surface. And the corneas of all their eyes. I think he took his gloves off, Jack."

"Jesus, Price'll have to gun it," Crawford said. "The funeral's this afternoon."

CHAPTER 3

"I THINK he had to touch her," Graham said in greeting.

Crawford handed him a Coke from the machine in Atlanta police headquarters. It was seven-fifty A.M.

"Sure, he moved her around," Crawford said. "There were grip marks on her wrists and behind her knees. But every print in the place is from nonporous gloves. Don't worry, Price is here. Grouchy old bastard. He's on his way to the funeral home now. The morgue released the bodies last night, but the funeral home's not doing anything yet. You look bushed. Did you get any sleep?"

"Maybe an hour. I think he had to touch her with his hands."

"I hope you're right, but the Atlanta lab swears he wore like surgeon's gloves the whole time," Crawford said. "The mirror pieces had those smooth prints. Forefinger on the back of the piece wedged in the labia, smudged thumb on the front."

"He polished it after he placed it, so he could see his damn face in there probably," Graham said.

"The one in her mouth was obscured with blood. Same with the eyes. He never took the gloves off."

"Mrs. Leeds was a good-looking woman," Graham said. "You've seen the family pictures, right? I'd want to touch her skin in an intimate situation, wouldn't you?"

"*Intimate?*" Distaste sounded in Crawford's voice before he could stop it. Suddenly he was busy rummaging in his pockets for change.

"Intimate—they had privacy. Everybody else was dead. He could have their eyes open or shut, however he liked."

"Any way he liked," Crawford said. "They tried her skin for prints, of course. Nothing. They did get a hand spread off her neck."

"The report didn't say anything about dusting nails."

"I expect her fingernails were smudged when they took scrapings. The scrapings were just where she cut her palms with them. She never scratched him."

"She had pretty feet," Graham said.

"Umm-hmm. Let's head upstairs," Crawford said. "The troops are about to muster."

➤

Jimmy Price had a lot of equipment—two heavy cases plus his camera bag and tripod. He made a clatter coming through the front door of the Lombard Funeral Home in Atlanta. He was a frail old man and his humor had not been improved by a long taxi ride from the airport in the morning rush.

An officious young fellow with styled hair hustled him into an office decorated in apricot and cream. The desk was bare except for a sculpture called *The Praying Hands.*

Price was examining the fingertips of the praying hands when Mr. Lombard himself came in. Lombard checked Price's credentials with extreme care.

"Your Atlanta office or agency or whatever called me, of course, Mr. Price. But last night we had to get the police to remove an obnoxious fellow who was trying to take pictures for *The National Tattler,* so I'm being very careful. I'm sure you understand. Mr. Price, the bodies were only released to us about one o'clock this morning, and the funeral is this afternoon at five. We simply can't delay it."

"This won't take a lot of time," Price said. "I need one reasonably intelligent assistant, if you have one. Have you touched the bodies, Mr. Lombard?"

"No."

"Find out who has. I'll have to print them all."

➤

The morning briefing of police detectives on the Leeds case was concerned mostly with teeth.

Atlanta Chief of Detectives R. J. (Buddy) Springfield, a burly man in shirtsleeves, stood by the door with Dr. Dominic Princi as the twenty-three detectives filed in.

"All right, boys, let's have the big grin as you come by," Springfield said. "Show Dr. Princi your teeth. That's right, let's see 'em all. Christ, Sparks, is that your tongue or are you swallowing a squirrel? Keep moving."

A large frontal view of a set of teeth, upper and lower, was tacked to the bulletin board at the front of the squad room. It reminded Graham of the celluloid strip of printed teeth in a dime-store jack-o'-lantern. He and Crawford sat down at the back of the room while the detectives took their places at schoolroom desks.

Atlanta Public Safety Commissioner Gilbert Lewis and his public-relations officer sat apart from them in folding chairs. Lewis had to face a news conference in an hour.

Chief of Detectives Springfield took charge.

"All right. Let's cease fire with the bullshit. If you read up this morning, you saw zero progress.

"House-to-house interviews will continue for a radius of four additional blocks around the scene. R & I has loaned us two clerks to help cross-matching airline reservations and car rentals in Birmingham and Atlanta.

"Airport and hotel details will make the rounds again today. Yes, again to*day*. Catch every maid and attendant as well as the desk people. He had to clean up somewhere and he may have left a mess. If you find somebody who cleaned up a mess, roust out whoever's in the room, seal it, and get on the horn to the laundry double quick. This time we've got something for you to show around. Dr. Princi?"

Dr. Dominic Princi, chief medical examiner for Fulton County, walked to the front and stood under the drawing of the teeth. He held up a dental cast.

"Gentlemen, this is what the subject's teeth look like. The Smithsonian in Washington reconstructed them from the impressions we took of bite marks on Mrs. Leeds and a clear bite mark in a piece of cheese from the Leedses' refrigerator," Princi said.

"As you can see, he has pegged lateral incisors—the teeth here and here." Princi pointed to the cast in his hand, then to the chart above him. "The teeth are crooked in alignment and a corner is missing from this central incisor. The other incisor is grooved, here. It looks like a 'tailor's notch,' the kind of wear you get biting thread."

"Snaggletoothed son of a bitch," somebody mumbled.

"How do you know for sure it was the perpetrator that bit the cheese, Doc?" a tall detective in the front row asked.

Princi disliked being called "Doc," but he swallowed it. "Saliva washes from the cheese and from the bite wounds matched for blood type," he said. "The victims' teeth and blood type didn't match."

"Fine, Doctor," Springfield said. "We'll pass out pictures of the teeth to show around."

"What about giving it to the papers?" The public-relations officer, Simpkins, was speaking. "A 'have-you-seen-these-teeth' sort of thing."

"I see no objection to that," Springfield said. "What about it, Commissioner?"

Lewis nodded.

Simpkins was not through. "Dr. Princi, the press is going to ask why it took four days to get this dental representation you have here. And why it all had to be done in Washington."

Special Agent Crawford studied the button on his ball-point pen.

Princi reddened but his voice was calm. "Bite marks on flesh are distorted when a body is moved, Mr. Simpson—"

"Simpkins."

"Simpkins, then. We couldn't make this using only the bite marks on the victims. That is the importance of the cheese. Cheese is relatively solid, but tricky to cast. You have to oil it first to keep the moisture out of the casting medium. Usually you get one shot at it. The Smithsonian has done it for the FBI crime lab before. They're better equipped to do a face bow registration and they have an anatomical articulator. They have a consulting forensic odontologist. We don't. Anything else?"

"Would it be fair to say that the delay was caused by the FBI lab and not here?"

Princi turned on him. "What it would be fair to say, Mr. Simpkins, is that a federal investigator, Special Agent Crawford, found the cheese in the refrigerator two days ago—after your people had been through the place. He expedited the lab work at my request. It would be fair to say I'm relieved that it wasn't one of you that bit the goddamned thing."

Commissioner Lewis broke in, his heavy voice booming in the squad room. "Nobody's questioning your judgment, Dr. Princi.

Simpkins, the last thing we need is to start a pissing contest with the FBI. Let's get on with it."

"We're all after the same thing," Springfield said. "Jack, do you fellows want to add anything?"

Crawford took the floor. The faces he saw were not entirely friendly. He had to do something about that.

"I just want to clear the air, Chief. Years ago there was a lot of rivalry about who got the collar. Each side, federal and local, held out on the other. It made a gap that crooks slipped through. That's not Bureau policy now, and it's not my policy. I don't give a damn who gets the collar. Neither does Investigator Graham. That's him sitting back there, if some of you are wondering. If the man who did this is run over by a garbage truck, it would suit me just fine as long as it puts him off the street. I think you feel the same way."

Crawford looked over the detectives and hoped they were mollified. He hoped they wouldn't hoard leads. Commissioner Lewis was talking to him.

"Investigator Graham has worked on this kind of thing before."

"Yes, sir."

"Can you add anything, Mr. Graham, suggest anything?"

Crawford raised his eyebrows at Graham.

"Would you come up to the front?" Springfield said.

Graham wished he had been given the chance to talk to Springfield in private. He didn't want to go to the front. He went, though.

Rumpled and sun-blasted, Graham didn't look like a federal investigator. Springfield thought he looked more like a house painter who had put on a suit to appear in court.

The detectives shifted from one buttock to the other.

When Graham turned to face the room, the ice-blue eyes were startling in his brown face.

"Just a couple of things," he said. "We can't assume he's a former mental patient or somebody with a record of sex offenses. There's a high probability that he doesn't have any kind of record. If he does, it's more likely to be breaking and entering than a minor sex offense.

"He may have a history of biting in lesser assaults—bar fights or child abuse. The biggest help we'll have on that will come from emergency-room personnel and the child-welfare people.

"Any bad bite they can remember is worth checking, regardless of who was bitten or how they said it happened. That's all I have."

The tall detective on the front row raised his hand and spoke at the same time.

"But he only bit women so far, right?"

"That's all we know about. He bites a lot, though. Six bad ones in Mrs. Leeds, eight in Mrs. Jacobi. That's way above average."

"What's average?"

"In a sex murder, three. He likes to bite."

"Women."

"Most of the time in sex assaults the bite mark has a livid spot in the center, a suck mark. These don't. Dr. Princi mentioned it in his autopsy report, and I saw it at the morgue. No suck marks. For him biting may be a fighting pattern as much as sexual behavior."

"Pretty thin," the detective said.

"It's worth checking," Graham said. "Any bite is worth checking. People lie about how it happened. Parents of a bitten child will claim an animal did it and let the child take rabies shots to cover for a snapper in the family—you've all seen that. It's worth asking at the hospitals—who's been referred for rabies shots.

"That's all I have." Graham's thigh muscles fluttered with fatigue when he sat down.

"It's worth asking, and we'll ask," Chief of Detectives Springfield said. "Now. The Safe and Loft Squad works the neighborhood along with Larceny. Work the dog angle. You'll see the update and the picture in the file. Find out if any stranger was seen with the dog. Vice and Narcotics, take the K-Y cowboys and the leather bars after you finish the day tour. Marcus and Whitman—heads up at the funeral. Do you have relatives, friends of the family, lined up to spot for you? Good. What about the photographer? All right. Turn in the funeral guest book to R & I. They've got the one from Birmingham already. The rest of the assignments are on the sheet. Let's go."

"One other thing," Commissioner Lewis said. The detectives sank back in their seats. "I have heard officers in this command referring to the killer as the 'Tooth Fairy.' I don't care what you call him among yourselves, I realize you have to call him something. But I had better not hear any police officer refer to him as the Tooth Fairy in public. It sounds flippant. Neither will you use that name on any internal memoranda.

"That's all."

Crawford and Graham followed Springfield back to his office. The chief of detectives gave them coffee while Crawford checked in with the switchboard and jotted down his messages.

"I didn't get a chance to talk to you when you got here yesterday," Springfield said to Graham. "This place has been a fucking madhouse. It's Will, right? Did the boys give you everything you need?"

"Yeah, they were fine."

"We don't have shit and we know it," Springfield said. "Oh, we developed a walking picture from the footprints in the flowerbed. He was walking around bushes and stuff, so you can't tell much more than his shoe size, maybe his height. The left print's a little deeper, so he may have been carrying something. It's busywork. We did get a burglar, though, a couple of years ago, off a walking picture. Showed Parkinson's disease. Princi picked it up. No luck this time."

"You have a good crew," Graham said.

"They are. But this kind of thing is out of our usual line, thank God. Let me get it straight, do you fellows work together all the time—you and Jack and Dr. Bloom—or do you just get together for one of these?"

"Just for these," Graham said.

"Some reunion. The commissioner was saying you were the one who nailed Lecter three years ago."

"We were all there with the Maryland police," Graham said. "The Maryland state troopers arrested him."

Springfield was bluff, not stupid. He could see that Graham was uncomfortable. He swiveled in his chair and picked up some notes.

"You asked about the dog. Here's the sheet on it. Last night a vet here called Leeds's brother. He had the dog. Leeds and his oldest boy brought it in to the vet the afternoon before they were killed. It had a puncture wound in the abdomen. The vet operated and it's all right. He thought it was shot at first, but he didn't find a bullet. He thinks it was stabbed with something like an ice pick or an awl. We're asking the neighbors if they saw anybody fooling with the dog, and we're working the phones today checking local vets for other animal mutilations."

"Was the dog wearing a collar with the Leeds name on it?"

"No."

"Did the Jacobis in Birmingham have a dog?" Graham asked.

"We're supposed to be finding that out," Springfield said. "Hold on, let me see." He dialed an inside number. "Lieutenant Flatt is our liaison with Birmingham . . . yeah, Flatt. What about the Jacobis' dog? Uh-huh . . . uh-huh. Just a minute." He put his hand over the phone. "No dog. They found a litter box in the downstairs bathroom with cat droppings in it. They didn't find any cat. The neighbors are watching for it."

"Could you ask Birmingham to check around in the yard and behind any outbuildings," Graham said. "If the cat was hurt, the children might not have found it in time and they might have buried it. You know how cats do. They hide to die. Dogs come home. And would you ask if it's wearing a collar?"

"Tell them if they need a methane probe, we'll send one," Crawford said. "Save a lot of digging."

Springfield relayed the request. The telephone rang as soon as he hung it up. The call was for Jack Crawford. It was Jimmy Price at the Lombard Funeral Home. Crawford punched on from the other phone.

"Jack, I got a partial that's probably a thumb and a fragment of a palm."

"Jimmy, you're the light of my life."

"I know. The partial's a tented arch, but it's smudged. I'll have to see what I can do with it when I get back. Came off the oldest kid's left eye. I never did that before. Never would have seen it, but it stood out against an eight-ball hemorrhage from the gunshot wound."

"Can you make an identification off it?"

"It's a very long shot, Jack. If he's in the single-print index, maybe, but that's like the Irish Sweepstakes, you know that. The palm came off the nail of Mrs. Leeds's left big toe. It's only good for comparison. We'll be lucky to get six points off it. The assistant SAC witnessed, and so did Lombard. He's a notary. I've got pictures *in situ.* Will that do it?"

"What about elimination prints on the funeral-home employees?"

"I inked up Lombard and all his Merry Men, major case prints whether they said they had touched her or not. They're scrubbing their hands and bitching now. Let me go home, Jack. I want to work these up in my own darkroom. Who knows what's in the water here— turtles—who knows?

"I can catch a plane to Washington in an hour and fax the prints down to you by early afternoon."

Crawford thought a moment. "Okay, Jimmy, but step on it. Copies to Atlanta and Birmingham PD's and Bureau offices."

"You got it. Now, something else we've got to get straight on your end."

Crawford rolled his eyes to the ceiling. "Gonna piss in my ear about the per diem, aren't you?"

"Right."

"Today, Jimmy my lad, nothing's too good for you."

Graham stared out the window while Crawford told them about the prints.

"That's by God remarkable," was all Springfield said.

Graham's face was blank; closed like a lifer's face, Springfield thought.

He watched Graham all the way to the door.

➤

The public-safety commissioner's news conference was breaking up in the foyer as Crawford and Graham left Springfield's office. The print reporters headed for the phones. Television reporters were doing "cutaways," standing alone before their cameras asking the best questions they had heard at the news conference and extending their microphones to thin air for a reply that would be spliced in later from film of the commissioner.

Crawford and Graham had started down the front steps when a small man darted ahead of them, spun and took a picture. His face popped up behind his camera.

"Will Graham!" he said. "Remember me—Freddy Lounds? I covered the Lecter case for the *Tattler*. I did the paperback."

"I remember," Graham said. He and Crawford continued down the steps, Lounds walking sideways ahead of them.

"When did they call you in, Will? What have you got?"

"I won't talk to you, Lounds."

"How does this guy compare with Lecter? Does he do them—?"

"Lounds." Graham's voice was loud and Crawford got in front of him fast. "Lounds, you write lying shit and *The National Tattler* is an asswipe. Keep away from me."

Crawford gripped Graham's arm. "Get away, Lounds. *Go on.* Will, let's get some breakfast. Come on, Will." They rounded the corner, walking swiftly.

"I'm sorry, Jack. I can't stand that bastard. When I was in the hospital, he came in and—"

"I know it," Crawford said. "I reamed him out, much good it did." Crawford remembered the picture in *The National Tattler* at the end of the Lecter case. Lounds had come into the hospital room while Graham was asleep. He flipped back the sheet and shot a picture of Graham's temporary colostomy. The paper ran it retouched with a black square covering Graham's groin. The caption said "Crazy Guts Cop."

The diner was bright and clean. Graham's hands trembled and he slopped coffee in his saucer.

He saw Crawford's cigarette smoke bothering a couple in the next booth. The couple ate in a peptic silence, their resentment hanging in the smoke.

Two women, apparently mother and daughter, argued at a table near the door. They spoke in low voices, anger ugly in their faces. Graham could feel their anger on his face and neck.

Crawford was griping about having to testify at a trial in Washington in the morning. He was afraid the trial could tie him up for several days. As he lit another cigarette, he peered across the flame at Graham's hands and his color.

"Atlanta and Birmingham can run the thumbprint against their known sex offenders," Crawford said. "So can we. And Price has dug a single print out of the files before. He'll program the FINDER with it—we've come a long way with that just since you left."

FINDER, the FBI's automated fingerprint reader and processor, might recognize the thumbprint on an incoming fingerprint card from some unrelated case.

"When we get him, that print and his teeth will put him away," Crawford said. "What we have to do, we have to figure on what he *could* be. We have to swing a wide loop. Indulge me, now. Say we've arrested a good suspect. You walk in and see him. What is there about him that doesn't surprise you?"

"I don't know, Jack. Goddammit, he's got no face for me. We could spend a lot of time looking for people we've invented. Have you talked to Bloom?"

"On the phone last night. Bloom doubts he's suicidal, and so does Heimlich. Bloom was only here a couple of hours the first day, but he and Heimlich have the whole file. Bloom's examining Ph.D.

candidates this week. He said tell you hello. Do you have his number in Chicago?"

"I have it."

Graham liked Dr. Alan Bloom, a small round man with sad eyes, a good forensic psychiatrist—maybe the best. Graham appreciated the fact that Dr. Bloom had never displayed professional interest in him. That was not always the case with psychiatrists.

"Bloom says he wouldn't be surprised if we heard from the Tooth Fairy. He might write us a note," Crawford said.

"On a bedroom wall."

"Bloom thinks he might be disfigured or he may believe he's disfigured. He told me not to give that a lot of weight. 'I won't set up a straw man to chase, Jack,' is what he told me. 'That would be a distraction and would diffuse the effort.' Said they taught him to talk like that in graduate school."

"He's right," Graham said.

"You could tell something about him or you wouldn't have found that fingerprint," Crawford said.

"That was the evidence on the damn wall, Jack. Don't put this on me. Look, don't expect too much from me all right?"

"Oh, we'll get him. You know we'll get him, don't you?"

"I know it. One way or the other."

"What's one way?"

"We'll find evidence we've overlooked."

"What's the other?"

"He'll do it and do it until one night he makes too much noise going in and the husband gets to a gun in time."

"No other possibilities?"

"You think I'm going to spot him across a crowded room? No, that's Ezio Pinza you're thinking about, does that. The Tooth Fairy will go on and on until we get smart or get lucky. He won't stop."

"Why?"

"Because he's got a genuine taste for it."

"See, you do know something about him," Crawford said.

Graham did not speak again until they were on the sidewalk. "Wait until the next full moon," he told Crawford. "Then tell me how much I know about him."

Graham went back to his hotel and slept for two and a half hours. He woke at noon, showered, and ordered a pot of coffee and a sandwich. It was time to make a close study of the Jacobi file from Birmingham. He scrubbed his reading glasses with hotel soap and settled in by the window with the file. For the first few minutes he looked up at every sound, footsteps in the hall, the distant thud of the elevator door. Then he knew nothing but the file.

The waiter with the tray knocked and waited, knocked and waited. Finally he left the lunch on the floor outside the door and signed the bill himself.

CHAPTER 4

HOYT LEWIS, meter reader for Georgia Power Company, parked his truck under a big tree in the alley and settled back with his lunch box. It was no fun opening his lunch now that he packed it himself. No little notes in there anymore, no surprise Twinkie.

He was halfway through his sandwich when a loud voice at his ear made him jump.

"I guess I used a thousand dollars' worth of electricity this month, is that right?"

Lewis turned and saw at the truck window the red face of H. G. Parsons. Parsons wore Bermuda shorts and carried a yard broom.

"I didn't understand what you said."

"I guess you'll say I used a thousand dollars' worth of electricity this month. Did you hear me that time?"

"I don't know what you've used because I haven't read your meter yet, Mr. Parsons. When I do read it, I'll put it down on this piece of paper right here."

Parsons was bitter about the size of the bill. He had complained to the power company that he was being prorated.

"I'm keeping up with what I use," Parsons said. "I'm going to the Public Service Commission with it, too."

"You want to read your meter with me? Let's go over there right now and —"

"I know how to read a meter. I guess you could read one too if it wasn't so much trouble."

"Just be quiet a minute, Parsons." Lewis got out of his truck. "Just

43

be quiet a minute now, dammit. Last year you put a magnet on your meter. Your wife said you was in the hospital, so I just took it off and didn't say anything. When you poured molasses in it last winter, I reported it. I notice you paid up when we charged you for it.

"Your bill went up after you did all that wiring yourself. I've told you until I'm blue in the face: something in that house is draining off current. Do you hire an electrician to find it? No, you call down to the office and bitch about me. I've about got a bait of you." Lewis was pale with anger.

"I'll get to the bottom of this," Parsons said, retreating down the alley toward his yard. "They're checking up on you, Mr. Lewis. I saw somebody reading your route ahead of you," he said across the fence. "Pretty soon you'll have to go to work like everybody else."

Lewis cranked his truck and drove on down the alley. Now he would have to find another place to finish his lunch. He was sorry. The big shade tree had been a good lunch place for years.

It was directly behind Charles Leeds's house.

➤

At five-thirty P.M. Hoyt Lewis drove in his own automobile to the Cloud Nine Lounge, where he had several boilermakers to ease his mind.

When he called his estranged wife, all he could think of to say was "I wish you was still fixing my lunch."

"You ought to have thought about that, Mr. Smarty," she said, and hung up.

He played a gloomy game of shuffleboard with some linemen and a dispatcher from Georgia Power and looked over the crowd. God-damned airline clerks had started coming in the Cloud Nine. All had the same little mustache and pinkie ring. Pretty soon they'd be fixing the Cloud Nine English with a damned dart board. You can't depend on nothing.

"Hey, Hoyt. I'll match you for a bottle of beer." It was his supervisor, Billy Meeks.

"Say, Billy, I need to talk to you."

"What's up?"

"You know that old son of a bitch Parsons that's all the time calling up?"

"Called me last week, as a matter of fact," Meeks said. "What about him?"

"He said somebody was reading my route ahead of me, like maybe somebody thought I wasn't making the rounds. You don't think I'm reading meters at home, do you?"

"Nope."

"You don't think that, do you? I mean, if I'm on a man's shit list I want him to come right out and say it."

"If you was on my shit list, you think I'd be scared to say so to your face?"

"No."

"All right, then. If anybody was checking your route, I'd know it. Your executives is always aware of a situation like that. Nobody's checking up on you, Hoyt. You can't pay any attention to Parsons, he's just old and contrary. He called me up last week and said, 'Congratulations on getting wise to that Hoyt Lewis.' I didn't pay him any mind."

"I wish we'd put the law on him about that meter," Lewis said. "I was just setting back there in the alley under a tree trying to eat my lunch today and he jumped me. What he needs is a good ass-kicking."

"I used to set back there myself when I had the route," Meeks said. "Boy, I tell you one time I seen Mrs. Leeds—well, it don't seem right to talk about it now she's dead—but one or two times she was out there sunning herself in the backyard in her swimming suit. Whooee. Had a cute little peter belly. That was a damn shame about them. She was a nice lady."

"Did they catch anybody yet?"

"Naw."

"Too bad he got the Leedses when old Parsons was right down the street convenient," Lewis observed.

"I'll tell you what, I don't let my old lady lay around out in the yard in no swimming suit. She goes 'Silly Billy, who's gonna see me?' I told her, I said you can't tell what kind of a insane bastard might jump over that hedge with his private out. Did the cops talk to you? Ast you had you seen anybody?"

"Yeah, I think they got everybody that has a route out there. Mailmen, everybody. I was working Laurelwood on the other side of Betty Jane Drive the whole week until today, though." Lewis picked at the label on his beer. "You say Parsons called you up last week?"

"Yep."

"Then he must have saw somebody reading his meter. He wouldn't have called in if he'd just made it up today to bother me. You say you didn't send nobody, and it sure wasn't me he saw."

"Might have been Southeastern Bell checking something."

"Might have been."

"We don't share poles out there, though."

"Reckon I ought to call the cops?"

"Wouldn't hurt nothing," Meeks said.

"Naw, it might do Parsons some good, talk with the law. Scare the shit out of him when they drive up, anyhow."

CHAPTER 5

GRAHAM WENT BACK to the Leeds house in the late afternoon. He entered through the front door and tried not to look at the ruin the killer had left. So far he had seen files, a killing floor and meat—all aftermath. He knew a fair amount about how they died. How they lived was on his mind today.

A survey, then. The garage contained a good ski boat, well used and well maintained, and a station wagon. Golf clubs were there, and a trail bike. The power tools were almost unused. Adult toys.

Graham took a wedge from the golf bag and had to choke up on the long shaft as he made a jerky swing. The bag puffed a smell of leather at him as he leaned it back against the wall. Charles Leeds's things.

Graham pursued Charles Leeds through the house. His hunting prints hung in the den. His set of the Great Books were all in a row. Sewanee annuals. H. Allen Smith and Perelman and Max Shulman on the bookshelves. Vonnegut and Evelyn Waugh. C. S. Forrester's *Beat to Quarters* was open on a table.

In the den closet a good skeet gun, a Nikon camera, a Bolex Super Eight movie camera and projector.

Graham, who owned almost nothing except basic fishing equipment, a third-hand Volkswagen, and two cases of Montrachet, felt a mild animosity toward the adult toys and wondered why.

Who was Leeds? A successful tax attorney, a Sewanee footballer, a rangy man who liked to laugh, a man who got up and fought with his throat cut.

Graham followed him through the house out of an odd sense of obligation. Learning about him first was a way of asking permission to look at his wife.

Graham felt that it was she who drew the monster, as surely as a singing cricket attracts death from the red-eyed fly.

Mrs. Leeds, then.

She had a small dressing room upstairs. Graham managed to reach it without looking around the bedroom. The room was yellow and appeared undisturbed except for the smashed mirror above the dressing table. A pair of L. L. Bean moccasins was on the floor in front of the closet, as though she had just stepped out of them. Her dressing gown appeared to have been flung on its peg, and the closet revealed the mild disorder of a woman who has many other closets to organize.

Mrs. Leeds's diary was in a plum velvet box on the dressing table. The key was taped to the lid along with a check tag from the police property room.

Graham sat on a spindly white chair and opened the diary at random:

December 23rd, Tuesday, Mama's house. The children are still asleep. When Mama glassed in the sun porch, I hated the way it changed the looks of the house, but it's very pleasant and I can sit here warm looking out at the snow. How many more Christmases can she manage a houseful of grandchildren? A lot, I hope.

A hard drive yesterday up from Atlanta, snowing after Raleigh. We had to creep. I was tired anyway from getting everyone ready. Outside Chapel Hill, Charlie stopped the car and got out. He snapped some icicles off a branch to make me a martini. He came back to the car, long legs lifting high in the snow, and there was snow in his hair and on his eyelashes and I remembered that I love him. It felt like something breaking with a little pain and spilling warm.

I hope the parka fits him. If he got me that tacky dinner ring, I'll die. I could kick Madelyn's big cellulite behind for showing hers and carrying on. Four ridiculously big diamonds the color of dirty ice. Icicle ice is so clear. The sun came through the car window and where the icicle was broken off it stuck up out of the glass and made a little prism. It made a spot of red and green on my hand holding the glass. I could feel the colors on my hand.

He asked me what I want for Christmas and I cupped my hands around his ear and whispered: Your big prick, silly, in as far as it will go.

The bald spot on the back of his head turned red. He's always afraid the children will hear. Men have no confidence in whispers.

The page was flecked with detective's cigar ash.

Graham read on as the light faded, through the daughter's tonsillectomy, and a scare in June when Mrs. Leeds found a small lump in her breast. *(Dear God, the children are so small.)*

Three pages later the lump was a small benign cyst, easily removed.

Dr. Janovich turned me loose this afternoon. We left the hospital and drove to the pond. We hadn't been there in a long while. There never seems to be enough time. Charlie had two bottles of champagne on ice and we drank them and fed the ducks while the sun went down. He stood at edge of the water with his back to me for a while and I think he cried a little.

Susan said she was afraid we were coming home from the hospital with another brother for her. Home!

Graham heard the telephone ring in the bedroom. A click and the hum of an answering machine. "Hello, this is Valerie Leeds. I'm sorry I can't come to the phone right now, but if you'll leave your name and number after the tone, we'll get back to you. Thank you."

Graham half-expected to hear Crawford's voice after the beep, but there was only the dial tone. The caller had hung up.

He had heard her voice; now he wanted to see her. He went down to the den.

➢

He had in his pocket a reel of Super Eight movie film belonging to Charles Leeds. Three weeks before his death, Leeds had left the film with a druggist who sent it away for processing. He never picked it up. Police found the receipt in Leeds's wallet and got the film from the druggist. Detectives viewed the home movie along with family snapshots developed at the same time and found nothing of interest.

Graham wanted to see the Leedses alive. At the police station, the detectives had offered Graham their projector. He wanted to watch the movie at the house. Reluctantly they let him check it out of the property room.

Graham found the screen and projector in the den closet, set them up, and sat down in Charles Leeds's big leather armchair to watch. He felt something tacky on the chair arm under his palm—a child's sticky fingerprints fuzzed with lint. Graham's hand smelled like candy.

It was a pleasant little silent home movie, more imaginative than most. It opened with a dog, a gray Scotty, asleep on the den rug. The dog was disturbed momentarily by the moviemaking and raised his head to look at the camera. Then he went to sleep again. A jumpy cut to the dog still asleep. Then the Scotty's ears perked up. He rose and barked, and the camera followed him into the kitchen as he ran to the door and stood expectantly, shivering and wagging his stumpy tail.

Graham bit his lower lip and waited too. On the screen, the door opened and Mrs. Leeds came in carrying groceries. She blinked and laughed in surprise and touched her tousled hair with her free hand. Her lips moved as she walked out of the picture, and the children came in behind her carrying smaller sacks. The girl was six, the boys eight and ten.

The younger boy, apparently a veteran of home movies, pointed to his ears and wiggled them. The camera was positioned fairly high. Leeds was seventy-five inches tall, according to the coroner's report.

Graham believed that this part of the movie must have been made in the early spring. The children wore windbreakers and Mrs. Leeds appeared pale. At the morgue she had a good tan and bathing-suit marks.

Brief scenes followed of the boys playing Ping-Pong in the basement and the girl, Susan, wrapping a present in her room, tongue curled over her upper lip in concentration and a wisp of hair down over her forehead. She brushed her hair back with her plump hand, as her mother had done in the kitchen.

A subsequent scene showed Susan in a bubble bath, crouched like a small frog. She wore a large shower cap. The camera angle was lower and the focus uncertain, clearly the work of a brother. The scene ended with her shouting soundlessly at the camera and covering her six-year-old chest as her shower cap slipped down over her eyes.

Not to be outdone, Leeds had surprised Mrs. Leeds in the shower. The shower curtain bumped and bulged as the curtain does before a grade-school theatrical. Mrs. Leeds's arm appeared around the curtain. In her hand was a large bath sponge. The scene closed with the lens obscured in soapsuds.

The film ended with a shot of Norman Vincent Peale speaking on television and a pan to Charles Leeds snoring in the chair where Graham now sat.

Graham stared at the blank square of light on the screen. He liked the Leedses. He was sorry that he had been to the morgue. He thought the madman who visited them might have liked them too. But the madman would like them better the way they were now.

➤

Graham's head felt stuffed and stupid. He swam in the pool at his hotel until he was rubber-legged, and came out of the water thinking of two things at once—a Tanqueray martini and the taste of Molly's mouth.

He made the martini himself in a plastic glass and telephoned Molly.

"Hello, hotshot."

"Hey, baby! Where are you?"

"In this damned hotel in Atlanta."

"Doing some good?"

"None you'd notice. I'm lonesome."

"Me too."

"Horny."

"Me too."

"Tell me about yourself."

"Well, I had a run-in with Mrs. Holper today. She wanted to return a dress with a huge big whiskey stain on the seat. I mean, obviously she had worn it to the Jaycee thing."

"And what did *you* say?"

"I told her I didn't sell it to her like that."

"And what did *she* say?"

"She said she never had any trouble returning dresses before, which was one reason she shopped at my place rather than some others that she knew about."

"And then what did *you* say?"

"Oh, I said I was upset because Will talks like a jackass on the phone."

"I see."

"Willy's fine. He's covering some turtle eggs the dogs dug up. Tell me what you're doing."

"Reading reports. Eating junk food."

"Thinking a good bit, I expect."

"Yep."

"Can I help you?"

"I just don't have a lock on anything, Molly. There's not enough information. Well, there's a lot of information, but I haven't done enough with it."

"Will you be in Atlanta for a while? I'm not bugging you about coming home, I just wonder."

"I don't know. I'll be here a few more days at least. I miss you."

"Want to talk about fucking?"

"I don't think I could stand it. I think maybe we better not do that."

"Do what?"

"Talk about fucking."

"Okay. You don't mind if I think about it, though?"

"Absolutely not."

"We've got a new dog."

"Oh hell."

"Looks like a cross between a basset hound and a Pekingese."

"Lovely."

"He's got big balls."

"Never mind about his balls."

"They almost drag the ground. He has to retract them when he runs."

"He can't do that."

"Yes he can. *You* don't know."

"Yes I do know."

"Can you retract yours?"

"I thought we were coming to that."

"Well?"

"If you must know, I retracted them once."

"When was that?"

"In my youth. I had to clear a barbed-wire fence in a hurry."

"Why?"

"I was carrying this watermelon that I had not cultivated."

"You were fleeing? From whom?"

"A swineherd of my acquaintance. Alerted by his dogs, he burst from his dwelling in his BVD's, waving a fowling piece. Fortunately, he tripped over a butterbean trellis and gave me a running start."

"Did he shoot at you?"

"I thought so at the time, yes. But the reports I heard might have issued from my behind. I've never been entirely clear on that."

"Did you clear the fence?"

"Handily."

"A criminal mind, even at that age."

"I don't have a criminal mind."

"Of course you don't. I'm thinking about painting the kitchen. What color do you like? Will? What color do you like? Are you there?"

"Yeah, uh, yellow. Let's paint it yellow."

"Yellow is a bad color for me. I'll look green at breakfast."

"Blue, then."

"Blue is cold."

"Well goddammit, paint it baby-shit tan for all I care. . . . No, look, I'll probably be home before long and we'll go to the paint store and get some chips and stuff, okay? And maybe some new handles and that."

"Let's do, let's get some handles. I don't know why I'm talking about this stuff. Look, I love you and I miss you and you're doing the right thing. It's costing you too, I know that. I'm here and I'll be here whenever you come home, or I'll meet you anywhere, anytime. That's what."

"Dear Molly. Dear Molly. Go to bed now."

"All right."

"Good night."

Graham lay with his hands behind his head and conjured dinners with Molly. Stone crab and Sancerre, the salt breeze mixed with the wine.

But it was his curse to pick at conversations, and he began to do it now. He had snapped at her after a harmless remark about his "criminal mind." Stupid.

Graham found Molly's interest in him largely inexplicable.

He called police headquarters and left word for Springfield that he wanted to start helping with the legwork in the morning. There was nothing else to do.

The gin helped him sleep.

CHAPTER 6

FLIMSY COPIES of the notes on all calls about the Leeds case were placed on Buddy Springfield's desk. Tuesday morning at seven o'clock when Springfield arrived at his office, there were sixty-three of them. The top one was red-flagged.

It said Birmingham police had found a cat buried in a shoebox behind the Jacobis' garage. The cat had a flower between its paws and was wrapped in a dish towel. The cat's name was written on the lid in a childish hand. It wore no collar. A string tied in a granny knot held the lid on.

The Birmingham medical examiner said the cat was strangled. He had shaved it and found no puncture wound.

Springfield tapped the earpiece of his glasses against his teeth.

They had found soft ground and dug it up with a shovel. Didn't need any damned methane probe. Still, Graham had been right.

The chief of detectives licked his thumb and started through the rest of the stack of flimsies. Most were reports of suspicious vehicles in the neighborhood during the past week, vague descriptions giving only vehicle type or color. Four anonymous telephone callers had told Atlanta residents: "I'm gonna do you like the Leedses."

Hoyt Lewis' report was in the middle of the pile.

Springfield called the overnight watch commander.

"What about the meter reader's report on this Parsons? Number forty-eight."

"We tried to check with the utilities last night, Chief, to see if they had anybody in that alley," the watch commander said. "They'll have to get back to us this morning."

"You have somebody get back to *them* now," Springfield said. "Check sanitation, the city engineer, check for construction permits along the alley and catch me in my car."

He dialed Will Graham's number. "Will? Meet me in front of your hotel in ten minutes and let's take a little ride."

At 7:45 A.M. Springfield parked near the end of the alley. He and Graham walked abreast in wheel tracks pressed in the gravel. Even this early the sun was hot.

"You need to get you a hat," Springfield said. His own snappy straw was tilted down over his eyes.

The chain-link fence at the rear of the Leeds property was covered with vines. They paused by the light meter on the pole.

"If he came down this way, he could see the whole back end of the house," Springfield said.

In only five days the Leeds property had begun to look neglected. The lawn was uneven, and wild onions sprouted above the grass. Small branches had fallen in the yard. Graham wanted to pick them up. The house seemed asleep, the latticed porch striped and dappled with the long morning shadows of the trees. Standing with Springfield in the alley, Graham could see himself looking in the back window, opening the porch door. Oddly, his reconstruction of the entry by the killer seemed to elude him now, in the sunlight. He watched a child's swing move gently in the breeze.

"That looks like Parsons," Springfield said.

H. G. Parsons was out early, grubbing in a flowerbed in his backyard, two houses down. Springfield and Graham went to Parsons' back gate and stood beside his garbage cans. The lids were chained to the fence.

Springfield measured the height of the light meter with a tape.

He had notes on all the Leedses' neighbors. His notes said Parsons had taken early retirement from the post office at his supervisor's request. The supervisor had reported Parsons to be "increasingly absentminded."

Springfield's notes contained gossip, too. The neighbors said Parsons' wife stayed with her sister in Macon as much as she could, and that his son never called him anymore.

"Mr. Parsons. Mr. Parsons," Springfield called.

Parsons leaned his tilling fork against the house and came to the fence. He wore sandals and white socks. Dirt and grass had stained the toes of his socks. His face was shiny pink.

Arteriosclerosis, Graham thought. He's taken his pill.

"Yes?"

"Mr. Parsons, could we talk to you for a minute? We were hoping you could help us," Springfield said.

"Are you from the power company?"

"No, I'm Buddy Springfield from the police department."

"It's about the murder, then. My wife and I were in Macon, as I told the officer—"

"I know, Mr. Parsons. We wanted to ask about your light meter. Did—"

"If that . . . meter reader said I did anything improper, he's just—"

"No, no. Mr. Parsons, did you see a stranger reading your meter last week?"

"No."

"Are you sure? I believe you told Hoyt Lewis that someone else read your meter ahead of him."

"I did. And it's about time. I'm keeping up with this, and the Public Service Commission will get a full report from me."

"Yes, sir. I'm sure they'll take care of it. Who did you see reading your meter?"

"It wasn't a stranger, it was somebody from Georgia Power."

"How do you know?"

"Well, he looked like a meter reader."

"What was he wearing?"

"What they all wear, I guess. What is it? A brown outfit and the cap."

"Did you see his face?"

"I can't remember if I did. I was looking out the kitchen window when I saw him. I wanted to talk to him, but I had to put on my robe, and by the time I got outside, he was gone."

"Did he have a truck?"

"I don't remember seeing one. What's going on? Why do you want to know?"

"We're checking everybody who was in this neighborhood last week. It's really important, Mr. Parsons. Try hard to remember."

"So it is about the murder. You haven't arrested anybody yet, have you?"

"No."

"I watched the street last night, and *fifteen minutes* went by without a single squad car passing. It was horrible, what happened to the Leedses. My wife has been beside herself. I wonder who'll buy their house. I saw some Negroes looking at it the other day. You know, I had to speak to Leeds a few times about his children, but they were all right. Of course, he wouldn't do anything I suggested about his lawn. The Department of Agriculture has some *excellent* pamphlets on the control of nuisance grasses. Finally I just put them in his mailbox. Honestly, when he mowed the wild onions were suffocating."

"Mr. Parsons, exactly when did you see this fellow in the alley?" Springfield asked.

"I'm not sure, I was trying to think."

"Do you recall the time of day? Morning? Noon? Afternoon?"

"I know the times of day, you don't have to name them. Afternoon, maybe. I don't remember."

Springfield rubbed the back of his neck. "Excuse me, Mr. Parsons, but I have to get this just right. Could we go in your kitchen and you show us just where you saw him from?"

"Let me see your credentials. Both of you."

In the house, silence, shiny surfaces, and dead air. Neat. Neat. The desperate order of an aging couple who see their lives begin to blur.

Graham wished he had stayed outside. He was sure the drawers held polished silver with egg between the tines.

Stop it and let's pump the old fart.

The window over the kitchen sink gave a good view of the backyard.

"There. Are you satisfied?" Parsons asked. "You *can* see out there from here. I never talked to him, I don't remember what he looked like. If that's all, I have a lot to do."

Graham spoke for the first time. "You said you went to get your robe, and when you came back he was gone. You weren't dressed, then?"

"No."

"In the middle of the afternoon? Were you not feeling well, Mr. Parsons?"

"What I do in my own house is my business. I can wear a kangaroo suit in here if I want to. Why aren't you out looking for the killer? Probably because it's cool in here."

"I understand you're retired, Mr. Parsons, so I guess it doesn't matter if you put on your clothes every day or not. A lot of days you just don't get dressed at all, am I right?"

Veins stood out in Parsons' temples. "Just because I'm retired doesn't mean I don't put my clothes on and get busy every day. I just got hot and I came in and took a shower. I was working. I was mulching, and I had done a day's work by afternoon, which is more than you'll do today."

"You were what?"

"Mulching."

"What day did you mulch?"

"Friday. It was last Friday. They delivered it in the morning, a big load, and I had . . . I had it all spread by afternoon. You can ask at the Garden Center how much it was."

"And you got hot and came in and took a shower. What were you doing in the kitchen?"

"Fixing a glass of iced tea."

"And you got out some ice? But the refrigerator is over there, away from the window."

Parsons looked from the window to the refrigerator, lost and confused. His eyes were dull, like the eyes of a fish in the market toward the end of the day. Then they brightened in triumph. He went to the cabinet by the sink.

"I was right here, getting some Sweet 'N Low when I saw him. That's it. That's all. Now, if you're through prying . . ."

"I think he saw Hoyt Lewis," Graham said.

"So do I," Springfield said.

"It was *not* Hoyt Lewis. It was *not*." Parsons' eyes were watering.

"How do you know?" Springfield said. "It might have been Hoyt Lewis, and you just *thought*—"

"Lewis is brown from the sun. He's got old greasy hair and those peckerwood sideburns." Parsons' voice had risen and he was talking so fast it was hard to understand him. "That's how I knew. Of course it wasn't Lewis. This fellow was paler and his hair was blond. He turned to write on his clipboard and I could see under the back of his hat. Blond. Cut off square on the back of his neck."

Springfield stood absolutely still and when he spoke his voice was still skeptical. "What about his face?"

"I don't know. He may have had a mustache."

"Like Lewis?"

"Lewis doesn't have a mustache."

"Oh," Springfield said. "Was he at eye level with the meter? Did he have to look up at it?"

"Eye level, I guess."

"Would you know him if you saw him again?"

"No."

"What age was he?"

"Not old. I don't know."

"Did you see the Leedses' dog anywhere around him?"

"No."

"Look, Mr. Parsons, I can see I was wrong," Springfield said. "You're a real big help to us. If you don't mind, I'm going to send our artist out here, and if you'd just let him sit right here at your kitchen table, maybe you could give him an idea of what this fellow looked like. It sure wasn't Lewis."

"I don't want my name in any newspapers."

"It won't be."

Parsons followed them outside.

"You've done a hell of a fine job on this yard, Mr. Parsons," Springfield said. "It ought to win some kind of a prize."

Parsons said nothing. His face was red and working, his eyes wet. He stood there in his baggy shorts and sandals and glared at them. As they left the yard, he grabbed his fork and began to grub furiously in the ground, hacking blindly through the flowers, scattering mulch on the grass.

➤

Springfield checked in on his car radio. None of the utilities or city agencies could account for the man in the alley on the day before the murders. Springfield reported Parsons' description and gave instructions for the artist. "Tell him to draw the pole and the meter first and go from there. He'll have to ease the witness along.

"Our artist doesn't much like to make house calls," the chief of detectives told Graham as he slid the stripline Ford through the traffic. "He likes for the secretaries to see him work, with the witness standing on one foot and then the other, looking over his shoulder. A police station is a damn poor place to question anybody that you don't need to scare. Soon as we get the picture, we'll door-to-door the neighborhood with it.

"I feel like we just got a whiff, Will. Just faint, but a whiff, don't you? Look, we did it to the poor old devil and he came through. Now let's do something with it."

"If the man in the alley is the one we want, it's the best news yet," Graham said. He was sick of himself.

"Right. It means he's not just getting off a bus and going whichever way his peter points. He's got a plan. He stayed in town overnight. He knows where he's going a day or two ahead. He's got some kind of an idea. Case the place, kill the pet, then the family. What the hell kind of an idea is that?" Springfield paused. "That's kind of your territory, isn't it?"

"It is, yes. If it's anybody's, I suppose it's mine."

"I know you've seen this kind of thing before. You didn't like it the other day when I asked you about Lecter, but I need to talk to you about it."

"All right."

"He killed nine people, didn't he, in all?"

"Nine that we know of. Two others didn't die."

"What happened to them?"

"One is on a respirator at a hospital in Baltimore. The other is in a private mental hospital in Denver."

"What made him do it, how was he crazy?"

Graham looked out the car window at the people on the sidewalk. His voice sounded detached, as though he were dictating a letter.

"He did it because he liked it. Still does. Dr. Lecter is not crazy, in any common way we think of being crazy. He did some hideous things because he enjoyed them. But he can function perfectly when he wants to."

"What did the psychologists call it—what was wrong with him."

"They say he's a sociopath, because they don't know what else to call him. He has some of the characteristics of what they call a sociopath. He has no remorse or guilt at all. And he had the first and worst sign—sadism to animals as a child."

Springfield grunted.

"But he doesn't have any of the other marks," Graham said. "He wasn't a drifter, he had no history of trouble with the law. He wasn't shallow and exploitive in small things, like most sociopaths are. He's not insensitive. They don't know what to call him. His electroencephalograms show some odd patterns, but they haven't been able to tell much from them."

"What would you call him?" Springfield asked.

Graham hesitated.

"Just to yourself, what do you call him?"

"He's a monster. I think of him as one of those pitiful things that are born in hospitals from time to time. They feed it, and keep it warm, but they don't put it on the machines and it dies. Lecter is the same way in his head, but he looks normal and nobody could tell."

"A couple of friends of mine in the chiefs' association are from Baltimore. I asked them how you spotted Lecter. They said they didn't know. How did you do it? What was the first indication, the first thing you felt?"

"It was a coincidence," Graham said. "The sixth victim was killed in his workshop. He had woodworking equipment and he kept his hunting stuff out there. He was laced to a pegboard where the tools hung, and he was really torn up, cut and stabbed, and he had arrows in him. The wounds reminded me of something. I couldn't think what it was."

"And you had to go on to the next ones."

"Yes. Lecter was very hot—he did the next three in nine days. But this sixth one, he had two old scars on his thigh. The pathologist checked with the local hospital and found he had fallen out of a tree blind five years before while he was bow hunting and stuck an arrow through his leg.

"The doctor of record was a resident surgeon, but Lecter had treated him first—he was on duty in the emergency room. His name was on the admissions log. It had been a long time since the accident, but I thought Lecter might remember if anything had seemed fishy about the arrow wound, so I went to his office to see him. We were grabbing at anything then.

"He was practicing psychiatry by that time. He had a nice office. Antiques. He said he didn't remember much about the arrow wound, that one of the victim's hunting buddies had brought him in, and that was it.

"Something bothered me, though. I thought it was something Lecter said, or something in the office. Crawford and I hashed it over. We checked the files, and Lecter had no record. I wanted some time in his office by myself, but we couldn't get a warrant. We had nothing to show. So I went back to see him.

"It was Sunday, he saw patients on Sunday. The building was empty except for a couple of people in his waiting room. He saw me right away. We were talking and he was making this polite effort to help me and I looked up at some very old medical books on the shelf above his head. And I knew it was him.

"When I looked at him again, maybe my face changed, I don't know. I knew it and *he knew* I knew it. I still couldn't think of the reason, though. I didn't trust it. I had to figure it out. So I mumbled something and got out of there, into the hall. There was a pay phone in the hall. I didn't want to stir him up until I had some help. I was talking to the police switchboard when he came out a service door behind me in his socks. I never heard him coming. I felt his breath was all, and then . . . there was the rest of it."

"How did you know, though?"

"I think it was maybe a week later in the hospital I finally figured it out. It was *Wound Man*—an illustration they used in a lot of the early medical books like the ones Lecter had. It shows different kinds of battle injuries, all in one figure. I had seen it in a survey course a pathologist was teaching at GWU. The sixth victim's position and his injuries were a close match to *Wound Man.*"

"*Wound Man*, you say? That's all you had?"

"Well, yeah. It was a coincidence that I had seen it. A piece of luck."

"That's some luck."

"If you don't believe me, what the fuck did you ask me for?"

"I didn't hear that."

"Good. I didn't mean to say it. That's the way it happened, though."

"Okay," Springfield said. "Okay. Thank you for telling me. I need to know things like that."

➤

Parsons' description of the man in the alley and the information on the cat and the dog were possible indications of the killer's methods: it seemed likely that he scouted as a meter reader and felt compelled to hurt the victims' pets before he came to kill the family.

The immediate problem the police faced was whether or not to publicize their theory.

With the public aware of the danger signals and watching, police might get advance warning of the killer's next attack— but the killer probably followed the news too.

He might change his habits.

There was strong feeling in the police department that the slender leads should be kept secret except for a special bulletin to veterinarians and animal shelters throughout the Southeast asking for immediate reports on pet mutilations.

That meant not giving the public the best possible warning. It was a moral question, and the police were not comfortable with it.

They consulted Dr. Alan Bloom in Chicago. Dr. Bloom said that if the killer read a warning in the newspapers, he would probably change his method of casing a house. Dr. Bloom doubted that the man could stop attacking the pets, regardless of the risk. The psychiatrist told the police that they should by no means assume they had twenty-five days to work—the period before the next full moon on August 25.

On the morning of July 31, three hours after Parsons gave his description, a decision was reached in a telephone conference among Birmingham and Atlanta police and Crawford in Washington: they would send the private bulletin to veterinarians, canvass for three days in the neighborhood with the artist's sketch, then release the information to the news media.

For those three days Graham and the Atlanta detectives pounded the sidewalks showing the sketch to householders in the area of the

Leeds home. There was only a suggestion of a face in the sketch, but they hoped to find someone who could improve it.

Graham's copy of the sketch grew soft around the edges from the sweat of his hands. Often it was difficult to get residents to answer the door. At night he lay in his room with powder on his heat rash, his mind circling the problem as though it were a hologram. He courted the feeling that precedes an idea. It would not come.

Meanwhile, there were four accidental injuries and one fatality in Atlanta as householders shot at relatives coming home late. Prowler calls multiplied and useless tips stacked up in the In baskets at police headquarters. Despair went around like the flu.

Crawford returned from Washington at the end of the third day and dropped in on Graham as he sat peeling off his wet socks.

"Hot work?"

"Grab a sketch in the morning and see," Graham said.

"No, it'll all be on the news tonight. Did you walk all day?"

"I can't drive through their yards."

"I didn't think anything would come of this canvass," Crawford said.

"Well, what the hell did you expect me to do?"

"The best you can, that's all." Crawford rose to leave. "Busywork's been a narcotic for me sometimes, especially after I quit the booze. For you too, I think."

Graham was angry. Crawford was right, of course.

Graham was a natural procrastinator, and he knew it. Long ago in school he had made up for it with speed. He was not in school now.

There was something else he could do, and he had known it for days. He could wait until he was driven to it by desperation in the last days before the full moon. Or he could do it now, while it might be of some use.

There was an opinion he wanted. A very strange view he needed to share; a mindset he had to recover after his warm round years in the Keys.

The reasons clacked like roller-coaster cogs pulling up to the first long plunge, and at the top, unaware that he clutched his belly, Graham said it aloud.

"I have to see Lecter."

CHAPTER 7

DR. FREDERICK CHILTON, chief of staff at the Chesapeake State Hospital for the Criminally Insane, came around his desk to shake Will Graham's hand.

Dr. Bloom called me yesterday, Mr. Graham—or should I call you Dr. Graham?"

- "I'm not a doctor."

"I was delighted to hear from Dr. Bloom, we've known each other for *years*. Take that chair."

"We appreciate your help, Dr. Chilton."

"Frankly, I sometimes feel like Lecter's secretary rather than his keeper," Chilton said. "The volume of his mail alone is a nuisance. I think among some researchers it's considered chic to correspond with him—I've seen his letters *framed* in psychology departments—and for a while it seemed that every Ph.D. candidate in the field wanted to interview him. Glad to cooperate with *you,* of course, and Dr. Bloom."

"I need to see Dr. Lecter in as much privacy as possible," Graham said. "I may need to see him again or telephone him after today."

Chilton nodded. "To begin with, Dr. Lecter will stay in his room. That is absolutely the only place where he is not put in restraints. One wall of his room is a double barrier which opens on the hall. I'll have a chair put there, and screens if you like.

"I must ask you not to pass him any objects whatever, other than paper free of clips or staples. No ring binders, pencils, or pens. He has his own felt-tipped pens."

"I might have to show him some material that could stimulate him," Graham said.

"You can show him what you like as long as it's on soft paper. Pass him documents through the sliding food tray. Don't hand anything through the barrier and do not accept anything he might extend through the barrier. He can return papers in the food tray. I insist on that. Dr. Bloom and Mr. Crawford assured me that you would cooperate on procedure."

"I will," Graham said. He started to rise.

"I know you're anxious to get on with it, Mr. Graham, but I want to tell you something first. This will interest you.

"It may seem gratuitous to warn *you*, of all people, about Lecter. But he's very disarming. For a year after he was brought here, he behaved perfectly and gave the appearance of cooperating with attempts at therapy. As a result—this was under the previous administrator—security around him was slightly relaxed.

"On the afternoon of July 8, 1976, he complained of chest pain. His restraints were removed in the examining room to make it easier to give him an electrocardiogram. One of his attendants left the room to smoke, and the other turned away for a second. The nurse was very quick and strong. She managed to save one of her eyes.

"You may find this curious." Chilton took a strip of EKG tape from a drawer and unrolled it on his desk. He traced the spiky line with his forefinger. "Here, he's resting on the examining table. Pulse seventy-two. Here, he grabs the nurse's head and pulls her down to him. Here, he is subdued by the attendant. He didn't resist, by the way, though the attendant dislocated his shoulder. Do you notice the strange thing? His pulse never got over eighty-five. Even when he tore out her tongue."

Chilton could read nothing in Graham's face. He leaned back in his chair and steepled his fingers under his chin. His hands were dry and shiny.

"You know, when Lecter was first captured we thought he might provide us with a singular opportunity to study a pure sociopath," Chilton said. "It's so rare to get one alive. Lecter is so lucid, so perceptive; he's trained in psychiatry . . . and he's a mass murderer.

He seemed cooperative, and we thought that he could be a window on this kind of aberration. We thought we'd be like Beaumont studying digestion through the opening in St. Martin's stomach.

"As it turned out, I don't think we're any closer to understanding him now than the day he came in. Have you ever talked with Lecter for any length of time?"

"No. I just saw him when . . . I saw him mainly in court. Dr. Bloom showed me his articles in the journals," Graham said.

"He's very familiar with *you*. He's given you a lot of thought."

"You had some sessions with him?"

"Yes. Twelve. He's impenetrable. Too sophisticated about the tests for them to register anything. Edwards, Fabré, even Dr. Bloom himself had a crack at him. I have their notes. He was an enigma to them too. It's impossible, of course, to tell what he's holding back or whether he understands more than he'll say. Oh, since his commitment he's done some brilliant pieces for *The American Journal of Psychiatry* and *The General Archives*. But they're always about problems he doesn't have. I think he's afraid that if we 'solve' him, nobody will be interested in him anymore and he'll be stuck in a back ward somewhere for the rest of his life."

Chilton paused. He had practiced using his peripheral vision to watch his subject in interviews. He believed that he could watch Graham this way undetected.

"The consensus around here is that the only person who has demonstrated any practical understanding of Hannibal Lecter is you, Mr. Graham. Can you tell me anything about him?"

"No."

"Some of the staff are curious about this: when you saw Dr. Lecter's murders, their 'style,' so to speak, were you able perhaps to reconstruct his fantasies? And did that help you identify him?"

Graham did not answer.

"We're woefully short of material on that sort of thing. There's one single piece in *The Journal of Abnormal Psychology*. Would you mind talking with some of the staff—no, no, not this trip—Dr. Bloom was very severe with me on that point. We're to leave you alone. Next trip, perhaps."

Dr. Chilton had seen a lot of hostility. He was seeing some at the moment.

Graham stood up. "Thank you, doctor. I want to see Lecter now."

➤

The steel door of the maximum-security section closed behind Graham. He heard the bolt slide home.

Graham knew that Lecter slept most of the morning. He looked down the corridor. At that angle he could not see into Lecter's cell, but he could tell that the lights inside were dimmed.

Graham wanted to see Dr. Lecter asleep. He wanted time to brace himself. If he felt Lecter's madness in his head, he had to contain it quickly, like a spill.

To cover the sound of his footsteps, he followed an orderly pushing a linen cart. Dr. Lecter is very difficult to slip up on.

Graham paused partway down the hall. Steel bars covered the entire front of the cell. Behind the bars, farther than arm's reach, was a stout nylon net stretched ceiling to floor and wall to wall. Through the barrier, Graham could see a table and chair bolted to the floor. The table was stacked with softcover books and correspondence. He walked up to the bars, put his hands on them, took his hands away.

Dr. Hannibal Lecter lay on his cot asleep, his head propped on a pillow against the wall. Alexandre Dumas' *Le Grand Dictionnaire de Cuisine* was open on his chest.

Graham had stared through the bars for about five seconds when Lecter opened his eyes and said, "That's the same atrocious after-shave you wore in court."

"I keep getting it for Christmas."

Dr. Lecter's eyes are maroon and they reflect the light redly in tiny points. Graham felt each hair bristle on his nape. He put his hand on the back of his neck.

"Christmas, yes," Lecter said. "Did you get my card?"

"I got it. Thank you."

Dr. Lecter's Christmas card had been forwarded to Graham from the FBI crime laboratory in Washington. He took it into the backyard, burned it, and washed his hands before touching Molly.

Lecter rose and walked over to his table. He is a small, lithe man. Very neat. "Why don't you have a seat, Will? I think there are some folding chairs in a closet just down that way. At least, that's where it sounds like they come from."

"The orderly's bringing one."

Lecter stood until Graham was seated in the hall. "And how is Officer Stewart?" he asked.

"Stewart's fine." Officer Stewart left law enforcement after he saw Dr. Lecter's basement. He managed a motel now. Graham did not mention this. He didn't think Stewart would appreciate any mail from Lecter.

"Unfortunate that his emotional problems got the better of him. I thought he was a very promising young officer. Do you ever have any problems, Will?"

"No."

"Of course you don't."

Graham felt that Lecter was looking through to the back of his skull. His attention felt like a fly walking around in there.

"I'm glad you came. It's been what now, three years? My callers are all professional. Banal clinical psychiatrists and grasping second-rate *doctors* of psychology from silo colleges somewhere. Pencil lickers trying to protect their tenure with pieces in the journals."

"Dr. Bloom showed me your article on surgical addiction in *The Journal of Clinical Psychiatry.*"

"And?"

"Very interesting, even to a layman."

"A layman . . . layman—layman. Interesting term," Lecter said. "So many learned fellows going about. So many *experts* on government grants. And you say you're a layman. But it was you who caught me, wasn't it, Will? Do you know how you did it?"

"I'm sure you've read the transcript. It's all in there."

"No it's not. Do you know how you did it, Will?"

"It's in the transcript. What does it matter now?"

"It doesn't matter to *me*, Will."

"I want you to help me, Dr. Lecter."

"Yes, I thought so."

"It's about Atlanta and Birmingham."

"Yes."

"You read about it, I'm sure."

"I've read the papers. I can't clip them. They won't let me have scissors, of course. Sometimes they threaten me with loss of books, you know. I wouldn't want them to think I was dwelling on anything morbid." He laughed. Dr. Lecter has small white teeth. "You want to know how he's choosing them, don't you?"

"I thought you would have some ideas. I'm asking you to tell me what they are."

"Why should I?"

Graham had anticipated the question. A reason to stop multiple murders would not occur readily to Dr. Lecter.

"There are things you don't have," Graham said. "Research materials, filmstrips even. I'd speak to the chief of staff."

"Chilton. You must have seen him when you came in. Gruesome, isn't it? Tell me the truth, he fumbles at your head like a freshman pulling at a panty girdle, doesn't he? Watched you out of the corner of his eye. Picked *that* up, didn't you? You may not believe this, but he actually tried to give *me* a Thematic Apperception Test. He was sitting there just like the Cheshire cat waiting for Mf 13 to come up. Ha. Forgive me, I forget that you're not among the anointed. It's a card with a woman in bed and a man in the foreground. I was supposed to avoid a sexual interpretation. I laughed. He puffed up and told everybody I avoided prison with a Ganser syndrome—never mind, it's boring."

"You'd have access to the AMA filmstrip library."

"I don't think you'd get me the things I want."

"Try me."

"I have quite enough to read as it is."

"You'd get to see the file on this case. There's another reason."

"Pray."

"I thought you might be curious to find out if you're smarter than the person I'm looking for."

"Then, by implication, you think you are smarter than I am, since you caught me."

"No. I know I'm not smarter than you are."

"Then how did you catch me, Will?"

"You had disadvantages."

"What disadvantages?"

"Passion. And you're insane."

"You're very tan, Will."

Graham did not answer.

"Your hands are rough. They don't look like a cop's hands anymore. That shaving lotion is something a child would select. It has a ship on the bottle, doesn't it?" Dr. Lecter seldom holds his head upright. He tilts it as he asks a question, as though he were screwing an auger of curiosity into your face. Another silence, and Lecter said, "Don't think you can persuade me with appeals to my intellectual vanity."

"I don't think I'll persuade you. You'll do it or you won't. Dr. Bloom is working on it anyway, and he's the most—"

"Do you have the file with you?"

"Yes."

"And pictures?"

"Yes."

"Let me have them, and I might consider it."

"No."

"Do you dream much, Will?"

"Good-bye, Dr. Lecter."

"You haven't threatened to take away my books yet."

Graham walked away.

"Let me have the file, then. I'll tell you what I think."

Graham had to pack the abridged file tightly into the sliding tray. Lecter pulled it through.

"There's a summary on top. You can read that now," Graham said.

"Do you mind if I do it privately? Give me an hour."

Graham waited on a tired plastic couch in a grim lounge. Orderlies came in for coffee. He did not speak to them. He stared at small objects in the room and was glad they held still in his vision. He had to go to the rest room twice. He was numb.

The turnkey admitted him to the maximum-security section again.

Lecter sat at his table, his eyes filmed with thought. Graham knew he had spent most of the hour with the pictures.

"This is a very shy boy, Will. I'd love to meet him. . . . Have you considered the possibility that he's disfigured? Or that he may believe he's disfigured?"

"The mirrors."

"Yes. You notice he smashed all the mirrors in the houses, not just enough to get the pieces he wanted. He doesn't just put the shards in place for the damage they cause. They're set so he can see himself. In their eyes—Mrs. Jacobi and . . . What was the other name?"

"Mrs. Leeds."

"Yes."

"That's interesting," Graham said.

"It's not 'interesting.' You'd thought of that before."

"I had considered it."

"You just came here to look at me. Just to get the old scent again, didn't you? Why don't you just smell yourself?"

"I want your opinion."

"I don't have one right now."

"When you do have one, I'd like to hear it."

"May I keep the file?"

"I haven't decided yet," Graham said.

"Why are there no descriptions of the grounds? Here we have frontal views of the houses, floor plans, diagrams of the rooms where the deaths occurred, and little mention of the grounds. What were the yards like?"

"Big backyards, fenced, with some hedges. Why?"

"Because, my dear Will, if this pilgrim feels a special relationship with the moon, he might like to go outside and look at it. Before he tidies himself up, you understand. Have you seen blood in the moonlight, Will? It appears quite black. Of course, it keeps the distinctive sheen. If one were nude, say, it would be better to have outdoor privacy for that sort of thing. One must show some consideration for the neighbors, hmmmm?"

"You think the yard might be a factor when he selects victims?"

"Oh yes. And there will be more victims, of course. Let me keep the file, Will. I'll study it. When you get more files, I'd like to see them, too. You can call me. On the rare occasions when my lawyer calls, they bring me a telephone. They used to patch him through on the intercom, but everyone listened of course. Would you like to give me your home number?"

"No."

"Do you know how you caught me, Will?"

"Good-bye, Dr. Lecter. You can leave messages for me at the number on the file." Graham walked away.

"Do you know how you caught me?"

Graham was out of Lecter's sight now, and he walked faster toward the far steel door.

"The reason you caught me is that we're *just alike*" was the last thing Graham heard as the steel door closed behind him.

He was numb except for dreading the loss of numbness. Walking with his head down, speaking to no one, he could hear his blood like a hollow drumming of wings. It seemed a very short distance to the outside. This was only a building; there were only five doors between Lecter and the outside. He had the absurd feeling that Lecter had walked out with him. He stopped outside the entrance and looked around him, assuring himself that he was alone.

From a car across the street, his long lens propped on the window sill, Freddy Lounds got a nice profile shot of Graham in the doorway and the words in stone above him: "Chesapeake State Hospital for the Criminally Insane."

As it turned out, *The National Tattler* cropped the picture to just Graham's face and the last two words in the stone.

CHAPTER 8

DR. HANNIBAL LECTER lay on his cot with the cell lights down after Graham left him. Several hours passed.

For a while he had textures; the weave of the pillowcase against his hands clasped behind his head, the smooth membrane that lined his cheek.

Then he had odors and let his mind play over them. Some were real, some were not. They had put Clorox in the drains; semen. They were serving chili down the hall; sweat-stiffened khaki. Graham would not give him his home telephone number; the bitter green smell of cut cocklebur and teaweed.

Lecter sat up. The man might have been civil. His thoughts had the warm brass smell of an electric clock.

Lecter blinked several times, and his eyebrows rose. He turned up the lights and wrote a note to Chilton asking for a telephone to call his counsel.

Lecter was entitled by law to speak with his lawyer in privacy and he hadn't abused the right. Since Chilton would never allow him to go to the telephone, the telephone was brought to him.

Two guards brought it, unrolling a long cord from the telephone jack at their desk. One of the guards had the keys. The other held a can of Mace.

"Go to the back of the cell, Dr. Lecter. Face the wall. If you turn

75

around or approach the barrier before you hear the lock snap, I'll Mace you in the face. Understand?"

"Yes indeed," Lecter said. "Thank you so much for bringing the telephone."

He had to reach through the nylon net to dial. Chicago information gave him numbers for the University of Chicago Department of Psychiatry and Dr. Alan Bloom's office number. He dialed the psychiatry department switchboard.

"I'm trying to reach Dr. Alan Bloom."

"I'm not sure he's in today, but I'll connect you."

"Just a second, I'm supposed to know his secretary's name and I'm embarrassed to say I've forgotten it."

"Linda King. Just a moment."

"Thank you."

The telephone rang eight times before it was picked up.

"Linda King's desk."

"Hi, Linda?"

"Linda doesn't come in on Saturday."

Dr. Lecter had counted on that. "Maybe you could help me, if you don't mind. This is Bob Greer at Blaine and Edwards Publishing Company. Dr. Bloom asked me to send a copy of the Overholser book, *The Psychiatrist and the Law*, to Will Graham, and Linda was supposed to send me the address and phone number, but she never did."

"I'm just a graduate assistant, she'll be in on Mon—"

"I have to catch Federal Express with it in about five minutes, and I hate to bother Dr. Bloom about it at home because he told Linda to send it and I don't want to get her in hot water. It's right there in her Rolodex or whatever. I'll dance at your wedding if you'll read it to me."

"She doesn't have a Rolodex."

"How about a Call Caddy with the slide on the side?"

"Yes."

"Be a darling and slide that rascal and I won't take up any more of your time."

"What was the name?"

"Graham. Will Graham."

"All right, his home number is 305 JL5-7002."

"I'm supposed to mail it to his house."

"It doesn't give the address of his house."

"What does it have?"

"Federal Bureau of Investigation, Tenth and Pennsylvania, Washington, D.C. Oh, and Post Office Box 3680, Marathon, Florida."

"That's fine, you're an angel."

"You're welcome."

Lecter felt much better. He thought he might surprise Graham with a call sometime, or if the man couldn't be civil, he might have a hospital-supply house mail Graham a colostomy bag for old times' sake.

CHAPTER 9

SEVEN HUNDRED MILES to the southwest, in the cafeteria at Gateway Film Laboratory of St. Louis, Francis Dolarhyde was waiting for a hamburger. The entrées offered in the steam table were filmed over. He stood beside the cash register and sipped coffee from a paper cup.

A red-haired young woman wearing a laboratory smock came into the cafeteria and studied the candy machine. She looked at Francis Dolarhyde's back several times and pursed her lips. Finally she walked over to him and said, "Mr. D.?"

Dolarhyde turned. He always wore red goggles outside the darkroom. She kept her eyes on the nosepiece of the goggles.

"Will you sit down with me a minute? I want to tell you something."

"What can you tell me, Eileen?"

"That I'm really sorry. Bob was just really drunk and, you know, clowning around. He didn't mean anything. Please come sit down. Just for a minute. Will you do that?"

"Mmmm-hmmm." Dolarhyde never said "yes," as he had trouble with the sibilant /s/.

They sat. She twisted a napkin in her hands.

"Everybody was having a good time at the party and we were glad you came by," she said. "Real glad, and surprised, too. You know how Bob is, he does voices all the time—he ought to be on the radio. He did two or three accents, telling jokes and all—he can talk just like a Negro. When he did that other voice, he didn't mean to make you feel bad. He was too drunk to know who was there."

"They were all laughing and then they . . . didn't laugh." Dolarhyde never said "stopped" because of the fricative /s/.

"That's when Bob realized what he had done."

"He went on, though."

"I know it," she said, managing to look from her napkin to his goggles without lingering on the way. "I got on his case about it, too. He said he didn't mean anything, he just saw he was into it and tried to keep up the joke. You saw how red his face got."

"He invited me to . . . perform a duet with him."

"He hugged you and tried to put his arm around you. He wanted you to laugh it off, Mr. D."

"I've laughed it off, Eileen."

"Bob feels terrible."

"Well, I don't want him to feel terrible. I don't want that. Tell him for me. And it won't make it any different here at the plant. Golly, if I had talent like Bob I'd make jo . . . a joke all the time." Dolarhyde avoided plurals whenever he could. "We'll all get together before long and he'll know how I feel."

"Good, Mr. D. You know he's really, under all the fun, he's a sensitive guy."

"I'll bet. Tender, I imagine." Dolarhyde's voice was muffled by his hand. When seated, he always pressed the knuckle of his forefinger under his nose.

"Pardon?"

"I think you're good for him, Eileen."

"I think so, I really do. He's not drinking but just on weekends. He just starts to relax and his wife calls the house. He makes faces while I talk to her, but I can tell he's upset after. A woman knows." She tapped Dolarhyde on the wrist and, despite the goggles, saw the touch register in his eyes. "Take it easy, Mr. D. I'm glad we had this talk."

"I am too, Eileen."

Dolarhyde watched her walk away. She had a suck mark on the back of her knee. He thought, correctly, that Eileen did not appreciate him. No one did, actually.

The great darkroom was cool and smelled of chemicals. Francis Dolarhyde checked the developer in the A tank. Hundreds of feet of home-movie film from all over the country moved through the tank hourly. Temperature and freshness of the chemicals were critical. This was his responsibility, along with all the other operations until the film had passed through the dryer. Many times a day he lifted samples of film from the tank and checked them frame by frame. The darkroom was quiet. Dolarhyde discouraged chatter among his assistants and communicated with them largely in gestures.

When the evening shift ended, he remained alone in the darkroom to develop, dry, and splice some film of his own.

➤

Dolarhyde got home about ten P.M. He lived alone in a big house his grandparents had left him. It stood at the end of a gravel drive that runs through an apple orchard north of St. Charles, Missouri, across the Missouri River from St. Louis. The orchard's absentee owner did not take care of it. Dead and twisted trees stood among the green ones. Now, in late July, the smell of rotting apples hung over the orchard. There were many bees in the daytime. The nearest neighbor was a half-mile away.

Dolarhyde always made an inspection tour of the house as soon as he got home; there had been an abortive burglary attempt some years before. He flicked on the lights in each room and looked around. A visitor would not think he lived alone. His grandparents' clothes still hung in the closets, his grandmother's brushes were on her dresser with combings of hair in them. Her teeth were in a glass on the bedside table. The water had long since evaporated. His grandmother had been dead for ten years.

(The funeral director had asked him, "Mr. Dolarhyde, wouldn't you like to bring me your grandmother's teeth?" He replied, "Just drop the lid.")

Satisfied that he was alone in the house, Dolarhyde went upstairs, took a long shower, and washed his hair.

He put on a kimono of a synthetic material that felt like silk and lay down on his narrow bed in the room he had occupied since childhood. His grandmother's hair dryer had a plastic cap and hose.

He put on the cap and, while he dried, he thumbed through a new high-fashion magazine. The hatred and brutishness in some of the photographs were remarkable.

He began to feel excited. He swiveled the metal shade of his reading lamp to light a print on the wall at the foot of the bed. It was William Blake's *The Great Red Dragon and the Woman Clothed with the Sun.*

The picture had stunned him the first time he saw it. Never before had he seen anything that approached his graphic thought. He felt that Blake must have peeked in his ear and seen the Red Dragon. For weeks Dolarhyde had worried that his thoughts might glow out his ears, might be visible in the darkroom, might fog the film. He put cotton balls in his ears. Then, fearing that cotton was too flammable, he tried steel wool. That made his ears bleed. Finally he cut small pieces of asbestos cloth from an ironing-board cover and rolled them into little pills that would fit in his ears.

The Red Dragon was all he had for a long time. It was not all he had now. He felt the beginnings of an erection.

He had wanted to go through this slowly, but now he could not wait.

Dolarhyde closed the heavy draperies over windows in the downstairs parlor. He set up his screen and projector. His grandfather had put a La-Z-Boy recliner in the parlor, over his grandmother's objections. (She had put a doily on the headrest.) Now Dolarhyde was glad. It was very comfortable. He draped a towel over the arm of the chair.

He turned out the lamps. Lying back in the dark room, he might have been anywhere. Over the ceiling fixture he had a good light machine which rotated, making varicolored dots of light crawl over the walls, the floor, his skin. He might have been reclining on the acceleration couch of a space vehicle, in a glass bubble out among the stars. When he closed his eyes he thought he could feel the points of light move over him, and when he opened them, those might be the lights of cities above or beneath him. There was no more down or up. The light machine turned faster as it got warm, and the dots swarmed over him, flowed over furniture in angular streams, fell in meteor showers down the walls. He might have been a comet plunging through the Crab Nebula.

There was one place shielded from the light. He had placed a piece of cardboard near the machine, and it cast a shadow over the movie screen.

Sometimes, in the future, he would smoke first to heighten the effect, but he did not need it now, this time.

He thumbed the drop switch at his side to start the projector. A white rectangle sprang on the screen, grayed and streaked as the leader moved past the lens, and then the gray Scotty perked up his ears and ran to the kitchen door, shivering and wagging his stump of a tail. A cut to the Scotty running beside a curb, turning to snap at his side as he ran.

Now Mrs. Leeds came into the kitchen carrying groceries. She laughed and touched her hair. The children came in behind her.

A cut to a badly lit shot in Dolarhyde's own bedroom upstairs. He is standing nude before the print of *The Great Red Dragon and the Woman Clothed with the Sun*. He is wearing "combat glasses," the close-fitting wraparound plastic glasses favored by hockey players. He has an erection, which he improves with his hand.

The focus blurs as he approaches the camera with stylized movements, hand reaching to change the focus as his face fills the frame. The picture quivers and sharpens suddenly to a close-up of his mouth, his disfigured upper lip rolled back, tongue out through the teeth, one rolling eye still in the frame. The mouth fills the screen, writhing lips pulled back from jagged teeth and darkness as his mouth engulfs the lens.

The difficulty of the next part was evident.

A bouncing blur in a harsh movie light became a bed and Charles Leeds thrashing, Mrs. Leeds sitting up, shielding her eyes, turning to Leeds and putting her hands on him, rolling toward the edge of the bed, legs tangled in the covers, trying to rise. The camera jerked toward the ceiling, molding whipping across the screen like a stave, and then the picture steadied, Mrs. Leeds back down on the mattress, a dark spot on her nightdress spreading and Leeds, hands to his neck and eyes wild rising. The screen went black for five beats, then the tic of a splice.

The camera was steady now, on a tripod. They were all dead now. Arranged. Two children seated against the wall facing the bed, one seated across the corner from them facing the camera. Mr. and Mrs.

Leeds in bed with the covers over them. Mr. Leeds propped up against the headboard, the sheet covering the rope around his chest and his head lolled to the side.

Dolarhyde came into the picture from the left with the stylized movements of a Balinese dancer. Blood-smeared and naked except for his glasses and gloves, he mugged and capered among the dead. He approached the far side of the bed, Mrs. Leeds's side, took the corner of the covers, whipped them off the bed and held the pose as though he had executed a veronica.

Now, watching in the parlor of his grandparents' house, Dolarhyde was covered with a sheen of sweat. His thick tongue ran out constantly, the scar on his upper lip wet and shiny and he moaned as he stimulated himself.

Even at the height of his pleasure he was sorry to see that in the film's ensuing scene he lost all his grace and elegance of motion, rooting piglike with his bottom turned carelessly to the camera. There were no dramatic pauses, no sense of pace or climax, just brutish frenzy.

It was wonderful anyway. Watching the film was wonderful. But not as wonderful as the acts themselves.

Two major flaws, Dolarhyde felt, were that the film did not actually show the deaths of the Leedses and that his own performance was poor toward the end. He seemed to lose all his values. That was not how the Red Dragon would do it.

Well. He had many films to make and, with experience, he hoped he could maintain some aesthetic distance, even in the most intimate moments.

He must bear down. This was his life's work, a magnificent thing. It would live forever.

He must press on soon. He must select his fellow performers. Already he had copied several films of Fourth of July family outings. The end of summer always brought a rush of business at the film-processing plant as vacation movies came in. Thanksgiving would bring another rush.

Families were mailing their applications to him every day.

CHAPTER 10

THE PLANE from Washington to Birmingham was half-empty. Graham took a window seat with no one beside him.

He declined the tired sandwich the stewardess offered and put his Jacobi file on the tray table. At the front he had listed the similarities between the Jacobis and the Leedses.

Both couples were in their late thirties, both had children—two boys and a girl. Edward Jacobi had another son, by a previous marriage, who was away at college when the family was killed.

Both parents in each case had college degrees, and both families lived in two-story houses in pleasant suburbs. Mrs. Jacobi and Mrs. Leeds were attractive women. The families had some of the same credit cards and they subscribed to some of the same popular magazines.

There the similarities ended. Charles Leeds was a tax attorney, while Edward Jacobi was an engineer and metallurgist. The Atlanta family were Presbyterian; the Jacobis were Catholic. The Leedses were lifelong Atlanta residents, while the Jacobis had lived in Birmingham only three months, transferred there from Detroit.

The word "random" sounded in Graham's head like a dripping faucet. "Random selection of victims," "no apparent motive"—

84

newspapers used those terms, and detectives spat them out in anger and frustration in homicide squad rooms.

"Random" wasn't accurate, though. Graham knew that mass murderers and serial murderers do not select their victims at random.

The man who killed the Jacobis and the Leedses saw something in them that drew him and drove him to do it. He might have known them well—Graham hoped so—or he might not have known them at all. But Graham was sure the killer saw them at some time before he killed them. He chose them because *something* in them spoke to him, and the women were at the core of it. What was it?

There were some differences in the crimes.

Edward Jacobi was shot as he came down the stairs carrying a flashlight—probably he was awakened by a noise.

Mrs. Jacobi and her children were shot in the head, Mrs. Leeds in the abdomen. The weapon was a nine-millimeter automatic pistol in all the shootings. Traces of steel wool from a homemade silencer were found in the wounds. The cartridge cases bore no fingerprints.

The knife had been used only on Charles Leeds. Dr. Princi believed it was thin-bladed and very keen, possibly a fileting knife.

The methods of entry were different too; a patio door pried open at the Jacobis', the glass cutter at the Leedses'.

Photographs of the crime in Birmingham did not show the quantity of blood found at the Leedses', but there were stains on the bedroom walls about two and one-half feet above the floor. So the killer had an audience in Birmingham too. The Birmingham police checked the bodies for fingerprints, including the fingernails, and found nothing. Burial for a summer month in Birmingham would destroy any prints like the one on the Leeds child.

In both places were the same blond hairs, same spit, same semen.

Graham propped photographs of the two smiling families against the seat back in front of him and stared at them for a long time in the hanging quiet of the airplane.

What could have attracted the murderer specifically to *them?* Graham wanted very much to believe there was a common factor and that he would find it soon.

Otherwise he would have to enter more houses and see what the Tooth Fairy had left for him.

➤

Graham got directions from the Birmingham field office and checked in with the police by telephone from the airport. The compact car he rented spit water from the air-conditioner vents onto his hands and arms.

His first stop was the Geehan Realty office on Dennison Avenue.

Geehan, tall and bald, made haste across his turquoise shag to greet Graham. His smile faded when Graham showed his identification and asked for the key to the Jacobi house.

"Will there be some cops in uniform out there today?" he asked, his hand on the top of his head.

"I don't know."

"I hope to God not. I've got a chance to show it twice this afternoon. It's a nice house. People see it and they forget this other. Last Thursday I had a couple from Duluth, substantial retired people hot on the Sun Belt. I had them down to the short rows—talking mortgages—I mean that man could have fronted a *third,* when the squad car rode up and in they came. Couple asked them questions and, boy, did they get some answers. These good officers gave 'em the whole tour—who was laying where. Then it was Good-bye, Geehan, much oblige for your trouble. I try to show 'em how safe we've fixed it, but they don't listen. There they go, jake-legged through the gravel, climbing back in their Sedan de Ville."

"Have any single men asked to look at it?"

"They haven't asked me. It's a multiple listing. I don't think so, though. Police wouldn't let us start painting until, I don't know, we just got finished inside last Tuesday. Took two coats of interior latex, three in places. We're still working outside. It'll be a genuine showplace."

"How can you sell it before the estate's probated?"

"I can't *close* until probate, but that doesn't mean I can't be ready. People could move in on a memorandum of understanding. I need to do something. A business associate of mine is holding the paper, and that interest just works all day and all night while you're asleep."

"Who is Mr. Jacobi's executor?"

"Byron Metcalf, firm of Metcalf and Barnes. How long you figure on being out there?"

"I don't know. Until I've finished."

"You can drop that key in the mail. You don't have to come back by."

➤

Graham had the flat feeling of a cold trail as he drove out to the Jacobi house. It was barely within the city limits in an area newly annexed. He stopped beside the highway once to check his map before he found the turnoff onto an asphalt secondary road.

More than a month had passed since they were killed. What had he been doing then? Putting a pair of diesels in a sixty-five foot Rybovich hull, signaling to Ariaga in the crane to come down another half-inch. Molly came over in the late afternoon and he and Molly and Ariaga sat under an awning in the cockpit of the half-finished boat and ate the big prawns Molly brought and drank cold Dos Equis beer. Ariaga explained the best way to clean crayfish, drawing the tail fan in sawdust on the deck, and the sunlight, broken on the water, played on the undersides of the wheeling gulls.

Water from the air conditioner squirted on the front of Graham's shirt and he was in Birmingham now and there were no prawns or gulls. He was driving, and pastures and wooded lots were on his right with goats and horses in them, and on his left was Stonebridge, a long-established residential area with a few elegant homes and a number of rich people's houses.

He saw the realtor's sign a hundred yards before he reached it. The Jacobi house was the only one on the right side of the road. Sap from the pecan trees beside the drive had made the gravel sticky, and it rattled inside the fenders of the car. A carpenter on a ladder was installing window guards. The workman raised a hand to Graham as he walked around the house.

A flagged patio at the side was shaded by a large oak tree. At night the tree would block out the floodlight in the side yard as well. This was where the Tooth Fairy had entered, through sliding glass doors. The doors had been replaced with new ones, the aluminum frames still bright and bearing the manufacturer's sticker. Covering the sliding doors was a new wrought-iron security gate. The basement door was new too—flush steel and secured by deadbolts. The components of a hot tub stood in crates on the flagstones.

Graham went inside. Bare floors and dead air. His footsteps echoed in the empty house.

The new mirrors in the bathrooms had never reflected the Jacobis' faces or the killer's. On each was a fuzzy white spot where the price had been torn off. A folded dropcloth lay in a corner of the master bedroom. Graham sat on it long enough for the sunlight through the bare windows to move one board-width across the floor.

There was nothing here. Nothing anymore.

If he had come here immediately after the Jacobis were killed, would the Leedses still be alive? Graham wondered. He tested the weight of that burden.

It did not lift when he was out of the house and under the sky again.

Graham stood in the shade of a pecan tree, shoulders hunched, hands in his pockets, and looked down the long drive to the road that passed in front of the Jacobi house.

How had the Tooth Fairy come to the Jacobi house? He had to drive. Where did he park? The gravel driveway was too noisy for a midnight visit, Graham thought. The Birmingham police did not agree.

He walked down the drive to the roadside. The asphalt road was bordered with ditches as far as he could see. It might be possible to pull across the ditch and hide a vehicle in the brush on the Jacobis' side of the road if the ground were hard and dry.

Facing the Jacobi house across the road was the single entrance to Stonebridge. The sign said that Stonebridge had a private patrol service. A strange vehicle would be noticed there. So would a man walking late at night. Scratch parking in Stonebridge.

Graham went back into the house and was surprised to find the telephone working. He called the Weather Bureau and learned that three inches of rain fell on the day before the Jacobis were killed. The ditches were full, then. The Tooth Fairy did not hide his vehicle beside the asphalt road.

A horse in the pasture beside the yard kept pace with Graham as he walked along the whitewashed fence toward the rear of the property. He gave the horse a Life-Saver and left him at the corner as he turned along the back fence behind the outbuildings.

He stopped when he saw the depression in the ground where the Jacobi children had buried their cat. Thinking about it in the Atlanta police station with Springfield, he had pictured the outbuildings as white. Actually they were dark green.

The children had wrapped the cat in a dish towel and buried it in a shoebox with a flower between its paws.

Graham rested his forearm on top of the fence and leaned his forehead against it.

A pet funeral, solemn rite of childhood. Parents going back into the house, ashamed to pray. The children looking at one another, discovering new nerves in the place loss pierces. One bows her head, then they all do, the shovel taller than any of them. Afterward a discussion of whether or not the cat is in heaven with God and Jesus, and the children don't shout for a while.

A certainty came to Graham as he stood, sun hot on the back of his neck: as surely as the Tooth Fairy killed the cat, he had watched the children bury it. He had to see that if he possibly could.

He did not make two trips out here, one to kill the cat and the second for the Jacobis. He came and killed the cat and waited for the children to find it.

There was no way to determine exactly where the children found the cat. The police had located no one who spoke to the Jacobis after noon, ten hours or so before they died.

How had the Tooth Fairy come, and where had he waited?

Behind the back fence the brush began, running head-high for thirty yards to the trees. Graham dug his wrinkled map out of his back pocket and spread it on the fence. It showed an unbroken strip of woods a quarter-mile deep running across the back of the Jacobi property and continuing in both directions. Beyond the woods, bounding them on the south, was a section line road that paralleled the one in front of the Jacobi house.

Graham drove from the house back to the highway, measuring the distance on his odometer. He went south on the highway and turned onto the section line road he had seen on the map. Measuring again, he drove slowly along it until the odometer showed him he was behind the Jacobi house on the other side of the woods.

Here the pavement ended at a low-income housing project so new it did not show on his map. He pulled into the parking lot. Most of the cars were old and sagging on their springs. Two were up on blocks.

Black children played basketball on the bare earth around a single netless goal. Graham sat on his fender to watch the game for a moment.

He wanted to take off his jacket, but he knew the .44 Special and the flat camera on his belt would attract attention. He always felt a curious embarrassment when people looked at his pistol.

There were eight players on the team wearing shirts. The skins had eleven, all playing at once. Refereeing was by acclamation.

A small skin, shoved down in the rebounding, stalked home mad. He came back fortified with a cookie and dived into the pack again.

The yelling and the thump of the ball lifted Graham's spirits.

One goal, one basketball. It struck him again how many *things* the Leedses had. The Jacobis too, according to the Birmingham police when they ruled out burglary. Boats and sporting equipment, camping equipment, cameras and guns and rods. It was another thing the families had in common.

And with the thought of the Leedses and the Jacobis alive came the thought of how they were afterward, and Graham couldn't watch basketball anymore. He took a deep breath and headed for the dark woods across the road.

The underbrush, heavy at the edge of the pine woods, thinned when Graham reached the deep shade and he had easy going over the pine needles. The air was warm and still. Blue jays in the trees ahead announced his coming.

The ground sloped gently to a dry streambed where a few cypresses grew and the tracks of raccoons and field mice were pressed into the red clay. A number of human footprints marked the streambed, some of them left by children. All were caved in and rounded, left several rains ago.

Past the streambed the land rose again, changing to sandy loam that supported ferns beneath the pines. Graham worked his way uphill in the heat until he saw the light beneath the trees at the edge of the woods.

Between the trunks he could see the upper story of the Jacobi house.

Undergrowth again, head-high from the edge of the woods to the Jacobis' back fence. Graham worked his way through it and stood at the fence looking into the yard.

The Tooth Fairy could have parked at the housing development and come through the woods to the brush behind the house. He could have lured the cat into the brush and choked it, the body limp in one hand as he crawled on his knees and other hand to the fence. Graham could see the cat in the air, never twisting to land on its feet, but hitting on its back with a thump in the yard.

The Tooth Fairy did that in daylight—the children would not have found or buried the cat at night.

And he waited to see them find it. Did he wait for the rest of the day in the heat of the underbrush? At the fence he would be visible through the rails. In order to see the yard from farther back in the brush, he would have to stand and face the windows of the house with the sun beating on him. Clearly he would go back to the trees. So did Graham.

The Birmingham police were not stupid. He could see where they had pushed through the brush, searching the area as a matter of course. But that was before the cat was found. They were looking for clues, dropped objects, tracks—not for a vantage point.

He went a few yards into the forest behind the Jacobi house and worked back and forth in the dappled shade. First he took the high ground that afforded a partial view of the yard and then worked his way down the tree line.

He had searched for more than an hour when a wink of light from the ground caught his eye. He lost it, found it again. It was the ring-pull tab from a soft-drink can half-buried in the leaves beneath an elm tree, one of the few elms among the pines.

He spotted it from eight feet away and went no closer for five minutes while he scanned the ground around the tree. He squatted and brushed the leaves away ahead of him as he approached the tree, duck-walking in the path he made to avoid ruining any impressions. Working slowly, he cleared the leaves all around the trunk. No footprints had pressed through the mat of last year's leaves.

Near the aluminum tab he found a dried apple core eaten thin by ants. Birds had pecked out the seeds. He studied the ground for ten more minutes. Finally he sat on the ground, stretched out his aching legs, and leaned back against the tree.

A cone of gnats swarmed in a column of sunlight. A caterpillar rippled along the underside of a leaf.

There was a wedge of red creek mud from the instep of a boot on the limb above his head.

Graham hung his coat on a branch and began to climb carefully on the opposite side of the tree, peering around the trunk at the limbs above the wedge of mud. At thirty feet he looked around the trunk, and there was the Jacobi house 175 yards away. It looked different from this height, the roof color dominant. He could see the backyard and the ground behind the outbuildings very well. A decent pair of field glasses would pick up the expression on a face easily at this distance.

Graham could hear traffic in the distance, and far away he heard a beagle on a case. A cicada started its numbing bandsaw buzz and drowned out the other sounds.

A thick limb just above him joined the trunk at a right angle to the Jacobi house. He pulled himself up until he could see, and leaned around the trunk to look at it.

Close by his cheek a soft-drink can was wedged between the limb and the trunk.

"I love it," Graham whispered into the bark. "Oh, sweet Jesus, yes. Come on, can."

Still, a child might have left it.

He climbed higher on his side of the tree, dicey work on small branches, and moved around until he could look down on the big limb.

A patch of outer bark on the upper side of the limb was shaved away, leaving a field of green inner bark the size of a playing card. Centered in the green rectangle, carved through to the white wood, Graham saw this:

It was done carefully and cleanly with a very sharp knife. It was not the work of a child.

Graham photographed the mark, carefully bracketing his exposures.

The view from the big limb was good, and it had been improved: the stub of a small branch jutted down from the limb above. It had been clipped off to clear the view. The fibers were compressed and the end slightly flattened in the cutting.

Graham looked for the severed branch. If it had been on the ground, he would have seen it. There, tangled in the limbs below, brown withered leaves amid the green foliage.

The laboratory would need both sides of the cut in order to measure the pitch of the cutting edges. That meant coming back here with a saw. He made several photographs of the stub. All the while he mumbled to himself.

I think that after you killed the cat and threw it into the yard, my man, you climbed up here and waited. I think you watched the children and passed the time whittling and dreaming. When night came, you saw them passing their bright windows and you watched the shades go down, and you saw the lights go out one by one. And after a while you climbed down and went in to them. Didn't you? It wouldn't be too hard a climb straight down from the big limb with a flashlight and the bright moon rising.

It was a hard enough climb for Graham. He stuck a twig into the opening of the soft-drink can, gently lifted it from the crotch of the tree, and descended, holding the twig in his teeth when he had to use both hands.

Back at the housing project, Graham found that someone had written "Levon is a doo-doo head" in the dust on the side of his car. The height of the writing indicated that even the youngest residents were well along in literacy.

He wondered if they had written on the Tooth Fairy's car.

Graham sat for a few minutes looking up at the rows of windows. There appeared to be about a hundred units. It was possible that someone might remember a white stranger in the parking lot late at night. Even though a month had passed, it was well worth trying. To ask every resident, and get it done quickly, he would need the help of the Birmingham police.

He fought the temptation to send the drink can straight to Jimmy Price in Washington. He had to ask the Birmingham police for manpower. It would be better to give them what he had. Dusting the can would be a straightforward job. Trying for fingerprints etched by acid sweat was another matter. Price could still do it after Birmingham dusted, as long as the can wasn't handled with bare fingers. Better give it to the police. He knew the FBI document section would fall on the carving like a rabid mongoose. Pictures of that for everybody, nothing lost there.

He called Birmingham Homicide from the Jacobi house. The detectives arrived just as the realtor, Geehan, was ushering in his prospective buyers.

CHAPTER 11

EILEEN WAS READING a *National Tattler* article called "Filth in Your Bread!" when Dolarhyde came into the cafeteria. She had eaten only the filling in her tuna-salad sandwich.

Behind the red goggles Dolarhyde's eyes zigged down the front page of the *Tattler*. Cover lines in addition to "Filth in Your Bread!" included "Elvis at Secret Love Retreat—Exclusive Pix!!" "Stunning Breakthrough for Cancer Victims!" and the big banner line "Hannibal the Cannibal Helps Lawmen—Cops Consult Fiend in 'Tooth Fairy' Murders."

He stood at the window absently stirring his coffee until he heard Eileen get up. She dumped her tray in the trash container and was about to throw in the *Tattler* when Dolarhyde touched her shoulder.

"May I have that paper, Eileen?"

"Sure, Mr. D. I just get it for the horoscopes."

Dolarhyde read it in his office with the door closed.

Freddy Lounds had two bylines in the same double-page center spread. The main story was a breathless reconstruction of the Jacobi and Leeds murders. Since the police had not divulged many of the specifics, Lounds consulted his imagination for lurid details.

Dolarhyde found them banal.

The sidebar was more interesting:

Insane Fiend Consulted in Mass Murders
by Cop He Tried to Kill
by
Freddy Lounds

CHESAPEAKE, MD.—Federal manhunters, stymied in their search for the "Tooth Fairy," psychopathic slayer of entire families in Birmingham and Atlanta, have turned to the most savage killer in captivity for help.

Dr. Hannibal Lecter, whose unspeakable practices were reported in these pages three years ago, was consulted this week in his maximum-security-asylum cell by ace investigator William (Will) Graham.

Graham suffered a near-fatal slashing at Lecter's hands when he unmasked the mass murderer.

He was brought back from early retirement to spearhead the hunt for the "Tooth Fairy."

What went on in this bizarre meeting of two mortal enemies? What was Graham after?

"It takes one to catch one," a high federal official told this reporter. He was referring to Lecter, known as "Hannibal the Cannibal," who is both a psychiatrist and a mass murderer.

OR WAS HE REFERRING TO GRAHAM???

The *Tattler* has learned that Graham, former instructor in forensics at the FBI Academy in Quantico, Va., was once confined to a mental institution for a period of four weeks. . . .

Federal officials refused to say why they placed a man with a history of mental instability at the forefront of a desperate manhunt.

The nature of Graham's mental problem was not revealed, but one former psychiatric worker called it "deep depression."

Garmon Evans, a paraprofessional formerly employed at Bethesda Naval Hospital, said Graham was admitted to the psychiatric wing soon after he killed Garrett Jacob Hobbs, the "Minnesota Shrike." Graham shot Hobbs to death in 1975, ending Hobbs's eight-month reign of terror in Minneapolis.

Evans said Graham was withdrawn and refused to eat or speak during the first weeks of his stay.

Graham has never been an FBI agent. Veteran observers attribute this to the Bureau's strict screening procedures, designed to detect instability.

Federal sources would reveal only that Graham originally worked in the FBI crime laboratory and was assigned teaching duties at the FBI Academy after outstanding work both in the laboratory and in the field, where he served as a "special investigator."

The *Tattler* learned that before his federal service, Graham was in the homicide division of the New Orleans police department, a post he left to attend graduate school in forensics at George Washington University.

One New Orleans officer who served with Graham commented, "Well, you can call him retired, but the feds like to know he's around. It's like having a king snake under the house. They may not see him much, but it's nice to know he's there to eat the moccasins."

Dr. Lecter is confined for the rest of his life. If he is ever declared sane, he will have to stand trial on nine counts of first-degree murder.

Lecter's attorney says the mass murderer spends his time writing useful articles for the scientific journals and has an "ongoing dialogue" by mail with some of the most respected figures in psychiatry.

Dolarhyde stopped reading and looked at the pictures. There were two of them above the sidebar. One showed Lecter pinned against the side of a state trooper's car. The other was the picture of Will Graham taken by Freddy Lounds outside the Chesapeake State Hospital. A small photograph of Lounds ran beside each of his bylines.

Dolarhyde looked at the pictures for a long time. He ran the tip of his forefinger over them slowly, back and forth, his touch exquisitely sensitive to the rough newsprint. Ink left a smudge on his fingertip. He wet the smudge with his tongue and wiped it off on a Kleenex. Then he cut out the sidebar and put it in his pocket.

➤

On his way home from the plant, Dolarhyde bought toilet paper of the quick-dissolving kind used in boats and campers, and a nasal inhaler.

He felt good despite his hay fever; like many people who have undergone extensive rhinoplasty, Dolarhyde had no hair in his nose and hay fever plagued him. So did upper respiratory infections.

When a stalled truck held him up for ten minutes on the Missouri River bridge to St. Charles, he sat patiently. His black van was carpeted, cool and quiet. Handel's Water Music played on the stereo.

He rippled his fingers on the steering wheel in time with the music and dabbed at his nose.

Two women in a convertible were in the lane beside him. They wore shorts and blouses tied across the midriff. Dolarhyde looked down into the convertible from his van. They seemed tired and bored squinting into the lowering sun. The woman on the passenger side had her head against the seat back and her feet on the dash. Her slumped posture made two creases across her bare stomach. Dolarhyde could see a suck mark on the inside of her thigh. She caught him looking, sat up and crossed her legs. He saw weary distaste in her face.

She said something to the woman at the wheel. Both looked straight ahead. He knew they were talking about him. He was *so* glad it did not make him angry. Few things made him angry anymore. He knew that he was developing a becoming dignity.

The music was very pleasant.

The traffic in front of Dolarhyde began to move. The lane beside him was still stalled. He looked forward to getting home. He tapped the wheel in time with the music and rolled down the window with his other hand.

He hawked and spit a blob of green phlegm into the lap of the woman beside him, hitting her just beside the navel. Her curses sounded high and thin over the Handel as he drove away.

➤

Dolarhyde's great ledger was at least a hundred years old. Bound in black leather with brass corners, it was so heavy a sturdy machine table supported it in the locked closet at the top of the stairs. From the moment he saw it at the bankruptcy sale of an old St. Louis printing company, Dolarhyde knew it should be his.

Now, bathed and in his kimono, he unlocked the closet and rolled it out. When the book was centered beneath the painting of the Great

Red Dragon, he settled himself in a chair and opened it. The smell of foxed paper rose to his face.

Across the first page, in large letters he had illuminated himself, were the words from Revelation: "And There Came a Great Red Dragon Also . . ."

The first item in the book was the only one not neatly mounted. Loose between the pages was a yellowed photograph of Dolarhyde as a small child with his grandmother on the steps of the big house. He is holding to Grandmother's skirt. Her arms are folded and her back is straight.

Dolarhyde turned past it. He ignored it as though it had been left there by mistake.

There were many clippings in the ledger, the earliest ones about the disappearances of elderly women in St. Louis and Toledo. Pages between the clippings were covered with Dolarhyde's writing—black ink in a fine copperplate script not unlike William Blake's own handwriting.

Fastened in the margins, ragged bites of scalp trailed their tails of hair like comets pressed in God's scrapbook.

The Jacobi clippings from Birmingham were there, along with film cartridges and slides set in pockets glued to the pages.

So were stories on the Leedses, with film beside them.

The term "Tooth Fairy" had not appeared in the press until Atlanta. The name was marked out in all the Leeds stories.

Now Dolarhyde did the same with his *Tattler* clipping, obliterating "Tooth Fairy" with angry slashes of a red marker pen.

He turned to a new, blank page in his ledger and trimmed the *Tattler* clipping to fit. Should Graham's picture go in? The words "Criminally Insane" carved in the stone above Graham offended Dolarhyde. He hated the sight of any place of confinement. Graham's face was closed to him. He set it aside for the time being.

But Lecter . . . Lecter. This was not a good picture of the doctor. Dolarhyde had a better one, which he fetched from a box in his closet. It was published upon Lecter's committal and showed the fine eyes. Still, it was not satisfactory. In Dolarhyde's mind, Lecter's likeness should be the dark portrait of a Renaissance prince. For Lecter, alone among all men, might have the sensitivity and experience to understand the glory, the majesty of Dolarhyde's Becoming.

Dolarhyde felt that Lecter knew the unreality of the people who die to help you in these things—understood that they are not flesh, but light and air and color and quick sounds quickly ended when you change them. Like balloons of color bursting. That they are more important for the changing, more important than the lives they scrabble after, pleading.

Dolarhyde bore screams as a sculptor bears dust from the beaten stone.

Lecter was capable of understanding that blood and breath were only elements undergoing change to fuel his Radiance. Just as the source of light is burning.

He would like to meet Lecter, talk and share with him, rejoice with him in their shared vision, be recognized by him as John the Baptist recognized the One who came after, sit on him as the Dragon sat on 666 in Blake's Revelation series, and film his death as, dying, he melded with the strength of the Dragon.

Dolarhyde pulled on a new pair of rubber gloves and went to his desk. He unrolled and discarded the outer layer of the toilet paper he had bought. Then he unrolled a strip of seven sheets and tore it off.

Printing carefully on the tissue with his left hand, he wrote a letter to Lecter.

Speech is never a reliable indicator of how a person writes; you never know. Dolarhyde's speech was bent and pruned by disabilities real and imagined, and the difference between his speech and his writing was startling. Still, he found he could not say the most important things he felt.

He wanted to hear from Lecter. He needed a personal response before he could tell Dr. Lecter the important things.

How could he manage that? He rummaged through his box of Lecter clippings, read them all again.

Finally a simple way occurred to him and he wrote again.

The letter seemed too diffident and shy when he read it over. He had signed it "Avid Fan."

He brooded over the signature for several minutes.

"Avid Fan" indeed. His chin rose an imperious fraction.

He put his gloved thumb in his mouth, removed his dentures, and placed them on the blotter.

The upper plate was unusual. The teeth were normal, straight and white, but the pink acrylic upper part was a tortuous shape cast to fit the twists and fissures of his gums. Attached to the plate was a soft plastic prosthesis with an obturator on top, which helped him close off his soft palate in speech.

He took a small case from his desk. It held another set of teeth. The upper casting was the same, but there was no prosthesis. The crooked teeth had dark stains between them and gave off a faint stench.

They were identical to Grandmother's teeth in the bedside glass downstairs.

Dolarhyde's nostrils flared at the odor. He opened his sunken smile and put them in place and wet them with his tongue.

He folded the letter across the signature and bit down hard on it. When he opened the letter again, the signature was enclosed in an oval bite mark; his notary seal, an imprimatur flecked with old blood.

CHAPTER 12

ATTORNEY BYRON METCALF took off his tie at five o'clock, made himself a drink, and put his feet up on his desk.

"Sure you won't have one?"

"Another time." Graham, picking the cockleburs off his cuffs, was grateful for the air conditioning.

"I didn't know the Jacobis very well," Metcalf said. "They'd only been here three months. My wife and I were there for drinks a couple of times. Ed Jacobi came to me for a new will soon after he was transferred here, that's how I met him."

"But you're his executor."

"Yes. His wife was listed first as executor, then me as alternate in case she was deceased or infirm. He has a brother in Philadelphia, but I gather they weren't close."

"You were an assistant district attorney."

"Yeah, 1968 to '72. I ran for DA in '72. It was close, but I lost. I'm not sorry now."

"How do you see what happened here, Mr. Metcalf?"

"The first thing I thought about was Joseph Yablonski, the labor leader?"

Graham nodded.

"A crime with a motive, power in that case, disguised as an insane

101

attack. We went over Ed Jacobi's papers with a fine-tooth comb—
Jerry Estridge from the DA's office and I.

"Nothing. Nobody stood to make much money off Ed Jacobi's
death. He made a big salary and he had some patents paying off, but
he spent it almost as fast as it came in. Everything was to go to the
wife, with a little land in California entailed to the kids and their
descendants. He had a small spendthrift trust set up for the surviving
son. It'll pay his way through three more years of college. I'm sure
he'll still be a freshman by then."

"Niles Jacobi."

"Yeah. The kid gave Ed a big pain in the ass. He lived with his
mother in California. Went to Chino for theft. I gather his mother's a
flake. Ed went out there to see about him last year. Brought him back
to Birmingham and put him in school at Bardwell Community
College. Tried to keep him at home, but he dumped on the other kids
and made it unpleasant for everybody. Mrs. Jacobi put up with it for a
while, but finally they moved him to a dorm."

"Where was he?"

"On the night of June 28?" Metcalf's eyes were hooded as he
looked at Graham. "The police wondered about that, and so did I. He
went to a movie and then back to school. It's verified. Besides, he has
type-O blood. Mr. Graham, I have to pick up my wife in half an
hour. We can talk tomorrow if you like. Tell me how I can help you."

"I'd like to see the Jacobis' personal effects. Diaries, pictures,
whatever."

"There's not much of that—they lost about everything in a fire in
Detroit before they moved down here. Nothing suspicious—Ed was
welding in the basement and the sparks got into some paint he had
stored down there and the house went up.

"There's some personal correspondence. I have it in the lockboxes
with the small valuables. I don't remember any diaries. Everything
else is in storage. Niles may have some pictures, but I doubt it. Tell
you what—I'm going to court at nine-thirty in the morning, but I
could get you into the bank to look at the stuff and come back by for
you afterward."

"Fine," Graham said. "One other thing. I could use copies of
everything to do with the probate: claims against the estate, any
contest of the will, correspondence. I'd like to have all the paper."

"The Atlanta DA's office asked me for that already. They're comparing with the Leeds estate in Atlanta, I know," Metcalf said.

"Still, I'd like copies for myself."

"Okay, copies to you. You don't really think it's money, though, do you?"

"No. I just keep hoping the same name will come up here and in Atlanta."

"So do I."

≻

Student housing at Bardwell Community College was four small dormitory buildings set around a littered quadrangle of beaten earth. A stereo war was in progress when Graham got there.

Opposing sets of speakers on the motel-style balconies blared at each other across the quad. It was Kiss versus the *1812 Overture*. A water balloon arched high in the air and burst on the ground ten feet from Graham.

He ducked under a clothesline and stepped over a bicycle to get through the sitting room of the suite Niles Jacobi shared. The door to Jacobi's bedroom was ajar and music blasted through the crack. Graham knocked.

No response.

He pushed open the door. A tall boy with a spotty face sat on one of the twin beds sucking on a four-foot bong pipe. A girl in dungarees lay on the other bed.

The boy's head jerked around to face Graham. He was struggling to think.

"I'm looking for Niles Jacobi."

The boy appeared stupefied. Graham switched off the stereo.

"I'm looking for Niles Jacobi."

"Just some stuff for my asthma, man. Don't you ever knock?"

"Where's Niles Jacobi?"

"Fuck if I know. What do you want him for?"

Graham showed him the tin. "Try real hard to remember."

"Oh, shit," the girl said.

"Narc, goddammit. I ain't worth it, look, let's talk about this a minute, man."

"Let's talk about where Jacobi is."

"I think I can find out for you," the girl said.

Graham waited while she asked in the other rooms. Everywhere she went, commodes flushed.

There were few traces of Niles Jacobi in the room—one photograph of the Jacobi family lay on a dresser. Graham lifted a glass of melting ice off it and wiped away the wet ring with his sleeve.

The girl returned. "Try the Hateful Snake," she said.

➢

The Hateful Snake bar was in a storefront with the windows painted dark green. The vehicles parked outside were an odd assortment, big trucks looking bobtailed without their trailers, compact cars, a lilac convertible, old Dodges and Chevrolets crippled with high rear ends for the drag-strip look, four full-dress Harley-Davidsons.

An air conditioner, mounted in the transom over the door, dripped steadily onto the sidewalk.

Graham ducked around the dribble and went inside.

The place was crowded and smelled of disinfectant and stale Canoe. The bartender, a husky woman in overalls, reached over heads at the service bar to hand Graham his Coke. She was the only woman there.

Niles Jacobi, dark and razor-thin, was at the jukebox. He put the money in the machine, but the man beside him pushed the buttons.

Jacobi looked like a dissolute schoolboy, but the one selecting the music did not.

Jacobi's companion was a strange mixture; he had a boyish face on a knobby, muscular body. He wore a T-shirt and jeans, worn white over the objects in his pockets. His arms were knotty with muscle, and he had large, ugly hands. One professional tattoo on his left forearm said "Born to Fuck." A crude jailhouse tattoo on his other arm said "Randy." His short jail haircut had grown out unevenly. As he reached for a button on the lighted jukebox, Graham saw a small shaved patch on his forearm.

Graham felt a cold place in his stomach.

He followed Niles Jacobi and "Randy" through the crowd to the back of the room. They sat in a booth.

Graham stopped two feet from the table.

"Niles, my name is Will Graham. I need to talk with you for a few minutes."

Randy looked up with a bright false smile. One of his front teeth was dead. "Do I know you?"

"No. Niles, I want to talk to you."

Niles arched a quizzical eyebrow. Graham wondered what had happened to him in Chino.

"We were having a private conversation here. Butt out," Randy said.

Graham looked thoughtfully at the marred muscular forearms, the dot of adhesive in the crook of the elbow, the shaved patch where Randy had tested the edge of his knife. Knife fighter's mange.

I'm afraid of Randy. Fire or fall back.

"Did you hear me?" Randy said. "Butt out."

Graham unbuttoned his jacket and put his identification on the table.

"Sit still, Randy. If you try to get up, you're gonna have two navels."

"I'm sorry, sir." Instant inmate sincerity.

"Randy, I want you to do something for me. I want you to reach in your left back pocket. Just use two fingers. You'll find a five-inch knife in there with a Flicket clamped to the blade. Put it on the table. . . . Thank you."

Graham dropped the knife into his pocket. It felt greasy.

"Now, in your other pocket is your wallet. Get it out. You sold some blood today, didn't you?"

"So what?"

"So hand me the slip they gave you, the one you show next time at the blood bank. Spread it out on the table."

Randy had type-O blood. Scratch Randy.

"How long have you been out of jail?"

"Three weeks."

"Who's your parole officer?"

"I'm not on parole."

"That's probably a lie." Graham wanted to roust Randy. He could get him for carrying a knife over the legal length. Being in a place with a liquor license was a parole violation. Graham knew he was angry at Randy because he had feared him.

"Randy."

"Yeah."

"Get out."

➤

"I don't know what I can tell you, I didn't know my father very well," Niles Jacobi said as Graham drove him to the school. "He left Mother when I was three, and I didn't see him after that—Mother wouldn't *have* it."

"He came to see you last spring."

"Yes."

"At Chino."

"You know about that."

"I'm just trying to get it straight. What happened?"

"Well, there he was in Visitors, uptight and trying not to look around—so many people treat it like the *zoo*. I'd heard a lot about him from Mother, but he didn't look so bad. He was just a man standing there in a tacky sport coat."

"What did he say?"

"Well, I *expected* him either to jump right in my shit or to be real guilty, that's the way it goes mostly in Visitors. But he just asked me if I thought I could go to school. He said he'd go custody if I'd go to school. And try. 'You have to help *yourself* a little. Try and help yourself, and I'll see you get in school,' and like that."

"How long before you got out?"

"Two weeks."

"Niles, did you ever talk about your family while you were in Chino? To your cellmates or anybody?"

Niles Jacobi looked at Graham quickly. "Oh. Oh, I see. No. Not about my *father*. I hadn't *thought* about him in years, why would I talk about him?"

"How about here? Did you ever take any of your friends over to your parents' house?"

"*Parent,* not parents. She was not my mother."

"Did you ever take anybody over there? School friends or . . ."

"Or rough trade, Officer Graham?"

"That's right."

"No."

"Never?"

"Not once."

"Did he ever mention any kind of threat, was he ever disturbed about anything in the last month or two before it happened?"

"He was disturbed the last time I talked to him, but it was just my grades. I had a lot of cuts. He bought me two alarm clocks. There wasn't anything else that I know of."

"Do you have any personal papers of his, correspondence, photographs, anything?"

"No."

"You have a picture of the family. It's on the dresser in your room. Near the bong."

"That's not my bong. I wouldn't put that filthy thing in my mouth."

"I need the picture. I'll have it copied and send it back to you. What else do you have?"

Jacobi shook a cigarette out of his pack and patted his pockets for matches. "That's all. I can't imagine why they gave *that* to me. My father smiling at *Mrs.* Jacobi and all the little Munchkins. You can have it. He never looked like that to me."

➤

Graham needed to know the Jacobis. Their new acquaintances in Birmingham were little help.

Byron Metcalf gave him the run of the lockboxes. He read the thin stack of letters, mostly business, and poked through the jewelry and the silver.

For three hot days he worked in the warehouse where the Jacobis' household goods were stored. Metcalf helped him at night. Every crate on every pallet was opened and their contents examined. Police photographs helped Graham see where things had been in the house.

Most of the furnishings were new, bought with the insurance from the Detroit fire. The Jacobis hardly had time to leave their marks on their possessions.

One item, a bedside table with traces of fingerprint powder still on it, held Graham's attention. In the center of the tabletop was a blob of green wax.

For the second time he wondered if the killer liked candlelight.

The Birmingham forensics unit was good about sharing.

The blurred print of the end of a nose was the best Birmingham and Jimmy Price in Washington could do with the soft-drink can from the tree.

The FBI laboratory's Firearms and Toolmarks section reported on the severed branch. The blades that clipped it were thick, with a shallow pitch: it had been done with a bolt cutter.

Document section had referred the mark cut in the bark to the Asian Studies department at Langley.

Graham sat on a packing case at the warehouse and read the long report. Asian Studies advised that the mark was a Chinese character which meant "You hit it" or "You hit it on the head"—an expression sometimes used in gambling. It was considered a "positive" or "lucky" sign. The character also appeared on a Mah-Jongg piece, the Asian scholars said. It marked the Red Dragon.

CHAPTER 13

CRAWFORD at FBI headquarters in Washington was on the telephone with Graham at the Birmingham airport when his secretary leaned into the office and flagged his attention.

"Dr. Chilton at Chesapeake Hospital on 2706. He says it's urgent."

Crawford nodded. "Hang on, Will." He punched the telephone. "Crawford."

"Frederick Chilton, Mr. Crawford, at the—"

"Yes, Doctor."

"I have a note here, or two pieces of a note, that appears to be from the man who killed those people in Atlanta and—"

"Where did you get it?"

"From Hannibal Lecter's cell. It's written on toilet tissue, of all things, and it has teeth marks pressed in it."

"Can you read it to me without handling it any more?"

Straining to sound calm, Chilton read it:

My dear Dr. Lecter,
    I wanted to tell you I'm delighted that you have taken an interest in me. And when I learned of your vast correspondence I thought *Dare I?* Of course I do. I don't believe you'd tell them who I am,

even if you knew. Besides, what particular body I currently occupy is trivia.

The important thing is what I am *Becoming*. I know that you alone can understand this. I have some things I'd love to show you. Someday, perhaps, if circumstances permit. I hope we can correspond . . .

"Mr. Crawford, there's a hole torn and punched out. Then it says:

I have admired you for *years* and have a complete collection of your press notices. Actually, I think of them as unfair reviews. As unfair as mine. They like to sling demeaning nicknames, don't they? The *Tooth Fairy*. What could be more inappropriate? It would shame me for you to see that if I didn't know you had suffered the same distortions in the press.

Investigator Graham interests me. Odd-looking for a flatfoot, isn't he? Not very handsome, but purposeful-looking.

You should have taught him not to meddle.

Forgive the stationery. I chose it because it will dissolve very quickly if you should have to swallow it.

"There's a piece missing here, Mr. Crawford. I'll read the bottom part:

If I hear from you, next time I might send you something wet. Until then I remain your

Avid Fan

Silence after Chilton finished reading. "Are you there?"

"Yes. Does Lecter know you have the note?"

"Not yet. This morning he was moved to a holding cell while his quarters were cleaned. Instead of using a proper rag, the cleaning man was pulling handfuls of toilet paper off the roll to wipe down the sink. He found the note wound up in the roll and brought it to me. They bring me anything they find hidden."

"Where's Lecter now?"

"Still in the holding cell."

"Can he see his quarters at all from there?"

"Let me think. . . . No, no, he can't."

"Wait a second, Doctor." Crawford put Chilton on hold. He stared at the two winking buttons on his telephone for several seconds without seeing them. Crawford, fisher of men, was watching his cork move against the current. He got Graham again.

"Will . . . a note, maybe from the Tooth Fairy, hidden in Lecter's cell at Chesapeake. Sounds like a fan letter. He wants Lecter's approval, he's curious about you. He's asking questions."

"How was Lecter supposed to answer?"

"Don't know yet. Part's torn out, part's scratched out. Looks like there's a chance of correspondence as long as Lecter's not aware that we know. I want the note for the lab and I want to toss his cell, but it'll be risky. If Lecter gets wise, who knows how he could warn the bastard? We need the link but we need the note too."

Crawford told Graham where Lecter was held, how the note was found. "It's eighty miles over to Chesapeake. I can't wait for you, buddy. What do you think?"

"Ten people dead in a month—we can't play a long mail game. I say go for it."

"I am," Crawford said.

"See you in two hours."

Crawford hailed his secretary. "Sarah, order a helicopter. I want the next thing smoking and I don't care whose it is—ours, DCPD or Marines. I'll be on the roof in five minutes. Call Documents, tell them to have a document case up there. Tell Herbert to scramble a search team. On the roof. Five minutes."

He picked up Chilton's line.

"Dr. Chilton, we have to search Lecter's cell without his knowledge and we need your help. Have you mentioned this to anybody else?"

"No."

"Where's the cleaning man who found the note?"

"He's here in my office."

"Keep him there, please, and tell him to keep quiet. How long has Lecter been out of his cell?"

"About half an hour."

"Is that unusually long?"

"No, not yet. But it takes only about a half-hour to clean it. Soon he'll begin to wonder what's wrong."

"Okay, do this for me: Call your building superintendent or engineer, whoever's in charge. Tell him to shut off the water in the building and to pull the circuit breakers on Lecter's hall. Have the super walk down the hall past the holding cell carrying tools. He'll be in a hurry, pissed off, too busy to answer any questions—got it? Tell him he'll get an explanation from me. Have the garbage pickup canceled for today if they haven't already come. Don't touch the note, okay? We're coming."

Crawford called the section chief, Scientific Analysis. "Brian, I have a note coming in on the fly, possibly from the Tooth Fairy. Number-one priority. It has to go back where it came from within the hour and unmarked. It'll go to Hair and Fiber, Latent Prints, and Documents, then to you, so coordinate with them, will you? . . . Yes. I'll walk it through. I'll deliver it to you myself."

➤

It was warm—the federally mandated eighty degrees—in the elevator when Crawford came down from the roof with the note, his hair blown silly by the helicopter blast. He was mopping his face by the time he reached the Hair and Fiber section of the laboratory.

Hair and Fiber is a small section, calm and busy. The common room is stacked with boxes of evidence sent by police departments all over the country; swatches of tape that have sealed mouths and bound wrists, torn and stained clothing, deathbed sheets.

Crawford spotted Beverly Katz through the window of an examining room as he wove his way between the boxes. She had a pair of child's coveralls suspended from a hanger over a table covered with white paper. Working under bright lights in the draft-free room, she brushed the overalls with a metal spatula, carefully working with the wale and across it, with the nap and against it. A sprinkle of dirt and sand fell to the paper. With it, falling through the still air more slowly than sand but faster than lint, came a tightly coiled hair. She cocked her head and looked at it with her bright robin's eye.

Crawford could see her lips moving. He knew what she was saying. "Gotcha."

That's what she always said.

Crawford pecked on the glass and she came out fast, stripping off her white gloves.

"It hasn't been printed yet, right?"

"No."

"I'm set up in the next examining room." She put on a fresh pair of gloves while Crawford opened the document case.

The note, in two pieces, was contained gently between two sheets of plastic film. Beverly Katz saw the tooth impressions and glanced up at Crawford, not wasting time with the question.

He nodded: the impressions matched the clear overlay of the killer's bite he had carried with him to Chesapeake.

Crawford watched through the window as she lifted the note on a slender dowel and hung it over white paper. She looked it over with a powerful glass, then fanned it gently. She tapped the dowel with the edge of a spatula and went over the paper beneath it with the magnifying glass.

Crawford looked at his watch.

Katz flipped the note over another dowel to get the reverse side up. She removed one tiny object from its surface with tweezers almost as fine as a hair.

She photographed the torn ends of the note under high magnification and returned it to its case. She put a clean pair of white gloves in the case with it. The white gloves—the signal not to touch—would always be beside the evidence until it was checked for fingerprints.

"That's it," she said, handing the case back to Crawford. "One hair, maybe a thirty-second of an inch. A couple of blue grains. I'll work it up. What else have you got?"

Crawford gave her three marked envelopes. "Hair from Lecter's comb. Whiskers from the electric razor they let him use. This is hair from the cleaning man. Gotta go."

"See you later," Katz said. "Love *your* hair."

≻

Jimmy Price in Latent Fingerprints winced at the sight of the porous toilet paper. He squinted fiercely over the shoulder of his technician operating the helium-cadmium laser as they tried to find a fingerprint and make it fluoresce. Glowing smudges appeared on the paper, perspiration stains, nothing.

Crawford started to ask him a question, thought better of it, waited with the blue light reflecting off his glasses.

"We know three guys handled this without gloves, right?" Price said.

"Yeah, the cleanup man, Lecter, and Chilton."

"The fellow scrubbing sinks probably had washed the oil off his fingers. But the others—this stuff is terrible." Price held the paper to the light, forceps steady in his mottled old hand. "I could fume it, Jack, but I couldn't guarantee the iodine stains would fade out in the time you've got."

"Ninhydrin? Boost it with heat?" Ordinarily, Crawford would not have ventured a technical suggestion to Price, but he was floundering for anything. He expected a huffy reply, but the old man sounded rueful and sad.

"No. We couldn't wash it after. I can't get you a print off this, Jack. There isn't one."

"Fuck," Crawford said.

The old man turned away. Crawford put his hand on Price's bony shoulder. "Hell, Jimmy. If there was one, you'd have found it."

Price didn't answer. He was unpacking a pair of hands that had arrived in another matter. Dry ice smoked in his wastebasket. Crawford dropped the white gloves into the smoke.

➤

Disappointment growling in his stomach, Crawford hurried on to Documents where Lloyd Bowman was waiting. Bowman had been called out of court and the abrupt shear in his concentration left him blinking like a man just wakened.

"I congratulate you on your hairstyle. A brave departure," Bowman said, his hands quick and careful as he transferred the note to his work surface. "How long do I have?"

"Twenty minutes max."

The two pieces of the note seemed to glow under Bowman's lights. His blotter showed dark green through a jagged oblong hole in the upper piece.

"The main thing, the first thing, is how Lecter was to reply," Crawford said when Bowman had finished reading.

"Instructions for answering were probably in the part torn out."

Bowman worked steadily with his lights and filters and copy camera as he talked. "Here in the top piece he says 'I hope we can correspond . . .' and then the hole begins. Lecter scratched over that with a felt-tip pen and then folded it and pinched most of it out."

"He doesn't have anything to cut with."

Bowman photographed the tooth impressions and the back of the note under extremely oblique light, his shadow leaping from wall to wall as he moved the light through 360 degrees around the paper and his hands made phantom folding motions in the air.

"Now we can mash just a little." Bowman put the note between two panes of glass to flatten the jagged edges of the hole. The tatters were smeared with vermilion ink. He was chanting under his breath. On the third repetition Crawford made out what he was saying. "You're so sly, but so am I."

Bowman switched filters on his small television camera and focused it on the note. He darkened the room until there was only the dull red glow of a lamp and the blue-green of his monitor screen.

The words "I hope we can correspond" and the jagged hole appeared enlarged on the screen. The ink smear was gone, and on the tattered edges appeared fragments of writing.

"Aniline dyes in colored inks are transparent to infrared," Bowman said. "These could be the tips of T's here and here. On the end is the tail of what could be an M or N, or possibly an R." Bowman took a photograph and turned the lights on. "Jack, there are just two common ways of carrying on a communication that's one-way blind—the phone and publication. Could Lecter take a fast phone call?"

"He can take calls, but it's slow and they have to come in through the hospital switchboard."

"Publication is the only safe way, then."

"We know this sweetheart reads the *Tattler*. The stuff about Graham and Lecter was in the *Tattler*. I don't know of any other paper that carried it."

"Three T's and an R in *Tattler*. Personal column, you think? It's a place to look."

Crawford checked with the FBI library, then telephoned instructions to the Chicago field office.

Bowman handed him the case as he finished.

"The *Tattler* comes out this evening," Crawford said. "It's printed in Chicago on Mondays and Thursdays. We'll get proofs of the classified pages."

"I'll have some more stuff—minor, I think," Bowman said.

"Anything useful, fire it straight to Chicago. Fill me in when I get back from the asylum," Crawford said on his way out the door.

CHAPTER 14

THE TURNSTILE at Washington's Metro Central spit Graham's fare card back to him and he came out into the hot afternoon carrying his flight bag.

The J. Edgar Hoover Building looked like a great concrete cage above the heat shimmer on Tenth Street. The FBI's move to the new headquarters had been under way when Graham left Washington. He had never worked there.

Crawford met him at the escort desk off the underground driveway to augment Graham's hastily issued credentials with his own. Graham looked tired and he was impatient with the signing-in. Crawford wondered how he felt, knowing that the killer was thinking about him.

Graham was issued a magnetically encoded tag like the one on Crawford's vest. He plugged it into the gate and passed into the long white corridors. Crawford carried his flight bag.

"I forgot to tell Sarah to send a car for you."

"Probably quicker this way. Did you get the note back to Lecter all right?"

"Yeah," Crawford said. "I just got back. We poured water on the hall floor. Faked a broken pipe and electrical short. We had Simmons—he's the assistant SAC Baltimore now—we had him mopping when Lecter was brought back to his cell. Simmons thinks he bought it."

"I kept wondering on the plane if Lecter wrote it himself."

"That bothered me too until I looked at it. Bite mark in the paper matches the ones on the women. Also it's ball-point, which Lecter doesn't have. The person who wrote it had read the *Tattler,* and Lecter hasn't had a *Tattler.* Rankin and Willingham tossed the cell. Beautiful job, but they didn't find diddly. They took Polaroids first to get everything back just right. Then the cleaning man went in and did what he always does."

"So what do you think?"

"As far as physical evidence toward an ID, the note is pretty much dreck," Crawford said. "Some way we've got to make the contact work for us, but damn if I know how yet. We'll get the rest of the lab results in a few minutes."

"You've got the mail and phone covered at the hospital?"

"Standing trace-and-tape order for any time Lecter's on the phone. He made a call Saturday afternoon. He told Chilton he was calling his lawyer. It's a damn WATS line, and I can't be sure."

"What did his lawyer say?"

"Nothing. We got a leased line to the hospital switchboard for Lecter's convenience in the future, so that won't get by us again. We'll fiddle with his mail both ways, starting next delivery. No problem with warrants, thank God."

Crawford bellied up to a door and stuck the tag on his vest into the lock slot. "My new office. Come on in. Decorator had some paint left over from a battleship he was doing. Here's the note. This print is exactly the size."

Graham read it twice. Seeing the spidery lines spell his name started a high tone ringing in his head.

"The library confirms the *Tattler* is the only paper that carried a story about Lecter and you," Crawford said, fixing himself an Alka-Seltzer. "Want one of these? Good for you. It was published Monday night a week ago. It was on the stands Tuesday nationwide—some areas not till Wednesday—Alaska and Maine and places. The Tooth Fairy got one—couldn't have done it before Tuesday. He reads it, writes to Lecter. Rankin and Willingham are still sifting the hospital trash for the envelope. Bad job. They don't separate the papers from the diapers at Chesapeake.

"All right, Lecter gets the note from the Tooth Fairy no sooner than Wednesday. He tears out the part about how to reply and scratches over and pokes out one earlier reference—I don't know why he didn't tear that out too."

"It was in the middle of a paragraph full of compliments," Graham said. "He couldn't stand to ruin them. That's why he didn't throw the whole thing away." He rubbed his temples with his knuckles.

"Bowman thinks Lecter will use the *Tattler* to answer The Tooth Fairy. He says that's probably the setup. You think he'd answer this thing?"

"Sure. He's a great correspondent. Pen pals all over."

"If they're using the *Tattler*, Lecter would barely have time to get his answer in the issue they'll print tonight, even if he sent it special delivery to the paper the same day he got the Tooth Fairy's note. Chester from the Chicago office is down at the *Tattler* checking the ads. The printers are putting the paper together right now."

"Please God don't stir the *Tattler* up," Graham said.

"The shop foreman thinks Chester's a realtor trying to get a jump on the ads. He's selling him the proof sheets under the table, one by one as they come off. We're getting everything, all the classifieds, just to blow some smoke. All right, say we find out how Lecter was to answer and we can duplicate the method. Then we can fake a message to the Tooth Fairy—but what do we say? How do we use it?"

"The obvious thing is to try to get him to come to a mail drop," Graham said. "Bait him with something he'd like to see. 'Important evidence' that Lecter knows about from talking to me. Some mistake he made that we're waiting for him to repeat."

"He'd be an idiot to go for it."

"I know. Want to hear what the best bait would be?"

"I'm not sure I do."

"Lecter would be the best bait," Graham said.

"Set up how?"

"It would be hell to do, I know that. We'd take Lecter into federal custody—Chilton would never sit still for this at Chesapeake—and we stash him in maximum security at a VA psychiatric hospital. We fake an escape."

"Oh, Jesus."

"We send the Tooth Fairy a message in next week's *Tattler*, after the big 'escape.' It would be Lecter asking him for a rendezvous."

"Why in God's name would anybody want to meet Lecter? I mean, even the Tooth Fairy?"

"To kill him, Jack." Graham got up. There was no window to look out of as he talked. He stood in front of the "Ten Most Wanted," Crawford's only wall decoration. "See, the Tooth Fairy could absorb him that way, engulf him, become more than he is."

"You sound pretty sure."

"I'm not sure. Who's sure? What he said in the note was 'I have some things I'd love to show you. Someday, perhaps, if circumstances permit.' Maybe it was a serious invitation. I don't think he was just being polite."

"Wonder what he's got to show? The victims were intact. Nothing missing but a little skin and hair, and that was probably . . . How did Bloom put it?"

"Ingested," Graham said. "God knows what he's got. Tremont, remember Tremont's costumes in Spokane? While he was strapped to a stretcher he was pointing with his chin, still trying to show them to the Spokane PD. I'm not sure Lecter would draw the Tooth Fairy, Jack. I say it's the best shot."

"We'd have a goddamn *stampede* if people thought Lecter was out. Papers all over us screaming. Best shot, maybe, but we'll save it for last."

"He probably wouldn't come near a mail drop, but he might be curious enough to *look* at a mail drop to see if Lecter had sold him. If he could do it from a distance. We could pick a drop that could be watched from only a few places a long way off and stake out the observation points." It sounded weak to Graham even as he said it.

"Secret Service has a setup they've never used. They'd let us have it. But if we don't put an ad in today, we'll have to wait until Monday before the next issue comes out. Presses roll at five our time. That gives Chicago another hour and fifteen minutes to come up with Lecter's ad, if there *is* one."

"What about Lecter's ad *order,* the letter he'd have sent the *Tattler* ordering the ad—could we get to that quicker?"

"Chicago put out some general feelers to the shop foreman," Crawford said. "The mail stays in the classified advertising manager's office. They sell the names and return addresses to mailing lists— outfits that sell products for lonely people, love charms, rooster pills, squack dealers, 'meet beautiful Asian girls,' personality courses, that sort of stuff.

"We might appeal to the ad manager's citizenship and all and get a look, request him to be quiet, but I don't want to chance it and risk the *Tattler* slobbering all over us. It would take a warrant to go in there and Bogart the mail. I'm thinking about it."

"If Chicago turns up nothing, we could put an ad in anyway. If we're wrong about the *Tattler,* we wouldn't lose anything," Graham said.

"And if we're right that the *Tattler* is the medium and we make up a reply based on what we have in this note and screw it up—if it doesn't look right to him—we're down the tubes. I didn't ask you about Birmingham. Anything?"

"Birmingham's shut down and over with. The Jacobi house has been painted and redecorated and it's on the market. Their stuff is in storage waiting for probate. I went through the crates. The people I talked to didn't know the Jacobis very well. The one thing they always mentioned was how affectionate the Jacobis were to each other. Always patting. Nothing left of them now but five pallet loads of stuff in a warehouse. I wish I had—"

"Quit wishing, you're on it now."

"What about the mark on the tree?"

"'You hit it on the head'? Means nothing to me," Crawford said. "The Red Dragon either. Beverly knows Mah-Jongg. She's sharp, and she can't see it. We know from his hair he's not Chinese."

"He cut the limb with a bolt cutter. I don't see—"

Crawford's telephone rang. He spoke into it briefly.

"Lab's ready on the note, Will. Let's go up to Zeller's office. It's bigger and not so gray."

Lloyd Bowman, dry as a document in spite of the heat, caught up with them in the corridor. He was flapping damp photographs in each hand and held a sheaf of Datafax sheets under his arm. "Jack, I have to be in court at four-fifteen," he said as he flapped ahead. "It's that paper hanger Nilton Eskew and his sweetheart, Nan. She could draw a Treasury note freehand. They've been driving me crazy for two years making their own traveler's checks on a color Xerox. Won't leave home without them. Will I make it in time, or should I call the prosecutor?"

"You'll make it," Crawford said. "Here we are."

Beverly Katz smiled at Graham from the couch in Zeller's office, making up for the scowl of Price beside her.

Scientific Analysis Section Chief Brian Zeller was young for his job, but already his hair was thinning and he wore bifocals. On the shelf behind Zeller's desk Graham saw H. J. Walls's forensic science text, Tedeschi's great *Forensic Medicine* in three volumes, and an antique edition of Hopkins' *The Wreck of the Deutschland.*

"Will, we met once at GWU I think," he said. "Do you know everybody? . . . Fine."

Crawford leaned against the corner of Zeller's desk, his arms folded. "Anybody got a blockbuster? Okay, does anything you found indicate the note did *not* come from the Tooth Fairy?"

"No," Bowman said. "I talked to Chicago a few minutes ago to give them some numerals I picked up from an impression on the back of the note. Six-six-six. I'll show you when we get to it. Chicago has over two hundred personal ads so far." He handed Graham a sheaf of Datafax copies. "I've read them and they're all the usual stuff— marriage offers, appeals to runaways. I'm not sure how we'd recognize the ad if it's here."

Crawford shook his head. "I don't know either. Let's break down the physical. Now, Jimmy Price did everything we could do and there was no print. What about you, Bev?"

"I got one whisker. Scale count and core size match samples from Hannibal Lecter. So does color. The color's markedly different from samples taken in Birmingham and Atlanta. Three blue grains and some dark flecks went to Brian's end." She raised her eyebrows at Brian Zeller.

"The grains were commercial granulated cleaner with chlorine," he said. "It must have come off the cleaning man's hands. There were several very minute particles of dried blood. It's definitely blood, but there's not enough to type."

"The tears at the end of the pieces wandered off the perforations," Beverly Katz continued. "If we find the roll in somebody's possession and he hasn't torn it again, we can get a definite match. I recommend issuing an advisory now, so the arresting officers will be sure to search for the roll."

Crawford nodded. "Bowman?"

"Sharon from my office went after the paper and got samples to match. It's toilet tissue for marine heads and motor homes. The texture matches brand name Wedeker manufactured in Minneapolis. It has nationwide distribution."

Bowman set up his photographs on an easel near the windows. His voice was surprisingly deep for his slight stature, and his bow tie moved slightly when he talked. "On the handwriting itself, this is a right-handed person using his left hand and printing in a deliberate block pattern. You can see the unsteadiness in the strokes and varying letter sizes.

"The proportions make me think our man has a touch of uncorrected astigmatism.

"The inks on both pieces of the note look like the same standard ball-point royal blue in natural light, but a slight difference appears under colored filters. He used two pens, changing somewhere in the missing section of the note. You can see where the first one began to skip. The first pen is not used frequently—see the blob it starts with? It might have been stored point-down and uncapped in a pencil jar or canister, which suggests a desk situation. Also the surface the paper lay on was soft enough to be a blotter. A blotter might retain impressions if you find it. I want to add the blotter to Beverly's advisory."

Bowman flipped to a photograph of the back of the note. The extreme enlargement made the paper look fuzzy. It was grooved with shadowed impressions. "He folded the note to write the bottom part, including what was later torn out. In this enlargement of the back side, oblique light reveals a few impressions. We can make out '666 an.' Maybe that's where he had pen trouble and had to bear down and overwrite. I didn't spot it until I had this high-contrast print. There's no 666 in any ad so far.

"The sentence structure is orderly, and there's no rambling. The folds suggest it was delivered in a standard letter-size envelope. These two dark places are printing-ink smudges. The note was probably folded inside some innocuous printed matter in the envelope.

"That's about it," Bowman said. "Unless you have questions, Jack, I'd better go to the courthouse. I'll check in after I testify."

"Sink 'em deep," Crawford said.

Graham studied the *Tattler* personals column. ("Attractive queen-size lady, young 52, seeks Christian Leo nonsmoker 40–70. No children please. Artificial limb welcomed. No phonies. Send photo first letter.")

Lost in the pain and desperation of the ads, he didn't notice that the others were leaving until Beverly Katz spoke to him.

"I'm sorry, Beverly. What did you say?" He looked at her bright eyes and kindly, well-worn face.

"I just said I'm glad to see you back, Champ. You're looking good."

"Thanks, Beverly."

"Saul's going to cooking school. He's still hit-or-miss, but when the dust settles come over and let him practice on you."

"I'll do it."

Zeller went away to prowl his laboratory. Only Crawford and Graham were left, looking at the clock.

"Forty minutes to *Tattler* press time," Crawford said. "I'm going after their mail. What do you say?"

"I think you have to."

Crawford passed the word to Chicago on Zeller's telephone. "Will, we need to be ready with a substitute ad if Chicago bingoes."

"I'll work on it."

"I'll set up the drop." Crawford called the Secret Service and talked at some length. Graham was still scribbling when he finished.

"Okay, the mail drop's a beauty," Crawford said at last. "It's an outside message box on a fire-extinguisher-service outfit in Annapolis. That's Lecter territory. The Tooth Fairy will see that it's something Lecter could know about. Alphabetical pigeonholes. The service people drive up to it and get assignments and mail. Our boy can check it out from a park across the street. Secret Service swears it looks good. They set it up to catch a counterfeiter, but it turned out they didn't need it. Here's the address. What about the message?"

"We have to use two messages in the same edition. The first one warns the Tooth Fairy that his enemies are closer than he thinks. It tells him he made a bad mistake in Atlanta and if he repeats the mistake he's doomed. It tells him Lecter has mailed 'secret information' I showed Lecter about what we're doing, how close we are, the leads we have. It directs the Tooth Fairy to a second message that begins with 'your signature.'

"The second message begins 'Avid Fan . . .' and contains the address of the mail drop. We have to do it that way. Even in roundabout language, the warning in the first message is going to excite some casual nuts. If they can't find out the address, they can't come to the drop and screw things up."

"Good. Damn good. Want to wait it out in my office?"

"I'd rather be doing something. I need to see Brian Zeller."

"Go ahead, I can get you in a hurry if I have to."

Graham found the section chief in Serology.

"Brian, could you show me a couple of things?"

"Sure, what?"

"The samples you used to type the Tooth Fairy."

Zeller looked at Graham through the close-range section of his bifocals. "Was there something in the report you didn't understand?"

"No."

"Was something unclear?"

"No."

"Something *incomplete?*" Zeller mouthed the word as if it had an unpleasant taste.

"Your report was fine, couldn't ask for better. I just want to hold the evidence in my hand."

"*Ah,* certainly. We can do that." Zeller believed that all field men retain the superstitions of the hunt. He was glad to humor Graham. "It's all together down at that end."

Graham followed him between the long counters of apparatus. "You're reading Tedeschi."

"Yes," Zeller said over his shoulder. "We don't do any forensic medicine here, as you know, but Tedeschi has a lot of useful things in there. Graham. Will Graham. You wrote the standard monograph on determining time of death by insect activity, didn't you. Or do I have the right Graham?"

"I did it." A pause. "You're right, Mant and Nuorteva in the Tedeschi are better on insects."

Zeller was surprised to hear his thought spoken. "Well, it does have more pictures and a table of invasion waves. No offense."

"Of course not. They're better. I told them so."

Zeller gathered vials and slides from a cabinet and a refrigerator and set them on the laboratory counter. "If you want to ask me anything, I'll be where you found me. The stage light on this microscope is on the side here."

Graham did not want the microscope. He doubted none of Zeller's findings. He didn't know what he wanted. He raised the vials and slides to the light, and a glassine envelope with two blond hairs found in Birmingham. A second envelope held three hairs found on Mrs. Leeds.

There were spit and hair and semen on the table in front of Graham and empty air where he tried to see an image, a face, something to replace the shapeless dread he carried.

A woman's voice came from a speaker in the ceiling. "Graham, Will Graham, to Special Agent Crawford's office. On Red."

He found Sarah in her headset typing, with Crawford looking over her shoulder.

"Chicago's got an ad order with 666 in it," Crawford said out of the side of his mouth. "They're dictating it to Sarah now. They said part of it looks like code."

The lines were climbing out of Sarah's typewriter.

> *Dear Pilgrim,*
> *You honor me . . .*

"That's it. That's it," Graham said. "Lecter called him a pilgrim when he was talking to me."

> *you're very beautiful . . .*

"Christ," Crawford said.

> *I offer 100 prayers for your safety.*
> *Find help in John 6:22, 8:16, 9:1; Luke 1:7, 3:1; Galatians 6:11,*
> *15:2; Acts 3:3; Revelation 18:7; Jonah 6:8 . . .*

The typing slowed as Sarah read back each pair of numbers to the agent in Chicago. When she had finished, the list of scriptural references covered a quarter of a page. It was signed "Bless you, 666."

"That's it," Sarah said.

Crawford picked up the phone. "Okay, Chester, how did it go down with the ad manager? . . . No, you did right. . . . A complete clam, right. Stand by at that phone, I'll get back to you."

"Code," Graham said.

"Has to be. We've got twenty-two minutes to get a message in if we can break it. Shop foreman needs ten minutes' notice and three hundred dollars to shoehorn one in this edition. Bowman's in his office, he got a recess. If you'll get him cracking, I'll talk to Cryptography at Langley. Sarah, shoot a telex of the ad to CIA cryptography section. I'll tell 'em it's coming."

Bowman put the message on his desk and aligned it precisely with the corners of his blotter. He polished his rimless spectacles for what seemed to Graham a very long time.

Bowman had a reputation for being quick. Even the explosives section forgave him for not being an ex-Marine and granted him that.

"We have twenty minutes," Graham said.

"I understand. You called Langley?"

"Crawford did."

Bowman read the message many times, looked at it upside down and sideways, ran down the margins with his finger. He took a Bible from his shelves. For five minutes the only sounds were the two men breathing and the crackle of onionskin pages.

"No," he said. "We won't make it in time. Better use what's left for whatever else you can do."

Graham showed him an empty hand.

Bowman swiveled around to face Graham and took off his glasses. He had a pink spot on each side of his nose. "Do you feel fairly confident the note to Lecter is the only communication he's had from your Tooth Fairy?"

"Right."

"The code is something simple then. They only needed cover against casual readers. Measuring by the perforations in the note to Lecter only about three inches is missing. That's not much room for instructions. The numbers aren't right for a jailhouse alphabet grid— the tap code. I'm guessing it's a book code."

Crawford joined them. "Book code?"

"Looks like it. The first numeral, that '100 prayers,' could be the page number. The paired numbers in the scriptural references could be line and letter. But what book?"

"Not the Bible?" Crawford said.

"No, not the Bible. I thought it might be at first. Galatians 6:11 threw me off. 'Ye see how large a letter I have written unto you with mine own hand.' That's appropriate, but it's coincidence because next he has Galatians 15:2. Galatians has only six chapters. Same with Jonah 6:8—Jonah has four chapters. He wasn't using a Bible."

"Maybe the book title could be concealed in the clear part of Lecter's message," Crawford said.

Bowman shook his head. "I don't think so."

"Then the Tooth Fairy named the book to use. He specified it in his note to Lecter," Graham said.

"It would appear so," Bowman said. "What about sweating Lecter? In a mental hospital I would think drugs—"

"They tried sodium amytal on him three years ago trying to find out where he buried a Princeton student," Graham said. "He gave them a recipe for dip. Besides, if we sweat him we lose the connection. If the Tooth Fairy picked the book, it's something he knew Lecter would have in his cell."

"I know for sure he didn't order one or borrow one from Chilton," Crawford said.

"What have the papers carried about that, Jack? About Lecter's books."

"That he has medical books, psychology books, cookbooks."

"Then it could be one of the standards in those areas, something so basic the Tooth Fairy knew Lecter would definitely have it," Bowman said. "We need a list of Lecter's books. Do you have one?"

"No." Graham stared at his shoes. "I could get Chilton . . . Wait. Rankin and Willingham, when they tossed his cell, they took Polaroids so they could get everything back in place."

"Would you ask them to meet me with the pictures of the books?" Bowman said, packing his briefcase.

"Where?"

"The Library of Congress."

Crawford checked with the CIA cryptography section one last time. The computer at Langley was trying consistent and progressive number-letter substitutions and a staggering variety of alphabet grids. No progress. The cryptographer agreed with Bowman that it was probably a book code.

Crawford looked at his watch. "Will, we're left with three choices and we've got to decide right now. We can pull Lecter's message out of the paper and run nothing. We can substitute our messages in plain language, inviting the Tooth Fairy to the mail drop. Or we can let Lecter's ad run as is."

"Are you sure we can still get Lecter's message out of the *Tattler?*"

"Chester thinks the shop foreman would chisel it for about five hundred dollars."

"I hate to put in a plain-language message, Jack. Lecter would probably never hear from him again."

"Yeah, but I'm leery of letting Lecter's message run without knowing what it says," Crawford said. "What could Lecter tell him that he doesn't know already? If he found out we have a partial thumbprint and his prints aren't on file anywhere, he could whittle his thumb and pull his teeth and give us a big gummy laugh in court."

"The thumbprint wasn't in the case summary Lecter saw. We better let Lecter's message run. At least it'll encourage the Tooth Fairy to contact him again."

"What if it encourages him to do something besides write?"

"We'll feel sick for a long time," Graham said. "We have to do it."

➤

Fifteen minutes later in Chicago the *Tattler's* big presses rolled, gathering speed until their thunder raised the dust in the pressroom. The FBI agent waiting in the smell of ink and hot newsprint took one of the first ones.

The cover lines included "Head Transplant!" and "Astronomers Glimpse God!"

The agent checked to see that Lecter's personal ad was in place and slipped the paper into an express pouch for Washington. He would see that paper again and remember his thumb smudge on the front page, but it would be years later, when he took his children through the special exhibits on a tour of FBI headquarters.

CHAPTER 15

IN THE HOUR before dawn Crawford woke from a deep sleep. He saw the room dark, felt his wife's ample bottom comfortably settled against the small of his back. He did not know why he had awakened until the telephone rang a second time. He found it with no fumbling.

"Jack, this is Lloyd Bowman. I solved the code. You need to know what it says right now."

"Okay, Lloyd." Crawford's feet searched for his slippers.

"It says: *Graham home Marathon, Florida. Save yourself. Kill them all.*"

"Goddammit. Gotta go."

"I know."

Crawford went to his den without stopping for his robe. He called Florida twice, the airport once, then called Graham at his hotel.

"Will, Bowman just broke the code."

"What did it say?"

"I'll tell you in a second. Now listen to me. Everything is okay. I've taken care of it, so stay on the phone when I tell you."

"Tell me now."

"It's your home address. Lecter gave the bastard your home address. *Wait*, Will. Sheriff's department has two cars on the way to Sugarloaf right now. Customs launch from Marathon is taking the ocean side. The Tooth Fairy couldn't have done anything in this short time. Hold

130

on. You can move faster with me helping you. Now, listen to this.

"The deputies aren't going to scare Molly. The sheriff's cars are just closing the road to the house. Two deputies will move up close enough to watch the house. You can call her when she wakes up. I'll pick you up in half an hour."

"I won't be here."

"The next plane in that direction doesn't go until eight. It'll be quicker to bring them up here. My brother's house on the Chesapeake is available to them. I've got a good plan, Will, wait and hear it. If you don't like it I'll put you on the plane myself."

"I need some things from the armory."

"We'll get it soon as I pick you up."

➢

Molly and Willy were among the first off the plane at National Airport in Washington. She spotted Graham in the crowd, did not smile, but turned to Willy and said something as they walked swiftly ahead of the stream of tourists returning from Florida.

She looked Graham up and down and came to him with a light kiss. Her brown fingers were cold on his cheek.

Graham felt the boy watching. Willy shook hands from a full arm's length away.

Graham made a joke about the weight of Molly's suitcase as they walked to the car.

"I'll carry it," Willy said.

A brown Chevrolet with Maryland plates moved in behind them as they pulled out of the parking lot.

Graham crossed the bridge at Arlington and pointed out the Lincoln and Jefferson memorials and the Washington Monument before heading east toward the Chesapeake Bay. Ten miles outside Washington the brown Chevrolet pulled up beside them in the inside lane. The driver looked across with his hand to his mouth and a voice from nowhere crackled in the car.

"Fox Edward, you're clean as a whistle. Have a nice trip."

Graham reached under the dash for the concealed microphone. "Roger, Bobby. Much obliged."

The Chevrolet dropped behind them and its turn signal came on.

"Just making sure no press cars or anything were following," Graham said.

"I see," Molly said.

They stopped in the late afternoon and ate crabs at a roadside restaurant. Willy went to look at the lobster tank.

"I hate it, Molly. I'm sorry," Graham said.

"Is he after you now?"

"We've had no reason to think so. Lecter just suggested it to him, urged him to do it."

"It's a clammy, sick feeling."

"I know it is. You and Willy are safe at Crawford's brother's house. Nobody in the world knows you're there but me and Crawford."

"I'd just as soon not talk about Crawford."

"It's a nice place, you'll see."

She took a deep breath and when she let it out the anger seemed to go with it, leaving her tired and calm. She gave him a crooked smile. "Hell, I just got mad there for a while. Do we have to put up with any Crawfords?"

"Nope." He moved the cracker basket to take her hand. "How much does Willy know?"

"Plenty. His buddy Tommy's mother had a trash newspaper from the supermarket at their house. Tommy showed it to Willy. It had a lot of stuff about you, apparently pretty distorted. About Hobbs, the place you were after that, Lecter, everything. It upset him. I asked him if he wanted to talk about it. He just asked me if I knew it all along. I said yes, that you and I talked about it once, that you told me everything before we got married. I asked him if he wanted me to tell him about it, the way it really was. He said he'd ask you to your face."

"Damn good. Good for him. What was it, the *Tattler?*"

"I don't know, I think so."

"Thanks a lot, Freddy." A swell of anger at Freddy Lounds lifted him from his seat. He washed his face with cold water in the rest room.

➤

Sarah was saying good night to Crawford in the office when the telephone rang. She put down her purse and umbrella to answer it.

"Special Agent Crawford's office. . . . No, Mr. Graham is not in the office, but let me . . . Wait, I'll be glad to . . . Yes, he'll be in tomorrow afternoon, but let me . . ."

The tone of her voice brought Crawford around his desk.

She held the receiver as though it had died in her hand. "He asked for Will and said he might call back tomorrow afternoon. I tried to hold him."

"Who?"

"He said, 'Just tell Graham it's the Pilgrim.' That's what Dr. Lecter called—"

"The Tooth Fairy," Crawford said.

➤

Graham went to the grocery store while Molly and Willy unpacked. He found canary melons at the market and a ripe cranshaw. He parked across the street from the house and sat for a few minutes, still gripping the wheel. He was ashamed that because of him Molly was rooted out of the house she loved and put among strangers.

Crawford had done his best. This was no faceless federal safe house with chair arms bleached by palm sweat. It was a pleasant cottage, freshly whitewashed, with impatiens blooming around the steps. It was the product of careful hands and a sense of order. The rear yard sloped down to the Chesapeake Bay and there was a swimming raft.

Blue-green television light pulsed behind the curtains. Molly and Willy were watching baseball, Graham knew.

Willy's father had been a baseball player, and a good one. He and Molly met on the school bus, married in college.

They trooped around the Florida State League while he was in the Cardinals' farm system. They took Willy with them and had a terrific time. Spam and spirit. He got a tryout with the Cardinals and hit safely in his first two games. Then he began to have difficulty swallowing. The surgeon tried to get it all, but it metastasized and ate him up. He died five months later, when Willy was six.

Willy still watched baseball whenever he could. Molly watched baseball when she was upset.

Graham had no key. He knocked.

"I'll get it." Willy's voice.

"Wait." Molly's face between the curtains. "All right."

Willy opened the door. In his fist, held close to his leg, was a fish billy.

Graham's eyes stung at the sight. The boy must have brought it in his suitcase.

Molly took the bag from him. "Want some coffee? There's gin, but not the kind you like."

When she was in the kitchen, Willy asked Graham to come outside.

From the back porch they could see the riding lights of boats anchored in the bay.

"Will, is there any stuff I need to know to see about Mom?"

"You're both safe here, Willy. Remember the car that followed us from the airport making sure nobody saw where we went? Nobody can find out where you and your mother are."

"This crazy guy wants to kill you, does he?"

"We don't know that. I just didn't feel easy with him knowing where the house is."

"You gonna kill him?"

Graham closed his eyes for a moment. "No. It's just my job to find him. They'll put him in a mental hospital so they can treat him and keep him from hurting anybody."

"Tommy's mother had this little newspaper, Will. It said you killed a guy in Minnesota and you were in a mental hospital. I never knew that. Is it true?"

"Yes."

"I started to ask Mom, but I figured I'd ask you."

"I appreciate your asking me straight out. It wasn't just a mental hospital; they treat everything." The distinction seemed important. "I was in the psychiatric wing. It bothers you, finding out I was in there. Because I'm married to your mom."

"I told my dad I'd take care of her. I'll do it, too."

Graham felt he had to tell Willy enough. He didn't want to tell him too much.

The lights went out in the kitchen. He could see Molly's dim outline inside the screen door and he felt the weight of her judgment. Dealing with Willy he was handling her heart.

Willy clearly did not know what to ask next. Graham did it for him.

"The hospital part was after the business with Hobbs."

"You shot him?"

"Yes."

"How'd it happen?"

"To begin with, Garrett Hobbs was insane. He was attacking college girls and he . . . killed them."

"How?"

"With a knife; anyway I found a little curly piece of metal in the clothes one of the girls had on. It was the kind of shred a pipe threader makes—remember when we fixed the shower outside?

"I was taking a look at a lot of steamfitters, plumbers and people. It took a long time. Hobbs had left this resignation letter at a construction job I was checking. I saw it and it was . . . peculiar. He wasn't working anywhere, and I had to find him at home.

"I was going up the stairs in Hobbs's apartment house. A uniformed officer was with me. Hobbs must have seen us coming. I was halfway up to his landing when he shoved his wife out the door and she came falling down the stairs dead."

"He had killed her?"

"Yeah. So I asked the officer I was with to call for SWAT, to get some help. But then I could hear kids in there and some screaming. I wanted to wait, but I couldn't."

"You went in the apartment?"

"I did. Hobbs had caught this girl from behind and he had a knife. He was cutting her with it. And I shot him."

"Did the girl die?"

"No."

"She got all right?"

"After a while, yes. She's all right now."

Willy digested this silently. Faint music came from an anchored sailboat.

Graham could leave things out for Willy, but he couldn't help seeing them again himself.

He left out Mrs. Hobbs on the landing clutching at him, stabbed so many times. Seeing she was gone, hearing the screaming from the apartment, prying the slick red fingers off and cracking his shoulder before the door gave in. Hobbs holding his own daughter busy cutting her neck when he could get to it, her struggling with her chin tucked down, the .38 knocking chunks out of him and he still cutting and he wouldn't go down. Hobbs sitting on the floor crying and the girl rasping. Holding her down and seeing Hobbs had gotten through the windpipe, but not the arteries. The daughter looked at him with wide glazed eyes and at her father sitting on the floor crying "See? See?" until he fell over dead.

That was where Graham lost his faith in .38's.

"Willy, the business with Hobbs, it bothered me a lot. You know, I kept it on my mind and I saw it over and over. I got so I couldn't think about much else. I kept thinking there must be some way I could have handled it better. And then I quit feeling anything. I couldn't eat and I stopped talking to anybody. I got really depressed. So a doctor asked me to go into the hospital, and I did. After a while I got some distance on it. The girl that got hurt in Hobbs's apartment came to see me. She was okay and we talked a lot. Finally I put it aside and went back to work."

"Killing somebody, even if you have to do it, it feels that bad?"

"Willy, it's one of the ugliest things in the world."

"Say, I'm going in the kitchen for a minute. You want something, a Coke?" Willy liked to bring Graham things, but he always made it a casual adjunct to something he was going to do anyway. No special trip or anything.

"Sure, a Coke."

"Mom ought to come out and look at the lights."

➤

Late in the night Graham and Molly sat in the back-porch swing. Light rain fell and the boat lights cast grainy halos on the mist. The breeze off the bay raised goose bumps on their arms.

"This could take a while, couldn't it?" Molly said.

"I hope it won't, but it might."

"Will, Evelyn said she could keep the shop for this week and four days next week. But I've got to go back to Marathon, at least for a day or two when my buyers come. I could stay with Evelyn and Sam. I should go to market in Atlanta myself. I need to be ready for September."

"Does Evelyn know where you are?"

"I just told her Washington."

"Good."

"It's hard to have anything, isn't it? Rare to get it, hard to keep it. This is a damn slippery planet."

"Slick as hell."

"We'll be back in Sugarloaf, won't we?"

"Yes we will."

"Don't get in a hurry and hang it out too far. You won't do that?"

"No."

"Are you going back early?"

He had talked to Crawford half an hour on the phone.

"A little before lunch. If you're going to Marathon at all, there's something we need to tend to in the morning. Willy can fish."

"He had to ask you about the other."

"I know, I don't blame him."

"Damn that reporter, what's his name?"

"Lounds. Freddy Lounds."

"I think maybe you hate him. And I wish I hadn't brought it up. Let's go to bed and I'll rub your back."

Resentment raised a minute blister in Graham. He had justified himself to an eleven-year-old. The kid said it was okay that he had been in the rubber Ramada. Now she was going to rub his back. Let's go to bed—it's okay with Willy.

When you feel strain, keep your mouth shut if you can.

"If you want to think awhile, I'll let you alone," she said.

He didn't want to think. He definitely did not. "You rub my back and I'll rub your front," he said.

"Go to it, Buster."

➤

Winds aloft carried the thin rain out over the bay and by nine A.M. the ground steamed. The far targets on the sheriff's department range seemed to flinch in the wavy air.

The rangemaster watched through his binoculars until he was sure the man and woman at the far end of the firing line were observing the safety rules.

The Justice Department credentials the man showed when he asked to use the range said "Investigator." That could be anything. The rangemaster did not approve of anyone other than a qualified instructor teaching pistolcraft.

Still, he had to admit the fed knew what he was doing.

They were only using a .22-caliber revolver but he was teaching the woman combat shooting from the Weaver stance, left foot slightly forward, a good two-handed grip on the revolver with isometric tension in the arms. She was firing at the silhouette target seven yards in front of her. Again and again she brought the weapon up from the outside pocket of her shoulderbag. It went on until the rangemaster was bored with it.

A change in the sound brought the rangemaster's glasses up again. They had the earmuffs on now and she was working with a short, chunky revolver. The rangemaster recognized the pop of the light target loads.

He could see the pistol extended in her hands and it interested him. He strolled along the firing line and stood a few yards behind them.

He wanted to examine the pistol, but this was not a good time to interrupt. He got a good look at it as she shucked out the empties and popped in five from a speedloader.

Odd arm for a fed. It was a Bulldog .44 Special, short and ugly with its startling big bore. It had been extensively modified by Mag Na Port. The barrel was vented near the muzzle to help keep the muzzle down on recoil, the hammer was bobbed and it had a good set of fat grips. He suspected it was throated for the speedloader. One hell of a mean pistol when it was loaded with what the fed had waiting. He wondered how the woman would stand up to it.

The ammunition on the stand beside them was an interesting progression. First there was a box of lightly loaded wadcutters. Then came regular service hardball, and last was something the rangemaster had read much about but had rarely seen. A row of Glaser Safety Slugs. The tips looked like pencil erasers. Behind each tip was a copper jacket containing number-twelve shot suspended in liquid Teflon.

The light projectile was designed to fly at tremendous velocity, smash into the target and release the shot. In meat the results were devastating. The rangemaster even recalled the figures. Ninety Glasers had been fired at men so far. All ninety were instant one-shot stops. In eighty-nine of the cases immediate death resulted. One man survived, surprising the doctors. The Glaser round had a safety advantage, too—no ricochets, and it would not go through a wall and kill someone in the next room.

The man was very gentle with her and encouraging, but he seemed sad about something.

The woman had worked up to the full service loads now and the rangemaster was pleased to see she handled the recoil very well, both eyes open and no flinch. True, it took her maybe four seconds to get the first one off, coming up from the bag, but three were in the X ring. Not bad for a beginner. She had some talent.

He had been back in the tower for some time when he heard the hellish racket of the Glasers going off.

She was pumping all five. It was not standard federal practice.

The rangemaster wondered what in God's name they saw in the silhouette that it would take five Glasers to kill.

Graham came to the tower to turn in the earmuffs, leaving his pupil sitting on a bench, head down, her elbows on her knees.

The rangemaster thought he should be pleased with her, and told him so. She had come a long way in one day. Graham thanked him absently. His expression puzzled the rangemaster. He looked like a man who had witnessed an irrevocable loss.

CHAPTER 16

THE CALLER, "Mr. Pilgrim," had said to Sarah that he might call again on the following afternoon. At FBI headquarters certain arrangements were made to receive the call.

Who was Mr. Pilgrim? Not Lecter—Crawford had made sure of that. Was Mr. Pilgrim the Tooth Fairy? Maybe so, Crawford thought.

The desks and telephones from Crawford's office had been moved overnight to a larger room across the hall.

Graham stood in the open doorway of a soundproof booth. Behind him in the booth was Crawford's telephone. Sarah had cleaned it with Windex. With the voiceprint spectrograph, tape recorders, and stress evaluator taking up most of her desk and another table beside it, and Beverly Katz sitting in her chair, Sarah needed something to do.

The big clock on the wall showed ten minutes before noon.

Dr. Alan Bloom and Crawford stood with Graham. They had adopted a sidelines stance, hands in their pockets.

A technician seated across from Beverly Katz drummed his fingers on the desk until a frown from Crawford stopped him.

Crawford's desk was cluttered with two new telephones, an open line to the Bell System's electronic switching center (ESS) and a hot line to the FBI communications room.

"How much time do you need for a trace?" Dr. Bloom asked.

"With the new switching it's a lot quicker than most people think,"

Crawford said. "Maybe a minute if it comes through all-electronic switching. More if it's from someplace where they have to swarm the frame."

Crawford raised his voice to the room. "If he calls at all, it'll be short, so let's play him perfect. Want to go over the drill, Will?"

"Sure. When we get to the point where I talk, I want to ask you a couple of things, Doctor."

Bloom had arrived after the others. He was scheduled to speak to the behavioral-science section at Quantico later in the day. Bloom could smell cordite on Graham's clothes.

"Okay," Graham said. "The phone rings. The circuit's completed immediately and the trace starts at ESS, but the tone generator continues the ringing noise so he doesn't know we've picked up. That gives us about twenty seconds on him." He pointed to the technician. "Tone generator to 'off' at the end of the fourth ring, got it?"

The technician nodded. "End of the fourth ring."

"Now, Beverly picks up the phone. Her voice is different from the one he heard yesterday. No recognition in the voice. Beverly sounds bored. He asks for me. Bev says, 'I'll have to page him, may I put you on hold?' Ready with that, Bev?" Graham thought it would be better not to rehearse the lines. They might sound flat by rote.

"All right, the line is open to us, dead to him. I think he'll hold longer than he'll talk."

"Sure you don't want to give him the hold music?" the technician asked.

"Hell no," Crawford said.

"We give him about twenty seconds of hold, then Beverly comes back on and tells him, 'Mr. Graham's coming to the phone, I'll connect you now.' I pick up." Graham turned to Dr. Bloom. "How would you play him, Doctor?"

"He'll expect you to be skeptical about it really being him. I'd give him some polite skepticism. I'd make a strong distinction between the nuisance of fake callers and the significance, the importance, of a call from the real person. The fakes are easy to recognize because they lack the *capacity* to understand what has happened, that sort of thing.

"Make him tell something to prove who he is." Dr. Bloom looked at the floor and kneaded the back of his neck.

"You don't know what he wants. Maybe he wants understanding, maybe he's fixed on you as the adversary and wants to gloat—we'll see. Try to pick up his mood and give him what he's after, a little at a time. I'd be very leery of appealing to him to come to us for help, unless you sense he's asking for that.

"If he's paranoid you'll pick it up fast. In that case I'd play into his suspicion or grievance. Let him air it. If he gets rolling on that, he may forget how long he's talked. That's all I know to tell you." Bloom put his hand on Graham's shoulder and spoke quietly. "Listen, this is not a pep talk or any bullshit; you can take him over the jumps. Never mind advice, do what seems right to you."

Waiting. Half an hour of silence was enough.

"Call or no call, we've got to decide where to go from here," Crawford said. "Want to try the mail drop?"

"I can't see anything better," Graham said.

"That would give us two baits, a stakeout at your house in the Keys and the drop."

The telephone was ringing.

Tone generator on. At ESS the trace began. Four rings. The technician hit the switch and Beverly picked up. Sarah was listening.

"Special Agent Crawford's office."

Sarah shook her head. She knew the caller, one of Crawford's cronies at Alcohol, Tobacco, and Firearms. Beverly got him off in a hurry and stopped the trace. Everyone in the FBI building knew to keep the line clear.

Crawford went over the details of the mail drop again. They were bored and tense at the same time. Lloyd Bowman came around to show them how the number pairs in Lecter's Scriptures fit page 100 of the softcover *Joy of Cooking*. Sarah passed around coffee in paper cups.

The telephone was ringing.

The tone generator took over and at ESS the trace began. Four rings. The technician hit the switch. Beverly picked up.

"Special Agent Crawford's office."

Sarah was nodding her head. Big nods.

Graham went into his booth and closed the door. He could see Beverly's lips moving. She punched "Hold" and watched the second hand on the wall clock.

Graham could see his face in the polished receiver. Two bloated faces in the earpiece and mouthpiece. He could smell cordite from the firing range in his shirt. *Don't hang up. Sweet Jesus, don't hang up.* Forty seconds had elapsed. The telephone moved slightly on his table when it rang. *Let it ring. Once more.* Forty-five seconds. *Now.*

"This is Will Graham, can I help you?"

Low laughter. A muffled voice: "I expect you can."

"Could I ask who's calling please?"

"Didn't your secretary tell you?"

"No, but she did call me out of a meeting, sir, and—"

"If you tell me you won't talk to Mr. Pilgrim, I'll hang up right now. Yes or no?"

"Mr. Pilgrim, if you have some problem I'm equipped to deal with, I'll be glad to talk with you."

"I think you have the problem, Mr. Graham."

"I'm sorry, I didn't understand you."

The second hand crawled toward one minute.

"You've been a busy boy, haven't you?" the caller said.

"Too busy to stay on the phone unless you state your business."

"My business is in the same place yours is. Atlanta and Birmingham."

"Do you know something about that?"

Soft laughter. "Know something about it? Are you interested in Mr. Pilgrim? Yes or no. I'll hang up if you lie."

Graham could see Crawford through the glass. He had a telephone receiver in each hand.

"Yes. But, see, I get a lot of calls, and most of them are from people who say they know things." One minute.

Crawford put one receiver down and scrawled on a piece of paper.

"You'd be surprised how many pretenders there are," Graham said. "Talk to them a few minutes and you can tell they don't have the capacity to even understand what's going on. Do you?"

Sarah held a sheet of paper to the glass for Graham to see. It said, "Chicago phone booth. PD scrambling."

"I'll tell you what, you tell me one thing you know about Mr. Pilgrim and maybe I'll tell you whether you're right or not," the muffled voice said.

"Let's get straight who we're talking about," Graham said.

"We're talking about Mr. Pilgrim."

"How do I know Mr. Pilgrim has done anything I'm interested in. Has he?"

"Let's say, yes."

"Are you Mr. Pilgrim?"

"I don't think I'll tell you that."

"Are you his friend?"

"Sort of."

"Well, prove it then. Tell me something that shows me how well you know him."

"You first. You show me yours." A nervous giggle. "First time you're wrong, I hang up."

"All right, Mr. Pilgrim is right-handed."

"That's a safe guess. Most people are."

"Mr. Pilgrim is misunderstood."

"No general crap, please."

"Mr. Pilgrim is really strong physically."

"Yes, you could say that."

Graham looked at the clock. A minute and a half. Crawford nodded encouragement.

Don't tell him anything that he could change.

"Mr. Pilgrim is white and about, say, five-feet-eleven. You haven't told me anything, you know. I'm not so sure you even know him at all."

"Want to stop talking?"

"No, but you said we'd trade. I was just going along with you."

"Do you think Mr. Pilgrim is crazy?"

Bloom was shaking his head.

"I don't think anybody who is as careful as he is could be crazy. I think he's different. I think a lot of people do believe he's crazy, and the reason for that is, he hasn't let people understand much about him."

"Describe exactly what you think he did to Mrs. Leeds and maybe I'll tell you if you're right or not."

"I don't want to do that."

"Good-bye."

Graham's heart jumped, but he could still hear breathing on the other end.

"I can't go into that until I know—"

Graham heard the telephone-booth door slam open in Chicago and the receiver fall with a clang. Faint voices and bangs as the receiver swung on its cord. Everyone in the office heard it on the speaker-phone.

"Freeze. Don't even twitch. Now lock your fingers behind your head and back out of the booth slowly. Slowly. Hands on the glass and spread 'em."

Sweet relief was flooding Graham.

"I'm not armed, Stan. You'll find my ID in my breast pocket. That tickles."

A confused voice loud on the telephone. "Who am I speaking to?"

"Will Graham, FBI."

"This is Sergeant Stanley Riddle, Chicago police department." Irritated now. "Would you tell me what the hell's going on?"

"You tell me. You have a man in custody?"

"Damn right. Freddy Lounds, the reporter. I've known him for ten years. . . . Here's your notebook, Freddy. . . . Are you preferring charges against him?"

Graham's face was pale. Crawford's was red. Dr. Bloom watched the tape reels go around.

"Can you hear me?"

"Yes, I'm preferring charges." Graham's voice was strangled. "Obstruction of justice. Please take him in and hold him for the U.S. attorney."

Suddenly Lounds was on the telephone. He spoke fast and clearly with the cotton wads out of his cheeks.

"Will, listen—"

"Tell it to the U.S. attorney. Put Sergeant Riddle on the phone."

"I know something—"

"Put Riddle on the goddamned telephone."

Crawford's voice came on the line. "Let me have it, Will."

Graham slammed his receiver down with a bang that made everyone in range of the speakerphone flinch. He came out of the booth and left the room without looking at anyone.

"Lounds, you have hubbed hell, my man," Crawford said.

"You want to catch him or not? I can help you. Let me talk one minute." Lounds hurried into Crawford's silence. "Listen, you just showed me how bad you need the *Tattler*. Before, I wasn't sure—now I am. That ad's part of the Tooth Fairy case or you wouldn't have gone balls-out to nail this call. Great. The *Tattler's* here for you. Anything you want."

"How did you find out?"

"The ad manager came to me. Said your Chicago office sent this suit-of-clothes over to check the ads. Your guy took five letters from the incoming ads. Said it was 'pursuant to mail fraud.' Mail fraud nothing. The ad manager made Xerox copies of the letters and envelopes before he let your guy have them.

"I looked them over. I knew he took five letters to smokescreen the one he really wanted. Took a day or two to check them all out. The answer was on the envelope. Chesapeake postmark. The postage-meter number was for Chesapeake State Hospital. I was over there you know, behind your friend with the wild hair up his ass. What else could it be?

"I had to be sure, though. That's why I called, to see if you'd come down on 'Mr. Pilgrim' with both feet, and you did."

"You made a large mistake, Freddy."

"You need the *Tattler* and I can open it up for you. Ads, editorial, monitoring incoming mail, anything. You name it. I can be discreet. I can. Cut me in, Crawford."

"There's nothing to cut you in on."

"Okay, then it won't make any difference if somebody happened to put in six personal ads next issue. All to 'Mr. Pilgrim' and signed the same way."

"I'll get an injunction slapped on you and a sealed indictment for obstruction of justice."

"And it might leak to every paper in the country." Lounds knew he was talking on tape. He didn't care anymore. "I swear to God, I'll do it, Crawford. I'll tear up your chance before I lose mine."

"Add interstate transmission of a threatening message to what I just said."

"Let me *help* you, Jack. I can, believe me."

"Run along to the police station, Freddy. Now put the sergeant back on the phone."

➤

Freddy Lounds's Lincoln Versailles smelled of hair tonic and after-shave, socks and cigars, and the police sergeant was glad to get out of it when they reached the station house.

Lounds knew the captain commanding the precinct and many of the patrolmen. The captain gave Lounds coffee and called the U.S. attorney's office to "try and clear this shit up."

No federal marshal came for Lounds. In half an hour he took a call from Crawford in the precinct commander's office. Then he was free to go. The captain walked him to his car.

Lounds was keyed up and his driving was fast and jerky as he crossed the Loop eastward to his apartment overlooking Lake Michigan. There were several things he wanted out of this story and he knew that he could get them. Money was one, and most of that would come from the paperback. He would have an instant paperback on the stands thirty-six hours after the capture. An exclusive story in the daily press would be a news coup. He would have the satisfaction of seeing the straight press—the Chicago *Tribune,* the Los Angeles *Times,* the sanctified Washington *Post* and the holy New York *Times*—run his copyrighted material under his byline with his picture credits.

And then the correspondents of those august journals, who looked down on him, who would not drink with him, could eat their fucking hearts out.

Lounds was a pariah to them because he had taken a different faith. Had he been incompetent, a fool with no other resource, the veterans of the straight press could have forgiven him for working on the *Tattler,* as one forgives a retarded geek. But Lounds was good. He had the qualities of a good reporter—intelligence, guts, and the good eye. He had great energy and patience.

Against him were the fact that he was obnoxious and therefore disliked by news executives, and his inability to keep himself out of his stories.

In Lounds was the lunging need to be noticed that is often miscalled ego. Lounds was lumpy and ugly and small. He had buck teeth and his rat eyes had the sheen of spit on asphalt.

He had worked in straight journalism for ten years when he realized that no one would ever send him to the White House. He saw that his publishers would wear his legs out, use him until it was time for him to become a broken-down old drunk manning a dead-end desk, drifting inevitably toward cirrhosis or a mattress fire.

They wanted the information he could get, but they didn't want Freddy. They paid him top scale, which is not very much money if you have to buy women. They patted his back and told him he had a lot of balls and they refused to put his name on a parking place.

One evening in 1969 while in the office working rewrite, Freddy had an epiphany.

Frank Larkin was seated near him taking dictation on the telephone. Dictation was the glue factory for old reporters on the paper where Freddy worked. Frank Larkin was fifty-five, but he looked seventy. He was oyster-eyed and he went to his locker every half-hour for a drink. Freddy could smell him from where he sat.

Larkin got up and shuffled over to the slot and spoke in a hoarse whisper to the news editor, a woman. Freddy always listened to other people's conversations.

Larkin asked the woman to get him a Kotex from the machine in the ladies' room. He had to use them on his bleeding behind.

Freddy stopped typing. He took the story out of his typewriter, replaced the paper and wrote a letter of resignation.

A week later he was working for the *Tattler.*

He started as cancer editor at a salary nearly double what he had earned before. Management was impressed with his attitude.

The *Tattler* could afford to pay him well because the paper found cancer very lucrative.

One in five Americans dies of it. The relatives of the dying, worn out, prayed out, trying to fight a raging carcinoma with pats and banana pudding and copper-tasting jokes, are desperate for anything hopeful.

Marketing surveys showed that a bold "New Cure for Cancer" or "Cancer Miracle Drug" cover line boosted supermarket sales of any *Tattler* issue by 22.3 percent. There was a six-percentile drop in those sales when the story ran on page one beneath the cover line, as the reader had time to scan the empty text while the groceries were being totaled.

Marketing experts discovered it was better to have the big cover line in color on the front and play the story in the middle pages, where it was difficult to hold the paper open and manage a purse and grocery cart at the same time.

The standard story featured an optimistic five paragraphs in ten-point type, then a drop to eight point, then to six point before mentioning that the "miracle drug" was unavailable or that animal research was just beginning.

Freddy earned his money turning them out, and the stories sold a lot of *Tattlers.*

In addition to increased readership, there were many spinoff sales of miracle medallions and healing cloths. Manufacturers of these paid a premium to get their ads located close to the weekly cancer story.

Many readers wrote to the paper for more information. Some additional revenue was realized by selling their names to a radio "evangelist," a screaming sociopath who wrote to them for money, using envelopes stamped "Someone You Love Will Die Unless . . ."

Freddy Lounds was good for the *Tattler*, and the *Tattler* was good to him. Now, after eleven years with the paper, he earned $72,000 a year. He covered pretty much what he pleased and spent the money trying to have a good time. He lived as well as he knew how to live.

The way things were developing, he believed he could raise the ante on his paperback deal, and there was movie interest. He had heard that Hollywood was a fine place for obnoxious fellows with money.

Freddy felt good. He shot down the ramp to the underground garage in his building and wheeled into his parking place with a spirited squeal of rubber. There on the wall was his name in letters a foot high, marking his private spot. Mr. Frederick Lounds.

Wendy was here already—her Datsun was parked next to his space. Good. He wished he could take her to Washington with him. That would make those flatfeet's eyes pop. He whistled in the elevator on his way upstairs.

➤

Wendy was packing for him. She had lived out of suitcases and she did a good job.

Neat in her jeans and plaid shirt, her brown hair gathered in a chipmunk tail on her neck, she might have been a farm girl except for her pallor and her shape. Wendy's figure was almost a caricature of puberty.

She looked at Lounds with eyes that had not registered surprise in years. She saw that he was trembling.

"You're working too hard, Roscoe." She liked to call him Roscoe, and it pleased him for some reason. "What are you taking, the six-o'clock shuttle?" She brought him a drink and moved her sequined jump suit and wig case off the bed so he could lie down. "I can take you to the airport. I'm not going to the club 'til six."

"Wendy City" was her own topless bar, and she didn't have to dance anymore. Lounds had cosigned the note.

"You sounded like Morocco Mole when you called me," she said.

"Who?"

"You know, on television Saturday morning, he's real mysterious and he helps Secret Squirrel. We watched it when you had the flu. . . . You really pulled one off today, didn't you? You're really pleased with yourself."

"Damn straight. I took a chance today, baby, and it paid off. I've got a chance at something sweet."

"You've got time for a nap before you go. You're running yourself in the ground."

Lounds lit a cigarette. He already had one burning in the ashtray.

"You know what?" she said. "I bet if you drink your drink and get it off, you could go to sleep."

Lounds's face, like a fist pressed against her neck, relaxed at last, became mobile as suddenly as a fist becomes a hand. His trembling stopped. He told her all about it, whispering into the buck jut of her augmented breasts; she tracing eights on the back of his neck with a finger.

"That is some kind of smart, Roscoe," she said. "You go to sleep now. I'll get you up for the plane. It'll be all right, all of it. And then we'll have a high old time."

They whispered about the places they would go. He went to sleep.

CHAPTER 17

DR. ALAN BLOOM and Jack Crawford sat on folding chairs, the only furniture left in Crawford's office.

"The cupboard is bare, Doctor."

Dr. Bloom studied Crawford's simian face and wondered what was coming. Behind Crawford's grousing and his Alka-Seltzers the doctor saw an intelligence as cold as an X-ray table.

"Where did Will go?"

"He'll walk around and cool off," Crawford said. "He hates Lounds."

"Did you think you might lose Will after Lecter published his home address? That he might go back to his family?"

"For a minute, I did. It shook him."

"Understandably," Dr. Bloom said.

"Then I realized—he can't go home, and neither can Molly and Willy, never, until the Tooth Fairy is out of the way."

"You've met Molly?"

"Yeah. She's great, I like her. She'd be glad to see me in hell with my back broken, of course. I'm having to duck her right now."

"She thinks you use Will?"

Crawford looked at Dr. Bloom sharply. "I've got some things I have to talk to him about. We'll need to check with you. When do you have to be at Quantico?"

"Not until Tuesday morning. I put it off." Dr. Bloom was a guest lecturer at the behavioral-science section of the FBI Academy.

"Graham likes you. He doesn't think you run any mind games on him," Crawford said. Bloom's remark about using Graham stuck in his craw.

"I don't. I wouldn't try," Dr. Bloom said. "I'm as honest with him as I'd be with a patient."

"Exactly."

"No, I want to be his friend, and I am. Jack, I owe it to my field of study to observe. Remember, though, when *you* asked me to give you a study on him, I refused."

"That was Petersen, upstairs, wanted the study."

"You were the one who asked for it. No matter, if I ever did anything on Graham, if there were ever anything that might be of therapeutic benefit to others, I'd abstract it in a form that would be totally unrecognizable. If I ever do anything in a scholarly way, it'll only be published posthumously."

"After you or after Graham?"

Dr. Bloom didn't answer.

"One thing I've noticed—I'm curious about this: you're never alone in a room with Graham, are you? You're smooth about it, but you're never one-on-one with him. Why's that? Do you think he's psychic, is that it?"

"No. He's an *eideteker*—he has a remarkable visual memory—but I don't think he's psychic. He wouldn't let Duke test him—that doesn't mean anything, though. He hates to be prodded and poked. So do I."

"But—"

"Will wants to think of this as purely an intellectual exercise, and in the narrow definition of forensics, that's what it is. He's good at that, but there are other people just as good, I imagine."

"Not many," Crawford said.

"What he has in addition is pure empathy and projection," Dr. Bloom said. "He can assume your point of view, or mine—and maybe some other points of view that scare and sicken him. It's an uncomfortable gift, Jack. Perception's a tool that's pointed on both ends."

"Why aren't you ever alone with him?"

"Because I have some professional curiosity about him and he'd pick that up in a hurry. He's fast."

"If he caught you peeking, he'd snatch down the shades."

"An unpleasant analogy, but accurate, yes. You've had sufficient revenge now, Jack. We can get to the point. Let's make it short. I don't feel very well."

"A psychosomatic manifestation, probably," Crawford said.

"Actually it's my gall bladder. What do you want?"

"I have a medium where I can speak to the Tooth Fairy."

"The *Tattler*," Dr. Bloom said.

"Right. Do you think there's any way to push him in a self-destructive way by what we say to him?"

"Push him toward suicide?"

"Suicide would suit me fine."

"I doubt it. In certain kinds of mental illness that might be possible. Here, I doubt it. If he were self-destructive, he wouldn't be so careful. He wouldn't protect himself so well. If he were a classic paranoid schizophrenic, you might be able to influence him to blow up and become visible. You might even get him to hurt himself. I wouldn't help you though." Suicide was Bloom's mortal enemy.

"No, I suppose you wouldn't," Crawford said. "Could we enrage him?"

"Why do you want to know? To what purpose?"

"Let me ask you this: could we enrage him and focus his attention?"

"He's already fixed on Graham as his adversary, and you know it. Don't fool around. You've decided to stick Graham's neck out, haven't you?"

"I think I have to do it. It's that or he gets his feet sticky on the twenty-fifth. Help me."

"I'm not sure you know what you're asking."

"Advice—that's what I'm asking."

"I don't mean from me," Dr. Bloom said. "What you're asking from Graham. I don't want you to misinterpret this, and normally I wouldn't say it, but you ought to know: what do you think one of Will's strongest drives is?"

Crawford shook his head.

"It's fear, Jack. The man deals with a huge amount of fear."

"Because he got hurt?"

"No, not entirely. Fear comes with imagination, it's a penalty, it's the price of imagination."

Crawford stared at his blunt hands folded on his stomach. He reddened. It was embarrassing to talk about it. "Sure. It's what you don't ever mention on the big boys' side of the playground, right? Don't worry about telling me he's afraid. I won't think he's not a 'stand-up guy.' I'm not a total asshole, Doctor."

"I never thought you were, Jack."

"I wouldn't put him out there if I couldn't cover him. Okay, if I couldn't cover him eighty percent. He's not bad himself. Not the best, but he's quick. Will you help us stir up the Tooth Fairy, Doctor? A lot of people are dead."

"Only if Graham knows the entire risk ahead of time and assumes it voluntarily. I have to hear him say that."

"I'm like you, Doctor. I never bullshit him. No more than we all bullshit each other."

➤

Crawford found Graham in the small workroom near Zeller's lab which he had commandeered and filled with photographs and personal papers belonging to the victims.

Crawford waited until Graham put down the *Law Enforcement Bulletin* he was reading.

"Let me fill you in on what's up for the twenty-fifth." He did not have to tell Graham that the twenty-fifth would bring the next full moon.

"When he does it again?"

"Yeah, if we have a problem on the twenty-fifth."

"Not if. When."

"Both times it's been on Saturday night. Birmingham, June 28, a full moon falling on a Saturday night. It was July 26 in Atlanta, that's one day short of a full moon, but also Saturday night. This time the full moon falls on Monday, August 25. He likes the weekend, though, so we're ready from Friday on."

"Ready? We're *ready?*"

"Correct. You know how it is in the textbooks—the ideal way to investigate a homicide?"

"I never saw it done that way," Graham said. "It never works out like that."

"No. Hardly ever. It would be great to be able to do it, though: Send one guy in. Just one. Let him go over the place. He's wired and dictating all the time. He gets the place absolutely cherry for as long as he needs. Just him. . . . just you."

A long pause.

"What are you telling me?"

"Starting the night of Friday, the twenty-second, we have a Grumman Gulfstream standing by at Andrews Air Force Base. I borrowed it from Interior. The basic lab stuff will be on it. We stand by—me, you, Zeller, Jimmy Price, a photographer, and two people to do interrogations. Soon as the call comes in, we're on our way. Anywhere in the East or South, we can be there in an hour and fifteen minutes."

"What about the locals? They don't have to cooperate. They won't wait."

"We're blanketing the chiefs of police and sheriffs' departments. Every one of them. We're asking orders to be posted on the dispatchers' consoles and the duty officers' desks."

Graham shook his head. "Balls. They'd never hold off. They couldn't."

"This is what we're asking—it's not so much. We're asking that when a report comes in, the first officers at the scene go in and look. Medical personnel go in and make sure nobody's left alive. They come back out. Roadblocks, interrogations, go on any way they like, but the *scene,* that's sealed off until we get there. We drive up, you go in. You're wired. You talk it out to us when you feel like it, don't say anything when you don't feel like it. Take as long as you want. Then we'll come in."

"The locals won't wait."

"Of course they won't. They'll send in some guys from Homicide. But the request will have *some* effect. It'll cut down on traffic in there, and you'll get it fresh."

Fresh. Graham tilted his head back against his chair and stared at the ceiling.

"Of course," Crawford said, "we've still got thirteen days before that weekend."

"Aw, Jack."

"'Jack' what?" Crawford said.

"You kill me, you really do."

"I don't follow you."

"Yes you do. What you've done, you've decided to use me for bait because you don't have anything else. So before you pop the question, you pump me up about how bad next time will be. Not bad psychology. To use on a fucking idiot. What did you think I'd say? You worried I don't have the onions for it since that with Lecter?"

"No."

"I wouldn't blame you for wondering. We both know people it happened to. I don't like walking around in a Kevlar vest with my butt puckered up. But hell, I'm in it now. We can't go home as long as he's loose."

"I never doubted you'd do it."

Graham saw that this was true. "It's something more then, isn't it?"

Crawford said nothing.

"No Molly. *No way.*"

"Jesus, Will, even *I* wouldn't ask you that."

Graham stared at him for a moment. "Oh, for Christ's sake, Jack. You've decided to play ball with Freddy Lounds, haven't you? You and little Freddy have cut a deal."

Crawford frowned at a spot on his tie. He looked up at Graham. "You know yourself it's the best way to bait him. The Tooth Fairy's gonna watch the *Tattler.* What else have we got?"

"It has to be Lounds doing it?"

"He's got the corner on the *Tattler.*"

"So I really bad-mouth the Tooth Fairy in the *Tattler* and then we give him a shot. You think it's better than the mail drop? Don't answer that, I know it is. Have you talked to Bloom about it?"

"Just in passing. We'll both get together with him. And Lounds. We'll run the mail drop on him at the same time."

"What about the setup? I think we'll have to give him a pretty good shot at it. Something open. Someplace where he can get close. I don't think he'd snipe. He might fool me, but I can't see him with a rifle."

"We'll have stillwatches on the high places."

They were both thinking the same thing. Kevlar body armor would stop the Tooth Fairy's nine-millimeter and his knife unless Graham got hit in the face. There was no way to protect him against a head shot if a hidden rifleman got the chance to fire.

"You talk to Lounds. I don't have to do that."

"He needs to interview you, Will," Crawford said gently. "He has to take your picture."

Bloom had warned Crawford he'd have trouble on that point.

CHAPTER 18

WHEN THE TIME CAME, Graham surprised both Crawford and Bloom. He seemed willing to meet Lounds halfway and his expression was affable beneath the cold blue eyes.

Being inside FBI headquarters had a salutary effect on Lounds's manners. He was polite when he remembered to be, and he was quick and quiet with his equipment.

Graham balked only once: he flatly refused to let Lounds see Mrs. Leeds's diary or any of the families' private correspondence.

When the interview began, he answered Lounds's questions in a civil tone. Both men consulted notes taken in conference with Dr. Bloom. The questions and answers were often rephrased.

➤

Alan Bloom had found it difficult to scheme toward hurt. In the end, he simply laid out his theories about the Tooth Fairy. The others listened like karate students at an anatomy lecture.

Dr. Bloom said the Tooth Fairy's acts and his letter indicated a projective delusional scheme which compensated for intolerable feelings of inadequacy. Smashing the mirrors tied these feelings to his appearance.

The killer's objection to the name "Tooth Fairy" was grounded in the homosexual implications of the word "fairy." Bloom believed he had an unconscious homosexual conflict, a terrible fear of being gay. Dr. Bloom's opinion was reinforced by one curious observation at the Leeds house: fold marks and covered bloodstains indicated the Tooth Fairy put a pair of shorts on Charles Leeds after he was dead. Dr. Bloom believed he did this to emphasize his lack of interest in Leeds.

The psychiatrist talked about the strong bonding of aggressive and sexual drives that occurs in sadists at a very early age.

The savage attacks aimed primarily at the women and performed in the presence of their families were clearly strikes at a maternal figure. Bloom, pacing, talking half to himself, called his subject "the child of a nightmare." Crawford's eyelids drooped at the compassion in his voice.

➤

In the interview with Lounds, Graham made statements no investigator would make and no straight newspaper would credit.

He speculated that the Tooth Fairy was ugly, impotent with persons of the opposite sex, and he claimed falsely that the killer had sexually molested his male victims. Graham said that the Tooth Fairy doubtless was the laughingstock of his acquaintances and the product of an incestuous home.

He emphasized that the Tooth Fairy obviously was not as intelligent as Hannibal Lecter. He promised to provide the *Tattler* with more observations and insights about the killer as they occurred to him. Many law-enforcement people disagreed with him, he said, but as long as he was heading the investigation, the *Tattler* could count on getting the straight stuff from him.

Lounds took a lot of pictures.

The key shot was taken in Graham's "Washington hideaway," an apartment he had "borrowed to use until he squashed the Fairy." It was the only place where he could "find solitude" in the "carnival atmosphere" of the investigation.

The photograph showed Graham in a bathrobe at a desk, studying late into the night. He was poring over a grotesque "artist's conception" of "the Fairy."

Behind him a slice of the floodlit Capitol dome could be seen through the window. Most importantly, in the lower-left corner of the window, blurred but readable, was the sign of a popular motel across the street.

The Tooth Fairy could find the apartment if he wanted to.

At FBI headquarters, Graham was photographed in front of a mass spectrometer. It had nothing to do with the case, but Lounds thought it looked impressive.

Graham even consented to have his picture taken with Lounds interviewing him. They did it in front of the vast gun racks in Firearms and Toolmarks. Lounds held a nine-millimeter automatic of the same type as the Tooth Fairy's weapon. Graham pointed to the homemade silencer, fashioned from a length of television-antenna mast.

Dr. Bloom was surprised to see Graham put a comradely hand on Lounds's shoulder just before Crawford clicked the shutter.

The interview and pictures were set to appear in the *Tattler* published the next day, Monday, August 11. As soon as he had the material, Lounds left for Chicago. He said he wanted to supervise the layout himself. He made arrangements to meet Crawford on Tuesday afternoon five blocks from the trap.

Starting Tuesday, when the *Tattler* became generally available, two traps would be baited for the monster.

Graham would go each evening to his "temporary residence" shown in the *Tattler* picture.

A coded personal notice in the same issue invited the Tooth Fairy to a mail drop in Annapolis watched around the clock. If he were suspicious of the mail drop, he might think the effort to catch him was concentrated there. Then Graham would be a more appealing target, the FBI reasoned.

Florida authorities provided a stillwatch at Sugarloaf Key.

There was an air of dissatisfaction among the hunters—two major stakeouts took manpower that could be used elsewhere, and Graham's presence at the trap each night would limit his movement to the Washington area.

Though Crawford's judgment told him this was the best move, the whole procedure was too passive for his taste. He felt they were playing games with themselves in the dark of the moon with less than two weeks to go before it rose full again.

Sunday and Monday passed in curiously jerky time. The minutes dragged and the hours flew.

➤

Spurgen, chief SWAT instructor at Quantico, circled the apartment block on Monday afternoon. Graham rode beside him. Crawford was in the back seat.

"The pedestrian traffic falls off around seven-fifteen. Everybody's settled in for dinner," Spurgen said. With his wiry, compact body and his baseball cap tipped back on his head, he looked like an infielder. "Give us a toot on the clear band tomorrow night when you cross the B&O railroad tracks. You ought to try to make it about eight-thirty, eight-forty or so."

He pulled into the apartment parking lot. "This setup ain't heaven, but it could be worse. You'll park here tomorrow night. We'll change the space you use every night after that, but it'll always be on this side. It's seventy-five yards to the apartment entrance. Let's walk it."

Spurgen, short and bandy-legged, went ahead of Graham and Crawford.

He's looking for places where he could get the bad hop, Graham thought.

"The walk is probably where it'll happen, if it happens," the SWAT leader said. "See, from here the direct line from your car to the entrance, the natural route, is across the center of the lot. It's as far as you can get from the line of cars that are here all day. He'll have to come across open asphalt to get close. How well do you hear?"

"Pretty well," Graham said. "Damn well on this parking lot."

Spurgen looked for something in Graham's face, found nothing he could recognize.

He stopped in the middle of the lot. "We're reducing the wattage on these streetlights a little to make it tougher on a rifleman."

"Tougher on your people too," Crawford said.

"Two of ours have Startron night scopes," Spurgen said. "I've got some clear spray I'll ask you to use on your suit jackets, Will. By the way, I don't care how hot it is, you will wear body armor each and every time. Correct?"

"Yes."

"What is it?"

"It's Kevlar—what, Jack?—Second Chance?"

"Second Chance," Crawford said.

"It's pretty likely he'll come up to you, probably from behind, or he may figure on meeting you and then turning around to shoot when he's passed you," Spurgen said. "Seven times he's gone for the head shot, right? He's seen that work. He'll do it with you too if you give him the time. *Don't give him the time.* After I show you a couple of things in the lobby and the flop, let's go to the range. Can you do that?"

"He can do that," Crawford said.

Spurgen was high priest on the range. He made Graham wear earplugs under the earmuffs and flashed targets at him from every angle. He was relieved to see that Graham did not carry the regulation .38, but he worried about the flash from the ported barrel. They worked for two hours. The man insisted on checking the cylinder crane and cylinder latch screws on Graham's .44 when he had finished firing.

Graham showered and changed clothes to get the smell of gunsmoke off him before he drove to the bay for his last free night with Molly and Willy.

He took his wife and stepson to the grocery store after dinner and made a considerable to-do over selecting melons. He made sure they bought plenty of groceries—the old *Tattler* was still on the racks beside the checkout stands and he hoped Molly would not see the new issue coming in the morning. He didn't want to tell her what was happening.

When she asked him what he wanted for dinner in the coming week, he had to say he'd be away, that he was going back to Birmingham. It was the first real lie he had ever told her and telling it made him feel as greasy as old currency.

He watched her in the aisles: Molly, his pretty baseball wife, with her ceaseless vigilance for lumps, her insistence on quarterly medical checkups for him and Willy, her controlled fear of the dark; her hard-bought knowledge that time is luck. She knew the value of their days. She could hold a moment by its stem. She had taught him to relish.

Pachelbel's Canon filled the sun-drowned room where they learned each other and there was the exhilaration too big to hold and even then the fear flickered across him like an osprey's shadow: this is too good to live for long.

Molly switched her bag often from shoulder to shoulder in the grocery aisles, as though the gun in it weighed much more than its nineteen ounces.

Graham would have been offended had he heard the ugly thing he mumbled to the melons: "I have to put that bastard in a rubber sack, that's all. I have to do that."

Variously weighted with lies, guns, and groceries, the three of them were a small and solemn troop.

Molly smelled a rat. She and Graham did not speak after the lights were out. Molly dreamed of heavy crazy footsteps coming in a house of changing rooms.

CHAPTER 19

THERE IS A NEWSSTAND in Lambert St. Louis International Airport which carries many of the major daily newspapers from all over the United States. The New York, Washington, Chicago, and Los Angeles papers come in by air freight and you can buy them on the same day they are published.

Like many newsstands, this one is owned by a chain and, along with the standard magazines and papers, the operator is required to take a certain amount of trash.

When the Chicago *Tribune* was delivered to the stand at ten o'clock on Monday night, a bundle of *Tattlers* thumped to the floor beside it. The bundle was still warm in the center.

The newsstand operator squatted in front of his shelves arranging the *Tribunes*. He had enough else to do. The day guys never did their share of straightening.

A pair of black zippered boots came into the corner of his vision. A browser. No, the boots were pointed at him. Somebody wanted some damn thing. The newsie wanted to finish arranging his *Tribunes* but the insistent attention made the back of his head prickle.

His trade was transient. He didn't have to be nice. "What is it?" he said to the knees.

"A *Tattler*."

"You'll have to wait until I bust the bundle."

The boots did not go away. They were too close.

"I said you'll have to wait until I bust the bundle. Understand? See I'm working here?"

A hand and a flash of bright steel and the twine on the bundle beside him parted with a pop. A Susan B. Anthony dollar rang on the floor in front of him. A clean copy of the *Tattler*, jerked from the center of the bundle, spilled the top ones to the floor.

The newsstand operator got to his feet. His cheeks were flushed. The man was leaving with the paper under his arm.

"Hey. Hey, you."

The man turned to face him. "Me?"

"Yeah, you. I told you—"

"You told me what?" He was coming back. He stood too close. "You told me what?"

Usually a rude merchant can fluster his customers. There was something awful in this one's calm.

The newsie looked at the floor. "You got a quarter coming back."

Dolarhyde turned his back and walked out. The newsstand operator's cheeks burned for half an hour. *Yeah, that guy was in here last week too. He comes in here again, I'll tell him where to fuckin' get off. I got somethin' under the counter for wise-asses.*

Dolarhyde did not look at the *Tattler* in the airport. Last Thursday's message from Lecter had left him with mixed feelings. Dr. Lecter had been right, of course, in saying that he was beautiful and it was thrilling to read. He *was* beautiful. He felt some contempt for the doctor's fear of the policeman. Lecter did not understand much better than the public.

Still, he was on fire to know if Lecter had sent him another message. He would wait until he got home to look. Dolarhyde was proud of his self-control.

He mused about the newsstand operator as he drove.

There was a time when he would have apologized for disturbing the man and never come back to the newsstand. For years he had taken shit unlimited from people. Not anymore. The man could have insulted Francis Dolarhyde: he could not face the Dragon. It was all part of Becoming.

➢

At midnight, the light above his desk still burned. The message from the *Tattler* was decoded and wadded on the floor. Pieces of the *Tattler* were scattered where Dolarhyde had clipped it for his journal. The great journal stood open beneath the painting of the Dragon, glue still drying where the new clippings were fastened. Beneath them, freshly attached, was a small plastic bag, empty as yet.

The legend beside the bag said: "With These He Offended Me."

But Dolarhyde had left his desk.

He was sitting on the basement stairs in the cool must of earth and mildew. The beam from his electric lantern moved over draped furniture, the dusty backs of the great mirrors that once hung in the house and now leaned against the walls, the trunk containing his case of dynamite.

The beam stopped on a tall draped shape, one of several in the far corner of the cellar. Cobwebs touched his face as he went to it. Dust made him sneeze when he pulled off the cloth cover.

He blinked back the tears and shone his light on the old oak wheelchair he had uncovered. It was high-backed, heavy, and strong, one of three in the basement. The county had provided them to Grandmother in the 1940's when she ran her nursing home here.

The wheels squeaked as he rolled the chair across the floor. Despite its weight, he carried it easily up the stairs. In the kitchen he oiled the wheels. The small front wheels still squeaked, but the back ones had good bearings and spun freely at a flip of his finger.

The searing anger in him was eased by the wheels' soothing hum. As he spun them, Dolarhyde hummed too.

CHAPTER 20

WHEN FREDDY LOUNDS LEFT the *Tattler* office at noon on Tuesday he was tired and high. He had put together the *Tattler* story on the plane to Chicago and laid it out in the composing room in thirty minutes flat.

The rest of the time he had worked steadily on his paperback, brushing off all callers. He was a good organizer and now he had fifty thousand words of solid background.

When the Tooth Fairy was caught, he'd do a whammo lead and an account of the capture. The background material would fit in neatly. He had arranged to have three of the *Tattler's* better reporters ready to go on short notice. Within hours of the capture they could be digging for details wherever the Tooth Fairy lived.

His agent talked very big numbers. Discussing the project with the agent ahead of time was, strictly speaking, a violation of his agreement with Crawford. All contracts and memos would be postdated after the capture to cover that up.

Crawford held a big stick—he had Lounds's threat on tape. Interstate transmission of a threatening message was an indictable offense outside any protection Lounds enjoyed under the First Amendment. Lounds also knew that Crawford, with one phone call, could give him a permanent problem with the Internal Revenue Service.

167

There were polyps of honesty in Lounds; he had few illusions about the nature of his work. But he had developed a near-religious fervor about this project.

He was possessed with a vision of a better life on the other side of the money. Buried under all the dirt he had ever done, his old hopes still faced east. Now they stirred and strained to rise.

Satisfied that his cameras and recording equipment were ready, he drove home to sleep for three hours before the flight to Washington, where he would meet Crawford near the trap.

A damned nuisance in the underground garage. The black van, parked in the space next to his, was over the line. It crowded into the space clearly marked "Mr. Frederick Lounds."

Lounds opened his door hard, banging the side of the van and leaving a dent and a mark. That would teach the inconsiderate bastard.

Lounds was locking his car when the van door opened behind him. He was turning, had half-turned when the flat sap thocked over his ear. He got his hands up, but his knees were going and there was tremendous pressure around his neck and the air was shut off. When his heaving chest could fill again it sucked chloroform.

➤

Dolarhyde parked the van behind his house, climbed out and stretched. He had fought a crosswind all the way from Chicago and his arms were tired. He studied the night sky. The Perseid meteor shower was due soon, and he must not miss it.

Revelation: And his tail drew the third part of the stars of heaven, and did cast them down to the earth . . .

His doing in another time. He must see it and remember.

Dolarhyde unlocked the back door and made his routine search of the house. When he came outside again he wore a stocking mask.

He opened the van and attached a ramp. Then he rolled out Freddy Lounds. Lounds wore nothing but his shorts and a gag and blindfold. Though he was only semiconscious, he did not slump. He sat up very straight, his head against the high back of the old oak wheelchair. From the back of his head to the soles of his feet he was bonded to the chair with epoxy glue.

Dolarhyde rolled him into the house and parked him in a corner of the parlor with his back to the room, as though he had misbehaved.

"Are you too cool? Would you like a blanket?"

Dolarhyde peeled off the sanitary napkins covering Lounds's eyes and mouth. Lounds didn't answer. The odor of chloroform hung on him.

"I'll get you a blanket." Dolarhyde took an afghan from the sofa and tucked it around Lounds up to the chin, then pressed an ammonia bottle under his nose.

Lounds's eyes opened wide on a blurred joining of walls. He coughed and started talking.

"Accident? Am I hurt bad?"

The voice behind him: "No, Mr. Lounds. You'll be just fine."

"My back hurts. My skin. Did I get burned? I hope to God I'm not burned."

"Burned? Burned. No. You just rest here. I'll be with you in a little while."

"Let me lie down. Listen, I want you to call my office. My God, I'm in a Striker frame. My back's broken—tell me the truth!"

Footsteps going away.

"What am I doing here?" The question shrill at the end.

The answer came from far behind him. "Atoning, Mr. Lounds."

Lounds heard footsteps mounting stairs. He heard a shower running. His head was clearer now. He remembered leaving the office and driving, but he couldn't remember after that. The side of his head throbbed and the smell of chloroform made him gag. Held rigidly erect, he was afraid he would vomit and drown. He opened his mouth wide and breathed deep. He could hear his heart.

Lounds hoped he was asleep. He tried to raise his arm from the armrest, increasing the pull deliberately until the pain in his palm and arm was enough to wake him from any dream. He was not asleep. His mind gathered speed.

By straining he could turn his eyes enough to see his arm for seconds at a time. He saw how he was fastened. This was no device to protect broken backs. This was no hospital. Someone had him.

Lounds thought he heard footsteps on the floor above, but they might have been his heartbeats.

He tried to think. Strained to think. *Keep cool and think,* he whispered. Cool and think.

The stairs creaked as Dolarhyde came down.

Lounds felt the weight of him in every step. A presence behind him now.

Lounds spoke several words before he could adjust the volume of his voice.

"I haven't seen your face. I couldn't identify you. I don't know what you look like. The *Tattler,* I work for *The National Tattler,* would pay a reward . . . a big reward for me. Half a million, a million maybe. A million dollars."

Silence behind him. Then a squeak of couch springs. He was sitting down, then.

"What do you think, Mr. Lounds?"

Put the pain and fear away and think. Now. For all time. To have some time. To have years. He hasn't decided to kill me. He hasn't let me see his face.

"What do you think, Mr. Lounds?"

"I don't know what's happened to me."

"Do you know Who I Am, Mr. Lounds?"

"No. I don't want to know, believe me."

"According to you, I'm a vicious, perverted sexual failure. An animal, you said. Probably turned loose from an asylum by a do-good judge." Ordinarily, Dolarhyde would have avoided the sibilant /s/ in "sexual." In the presence of this audience, very far from laughter, he was freed. "You know now, don't you?"

Don't lie. Think fast. "Yes."

"Why do you write lies, Mr. Lounds? Why do you say I'm crazy? Answer now."

"When a person . . . when a person does things that most people can't understand, they call him . . ."

"Crazy."

"They called, like . . . the Wright brothers. All through history—"

"History. Do you understand what I'm doing, Mr. Lounds?"

Understand. There it was. A chance. Swing hard. "No, but I think I've got an opportunity to understand, and then *all my readers could understand too.*"

"Do you feel privileged?"

"It's a privilege. But I have to tell you, man to man, that I'm scared. It's hard to concentrate when you're scared. If you have a great idea, you wouldn't have to scare me for me to really be impressed."

"Man to man. Man to man. You use that expression to imply

frankness, Mr. Lounds, I appreciate that. But you see, I am not a man. I began as one but by the Grace of God and my own Will, I have become Other and More than a man. You say you're frightened. Do you believe that God is in attendance here, Mr. Lounds?"

"I don't know."

"Are you praying to Him now?"

"Sometimes I pray. I have to tell you, I just pray mostly when I'm scared."

"And does God help you?"

"I don't know. I don't think about it after. I ought to."

"You ought to. Um-hmmmm. There are so many things you ought to understand. In a little while I'll help you understand. Will you excuse me now?"

"Certainly."

Footsteps out of the room. The slide and rattle of a kitchen drawer. Lounds had covered many murders committed in kitchens where things are handy. Police reporting can change forever your view of kitchens. Water running now.

Lounds thought it must be night. Crawford and Graham were expecting him. Certainly he had been missed by now. A great, hollow sadness pulsed briefly with his fear.

Breathing behind him, a flash of white caught by his rolling eye. A hand, powerful and pale. It held a cup of tea with honey. Lounds sipped it through a straw.

"I'd do a big story," he said between sips. "Anything you want to say. Describe you any way you want, or no description, no description."

"Shhhh." A single finger tapped the top of his head. The lights brightened. The chair began to turn.

"No. I don't want to see you."

"Oh, but you must, Mr. Lounds. You're a reporter. You're here to report. When I turn you around, open your eyes and look at me. If you won't open them yourself, I'll staple your eyelids to your forehead."

A wet mouth noise, a snapping click and the chair spun. Lounds faced the room, his eyes tight shut. A finger tapped insistently on his chest. A touch on his eyelids. He looked.

To Lounds, seated, he seemed very tall standing in his kimono. A stocking mask was rolled up to his nose. He turned his back to Lounds and dropped the robe. The great back muscles flexed above the brilliant tattoo of the tail that ran down his lower back and wrapped around the leg.

The Dragon turned his head slowly, looked over his shoulder at Lounds and smiled, all jags and stains.

"Oh my dear God Jesus," Lounds said.

Lounds now in the center of the room where he can see the screen. Dolarhyde, behind him, has put on his robe and put in the teeth that allow him to speak.

"Do you want to know What I Am?"

Lounds tried to nod; the chair jerked his scalp. "More than anything. I was afraid to ask."

"Look."

The first slide was Blake's painting, the great Man-Dragon, wings flared and tail lashing, poised above the Woman Clothed with the Sun.

"Do you see now?"

"I see."

Rapidly Dolarhyde ran through his other slides.

Click. Mrs. Jacobi alive. "Do you see?"

"Yes."

Click. Mrs. Leeds alive. "Do you see?"

"Yes."

Click. Dolarhyde, the Dragon rampant, muscles flexed and tail tattoo above the Jacobis' bed. "Do you see?"

"Yes."

Click. Mrs. Jacobi waiting. "Do you see?"

"Yes."

Click. Mrs. Jacobi after. "Do you see?"

"Yes."

Click. The Dragon rampant. "Do you see?"

"Yes."

Click. Mrs. Leeds waiting, her husband slack beside her. "Do you see?"

"Yes."

Click. Mrs. Leeds after, harlequined with blood. "Do you see?"

"Yes."

Click. Freddy Lounds, a copy of a *Tattler* photograph. "Do you see?"

"Oh God."

"Do you see?"

"Oh my God." The words drawn out, as a child speaks crying.

"Do you see?"

"Please no."

"No what?"

"Not me."

"No what? You're a man, Mr. Lounds. Are you a man?"

"Yes."

"Do you imply that I'm some kind of queer?"

"God no."

"Are you a queer, Mr. Lounds?"

"No."

"Are you going to write more lies about me, Mr. Lounds?"

"Oh no, no."

"Why did you write lies, Mr. Lounds?"

"The police told me. It was what they said."

"You quote Will Graham."

"Graham told me the lies. Graham."

"Will you tell the truth now? About Me. My Work. My Becoming. My *Art*, Mr. Lounds. Is this Art?"

"Art."

The fear in Lounds's face freed Dolarhyde to speak and he could fly on sibilants and fricatives; plosives were his great webbed wings.

"You said that I, who see more than you, am insane. I, who pushed the world so much further than you, am insane. I have dared more than you, I have pressed my unique seal so much deeper in the earth, where it will last longer than your dust. Your life to mine is a slug track on stone. A thin silver mucus track in and out of the letters on my monument." The words Dolarhyde had written in his journal swarmed in him now.

"I am the Dragon and you call me *insane?* My movements are followed and recorded as avidly as those of a mighty guest star. Do you know about the guest star in 1054? Of course not. Your readers follow you like a child follows a slug track with his finger, and in the same tired loops of reason. Back to your shallow skull and potato face as a slug follows his own slime back home.

"Before Me you are a slug in the sun. You are privy to a great Becoming and you recognize nothing. You are an ant in the afterbirth.

"It is in your nature to do one thing correctly: before Me you rightly tremble. Fear is not what you owe Me, Lounds, you and the other pismires. *You owe Me awe.*"

Dolarhyde stood with his head down, his thumb and forefinger against the bridge of his nose. Then he left the room.

He didn't take off the mask, Lounds thought. *He didn't take off the mask. If he comes back with it off, I'm dead. God, I'm wet all over.* He rolled his eyes toward the doorway and waited through the sounds from the back of the house.

When Dolarhyde returned, he still wore the mask. He carried a lunch box and two thermoses. "For your trip back home." He held up a thermos. "Ice, we'll need that. Before we go, we'll tape a little while."

He clipped a microphone to the afghan near Lounds's face. "Repeat after me."

They taped for half an hour. Finally, "That's all, Mr. Lounds. You did very well."

"You'll let me go now?"

"I will. There's one way, though, that I can help you better understand and remember." Dolarhyde turned away.

"I want to understand. I want you to know I appreciate you turning me loose. I'm really going to be fair from now on, you know that."

Dolarhyde could not answer. He had changed his teeth.

The tape recorder was running again.

He smiled at Lounds, a brown-stained smile. He placed his hand on Lounds's heart and, leaning to him intimately as though to kiss him, he bit Lounds's lips off and spit them on the floor.

CHAPTER 21

DAWN IN CHICAGO, heavy air and the gray sky low.

A security guard came out of the lobby of the *Tattler* building and stood at the curb smoking a cigarette and rubbing the small of his back. He was alone on the street and in the quiet he could hear the clack of the traffic light changing at the top of the hill, a long block away.

Half a block north of the light, out of the guard's sight, Francis Dolarhyde squatted beside Lounds in the back of the van. He arranged the blanket in a deep cowl that hid Lounds's head.

Lounds was in great pain. He appeared stuporous, but his mind was racing. There were things he must remember. The blindfold was tented across his nose and he could see Dolarhyde's fingers checking the crusted gag.

Dolarhyde put on the white jacket of a medical orderly, laid a thermos in Lounds's lap and rolled him out of the van. When he locked the wheels of the chair and turned to put the ramp back in the van, Lounds could see the end of the van's bumper beneath his blindfold.

Turning now, seeing the bumper guard . . . Yes! the license plate. Only a flash, but Lounds burned it into his mind.

Rolling now. Sidewalk seams. Around a corner and down a curb. Paper crackled under the wheels.

Dolarhyde stopped the wheelchair in a bit of littered shelter between a garbage dumpster and a parked truck. He pulled at the blindfold. Lounds closed his eyes. An ammonia bottle under his nose.

The soft voice close beside him.

"Can you hear me? You're almost there." The blindfold off now. "Blink if you can hear me."

Dolarhyde opened his eye with a thumb and forefinger. Lounds was looking at Dolarhyde's face.

"I told you one fib." Dolarhyde tapped the thermos. "I don't *really* have your lips on ice." He whipped off the blanket and opened the thermos.

Lounds strained hard when he smelled the gasoline, separating the skin from under his forearms and making the stout chair groan. The gas was cold all over him, fumes filling his throat and they were rolling toward the center of the street.

"Do you like being Graham's pet, Freeeeedeeeee?"

Lit with a whump and shoved, sent rolling down on the *Tattler*, eeek, eeek, eeekeeekeeek the wheels.

The guard looked up as a scream blew the burning gag away. He saw the fireball coming, bouncing on the potholes, trailing smoke and sparks and the flames blown back like wings, disjointed reflections leaping along the shop windows.

It veered, struck a parked car and overturned in front of the building, one wheel spinning and flames through the spokes, blazing arms rising in the fighting posture of the burned.

The guard ran back into the lobby. He wondered if it would blow up, if he should get away from the windows. He pulled the fire alarm. What else? He grabbed the fire extinguisher off the wall and looked outside. It hadn't blown up yet.

The guard approached cautiously through the greasy smoke spreading low over the pavement and, at last, sprayed foam on Freddy Lounds.

CHAPTER 22

THE SCHEDULE called for Graham to leave the staked-out apartment in Washington at 5:45 A.M., well ahead of the morning rush.

Crawford called while he was shaving.

"Good morning."

"Not so good," Crawford said. "The Tooth Fairy got Lounds in Chicago."

"Oh hell no."

"He's not dead yet and he's asking for you. He can't wait long."

"I'll go."

"Meet me at the airport. United 245. It leaves in forty minutes. You can be back for the stakeout, if it's still on."

➤

Special Agent Chester from the Chicago FBI office met them at O'Hare in a downpour. Chicago is a city used to sirens. The traffic parted reluctantly in front of them as Chester howled down the expressway, his red light flashing pink on the driving rain.

He raised his voice above the siren. "Chicago PD says he was jumped in his garage. My stuff is secondhand. We're not popular around here today."

"How much is out?" Crawford said.

177

"The whole thing, trap, all of it."

"Did Lounds get a look at him?"

"I haven't heard a description. Chicago PD put out an all-points bulletin for a license number about six-twenty."

"Did you get hold of Dr. Bloom for me?"

"I got his wife, Jack. Dr. Bloom had his gall bladder taken out this morning."

"Glorious," Crawford said.

Chester pulled under the dripping hospital portico. He turned in his seat. "Jack, Will, before you go up . . . I hear this fruit really trashed Lounds. You ought to be ready for that."

Graham nodded. All the way to Chicago he had tried to choke his hope that Lounds would die before he had to see him.

The corridor of Paege Burn Center was a tube of spotless tile. A tall doctor with a curiously old-young face beckoned Graham and Crawford away from the knot of people at Lounds's door.

"Mr. Lounds's burns are fatal," the doctor said. "I *can* help him with the pain, and I intend to do it. He breathed flames and his throat and lungs are damaged. He may not regain consciousness. In his condition, that would be a blessing.

"In the event that he does regain consciousness, the city police have asked me to take the airway out of his throat so that he might possibly answer questions. I've agreed to try that—briefly.

"At the moment his nerve endings are anesthetized by fire. A lot of pain is coming, if he lives that long. I made this clear to the police and I want to make it clear to you: I'll interrupt any attempted questioning to sedate him if he wants me to. Do you understand me?"

"Yes," Crawford said.

With a nod to the patrolman in front of the door, the doctor clasped his hands behind his white lab coat and moved away like a wading egret.

Crawford glanced at Graham. "You okay?"

"I'm okay. *I* had the SWAT team."

Lounds's head was elevated in the bed. His hair and ears were gone and compresses over his sightless eyes replaced the burned-off lids. His gums were puffed with blisters.

The nurse beside him moved an IV stand so Graham could come close. Lounds smelled like a stable fire.

"Freddy, it's Will Graham."

Lounds arched his neck against the pillow.

"The movement's just reflex, he's not conscious," the nurse said.

The plastic airway holding open his scorched and swollen throat hissed in time with the respirator.

A pale detective sergeant sat in the corner with a tape recorder and a clipboard on his lap. Graham didn't notice him until he spoke.

"Lounds said your name in the emergency room before they put the airway in."

"You were there?"

"Later I was there. But I've got what he said on tape. He gave the firemen a license number when they first got to him. He passed out, and he was out in the ambulance, but he came around for a minute in the emergency room when they gave him a shot in the chest. Some *Tattler* people had followed the ambulance—they were there. I have a copy of their tape."

"Let me hear it."

The detective fiddled with his tape recorder. "I think you want to use the earphone," he said, his face carefully blank. He pushed the button.

Graham heard voices, the rattle of casters, ". . . put him in three," the bump of a litter on a swinging door, a retching cough and a voice croaking, speaking without lips.

"*Tooth Hairy.*"

"Freddy, did you see him? What did he look like, Freddy?"

"*Wendy? Hlease Wendy. Grahan set ne uh. The cunt knew it. Grahan set ne uh. Cunt tut his hand on ne in the ticture like a hucking tet. Wendy?*"

A noise like a drain sucking. A doctor's voice: "That's it. Let me get there. Get out of the way. *Now.*"

That was all.

Graham stood over Lounds while Crawford listened to the tape.

"We're running down the license number," the detective said. "Could you understand what he was saying?"

"Who's Wendy?" Crawford asked.

"That hooker in the hall. The blonde with the chest. She's been trying to see him. She doesn't know anything."

"Why don't you let her in?" Graham said from the bedside. His back was to them.

"No visitors."

"The man's dying."

"Think I don't know it? I've been here since a quarter to fucking six o'clock—excuse me, Nurse."

"Take a few minutes," Crawford said. "Get some coffee, put some water on your face. He can't say anything. If he does, I'll be here with the recorder."

"Okay, I could use it."

When the detective was gone, Graham left Crawford at the bedside and approached the woman in the hall.

"Wendy?"

"Yeah."

"If you're sure you want to go in there, I'll take you."

"I want to. Maybe I ought to go comb my hair."

"It doesn't matter," Graham said.

When the policeman returned, he didn't try to put her out.

Wendy of Wendy City held Lounds's blackened claw and looked straight at him. He stirred once, a little before noon.

"It's gonna be just fine, Roscoe," she said. "We'll have us some high old times."

Lounds stirred again and died.

CHAPTER 23

CAPTAIN OSBORNE of Chicago Homicide had the gray, pointed face of a stone fox. Copies of the *Tattler* were all over the police station. One was on his desk.

He didn't ask Crawford and Graham to sit down.

"You had nothing at all working with Lounds in the city of Chicago?"

"No, he was coming to Washington," Crawford said. "He had a plane reservation. I'm sure you've checked it."

"Yeah, I got it. He left his office about one-thirty yesterday. Got jumped in the garage of his building, must have been about ten of two."

"Anything in the garage?"

"His keys got kicked under his car. There's no garage attendant—they had a radio-operated door but it came down on a couple of cars and they took it out. Nobody saw it happen. That's getting to be the refrain today. We're working on his car."

"Can we help you there?"

"You can have the results when I get 'em. You haven't said much, Graham. You had plenty to say in the paper."

"I haven't heard much either, listening to you."

"You pissed off, Captain?" Crawford said.

"Me? Why should I be? We run down a phone trace for you and

181

collar a fucking news reporter. Then you've got no charges against him. You *have* got some deal with him, gets him cooked in front of this scandal sheet. Now the other papers adopt him like he was their own.

"Now we've got our own Tooth Fairy murder right here in Chicago. That's great. 'Tooth Fairy in Chicago,' boy. Before midnight we'll have six accidental domestic shootings, guy trying to sneak in his own house drunk, wife hears him, bang. The Tooth Fairy may like Chicago, decide to stick around, have some fun."

"We can do like this," Crawford said. "Butt heads, get the police commissioner and the U.S. attorney all stirred up, get all the assholes stirred up, yours and mine. Or we can settle down and try to catch the bastard. This was my operation and it went to shit, I know that. You ever have that happen right here in Chicago? I don't want to fight you, Captain. We want to catch him and go home. What do you want?"

Osborne moved a couple of items on his desk, a penholder, a picture of a fox-faced child in band uniform. He leaned back in his chair, pursed his lips and blew out some air.

"Right now I want some coffee. You guys want some?"

"I'd like some," Crawford said.

"So would I," Graham said.

Osborne passed around the Styrofoam cups. He pointed to some chairs.

"The Tooth Fairy had to have a van or a panel truck to move Lounds around in that wheelchair," Graham said.

Osborne nodded. "The license plate Lounds saw was stolen off a TV repair truck in Oak Park. He took a commercial plate, so he was getting it for a truck or a van. He *replaced* the plate on the TV truck with another stolen plate so it wouldn't be noticed so fast. Very sly, this boy. One thing we do know—he got the plate off the TV truck sometime after eight-thirty yesterday morning. The TV repair guy bought gas first thing yesterday and he used a credit card. The attendant copied the correct license number on the slip, so the plate was stolen after that."

"Nobody saw any kind of truck or van?" Crawford said.

"Nothing. The guard at the *Tattler* saw zip. He could referee wrestling he sees so little. The fire department responded first to the *Tattler*. They were just looking for fire. We're canvassing the overnight workers in the *Tattler* neighborhood and the neighborhoods where the TV guy worked Tuesday morning. We hope somebody saw him cop the plate."

"I'd like to see the chair again," Graham said.

"It's in our lab. I'll call them for you." Osborne paused. "Lounds was a ballsy little guy, you have to give him that. Remembering the license number and spitting it out, the shape he was in. You listened to what Lounds said at the hospital?"

Graham nodded.

"I don't mean to rub this in, but I want to know if we heard it the same way. What does it sound like to you?"

Graham quoted in a monotone: "'Tooth Fairy. Graham set me up. The cunt knew it. Graham set me up. Cunt put his hand on me in the picture like a fucking pet.'"

Osborne could not tell how Graham felt about it. He asked another question.

"He was talking about the picture of you and him in the *Tattler?*"

"Had to be."

"Where would he get that idea?"

"Lounds and I had a few run-ins."

"But you looked friendly toward Lounds in the picture. The Tooth Fairy kills the pet first, is that it?"

"That's it." The stone fox was pretty fast, Graham thought.

"Too bad you didn't stake him out."

Graham said nothing.

"Lounds was supposed to be with us by the time the Tooth Fairy saw the *Tattler*," Crawford said.

"Does what he said mean anything else to you, anything we can use?"

Graham came back from somewhere and had to repeat Osborne's question in his mind before he answered. "We know from what Lounds said that the Tooth Fairy saw the *Tattler* before he hit Lounds, right?"

"Right."

"If you start with the idea that the *Tattler* set him off, does it strike you that he set this up in a hell of a hurry? The thing came off the press Monday night, he's in Chicago stealing license plates sometime Tuesday, probably Tuesday morning, and he's on top of Lounds

Tuesday afternoon. What does that say to you?"

"That he saw it early or he didn't have far to come," Crawford said. "Either he saw it here in Chicago or he saw it someplace else Monday night. Bear in mind, he'd be watching for it to get the personal column."

"Either he was already here, or he came from driving distance," Graham said. "He was on top of Lounds too fast with a big old wheelchair you couldn't carry on a plane—it doesn't even fold. And he didn't fly here, steal a van, steal plates for it, and go around looking for an antique wheelchair to use. He had to have an old wheelchair—a new one wouldn't work for what he did." Graham was up, fiddling with the cord on the venetian blinds, staring at the brick wall across the airshaft. "He already had the wheelchair or he saw it all the time."

Osborne started to ask a question, but Crawford's expression cautioned him to wait.

Graham was tying knots in the blind cord. His hands were not steady.

"He saw it all the time . . ." Crawford prompted.

"Um-hmm," Graham said. "You can see how . . . the idea starts with the wheelchair. From the sight and thought of the wheelchair. That's where the idea would come from when he's thinking what he'll do to those fuckers. Freddy rolling down the street on fire, it must have been quite a sight."

"Do you think he watched it?"

"Maybe. He certainly saw it before he did it, when he was making up his mind what he'd do."

Osborne watched Crawford. Crawford was solid. Osborne knew Crawford was solid, and Crawford was going along with this.

"If he had the chair, or he saw it all the time . . . we can check around the nursing homes, the VA," Osborne said.

"It was perfect to hold Freddy still," Graham said.

"For a long time. He was gone fifteen hours and twenty-five minutes, more or less," Osborne said.

"If he had just wanted to snuff Freddy, he could have done that in the garage," Graham said. "He could have burned him in his car. He wanted to talk to Freddy, or hurt him for a while."

"Either he did it in the back of the van or he took him somewhere," Crawford said. "That length of time, I'd say he took him somewhere."

"It had to be somewhere safe. If he bundled him up good, he

wouldn't attract much notice around a nursing home, going in and out," Osborne said.

"He'd have the racket, though," Crawford said. "A certain amount of cleaning up to do. Assume he had the chair, and he had access to the van, and he had a safe place to take him to work on him. Does that sound like . . . home?"

Osborne's telephone rang. He growled into it.

"What? . . . No, I don't want to talk to the *Tattler* . . . Well, it better not be bullshit. Put her on. . . . Captain Osborne, yes . . . What time? Who answered the phone initially—at the switchboard? Take her off the switchboard, please. Tell me again what he said. . . . I'll have an officer there in five minutes."

Osborne looked at his telephone thoughtfully after he hung up.

"Lounds's secretary got a call about five minutes ago," he said. "She swears it was Lounds's voice. He said something, something she didn't get, '. . . strength of the Great Red Dragon.' That's what she thought he said."

CHAPTER 24

DR. FREDERICK CHILTON stood in the corridor outside Hannibal Lecter's cell. With Chilton were three large orderlies. One carried a straitjacket and leg restraints and another held a can of Mace. The third loaded a tranquilizer dart into his air rifle.

Lecter was reading an actuarial chart at his table and taking notes. He had heard the footsteps coming. He heard the rifle breech close behind him, but he continued to read and gave no sign that he knew Chilton was there.

Chilton had sent him the newspapers at noon and let him wait until night to find out his punishment for helping the Dragon.

"Dr. Lecter," Chilton said.

Lecter turned around. "Good evening, Dr. Chilton." He didn't acknowledge the presence of the guards. He looked only at Chilton.

"I've come for your books. *All* your books."

"I see. May I ask how long you intend to keep them?"

"That depends on your attitude."

"Is this *your* decision?"

"I decide the punitive measures here."

"Of course you do. It's not the sort of thing Will Graham would request."

"Back up to the net and slip these on, Dr. Lecter. I won't ask you twice."

"Certainly, Dr. Chilton. I hope that's a thirty-nine—the thirty-sevens are snug around the chest."

186

Dr. Lecter put on the restraints as though they were dinner clothes. An orderly reached through the barrier and fastened them from the back.

"Help him to his cot," Chilton said.

While the orderlies stripped the bookshelves, Chilton polished his glasses and stirred Lecter's personal papers with a pen.

Lecter watched from the shadowed corner of his cell. There was a curious grace about him, even in restraints.

"Beneath the yellow folder," Lecter said quietly, "you'll find a rejection slip the *Archives* sent you. It was brought to me by mistake with some of my *Archives* mail, and I'm afraid I opened it without looking at the envelope. Sorry."

Chilton reddened. He spoke to an orderly. "I think you'd better take the seat off Dr. Lecter's toilet."

Chilton looked at the actuarial table. Lecter had written his age at the top: forty-one. "And what do you have here?" Chilton asked.

"Time," Dr. Lecter said.

➤

Section Chief Brian Zeller took the courier's case and the wheelchair wheels into Instrumental Analysis, walking at a rate that made his gabardine pants whistle.

The staff, held over from the day shift, knew that whistling sound very well: Zeller in a hurry.

There had been enough delays. The weary courier, his flight from Chicago delayed by weather and then diverted to Philadelphia, had rented a car and driven down to the FBI laboratory in Washington.

The Chicago police laboratory is efficient, but there are things it is not equipped to do. Zeller prepared to do them now.

At the mass spectrometer he dropped off the paint flecks from Lounds's car door.

Beverly Katz in Hair and Fiber got the wheels to share with others in the section.

Zeller's last stop was the small hot room where Liza Lake bent over her gas chromatograph. She was testing ashes from a Florida arson case, watching the stylus trace its spiky line on the moving graph.

"Ace lighter fluid," she said. "That's what he lit it with." She had looked at so many samples that she could distinguish brands without searching through the manual.

Zeller took his eyes off Liza Lake and rebuked himself severely for feeling pleasure in the office. He cleared his throat and held up the two shiny paint cans.

"Chicago?" she said.

Zeller nodded.

She checked the condition of the cans and the seal of the lids. One can contained ashes from the wheelchair; the other, charred material from Lounds.

"How long has it been in the cans?"

"Six hours anyway," Zeller said.

"I'll headspace it."

She pierced the lid with a heavy-duty syringe, extracted air that had been confined with the ashes, and injected the air directly into the gas chromatograph. She made minute adjustments. As the sample moved along the machine's five-hundred-foot column, the stylus jiggled on the wide graph paper.

"Unleaded . . ." she said. "It's gasohol, unleaded gasohol. Don't see much of that." She flipped quickly through a looseleaf file of sample graphs. "I can't give you a brand yet. Let me do it with pentane and I'll get back to you."

"Good," Zeller said. Pentane would dissolve the fluids in the ashes, then fractionate early in the chromatograph, leaving the fluids for fine analysis.

➤

By one A.M. Zeller had all he could get.

Liza Lake succeeded in naming the gasohol: Freddy Lounds was burned with a "Servco Supreme" blend.

Patient brushing in the grooves of the wheelchair treads yielded two kinds of carpet fiber—wool and synthetic. Mold in dirt from the treads indicated the chair had been stored in a cool, dark place.

The other results were less satisfactory. The paint flecks were not original factory paint. Blasted in the mass spectrometer and compared with the national automotive paint file, the paint proved to be high-quality Duco enamel manufactured in a lot of 186,000 gallons during the first quarter of 1978 for sale to several auto-paintshop chains.

Zeller had hoped to pinpoint a make of vehicle and the approximate time of manufacture.

He telexed the results to Chicago.

The Chicago police department wanted its wheels back. The wheels made an awkward package for the courier. Zeller put written lab reports in his pouch along with mail and a package that had come for Graham.

"Federal Express I'm not," the courier said when he was sure Zeller couldn't hear him.

➤

The Justice Department maintains several small apartments near Seventh District Court in Chicago for the use of jurists and favored expert witnesses when court is in session. Graham stayed in one of these, with Crawford across the hall.

He came in at nine P.M., tired and wet. He had not eaten since breakfast on the plane from Washington and the thought of food repelled him.

Rainy Wednesday was over at last. It was as bad a day as he could remember.

With Lounds dead, it seemed likely that he was next and all day Chester had watched his back; while he was in Lounds's garage, while he stood in the rain on the scorched pavement where Lounds was burned. With strobe lights flashing in his face, he told the press he was "grieved at the loss of his friend Frederick Lounds."

He was going to the funeral, too. So were a number of federal agents and police, in the hope that the killer would come to see Graham grieve.

Actually he felt nothing he could name, just cold nausea and an occasional wave of sickly exhilaration that he had not burned to death instead of Lounds.

It seemed to Graham that he had learned nothing in forty years: he had just gotten tired.

He made a big martini and drank it while he undressed. He had another after his shower while he watched the news.

("An FBI trap to catch the Tooth Fairy backfires and a veteran reporter is dead. We'll be back with details on Eyewitness News after this.")

They were referring to the killer as "the Dragon" before the newscast was over. The *Tattler* had spilled it all to the networks. Graham wasn't surprised. Thursday's edition should sell well.

He made a third martini and called Molly.

She had seen the television news at six and ten o'clock and she had seen a *Tattler*. She knew that Graham had been the bait in a trap.

"You should have told me, Will."

"Maybe. I don't think so."

"Will he try to kill you now?"

"Sooner or later. It would be hard for him now, since I'm moving around. I'm covered all the time, Molly, and he knows it. I'll be okay."

"You sound a little slurry, have you been to see your friend in the fridge?"

"I had a couple."

"How do you feel?"

"Fairly rotten."

"The news said the FBI didn't have any protection for the reporter."

"He was supposed to be with Crawford by the time the Tooth Fairy got the paper."

"The news is calling him the Dragon now."

"That's what he calls himself."

"Will, there's something . . . I want to take Willy and leave here."

"And go where?"

"His grandparents'. They haven't seen him in a while, they'd like to see him."

"Oh, um-hmm."

Willy's father's parents had a ranch on the Oregon coast.

"It's creepy here. I know it's supposed to be safe—but we're not sleeping a whole lot. Maybe the shooting lessons spooked me, I don't know."

"I'm sorry, Molly." I wish I could tell you how sorry.

"I'll miss you. We both will."

So she had made up her mind.

"When are you going?"

"In the morning."

"What about the shop?"

"Evelyn wants to take it. I'll underwrite the fall stuff with the wholesalers, just for the interest, and she can keep what she makes."

"The dogs?"

"I asked her to call the county, Will. I'm sorry, but maybe somebody will take some of them."

"Molly, I—"

"If staying here I could keep something bad from happening to you, I'd stay. But you can't save anybody, Will, I'm not helping you here. With us up there, you can just think about taking care of yourself. I'm not carrying this damned pistol the rest of my life, Will."

"Maybe you can get down to Oakland and watch the A's." Didn't mean to say that. Oh boy, this silence is getting pretty long.

"Well, look, I'll call you," she said, "or I guess you'll have to call me up there."

Graham felt something tearing. He felt short of breath.

"Let me get the office to make the arrangements. Have you made a reservation already?"

"I didn't use my name. I thought maybe the newspapers . . ."

"Good. Good. Let me get somebody to see you off. You wouldn't have to board through the gate, and you'd get out of Washington absolutely clean. Can I do that? Let me do that. What time does the plane go?"

"Nine-forty. American 118."

"Okay, eight-thirty . . . behind the Smithsonian. There's a Park-Rite. Leave the car there. Somebody'll meet you. He'll listen to his watch, put it to his ear when he gets out of his car, okay?"

"That's fine."

"Say, do you change at O'Hare? I could come out—"

"No. Change in Minneapolis."

"Oh, Molly. Maybe I could come up there and get you when it's over?"

"That would be very nice."

Very nice.

"Do you have enough money?"

"The bank's wiring me some."

"What?"

"To Barclay's at the airport. Don't worry."

"I'll miss you."

"Me too, but that'll be the same as now. Same distance by phone. Willy says hi."

"Hi to Willy."

"Be careful, darling."

She had never called him darling before. He didn't care for it. He didn't care for new names; darling, Red Dragon.

The night-duty officer in Washington was glad to make the arrangements for Molly. Graham pressed his face to the cool window and watched sheets of rain whip over the muffled traffic below him, the street leaping from gray to sudden color in the lightning flashes. His face left a print of forehead, nose, lips, and chin on the glass.

Molly was gone.

The day was over and there was only the night to face, and the lipless voice accusing him.

Lounds's woman held what was left of his hand until it was over.

"Hello, this is Valerie Leeds. I'm sorry I can't come to the phone right now . . ."

"I'm sorry too," Graham said.

Graham filled his glass again and sat at the table by the window, staring at the empty chair across from him. He stared until the space in the opposite chair assumed a man-shape filled with dark and swarming motes, a presence like a shadow on suspended dust. He tried to make the image coalesce, to see a face. It would not move, had no countenance but, faceless, faced him with palpable attention.

"I know it's tough," Graham said. He was intensely drunk. "You've got to try to stop, just hold off until we find you. If you've got to do something, fuck, come after me. I don't give a shit. It'll be better after that. They've got some things now to help you make it stop. To help you stop *wanting to* so bad. Help me. Help me a little. Molly's gone, old Freddy's dead. It's you and me now, sport." He leaned across the table, his hand extended to touch, and the presence was gone.

Graham put his head down on the table, his cheek on his arm. He could see the print of his forehead, nose, mouth, and chin on the window as the lightning flashed behind it; a face with drops crawling through it down the glass. Eyeless. A face full of rain.

Graham had tried hard to understand the Dragon.

At times, in the breathing silence of the victims' houses, the very spaces the Dragon had moved through tried to speak.

Sometimes Graham felt close to him. A feeling he remembered from other investigations had settled over him in recent days: the taunting sense that he and the Dragon were doing the same things at various times of the day, that there were parallels in the quotidian

details of their lives. Somewhere the Dragon was eating, or shower-
ing, or sleeping at the same time he did.

Graham tried hard to know him. He tried to see him past the
blinding glint of slides and vials, beneath the lines of police reports,
tried to see his face through the louvers of print. He tried as hard as he
knew how.

But to begin to understand the Dragon, to hear the cold drips in his
darkness, to watch the world through his red haze, Graham would
have had to see things he could never see, and he would have had to
fly through time. . . .

CHAPTER 25

SPRINGFIELD, MISSOURI, June 14, 1938.

Marian Dolarhyde Trevane, tired and in pain, got out of a taxi at City Hospital. Hot wind whipped grit against her ankles as she climbed the steps. The suitcase she lugged was better than her loose wash dress, and so was the mesh evening bag she pressed to her swollen belly. She had two quarters and a dime in her bag. She had Francis Dolarhyde in her belly.

She told the admitting officer her name was Betty Johnson, a lie. She said her husband was a musician, but she did not know his whereabouts, which was true.

They put her in the charity section of the maternity ward. She did not look at the patients on either side of her. She looked across the aisle at the soles of feet.

In four hours she was taken to the delivery room, where Francis Dolarhyde was born. The obstetrician remarked that he looked "more like a leaf-nosed bat than a baby," another truth. He was born with bilateral fissures in his upper lip and in his hard and soft palates. The center section of his mouth was unanchored and protruded. His nose was flat.

The hospital supervisors decided not to show him to his mother immediately. They waited to see if the infant could survive without oxygen. They put him in a bed at the rear of the infant ward and faced

194

him away from the viewing window. He could breathe, but he could not feed. With his palate cleft, he could not suck.

His crying on the first day was not as continuous as that of a heroin-addicted baby, but it was as piercing.

By the afternoon of the second day a thin keening was all he could produce.

When the shifts changed at three P.M., a wide shadow fell across his bed. Prince Easter Mize, 260 pounds, cleaning woman and aide in the maternity ward, stood looking at him, her arms folded on top of her bosom. In twenty-six years in the nursery she had seen about thirty-nine thousand infants. This one would live if he ate.

Prince Easter had received no instructions from the Lord about letting this infant die. She doubted that the hospital had received any either. She took from her pocket a rubber stopper pierced with a curved glass drinking straw. She pushed the stopper into a bottle of milk. She could hold the baby and support his head in one great hand. She held him to her breast until she knew he felt her heartbeat. Then she flipped him over and popped the tube down his throat. He took about two ounces and went to sleep.

"Um-hum," she said. She put him down and went about her assigned duties with the diaper pails.

➤

On the fourth day the nurses moved Marian Dolarhyde Trevane to a private room. Hollyhocks left over from a previous occupant were in an enamel pitcher on the washstand. They had held up pretty well.

Marian was a handsome girl and the puffiness was leaving her face. She looked at the doctor when he started talking to her, his hand on her shoulder. She could smell strong soap on his hand and she thought about the crinkles at the corners of his eyes until she realized what he was saying. Then she closed her eyes and did not open them while they brought the baby in.

Finally she looked. They shut the door when she screamed. Then they gave her a shot.

On the fifth day she left the hospital alone. She didn't know where to go. She could never go home again; her mother had made that clear.

Marian Dolarhyde Trevane counted the steps between the light poles. Each time she passed three poles, she sat on the suitcase to rest. At least she had the suitcase. In every town there was a pawn shop near the bus station. She had learned that traveling with her husband.

➤

Springfield in 1938 was not a center for plastic surgery. In Springfield, you wore your face as it was.

A surgeon at City Hospital did the best he could for Francis Dolarhyde, first retracting the front section of his mouth with an elastic band, then closing the clefts in his lip by a rectangular flap technique that is now outmoded. The cosmetic results were not good.

The surgeon had troubled to read up on the problem and decided, correctly, that repair of the infant's hard palate should wait until he was five. To operate sooner would distort the growth of his face.

A local dentist volunteered to make an obturator, which plugged the baby's palate and permitted him to feed without flooding his nose.

The infant went to the Springfield Foundling Home for a year and a half and then to Morgan Lee Memorial Orphanage.

Reverend S. B. "Buddy" Lomax was head of the orphanage. Brother Buddy called the other boys and girls together and told them that Francis was a harelip but they must be careful never to call him a harelip.

Brother Buddy suggested they pray for him.

➤

Francis Dolarhyde's mother learned to take care of herself in the years following his birth.

Marian Dolarhyde first found a job typing in the office of a ward boss in the St. Louis Democratic machine. With his help she had her marriage to the absent Mr. Trevane annulled.

There was no mention of a child in the annulment proceedings.

She had nothing to do with her mother. ("I didn't raise you to slut for that Irish trash" were Mrs. Dolarhyde's parting words to Marian when she left home with Trevane.)

Marian's ex-husband called her once at the office. Sober and pious, he told her he had been saved and wanted to know if he, Marian, and the child he "never had the joy of knowing" might make a new life together. He sounded broke.

Marian told him the child was born dead and she hung up.

He showed up drunk at her boardinghouse with his suitcase. When she told him to go away, he observed that it was her fault the marriage failed and the child was stillborn. He expressed doubt that the child was his.

In a rage Marian Dolarhyde told Michael Trevane exactly what he had fathered and told him he was welcome to it. She reminded him that there were two cleft palates in the Trevane family.

She put him in the street and told him never to call her again. He didn't. But years later, drunk and brooding over Marian's rich new husband and her fine life, he did call Marian's mother.

He told Mrs. Dolarhyde about the deformed child and said her snag teeth proved the hereditary fault lay with the Dolarhydes.

A week later a Kansas City streetcar cut Michael Trevane in two.

When Trevane told Mrs. Dolarhyde that Marian had a hidden son, she sat up most of the night. Tall and lean in her rocker, Grandmother Dolarhyde stared into the fire. Toward dawn she began a slow and purposeful rocking.

Somewhere upstairs in the big house, a cracked voice called out of sleep. The floor above Grandmother Dolarhyde creaked as someone shuffled toward the bathroom.

A heavy thump on the ceiling—someone falling—and the cracked voice called in pain.

Grandmother Dolarhyde never took her eyes off the fire. She rocked faster and, in time, the calling stopped.

➢

Near the end of his fifth year, Francis Dolarhyde had his first and only visitor at the orphanage.

He was sitting in the thick reek of the cafeteria when an older boy came for him and took him to Brother Buddy's office.

The lady waiting with Brother Buddy was tall and middle-aged, dredged in powder, her hair in a tight bun. Her face was stark white. There were touches of yellow in the gray hair and in the eyes and teeth.

What struck Francis, what he would always remember: she smiled with pleasure when she saw his face. That had never happened before. No one would ever do it again.

"This is your grandmother," Brother Buddy said.

"Hello," she said.

Brother Buddy wiped his own mouth with a long hand. "Say 'hello.' Go ahead."

Francis had learned to say some things by occluding his nostrils with his upper lip, but he did not have much occasion for "hello." "Lhho" was the best he could do.

Grandmother seemed even more pleased with him. "Can you say 'grandmother'?"

"Try to say 'grandmother,'" Brother Buddy said.

The plosive G defeated him. Francis strangled easily on tears.

A red wasp buzzed and tapped against the ceiling.

"Never mind," his grandmother said. "I'll just bet you can say your name. I just know a big boy like you can say his name. Say it for me."

The child's face brightened. The big boys had helped him with this. He wanted to please. He collected himself.

"Cunt Face," he said.

➤

Three days later Grandmother Dolarhyde called for Francis at the orphanage and took him home with her. She began at once to help him with his speech. They concentrated on a single word. It was "Mother."

➤

Within two years of the annulment, Marian Dolarhyde met and married Howard Vogt, a successful lawyer with solid connections to the St. Louis machine and what was left of the old Pendergast machine in Kansas City.

Vogt was a widower with three young children, an affable ambitious man fifteen years older than Marian Dolarhyde. He hated nothing in the world except the St. Louis *Post-Dispatch*, which had singed his feathers in the voter-registration scandal of 1936 and blasted the attempt in 1940 by the St. Louis machine to steal the governorship.

By 1943 Vogt's star was rising again. He was a brewery candidate for · the state legislature and was mentioned as a possible delegate to the upcoming state constitutional convention.

Marian was a useful and attractive hostess and Vogt bought her a handsome, half-timbered house on Olive Street that was perfect for entertaining.

Francis Dolarhyde had lived with his grandmother for a week when she took him there.

Grandmother had never seen her daughter's house. The maid who answered the door did not know her.

"I'm Mrs. Dolarhyde," she said, barging past the servant. Her slip was showing three inches in the back. She led Francis into a big living room with a pleasant fire.

"Who is it, Viola?" A woman's voice from upstairs.

Grandmother cupped Francis' face in her hand. He could smell the cold leather glove. An urgent whisper. "Go see Mother, Francis. Go see Mother. Run!"

He shrank from her, twisting on the tines of her eyes.

"Go see Mother. Run!" She gripped his shoulders and marched him toward the stairs. He trotted up to the landing and looked back down at her. She motioned upward with her chin.

Up to the strange hallway toward the open bedroom door.

Mother was seated at her dressing table checking her makeup in a mirror framed with lights. She was getting ready for a political rally, and too much rouge wouldn't do. Her back was to the door.

"Muhner," Francis piped, as he had been taught. He tried hard to get it right. "Muhner."

She saw him in the mirror then. "If you're looking for Ned, he isn't home from . . ."

"Muhner." He came into the heartless light.

Marian heard her mother's voice downstairs demanding tea. Her eyes widened and she sat very still. She did not turn around. She turned out the makeup lights and vanished from the mirror. In the darkened room she gave a single low keening that ended in a sob. It might have been for herself, or it might have been for him.

➤

Grandmother took Francis to all the political rallies after that and explained who he was and where he came from. She had him say hello to everyone. They did not work on "hello" at home.

Mr. Vogt lost the election by eighteen hundred votes.

CHAPTER 26

AT GRANDMOTHER'S HOUSE, Francis Dolarhyde's new world was a forest of blue-veined legs.

Grandmother Dolarhyde had been running her nursing home for three years when he came to live with her. Money had been a problem since her husband's death in 1936; she had been brought up a lady and she had no marketable skills.

What she had was a big house and her late husband's debts. Taking in boarders was out. The place was too isolated to be a successful boardinghouse. She was threatened with eviction.

The announcement in the newspaper of Marian's marriage to the affluent Mr. Howard Vogt had seemed a godsend to Grandmother. She wrote to Marian repeatedly for help, but received no answer. Every time she telephoned, a servant told her Mrs. Vogt was out.

Finally, bitterly, Grandmother Dolarhyde made an arrangement with the county and began to take in elderly indigent persons. For each one she received a sum from the county and erratic payments from such relatives as the county could locate. It was hard until she began to get some private patients from middle-class families.

No help from Marian all this time—and Marian could have helped.

Now Francis Dolarhyde played on the floor in the forest of legs. He played cars with Grandmother's Mah-Jongg pieces, pushing them among feet twisted like gnarled roots.

Mrs. Dolarhyde could keep clean wash dresses on her residents, but she despaired at trying to make them keep on their shoes.

The old people sat all day in the living room listening to the radio. Mrs. Dolarhyde had put in a small aquarium for them to watch as well, and a private contributor had helped her cover her parquet floors with linoleum against the inevitable incontinence.

They sat in a row on the couches and in wheelchairs listening to the radio, their faded eyes fixed on the fish or on nothing or something they saw long ago.

Francis would always remember the shuffle of feet on linoleum in the hot and buzzing day, and the smell of stewed tomatoes and cabbage from the kitchen, the smell of the old people like meat wrappers dried in the sun, and always the radio.

> *Rinso white, Rinso bright*
> *Happy little washday song.*

Francis spent as much time as he could in the kitchen, because his friend was there. The cook, Queen Mother Bailey, had grown up in the service of the late Mr. Dolarhyde's family. She sometimes brought Francis a plum in her apron pocket, and she called him "Little Possum, always dreamin'." The kitchen was warm and safe. But Queen Mother Bailey went home at night. . . .

➤

December 1943.

Francis Dolarhyde, five years old, lay in bed in his upstairs room in Grandmother's house. The room was pitch dark with its blackout curtains against the Japanese. He could not say "Japanese." He needed to pee. He was afraid to get up in the dark.

He called to his grandmother in bed downstairs.

"Aayma. Aayma." He sounded like an infant goat. He called until he was tired. "Mleedse Aayma."

It got away from him then, hot on his legs and under his seat, and then cold, his nightdress sticking to him. He didn't know what to do. He took a deep breath and rolled over to face the door. Nothing happened to him. He put his foot on the floor. He stood up in the dark, nightdress plastered to his legs, face burning. He ran for the door. The doorknob caught him over the eye and he sat down in wetness, jumped up and ran down the stairs, fingers squealing on the banister. To his grandmother's room. Crawling across her in the dark and under the covers, warm against her now.

Grandmother stirred, tensed, her back hardened against his cheek, voice hissing. "I've never sheen . . ." A clatter on the bedside table as she found her teeth, clacket as she put them in. "I've never seen a child as disgusting and dirty as you. Get *out*, get out of this bed."

She turned on the bedside lamp. He stood on the carpet shivering. She wiped her thumb across his eyebrow. Her thumb came away bloody.

"Did you break something?"

He shook his head so fast droplets of blood fell on Grandmother's nightgown.

"Upstairs. Go on."

The dark came down over him as he climbed the stairs. He couldn't turn on the lights because Grandmother had cut the cords off short so only she could reach them. He did not want to get back in the wet bed. He stood in the dark holding on to the footboard for a long time. He thought she wasn't coming. The blackest corners in the room knew she wasn't coming.

She came, snatching the short cord on the ceiling light, her arms full of sheets. She did not speak to him as she changed the bed.

She gripped his upper arm and pulled him down the hall to the bathroom. The light was over the mirror and she had to stand on tiptoe to reach it. She gave him a washcloth, wet and cold.

"Take off your nightshirt and wipe yourself off."

Smell of adhesive tape and the bright sewing scissors clicking. She snipped out a butterfly of tape, stood him on the toilet lid and closed the cut over his eye.

"Now," she said. She held the sewing scissors under his round belly and he felt cold down there.

"Look," she said. She grabbed the back of his head and bent him over to see his little penis lying across the bottom blade of the open scissors. She closed the scissors until they began to pinch him.

"Do you want me to cut it off?"

He tried to look up at her, but she gripped his head. He sobbed and spit fell on his stomach.

"*Do* you?"

"No, Aayma. No, Aayma."

"I pledge you my word, if you ever make your bed dirty again I'll cut it off. Do you understand?"

"Yehn, Aayma."

"You can find the toilet in the dark and you can sit on it like a good boy. You don't have to stand up. Now go back to bed."

➤

At two A.M. the wind rose, gusting warm out of the southeast, clacking together the branches of the dead apple trees, rustling the leaves of the live ones. The wind drove warm rain against the side of the house where Francis Dolarhyde, forty-two years old, lay sleeping.

He lay on his side sucking his thumb, his hair damp and flat on his forehead and his neck.

Now he awakes. He listens to his breathing in the dark and the tiny clicks of his blinking eyes. His fingers smell faintly of gasoline. His bladder is full.

He feels on the bedside table for the glass containing his teeth.

Dolarhyde always puts in his teeth before he rises. Now he walks to the bathroom. He does not turn on the light. He finds the toilet in the dark and sits down on it like a good boy.

CHAPTER 27

THE CHANGE in Grandmother first became apparent in the winter of 1947, when Francis was eight.

She stopped taking meals in her room with Francis. They moved to the common table in the dining room, where she presided over meals with the elderly residents.

Grandmother had been trained as a girl to be a charming hostess, and now she unpacked and polished her silver bell and put it beside her plate.

Keeping a luncheon table going, pacing the service, managing conversation, batting easy conversational lobs to the strong points of the shy ones, turning the best facets of the bright ones in the light of the other guests' attention is a considerable skill and one now sadly in decline.

Grandmother had been good at it in her time. Her efforts at this table did brighten meals initially for the two or three among the residents who were capable of linear conversation.

Francis sat in the host's chair at the other end of the avenue of nodding heads as Grandmother drew out the recollections of those who could remember. She expressed keen interest in Mrs. Floder's honeymoon trip to Kansas City, went through the yellow fever with Mr. Eaton a number of times, and listened brightly to the random unintelligible sounds of the others.

"Isn't that interesting, Francis?" she said, and rang the bell for the next course. The food was a variety of vegetable and meat mushes, but she divided it into courses, greatly inconveniencing the kitchen help.

Mishaps at the table were never mentioned. A ring of the bell and a gesture in mid-sentence took care of those who had spilled or gone to sleep or forgotten why they were at the table. Grandmother always kept as large a staff as she could pay.

As Grandmother's general health declined, she lost weight and was able to wear dresses that had long been packed away. Some of them were elegant. In the cast of her features and her hairstyle, she bore a marked resemblance to George Washington on the dollar bill.

Her manners had slipped somewhat by spring. She ruled the table and permitted no interruptions as she told of her girlhood in St. Charles, even revealing personal matters to inspire and edify Francis and the others.

It was true that Grandmother had enjoyed a season as a belle in 1907 and was invited to some of the better balls across the river in St. Louis.

There was an "object lesson" in this for everyone, she said. She looked pointedly at Francis, who crossed his legs beneath the table.

"I came up at a time when little could be done medically to overcome the little accidents of nature," she said. "I had lovely skin and hair and I took full advantage of them. I overcame my teeth with force of personality and bright spirits—so successfully, in fact, that they became my 'beauty spot.' I think you might even call them my 'charming trademark.' I wouldn't have traded them for the world."

She distrusted doctors, she explained at length, but when it became clear that gum problems would cost her her teeth, she sought out one of the most renowned dentists in the Midwest, Dr. Felix Bertl, a Swiss. Dr. Bertl's "Swiss teeth" were very popular with a certain class of people, Grandmother said, and he had a remarkable practice.

Opera singers fearing that new shapes in their mouths would affect their tone, actors and others in public life came from as far away as San Francisco to be fitted.

Dr. Bertl could reproduce a patient's natural teeth exactly and had experimented with various compounds and their effect on resonance.

When Dr. Bertl had completed her dentures, her teeth appeared just as they had before. She overcame them with personality and lost none of her unique charm, she said with a spiky smile.

If there was an object lesson in all this, Francis did not appreciate it until later; there would be no further surgery for him until he could pay for it himself.

Francis could make it through dinner because there was something he looked forward to afterward.

Queen Mother Bailey's husband came for her each evening in the mule-drawn wagon he used to haul firewood. If Grandmother was occupied upstairs, Francis could ride with them down the lane to the main road.

He waited all day for the evening ride: sitting on the wagon seat beside Queen Mother, her tall flat husband silent and almost invisible in the dark, the iron tires of the wagon loud in the gravel behind the jingle of the bits. Two mules, brown and sometimes muddy, their cropped manes standing up like brushes, swishing their tails across their rumps. The smell of sweat and boiled cotton cloth, snuff and warm harness. There was the smell of woodsmoke when Mr. Bailey had been clearing new ground and sometimes, when he took his shotgun to the new ground, a couple of rabbits or squirrels lay in the wagon box, stretched long as though they were running.

They did not talk on the ride down the lane; Mr. Bailey spoke only to the mules. The wagon motion bumped the boy pleasantly against the Baileys. Dropped off at the end of the lane, he gave his nightly promise to walk straight back to the house and watched the lantern on the wagon move away. He could hear them talking down the road. Sometimes Queen Mother made her husband laugh and she laughed with him. Standing in the dark, it was pleasant to hear them and know they were not laughing at him.

Later he would change his mind about that. . . .

➤

Francis Dolarhyde's occasional playmate was the daughter of a sharecropper who lived three fields away. Grandmother let her come to play because it amused her now and then to dress the child in the clothing Marian had worn when she was small.

She was a red-haired listless child and she was too tired to play much of the time.

One hot June afternoon, bored with fishing for doodlebugs in the chicken yard with straws, she asked to see Francis' private parts.

In a corner between the chicken house and a low hedge that shielded them from the lower windows of the house, he showed her. She reciprocated by showing him her own, standing with her pilled cotton underwear around her ankles. As he squatted on his heels to see, a headless chicken flapped around the corner, traveling on its back, flapping up the dust. The hobbled girl hopped backward as it spattered blood on her feet and legs.

Francis jumped to his feet, his trousers still down, as Queen Mother Bailey came around the corner after the chicken and saw them.

"Look here, boy," she said calmly, "you want to see what's what, well now you see, so go on and find yourselves something else to do. Occupy yourself with children's doings and keep your clothes on. You and that child help me catch that rooster."

The children's embarrassment quickly passed as the rooster eluded them. But Grandmother was watching from the upstairs window. . . .

➤

Grandmother watched Queen Mother come back inside. The children went into the chicken house. Grandmother waited five minutes, then came up on them silently. She flung open the door and found them gathering feathers for headdresses.

She sent the girl home and led Francis into the house.

She told him he was going back to Brother Buddy's orphanage after she had punished him. "Go upstairs. Go to your room and take your trousers off and wait for me while I get my scissors."

He waited for hours in his room, lying on the bed with his trousers off, clutching the bedspread and waiting for the scissors. He waited through the sounds of supper downstairs and he heard the creak and clop of the firewood wagon and the snort of the mules as Queen Mother's husband came for her.

Sometime toward morning he slept, and woke in starts to wait.

Grandmother never came. Perhaps she had forgotten.

He waited through the routine of the days that followed, remembering many times a day in a rush of freezing dread. He would never cease from waiting.

He avoided Queen Mother Bailey, would not speak to her and wouldn't tell her why: he mistakenly believed that she had told

Grandmother what she saw in the chicken yard. Now he was convinced that the laughter he heard while he watched the wagon lantern diminish down the road was about him. Clearly he could trust no one.

➤

It was hard to lie still and go to sleep when it was there to think about. It was hard to lie still on such a bright night.

Francis knew that Grandmother was right. He had hurt her so. He had shamed her. Everyone must know what he had done—even as far away as St. Charles. He was not angry at Grandmother. He was not angry at Grandmother. He knew that he Loved her very much. He wanted to do right.

He imagined that burglars were breaking in and he protected Grandmother and she took back what she said. "You're not a Child of the Devil after all, Francis. You are my good boy."

He thought about a burglar breaking in. Coming in the house determined to show Grandmother his private parts.

How would Francis protect her? He was too small to fight a big burglar.

He thought about it. There was Queen Mother's hatchet in the pantry. She wiped it with newspaper after she killed a chicken. He should see about the hatchet. It was his responsibility. He would fight his fear of the dark. If he really Loved Grandmother, he should be the thing to be afraid of in the dark. The thing for the *burglar* to be afraid of.

He crept downstairs and found the hatchet hanging on its nail. It had a strange smell, like the smell at the sink when they were drawing a chicken. It was sharp and its weight was reassuring in his hand.

He carried the hatchet to Grandmother's room to be sure there were no burglars.

Grandmother was asleep. It was very dark but he knew exactly where she was. If there was a burglar, he would hear him breathing just as he could hear Grandmother breathing. He would know where his neck was just as surely as he knew where Grandmother's neck was. It was just below the breathing.

If there was a burglar, he would come up on him quietly like this. He would raise the hatchet over his head with both hands like this.

Francis stepped on Grandmother's slipper beside the bed. The hatchet swayed in the dizzy dark and pinged against the metal shade of her reading lamp.

Grandmother rolled over and made a wet noise with her mouth. Francis stood still. His arms trembled from the effort of holding up the hatchet. Grandmother began to snore.

The Love Francis felt almost burst him. He crept out of the room. He was frantic to be ready to protect her. He must do something. He did not fear the dark house now, but it was choking him.

He went out the back door and stood in the brilliant night, face upturned, gasping as though he could breathe the light. A tiny disk of moon, distorted on the whites of his rolled-back eyes, rounded as the eyes rolled down and was centered at last in his pupils.

The Love swelled in him unbearably tight and he could not gasp it out. He walked toward the chicken house, hurrying now, the ground cold under his feet, the hatchet bumping cold against his leg, running now before he burst. . . .

➤

Francis, scrubbing himself at the chicken-yard pump, had never felt such sweet and easy peace. He felt his way cautiously into it and found that the peace was endless and all around him.

What Grandmother kindly had not cut off was still there like a prize when he washed the blood off his belly and legs. His mind was clear and calm.

He should do something about the nightshirt. Better hide it under the sacks in the smokehouse.

➤

Discovery of the dead chicken puzzled Grandmother. She said it didn't look like a fox job.

A month later Queen Mother found another one when she went to gather eggs. This time the head had been wrung off.

Grandmother said at the dinner table that she was convinced it was done for spite by some "sorry help I ran off." She said she had called the sheriff about it.

Francis sat silent at his place, opening and closing his hand on the memory of an eye blinking against his palm. Sometimes in bed he held himself to be sure he hadn't been cut. Sometimes when he held himself he thought he felt a blink.

➤

Grandmother was changing rapidly. She was increasingly contentious and could not keep household help. Though she was short of housekeepers, it was the kitchen where she took personal charge, directing Queen Mother Bailey to the detriment of the food. Queen Mother, who had worked for the Dolarhydes all her life, was the only constant on the staff.

Red-faced in the kitchen heat, Grandmother moved restlessly from one task to the next, often leaving dishes half-made, never to be served. She made casseroles of leftovers while vegetables wilted in the pantry.

At the same time, she became fanatical about waste. She reduced the soap and bleach in the wash until the sheets were dingy gray.

In the month of November she hired five different black women to help in the house. They would not stay.

Grandmother was furious the evening the last one left. She went through the house yelling. She came into the kitchen and saw that Queen Mother Bailey had left a teaspoonful of flour on the board after rolling out some dough.

In the steam and heat of the kitchen a half-hour before dinner she walked up to Queen Mother and slapped her face.

Queen Mother dropped her ladle, shocked. Tears sprang into her eyes. Grandmother drew back her hand again. A big pink palm pushed her away.

"Don't you *ever* do that. You're not yourself, Mrs. Dolarhyde, but don't you *ever* do that."

Screaming insults, Grandmother with her bare hand shoved over a kettle of soup to slop and hiss down through the stove. She went to her room and slammed the door. Francis heard her cursing in her room and objects thrown against the walls. She didn't come out again all evening.

Queen Mother cleaned up the soup and fed the old people. She got her few things together in a basket and put on her old sweater and stocking cap. She looked for Francis but couldn't find him.

She was in the wagon when she saw the boy sitting in the corner of the porch. He watched her climb down heavily and come back to him.

"Possum, I'm going now. I won't be back here. Sironia at the feed store, she'll call your mama for me. You need me before your mama get here, you come to my house."

He twisted away from the touch on his cheek.

Mr. Bailey clucked to the mules. Francis watched the wagon lantern move away. He had watched it before, with a sad and empty feeling since he understood that Queen Mother betrayed him. Now he didn't care. He was glad. A feeble kerosene wagon light fading down the road. It was nothing to the moon.

He wondered how it feels to kill a mule.

➤

Marian Dolarhyde Vogt did not come when Queen Mother Bailey called her.

She came two weeks later after a call from the sheriff in St. Charles. She arrived in midafternoon, driving herself in a prewar Packard. She wore gloves and a hat.

A deputy sheriff met her at the end of the lane and stooped to the car window.

"Mrs. Vogt, your mother called our office around noon, saying something about the help stealing. When I come out here, you'll excuse me but she was talking out of her head and it looked like things wasn't tended to. Sheriff thought he ought to get ahold of y'all first, if you understand me. Mr. Vogt being before the public and all."

Marian understood him. Mr. Vogt was commissioner of public works in St. Louis now and was not in the party's best graces.

"To my knowledge, nobody else has saw the place," the deputy said.

Marian found her mother asleep. Two of the old people were still sitting at the table waiting for lunch. One woman was out in the backyard in her slip.

Marian telephoned her husband. "How often do they inspect these places? . . . They must not have seen anything. . . . I don't *know* if any relatives have complained, I don't think these people have any relatives. . . . No. You stay away. I need some Negroes. Get me some Negroes . . . and Dr. Waters. I'll take care of it."

The doctor with an orderly in white arrived in forty-five minutes, followed by a panel truck bringing Marian's maid and five other domestics.

Marian, the doctor, and the orderly were in Grandmother's room when Francis came home from school. Francis could hear his grandmother cursing. When they rolled her out in one of the nursing-home wheelchairs, she was glassy-eyed and a piece of cotton was taped to her arm. Her face looked sunken and strange without her teeth. Marian's arm was bandaged too; she had been bitten.

Grandmother rode away in the doctor's car, sitting in the backseat with the orderly. Francis watched her go. He started to wave, but let his hand fall back to his side.

Marian's cleaning crew scrubbed and aired the house, did a tremendous wash, and bathed the old people. Marian worked alongside them and supervised a sketchy meal.

She spoke to Francis only to ask where things were.

Then she sent the crew away and called the county authorities. Mrs. Dolarhyde had suffered a stroke, she explained.

It was dark when the welfare workers came for the patients in a school bus. Francis thought they would take him too. He was not discussed.

Only Marian and Francis remained at the house. She sat at the dining-room table with her head in her hands. He went outside and climbed a crabapple tree.

Finally Marian called him. She had packed a small suitcase with his clothes.

"You'll have to come with me," she said, walking to the car. "Get in. Don't put your feet on the seat."

They drove away in the Packard and left the empty wheelchair standing in the yard.

There was no scandal. The county authorities said it was sure a shame about Mrs. Dolarhyde, she sure kept things nice. The Vogts remained untarnished.

Grandmother was confined to a private nerve sanatorium. It would be fourteen years before Francis went home to her again.

➢

"Francis, here are your stepsisters and stepbrother," his mother said. They were in the Vogts' library.

Ned Vogt was twelve, Victoria thirteen, and Margaret nine. Ned and Victoria looked at each other. Margaret looked at the floor.

Francis was given a room at the top of the servants' stairs. Since the disastrous election of 1944 the Vogts no longer employed an upstairs maid.

He was enrolled in Potter Gerard Elementary School, within walking distance of the house and far from the Episcopal private school the other children attended.

The Vogt children ignored him as much as possible during the first few days, but at the end of the first week Ned and Victoria came up the servants' stairs to call.

Francis heard them whispering for minutes before the knob turned on his door. When they found it bolted, they didn't knock. Ned said, "Open this door."

Francis opened it. They did not speak to him again while they looked through his clothes in the wardrobe. Ned Vogt opened the drawer in the small dressing table and picked up the things he found with two fingers: birthday handkerchiefs with F.D. embroidered on them, a capo for a guitar, a bright beetle in a pill bottle, a copy of *Baseball Joe in the World Series* which had once been wet, and a get-well card signed "Your classmate, Sarah Hughes."

"What's this?" Ned asked.

"A capo."

"What's it for?"

"A guitar."

"Do you have a guitar?"

"No."

"What do you have it for?" Victoria asked.

"My father used it."

"I can't understand you. What did you say? Make him say it again, Ned."

"He said it belonged to his father." Ned blew his nose on one of the handkerchiefs and dropped it back in the drawer.

"They came for the ponies today," Victoria said. She sat on the narrow bed. Ned joined her, his back against the wall, his feet on the quilt.

"No more ponies," Ned said. "No more lake house for the

summer. Do you know why? Speak up, you little bastard."

"Father is sick a lot and doesn't make as much money," Victoria said. "Some days he doesn't go to the office at all."

"Know why he's sick, you little bastard?" Ned asked. "Talk where I can understand you."

"Grandmother said he's a drunk. Understand that all right?"

"He's sick because of your ugly face," Ned said.

"That's why people didn't vote for him, too," Victoria said.

"Get out," Francis said. When he turned to open the door, Ned kicked him in the back. Francis tried to reach his kidney with both hands, which saved his fingers as Ned kicked him in the stomach.

"Oh, Ned," Victoria said. "Oh, Ned."

Ned grabbed Francis by the ears and held him close to the mirror over the dressing table.

"That's why he's sick!" Ned slammed his face into the mirror. "That's why he's sick!" Slam. "That's why he's sick!" Slam. The mirror was smeared with blood and mucus. Ned let him go and he sat on the floor. Victoria looked at him, her eyes wide, holding her lower lip between her teeth. They left him there. His face was wet with blood and spit. His eyes watered from the pain, but he did not cry.

CHAPTER 28

RAIN IN CHICAGO drums through the night on the canopy over the open grave of Freddy Lounds.

Thunder jars Will Graham's pounding head as he weaves from the table to a bed where dreams coil beneath the pillow.

The old house above St. Charles, shouldering the wind, repeats its long sigh over the hiss of rain against the windows and the bump of thunder.

The stairs are creaking in the dark. Mr. Dolarhyde is coming down them, his kimono whispering over the treads, his eyes wide with recent sleep.

His hair is wet and neatly combed. He has brushed his nails. He moves smoothly and slowly, carrying his concentration like a brimming cup.

Film beside his projector. Two subjects. Other reels are piled in the wastebasket for burning. Two left, chosen from the dozens of home movies he has copied at the plant and brought home to audition.

Comfortable in his reclining chair with a tray of cheese and fruit beside him, Dolarhyde settles in to watch.

The first film is a picnic from the Fourth of July weekend. A handsome family; three children, the father bull-necked, dipping into the pickle jar with his thick fingers. And the mother.

The best view of her is in the softball game with the neighbors' children. Only about fifteen seconds of her; she takes a lead off second base, faces the pitcher and the plate, feet apart ready to dash either way, her breasts swaying beneath her pullover as she leans forward from the waist. An annoying interruption as a child swings a bat. The woman again, walking back to tag up. She puts one foot on the boat cushion they use for a base and stands hip-shot, the thigh muscle tightening in her locked leg.

Over and over Dolarhyde watches the frames of the woman. Foot on the base, pelvis tilts, thigh muscle tightens under the cutoff jeans.

He freezes the last frame. The woman and her children. They are dirty and tired. They hug, and a dog wags among their legs.

A terrific crash of thunder clinks the cut crystal in Grandmother's tall cabinet. Dolarhyde reaches for a pear.

The second film is in several segments. The title, *The New House,* is spelled out in pennies on a shirt cardboard above a broken piggy bank. It opens with Father pulling up the "For Sale" sign in the yard. He holds it up and faces the camera with an embarrassed grin. His pockets are turned out.

An unsteady long shot of Mother and three children on the front steps. It is a handsome house. A cut to the swimming pool. A child, sleek-headed and small, pads around to the diving board, leaving wet footprints on the tile. Heads bob in the water. A small dog paddles toward a daughter, his ears back, chin high, and the whites of his eyes showing.

Mother in the water holds to the ladder and looks up at the camera. Her curly black hair has the gloss of pelt, her bosom swelling shining wet above her suit, her legs wavy below the surface, scissoring.

Night. A badly exposed shot across the pool to the lighted house, the lights reflected in the water.

Indoors and family fun. Boxes everywhere, and packing materials. An old trunk, not yet stored in the attic.

A small daughter is trying on Grandmother's clothes. She has on a big garden-party hat. Father is on the sofa. He looks a little drunk. Now Father must have the camera. It is not quite level. Mother is at the mirror in the hat.

The children jostle around her, the boys laughing and plucking at the old finery. The girl watches her mother coolly, appraising herself in time to come.

A close-up. Mother turns and strikes a pose for the camera with an arch smile, her hand at the back of her neck. She is quite lovely. There is a cameo at her throat.

Dolarhyde freezes the frame. He backs up the film. Again and again she turns from the mirror and smiles.

Absently Dolarhyde picks up the film of the softball game and drops it in the wastebasket.

He takes the reel from the projector and looks at the Gateway label on the box: *Bob Sherman, Star Route 7, Box 603, Tulsa, Okla.*

An easy drive, too.

Dolarhyde holds the film in his palm and covers it with his other hand as though it were a small living thing that might struggle to escape. It seems to jump against his palm like a cricket.

He remembers the jerkiness, the haste at the Leeds house when the lights came on. He had to deal with Mr. Leeds before turning on his movie lights.

This time he wants a smoother progression. It would be wonderful to crawl in between the sleepers with the camera going and snuggle up a little while. Then he could strike in the dark and sit up between them happily getting wet.

He can do that with infrared film, and he knows where to get some.

The projector is still on. Dolarhyde sits holding the film between his hands while on the bright blank screen other images move for him to the long sigh of the wind.

There is no sense of vengeance in him, only Love and thoughts of the Glory to come; hearts becoming faint and fast, like footsteps fleeing into silence.

Him rampant. Him rampant, filled with Love, the Shermans opening to him.

The past does not occur to him at all; only the Glory to come. He does not think of his mother's house. In fact, his conscious memories of that time are remarkably few and indistinct.

Sometime in his twenties Dolarhyde's memories of his mother's house sank out of sight, leaving a slick on the surface of his mind.

He knew that he had lived there only a month. He did not recall that he was sent away at the age of nine for hanging Victoria's cat.

One of the few images he retained was the house itself, lighted, viewed from the street in winter twilight as he passed it going from

Potter Gerard Elementary School to the house where he was boarded a mile away.

He could remember the smell of the Vogt library, like a piano just opened, when his mother received him there to give him holiday things. He did not remember the faces at the upstairs windows as he walked away, down the frozen sidewalk, the practical gifts burning hateful under his arm; hurrying home to a place inside his head that was quite different from St. Louis.

At the age of eleven his fantasy life was active and intense and when the pressure of his Love grew too great, he relieved it. He preyed on pets, carefully, with a cool eye to consequence. They were so tame that it was easy. The authorities never linked him with the sad little bloodstains soaked into the dirt floors of garages.

At forty-two he did not remember that. Nor did he ever think about the people in his mother's house—his mother, stepsisters, or step-brother.

Sometimes he saw them in his sleep, in the brilliant fragments of a fever dream; altered and tall, faces and bodies in bright parrot colors, they poised over him in a mantis stance.

When he chose to reflect, which was seldom, he had many satisfactory memories. They were of his military service.

Caught at seventeen entering the window of a woman's house for a purpose never established, he was given the choice of enlisting in the Army or facing criminal charges. He took the Army.

After basic training he was sent to specialist school in darkroom operation and shipped to San Antonio, where he worked on medical-corps training films at Brooke Army Hospital.

Surgeons at Brooke took an interest in him and decided to improve his face.

They performed a Z-plasty on his nose, using ear cartilage to lengthen the columella, and repaired his lip with an interesting Abbé flap procedure that drew an audience of doctors to the operating theater.

The surgeons were proud of the result. Dolarhyde declined the mirror and looked out the window.

Records at the film library show Dolarhyde checked out many films, mainly on trauma, and kept them overnight.

He reenlisted in 1958 and in his second hitch he found Hong Kong. Stationed at Seoul, Korea, developing film from the tiny spotter planes the Army floated over the thirty-eighth parallel in the late 1950's, he was able to go to Hong Kong twice on leave. Hong Kong and Kowloon could satisfy any appetite in 1959.

➤

Grandmother was released from the sanatorium in 1961 in a vague Thorazine peace. Dolarhyde asked for and received a hardship discharge two months before his scheduled separation date and went home to take care of her.

It was a curiously peaceful time for him as well. With his new job at Gateway, Dolarhyde could hire a woman to stay with Grandmother in the daytime. At night they sat in the parlor together, not speaking. The tick of the old clock and its chimes were all that broke the silence.

He saw his mother once, at Grandmother's funeral in 1970. He looked through her, past her, with his yellow eyes so startlingly like her own. She might have been a stranger.

His appearance surprised his mother. He was deep-chested and sleek, with her fine coloring and a neat mustache which she suspected was hair transplanted from his head.

She called him once in the next week and heard the receiver slowly replaced.

➤

For nine years after Grandmother's death Dolarhyde was un-troubled and he troubled no one. His forehead was as smooth as a seed. He knew that he was waiting. For what, he didn't know.

One small event, which occurs to everyone, told the seed in his skull it was Time: standing by a north window, examining some film, he noticed aging in his hands. It was as though his hands, holding the film, had suddenly appeared before him and he saw in that good north light that the skin had slackened over the bones and tendons and his hands were creased in diamonds as small as lizard scales.

As he turned them in the light, an intense odor of cabbage and stewed tomatoes washed over him. He shivered though the room was warm. That evening he worked out harder than usual.

A full-length mirror was mounted on the wall of Dolarhyde's attic gym beside his barbells and weight bench. It was the only mirror hanging in his house, and he could admire his body in it comfortably because he always worked out in a mask.

He examined himself carefully while his muscles were pumped up. At forty, he could have competed successfully in regional body-building competition. He was not satisfied.

Within the week he came upon the Blake painting. It seized him instantly.

He saw it in a large, full-color photograph in *Time* magazine illustrating a report on the Blake retrospective at the Tate Museum in London. The Brooklyn Museum had sent *The Great Red Dragon and the Woman Clothed with the Sun* to London for the show.

Time's critic said: "Few demonic images in Western art radiate such a nightmarish charge of sexual energy. . . ." Dolarhyde didn't have to read the text to find that out.

He carried the picture with him for days, photographed and enlarged it in the darkroom late at night. He was agitated much of the time. He posted the painting beside his mirror in the weight room and stared at it while he pumped. He could sleep only when he had worked out to exhaustion and watched his medical films to aid him in sexual relief.

He had known since the age of nine that essentially he was alone and that he would always be alone, a conclusion more common to the forties.

Now, in his forties, he was seized by a fantasy life with the brilliance and freshness and immediacy of childhood. It took him a step beyond Alone.

At a time when other men first see and fear their isolation, Dolarhyde's became understandable to him: he was alone because he was Unique. With the fervor of conversion he saw that if he worked at it, if he followed the true urges he had kept down for so long—cultivated them as the inspirations they truly were—he could Become.

The Dragon's face is not visible in the painting, but increasingly Dolarhyde came to know how it looked.

Watching his medical films in the parlor, pumped up from lifting, he stretched his jaw wide to hold in Grandmother's teeth. They did not fit his distorted gums and his jaw cramped quickly.

He worked on his jaw in private moments, biting on a hard rubber block until the muscles stood out in his cheeks like walnuts.

In the fall of 1979, Francis Dolarhyde withdrew part of his considerable savings and took a three-month leave of absence from Gateway. He went to Hong Kong and he took with him his grandmother's teeth.

When he returned, red-haired Eileen and his other fellow workers agreed that the vacation had done him good. He was calm. They hardly noticed that he never used the employees' locker room or shower anymore—he had never done that often anyway.

His grandmother's teeth were back in the glass beside her bed. His own new ones were locked in his desk upstairs.

If Eileen could have seen him before his mirror, teeth in place, new tattoo brilliant in the harsh gym light, she would have screamed. Once.

There was time now; he did not have to hurry now. He had forever. It was five months before he selected the Jacobis.

The Jacobis were the first to help him, the first to lift him into the Glory of his Becoming. The Jacobis were better than anything, better than anything he ever knew.

Until the Leedses.

And now, as he grew in strength and Glory, there were the Shermans to come and the new intimacy of infrared. Most promising.

CHAPTER 29

FRANCIS DOLARHYDE had to leave his own territory at Gateway Film Processing to get what he needed.

Dolarhyde was production chief of Gateway's largest division—home-movie processing—but there were four other divisions.

The recessions of the 1970's cut deeply into home moviemaking, and there was increasing competition from home video recorders. Gateway had to diversify.

The company added departments which transferred film to videotape, printed aerial survery maps, and offered custom services to small-format commercial filmmakers.

In 1979 a plum fell to Gateway. The company contracted jointly with the Department of Defense and the Department of Energy to develop and test new emulsions for infrared photography.

The Department of Energy wanted sensitivie infrared film for its heat-conservation studies. Defense wanted it for night reconnaissance.

Gateway bought a small company next door, Baeder Chemical, in late 1979 and set up the project there.

Dolarhyde walked across to Baeder on his lunch hour under a scrubbed blue sky, carefully avoiding the reflecting puddles on the asphalt. Lounds's death had put him in an excellent humor.

Everyone at Baeder seemed to be out for lunch.

He found the door he wanted at the end of a labyrinth of halls. The sign beside the door said "Infrared Sensitive Materials in Use. NO Safelights, NO Smoking, NO hot beverages." The red light was on above the sign.

Dolarhyde pushed a button and, in a moment, the light turned green. He entered the light trap and rapped on the inner door.

"Come." A woman's voice.

Cool, absolute darkness. The gurgle of water, the familiar smell of D-76 developer, and a trace of perfume.

"I'm Francis Dolarhyde. I came about the dryer."

"Oh, good. Excuse me, my mouth's full. I was just finishing lunch."

He heard papers wadded and dropped in a wastebasket.

"Actually, Ferguson wanted the dryer," said the voice in the dark. "He's on vacation, but I know where it goes. You have one over at Gateway?"

"I have two. One is larger. He didn't say how much room he has." Dolarhyde had seen a memo about the dryer problem weeks ago.

"I'll show you, if you don't mind a short wait."

"All right."

"Put your back against the door"—her voice took on a touch of the lecturer's practiced tone—"come forward three steps, until you feel the tile under your feet, and there'll be a stool just to your left."

He found it. He was closer to her now. He could hear the rustle of her lab apron.

"Thanks for coming down," she said. Her voice was clear, with a faint ring of iron in it. "You're head of processing over in the big building, right?"

"Um-humm."

"The same 'Mr. D.' who sends the rockets when the requisitions are filed wrong?"

"The very one."

"I'm Reba McClane. Hope there's nothing wrong over here."

"Not my project anymore. I just planned the darkroom construction when we bought this place. I haven't been over here in six months." A long speech for him, easier in the dark.

"Just a minute more and we'll get you some light. Do you need a tape measure?"

"I have one."

Dolarhyde found it rather pleasant, talking to the woman in the dark. He heard the rattle of a purse being rummaged, the click of a compact.

He was sorry when the timer rang.

"There we go. I'll put this stuff in the Black Hole," she said.

He felt a breath of cold air, heard a cabinet close on rubber seals and the hiss of a vacuum lock. A puff of air, and fragrance touched him as she passed.

Dolarhyde pressed his knuckle under his nose, put on his thoughtful expression and waited for the light.

The lights came on. She stood by the door smiling in his approximate direction. Her eyes made small random movements behind the closed lids.

He saw her white cane propped in the corner. He took his hand away from his face and smiled.

"Do you think I could have a plum?" he said. There were several on the counter where she had been sitting.

"Sure, they're really good."

Reba McClane was about thirty, with a handsome prairie face shaped by good bones and resolution. She had a small star-shaped scar on the bridge of her nose. Her hair was a mixture of wheat and red-gold, cut in a pageboy that looked slightly out-of-date, and her face and hands were pleasantly freckled by the sun. Against the tile and stainless steel of the darkroom she was as bright as Fall.

He was free to look at her. His gaze could move over her as freely as the air. She had no way to parry eyes.

Dolarhyde often felt warm spots, stinging spots on his skin when he talked to a woman. They moved over him to wherever he thought the woman was looking. Even when a woman looked away from him, he suspected that she saw his reflection. He was always aware of reflective surfaces, knew the angles of reflection as a pool shark knows the banks.

His skin now was cool. Hers was freckled, pearly on her throat and the insides of her wrists.

"I'll show you the room where he wants to put it," she said. "We can get the measuring done."

They measured.

"Now, I want to ask a favor," Dolarhyde said.

"Okay."

"I need some infrared movie film. Hot film, sensitive up around one thousand nanometers."

"You'll have to keep it in the freezer and put it back in the cold after you shoot."

"I know."

"Could you give me an idea of the conditions, maybe I—"

"Shooting at maybe eight feet, with a pair of Wratten filters over the lights." It sounded too much like a surveillance rig. "At the zoo," he said. "In the World of Darkness. They want to photograph the nocturnal animals."

"They must really be spooky if you can't use commercial infrared."

"Ummm-hmmmm."

"I'm sure we can fix you up. One thing, though. You know a lot of our stuff is under the DD contract. Anything that goes out of here, you have to sign for."

"Right."

"When do you need it?"

"About the twentieth. No later."

"I don't have to tell you—the more sensitive it is, the meaner it is to handle. You get into coolers, dry ice, all that. They're screening some samples about four o'clock, if you want to look. You can pick the tamest emulsion that'll do what you want."

"I'll come."

Reba McClane counted her plums after Dolarhyde left. He had taken one.

Strange man, Mr. Dolarhyde. There had been no awkward pause of sympathy and concern in his voice when she turned on the lights. Maybe he already knew she was blind. Better yet, maybe he didn't give a damn.

That would be refreshing.

CHAPTER 30

IN CHICAGO, Freddy Lounds's funeral was under way. *The National Tattler* paid for the elaborate service, rushing the arrangements so that it could be held on Thursday, the day after his death. Then the pictures would be available for the *Tattler* edition published Thursday night.

The funeral was long in the chapel and it was long at the graveside.

A radio evangelist went on and on in fulsome eulogy. Graham rode the greasy swells of his hangover and tried to study the crowd.

The hired choir at graveside gave full measure for the money while the *Tattler* photographers' motor-driven cameras whizzed. Two TV crews were present with fixed cameras and creepy-peepies. Police photographers with press credentials photographed the crowd.

Graham recognized several plainclothes officers from Chicago Homicide. Theirs were the only faces that meant anything to him.

And there was Wendy of Wendy City, Lounds's girlfriend. She was seated beneath the canopy, nearest the coffin. Graham hardly recognized her. Her blonde wig was drawn back in a bun and she wore a black tailored suit.

During the last hymn she rose, went forward unsteadily, knelt and laid her head on the casket, her arms outstretched in the pall of chrysanthemums as the strobe lights flashed.

The crowd made little noise moving over the spongy grass to the cemetery gates.

Graham walked beside Wendy. A crowd of the uninvited stared at them through the bars of the high iron fence.

"Are you all right?" Graham asked.

They stopped among the tombstones. Her eyes were dry, her gaze level.

"Better than you," she said. "Got drunk, didn't you?"

"Yep. Is somebody keeping an eye on you?"

"The precinct sent some people over. They've got plainclothes in the club. Lot of business now. More weirdos than usual."

"I'm sorry you had this. You did . . . I thought you were fine at the hospital. I admired that."

She nodded. "Freddy was a sport. He shouldn't have to go out that hard. Thanks for getting me in the room." She looked into the distance, blinking, thinking, eye shadow like stone dust on her lids. She faced Graham. "Look, the *Tattler's* giving me some money, you figured that, right? For an interview and the dive at the graveside. I don't think Freddy would mind."

"He'd have been mad if you passed it up."

"That's what I thought. They're jerks, but they pay. What it is, they tried to get me to say that I think you deliberately turned this freak on to Freddy, chumming with him in that picture. I didn't say it. If they print that I did say it, well that's bullshit."

Graham said nothing as she scanned his face.

"You didn't like him, maybe—it doesn't matter. But if you thought this could happen, you wouldn't have missed the shot at the Fairy, right?"

"Yeah, Wendy, I'd have staked him out."

"Do you have anything at all? I hear noise from these people and that's about it."

"We don't have much. A few things from the lab we're following up. It was a clean job and he's lucky."

"Are you?"

"What?"

"Lucky."

"Off and on."

"Freddy was never lucky. He told me he'd clean up on this. Big deals everywhere."

"He probably would have, too."

"Well look, Graham, if you ever, you know, feel like a drink, I've got one."

"Thanks."

"But stay sober on the street."

"Oh yes."

Two policemen cleared a path for Wendy through the crowd of curiosity-seekers outside the gate. One of the gawkers wore a printed T-shirt reading "The Tooth Fairy Is a One-Night Stand." He whistled at Wendy. The woman beside him slapped his face.

A big policeman squeezed into the 280ZX beside Wendy and she pulled into the traffic. A second policeman followed in an unmarked car.

Chicago smelled like a spent skyrocket in the hot afternoon.

Graham was lonely, and he knew why; funerals often make us want sex—it's one in the eye for death.

The wind rattled the dry stalks of a funeral arrangement near his feet. For a hard second he remembered palm fronds rustling in the sea wind. He wanted very much to go home, knowing that he would not, could not, until the Dragon was dead.

CHAPTER 31

THE PROJECTION ROOM at Baeder Chemical was small—five rows of folding chairs with an aisle in the middle.

Dolarhyde arrived late. He stood at the back with his arms folded while they screened gray cards, color cards, and cubes variously lighted, filmed on a variety of infrared emulsions.

His presence disturbed Dandridge, the young man in charge. Dolarhyde carried an air of authority at work. He was the recognized darkroom expert from the parent company next door, and he was known to be a perfectionist.

Dandridge had not consulted him in months, a petty rivalry that had gone on since Gateway bought Baeder Chemical.

"Reba, give us the development dope on sample . . . eight," Dandridge said.

Reba McClane sat at the end of a row, a clipboard in her lap. Speaking in a clear voice, her fingers moving over the clipboard in the semidarkness, she outlined the mechanics of the development—chemicals, temperature and time, and storage procedures before and after filming.

Infrared-sensitive film must be handled in total darkness. She had done all the darkroom work, keeping the many samples straight by touch code and keeping a running record in the dark. It was easy to see her value to Baeder.

230

The screening ran through quitting time.

Reba McClane kept her seat as the others were filing out. Dolarhyde approached her carefully. He spoke to her at a distance while there were others in the room. He didn't want her to feel watched.

"I thought you hadn't made it," she said.

"I had a machine down. It made me late."

The lights were on. Her clean scalp glistened in the part of her hair as he stood over her.

"Did you get to see the 1000C sample?"

"I did."

"They said it looked all right. It's a lot easier to handle than the 1200 series. Think it'll do?"

"It will."

She had her purse with her, and a light raincoat. He stood back when she came into the aisle behind her searching cane. She didn't seem to expect any help. He didn't offer any.

Dandridge stuck his head back into the room.

"Reba, dear, Marcia had to fly. Can you manage?"

Spots of color appeared in her cheeks. "I can manage very well, thank you, Danny."

"I'd drop you, love, but I'm late already. Say, Mr. Dolarhyde, if it wouldn't be too much trouble, could you—"

"Danny, I have a ride home." She held in her anger. The nuances of expression were denied her, so she kept her face relaxed. She couldn't control her color, though.

Watching with his cold yellow eyes, Dolarhyde understood her anger perfectly; he knew that Dandridge's limp sympathy felt like spit on her cheek.

"I'll take you," he said, rather late.

"No, but thank you." She had thought he might offer and had intended to accept. She wouldn't have anybody forced into it. Damn Dandridge, damn his fumbling, she'd ride the damned bus, dammit. She had the fare and she knew the way and she could go anywhere she fucking pleased.

She stayed in the women's room long enough for the others to leave the building. The janitor let her out.

She followed the edge of a dividing strip across the parking lot toward the bus stop, her raincoat over her shoulders, tapping the edge with her cane and feeling for the slight resistance of the puddles when the cane swished through them.

Dolarhyde watched her from his van. His feelings made him uneasy; they were dangerous in daylight.

For a moment under the lowering sun, windshields, puddles, high steel wires splintered the sunlight into the glint of scissors.

Her white cane comforted him. It swept the light of scissors, swept scissors away, and the memory of her harmlessness eased him. He was starting the engine.

Reba McClane heard the van behind her. It was beside her now.

"Thank you for inviting me."

She nodded, smiled, tapped along.

"Ride with me."

"Thanks, but I take the bus all the time."

"Dandridge is a fool. Ride with me . . ."—*what would someone say?*—"for my pleasure."

She stopped. She heard him get out of the van.

People usually grasped her upper arm, not knowing what else to do. Blind people do not like to have their balance disturbed by a firm hold on their triceps. It is as unpleasant for them as standing on wiggly scales to weigh. Like anyone else, they don't like to be propelled.

He didn't touch her. In a moment she said, "It's better if *I* take *your* arm."

She had wide experience of forearms, but his surprised her fingers. It was as hard as an oak banister.

She could not know the amount of nerve he summoned to let her touch him.

The van felt big and high. Surrounded by resonances and echoes unlike those of a car, she held to the edges of the bucket seat until Dolarhyde fastened her safety belt. The diagonal shoulder belt pressed one of her breasts. She moved it until it lay between them.

They said little during the drive. Waiting at the red lights, he could look at her.

She lived in the left side of a duplex on a quiet street near Washington University.

"Come in and I'll give you a drink."

In his life, Dolarhyde had been in fewer than a dozen private homes. In the past ten years he had been in four; his own, Eileen's briefly, the Leedses', and the Jacobis'. Other people's houses were exotic to him.

She felt the van rock as he got out. Her door opened. It was a long step down from the van. She bumped into him lightly. It was like bumping into a tree. He was much heavier, more solid than she would have judged from his voice and his footfalls. Solid and light on his feet. She had known a Bronco linebacker once in Denver who came out to film a United Way appeal with some blind kids . . .

Once inside her front door, Reba McClane stood her cane in the corner and was suddenly free. She moved effortlessly, turning on music, hanging up her coat.

Dolarhyde had to reassure himself that she was blind. Being in a home excited him.

"How about a gin and tonic?"

"Tonic will be fine."

"Would you rather have juice?"

"Tonic."

"You're not a drinker, are you?"

"No."

"Come on in the kitchen." She opened the refrigerator. "How about . . ."—she made a quick inventory with her hands—"a piece of pie, then? Karo pecan, it's dynamite."

"Fine."

She took a whole pie from the icebox and put it on the counter.

Hands pointing straight down, she spread her fingers along the edge of the pie tin until its circumference told her that her middle fingers were at nine and three o'clock. Then she touched her thumbtips together and brought them down to the surface of the pie to locate its exact center. She marked the center with a toothpick.

Dolarhyde tried to make conversation to keep her from feeling his stare. "How long have you been at Baeder?" No S's in that one.

"Three months. Didn't you know?"

"They tell me the minimum."

She grinned. "You probably stepped on some toes when you laid out the darkrooms. Listen, the techs love you for it. The plumbing works and there are plenty of outlets. Two-twenty wherever you need it."

She put the middle finger of her left hand on the toothpick, her thumb on the edge of the tin and cut him a slice of pie, guiding the knife with her left index finger.

He watched her handle the bright knife. Strange to look at the front of a woman as much as he liked. How often in company can one look where he wants to look?

She made herself a stiff gin and tonic and they went into the living room. She passed her hand over a floor lamp, felt no heat, switched it on.

Dolarhyde ate his pie in three bites and sat stiffly on the couch, his sleek hair shining under the lamp, his powerful hands on his knees.

She put her head back in her chair and propped her feet on an ottoman.

"When will they film at the zoo?"

"Maybe next week." He was glad he had called the zoo and offered the infrared film: Dandridge might check.

"It's a great zoo. I went with my sister and my niece when they came to help me move in. They have the contact area, you know. I hugged this llama. It felt nice, but talk about *aroma,* boy . . . I thought I was being followed by a llama until I changed my shirt."

This was Having a Conversation. He had to say something or leave. "How did you come to Baeder?"

"They advertised at the Reiker Institute in Denver where I was working. I was checking the bulletin board one day and just happened to come across this job. Actually, what happened, Baeder had to shape up their employment practices to keep this Defense contract. They managed to pack six women, two blacks, two chicanos, an oriental, a paraplegic, and me into a total of eight hirings. We all count in at least two categories, you see."

"You worked out well for Baeder."

"The others did too. Baeder's not giving anything away."

"Before that?" He was sweating a little. Conversation was hard. Looking was good, though. She had good legs. She had nicked an ankle shaving. Along his arms a sense of the weight of her legs, limp.

"I trained newly blind people at the Reiker Institute in Denver for ten years after I finished school. This is my first job on the outside."

"Outside of what?"

"Out in the big world. It was really insular at Reiker. I mean, we were training people to live in the sighted world and we didn't live in it ourselves. We talked to each other too much. I thought I'd get out and knock around a little. Actually, I had intended to go into speech therapy, for speech-and-hearing-impaired children. I expect I'll go back to that, one of these days." She drained her glass. "Say, I've got some Mrs. Paul's crab-ball miniatures in here. They're pretty good. I shouldn't have served dessert first. Want some?"

"Um-hmmm."

"Do you cook?"

"Um-hmmm."

A tiny crease appeared in her forehead. She went into the kitchen. "How about coffee?" she called.

"Uh-huh."

She made small talk about grocery prices and got no reply. She came back into the living room and sat on the ottoman, her elbows on her knees.

"Let's talk about something for a minute and get it out of the way, okay?"

Silence.

"You haven't said anything lately. In fact, you haven't said anything since I mentioned speech therapy." Her voice was kind, but firm. It carried no taint of sympathy. "I understand you fine because you speak very well and because I listen. People don't pay attention. They ask me *what? what?* all the time. If you don't want to talk, okay. But I hope you will talk. Because you can, and I'm interested in what you have to say."

"Ummm. That's good," Dolarhyde said softly. Clearly this little speech was very important to her. Was she inviting him into the two-category club with her and the Chinese paraplegic? He wondered what his second category was.

Her next statement was incredible to him.

"May I touch your face? I want to know if you're smiling or frowning." Wryly, now. "I want to know whether to just shut up or not."

She raised her hand and waited.

How well would she get around with her fingers bitten off? Dolarhyde mused. Even in street teeth he could do it as easily as biting off breadsticks. If he braced his heels on the floor, his weight back on the couch, and locked both hands on her wrist, she could never pull away from him in time. Crunch, crunch, crunch, crunch, maybe leave the thumb. For measuring pies.

He took her wrist between his thumb and forefinger and turned her shapely, hard-used hand in the light. There were many small scars on it, and several new nicks and abrasions. A smooth scar on the back might have been a burn.

Too close to home. Too early in his Becoming. She wouldn't be there to look at anymore.

To ask this incredible thing, she could know nothing personal about him. She had not gossiped.

"Take my word that I'm smiling," he said. Okay on the S. It was true that he had a sort of smile which exposed his handsome public teeth.

He held her wrist above her lap and released it. Her hand settled to her thigh and half-closed, fingers trailing on the cloth like an averted glance.

"I think the coffee's ready," she said.

"I'm going." Had to go. Home for relief.

She nodded. "If I offended you, I didn't mean to."

"No."

She stayed on the ottoman, listened to be sure the lock clicked as he left.

Reba McClane made herself another gin and tonic. She put on some Segovia records and curled up on the couch. Dolarhyde had left a warm dent in the cushion. Traces of him remained in the air—shoe polish, a new leather belt, good shaving lotion.

What an intensely private man. She had heard only a few references to him at the office—Dandridge saying "that son of a bitch Dolarhyde" to one of his toadies.

Privacy was important to Reba. As a child, learning to cope after she lost her sight, she had had no privacy at all.

Now, in public, she could never be sure that she was not watched. So Francis Dolarhyde's sense of privacy appealed to her. She had not felt one ion of sympathy from him, and that was good.

So was this gin.

Suddenly the Segovia sounded busy. She put on her whale songs.

Three tough months in a new town. The winter to face, finding curbs in the snow. Reba McClane, leggy and brave, damned self-pity.

She would not have it. She was aware of a deep vein of cripple's anger in her and, while she could not get rid of it, she made it work for her, fueling her drive for independence, strengthening her determination to wring all she could from every day.

In her way, she was a hard one. Faith in any sort of natural justice was nothing but a night-light; she knew that. Whatever she did, she would end the same way everyone does: flat on her back with a tube in her nose, wondering "Is this all?"

She knew that she would never have the light, but there were things she *could* have. There were things to enjoy. She had gotten pleasure from helping her students, and the pleasure was oddly intensified by the knowledge that she would be neither rewarded nor punished for helping them.

In making friends she was ever wary of people who foster dependency and feed on it. She had been involved with a few—the blind attract them, and they are the enemy.

Involved. Reba knew that she was physically attractive to men— God knows enough of them copped a feel with their knuckles when they grabbed her upper arm.

She liked sex very much, but years ago she had learned something basic about men; most of them are terrified of entailing a burden. Their fear was augmented in her case.

She did not like for a man to creep in and out of her bed as though he were stealing chickens.

Ralph Mandy was coming to take her to dinner. He had a particularly cowardly mew about being so scarred by life that he was incapable of love. Careful Ralph told her that too often, and it scalded her. Ralph was amusing, but she didn't want to own him.

She didn't want to see Ralph. She didn't feel like making conversation and hearing the hitches in conversations around them as people watched her eat.

It would be so nice to be wanted by someone with the courage to get his hat or stay as he damn pleased, and who gave her credit for the same. Someone who didn't *worry* about her.

Francis Dolarhyde—shy, with a linebacker's body and no bullshit.

She had never seen or touched a cleft lip and had no visual associations with the sound. She wondered if Dolarhyde thought she understood him easily because "blind people hear so much better than we do." That was a common myth. Maybe she should have explained to him that it was not true, that blind people simply pay more attention to what they hear.

There were so many misconceptions about the blind. She wondered if Dolarhyde shared the popular belief that the blind are "purer in spirit" than most people, that they are somehow sanctified by their affliction. She smiled to herself. That one wasn't true either.

CHAPTER 32

THE CHICAGO POLICE worked under a media blitz, a nightly news "countdown" to the next full moon. Eleven days were left.

Chicago families were frightened.

At the same time, attendance rose at horror movies that should have died at the drive-ins in a week. Fascination and horror. The entrepreneur who hit the punk-rock market with "Tooth Fairy" T-shirts came out with an alternate line that said "The Red Dragon Is a One-Night Stand." Sales were divided about equally between the two.

Jack Crawford himself had to appear at a news conference with police officials after the funeral. He had received orders from Above to make the federal presence more visible; he did not make it more audible, as he said nothing.

When heavily manned investigations have little to feed on, they tend to turn upon themselves, covering the same ground over and over, beating it flat. They take on the circular shape of a hurricane or a zero.

Everywhere Graham went he found detectives, cameras, a rush of uniformed men and the incessant crackle of radios. He needed to be still.

Crawford, ruffled from his news conference, found Graham at nightfall in the quiet of an unused jury room on the floor above the U.S. prosecutor's office.

Good lights hung low over the green felt jury table where Graham spread out his papers and photographs. He had taken off his coat and tie and he was slumped in a chair staring at two photographs. The Leedses' framed picture stood before him and beside it, on a clipboard propped against a carafe, was a picture of the Jacobis.

Graham's pictures reminded Crawford of a bullfighter's folding shrine, ready to be set up in any hotel room. There was no photograph of Lounds. He suspected that Graham had not been thinking about the Lounds case at all. He didn't need trouble with Graham.

"Looks like a poolroom in here," Crawford said.

"Did you knock 'em dead?" Graham was pale but sober. He had a quart of orange juice in his fist.

"Jesus." Crawford collapsed in a chair. "You try to think out there, it's like trying to take a piss on the train."

"Any news?"

"The commissioner was popping sweat over a question and scratched his balls on television, that's the only notable thing I saw. Watch at six and eleven if you don't believe it."

"Want some orange juice?"

"I'd just as soon swallow barbed wire."

"Good. More for me." Graham's face was drawn. His eyes were too bright. "How about the gas?"

"God bless Liza Lake. There're forty-one Servco Supreme franchise stations in greater Chicago. Captain Osborne's boys swarmed those, checking sales in containers to people driving vans and trucks. Nothing yet, but they haven't seen all shifts. Servco has 186 other stations—they're scattered over eight states. We've asked for help from the local jurisdictions. It'll take a while. If God loves me, he used a credit card. There's a chance."

"Not if he can suck a siphon hose, there isn't."

"I asked the commissioner not to say anything about the Tooth Fairy maybe living in this area. These people are spooked enough. If he told them that, this place would sound like Korea tonight when the drunks come home."

"You still think he's close?"

"Don't you? It figures, Will." Crawford picked up the Lounds autopsy report and peered at it through his half-glasses.

"The bruise on his head was older than the mouth injuries. Five to eight hours older, they're not sure. Now, the mouth injuries were hours old when they got Lounds to the hospital. They were burned over too, but inside his mouth they could tell. He retained some chloroform in his . . . hell, someplace in his wheeze. You think he was unconscious when the Tooth Fairy bit him?"

"No. He'd want him awake."

"That's what I figure. All right, he takes him out with a lick on the head—that's in the garage. He has to keep him quiet with chloroform until he gets him someplace where the noise won't matter. Brings him back and gets here hours after the bite."

"He could have done it all in the back of the van, parked way out somewhere," Graham said.

Crawford massaged the sides of his nose with his fingers, giving his voice a megaphone effect. "You're forgetting about the wheels on the chair. Bev got two kinds of carpet fuzz, wool and synthetic. Synthetic's from a van, maybe, but when have you ever seen a wool rug in a van? How many wool rugs have you seen in someplace you can rent? Damn few. Wool rug is a house, Will. And the dirt and mold were from a dark place where the chair was stored, a dirt-floored cellar."

"Maybe."

"Now, look at this." Crawford pulled a Rand McNally road atlas out of his briefcase. He had drawn a circle on the "United States mileage and driving time" map. "Freddy was gone a little over fifteen hours, and his injuries are spaced over that time. I'm going to make a couple of assumptions. I don't like to do that, but here goes. . . . What are you laughing at?"

"I just remembered when you ran those field exercises at Quantico—when that trainee told you he *assumed* something."

"I don't remember that. Here's—"

"You made him write 'assume' on the blackboard. You took the chalk and started underlining and yelling in his face. 'When you assume, you make an *ASS* out of *U* and *ME* both,' that's what you told him, as I recall."

"He needed a boot in the ass to shape up. Now, look at this. Figure he had Chicago traffic on Tuesday afternoon, going out of town with Lounds. Allow a couple of hours to fool with Lounds at the location where he took him, and then the time driving back. He couldn't have gone much farther than six hours' driving time out of Chicago. Okay, this circle around Chicago is six hours' driving time. See, it's wavy because some roads are faster than others."

"Maybe he just stayed here."

"Sure, but this is the farthest away he *could* be."

"So you've narrowed it down to Chicago, or inside a circle covering Milwaukee, Madison, Dubuque, Peoria, St. Louis, Indianapolis, Cincinnati, Toledo, and Detroit, to name a few."

"Better than that. We know he got a *Tattler* very fast. Monday night, probably."

"He could have done that in Chicago."

"I know it, but once you get out of town the *Tattlers* aren't available on Monday night in a lot of locations. Here's a list from the *Tattler* circulation department—places *Tattlers* are air-freighted or trucked inside the circle on Monday night. See, that leaves Milwaukee, St. Louis, Cincinnati, Indianapolis, and Detroit. They go to the airports and maybe ninety newsstands that stay open all night, not counting the ones in Chicago. I'm using the field offices to check them. Some newsie might remember an odd customer on Monday night."

"Maybe. That's a good move, Jack."

Clearly Graham's mind was elsewhere.

If Graham were a regular agent, Crawford would have threatened him with a lifetime appointment to the Aleutians. Instead he said, "My brother called this afternoon. Molly left his house, he said."

"Yeah."

"Someplace safe, I guess?"

Graham was confident Crawford knew exactly where she went. "Willy's grandparents.'"

"Well, they'll be glad to see the kid." Crawford waited.

No comment from Graham.

"Everything's okay, I hope."

"I'm working, Jack. Don't worry about it. No, look, it's just that she got jumpy over there."

Graham pulled a flat package tied with string from beneath a stack of funeral pictures and began to pick at the knot.

"What's that?"

"It's from Byron Metcalf, the Jacobis' lawyer. Brian Zeller sent it on. It's okay."

"Wait a minute, let me see." Crawford turned the package in his hairy fingers until he found the stamp and signature of S. F. "Semper

Fidelis" Aynesworth, head of the FBI's explosives section, certifying that the package had been fluoroscoped.

"Always check. Always check."

"I always check, Jack."

"Did Chester bring you this?"

"Yes."

"Did he show you the stamp before he handed it to you?"

"He checked it and showed me."

Graham cut the string. "It's copies of all the probate business in the Jacobi estate. I asked Metcalf to send it to me—we can compare with the Leeds stuff when it comes in."

"We have a lawyer doing that."

"*I* need it. I don't know the Jacobis, Jack. They were new in town. I got to Birmingham a month late, and their stuff was scattered to shit and gone. I've got a feel for the Leedses. I don't for the Jacobis. I need to know them. I want to talk to people they knew in Detroit, and I want a couple of days more in Birmingham."

"I need you here."

"Listen, Lounds was a straight snuff. We made him mad at Lounds. The only connection to Lounds is one we made. There's a little hard evidence with Lounds, and the police are handling it. Lounds was just an annoyance to him, but the Leedses and the Jacobis are *what he needs*. We've got to have the connection between them. If we ever get him, that's how we'll do it."

"So you have the Jacobi paper to use here," Crawford said. "What are you looking for? What kind of thing?"

"Any damn thing, Jack. Right now, a medical deduction." Graham pulled the IRS estate-tax form from the package. "Lounds was in a wheelchair. Medical. Valerie Leeds had surgery about six weeks before she died—remember in her diary? A small cyst in her breast. Medical again. I was wondering if Mrs. Jacobi had surgery too."

"I don't remember anything about surgery in the autopsy report."

"No, but it might have been something that didn't show. Her medical history was split between Detroit and Birmingham. Something might have gotten lost there. If she had anything done, there'll be a deduction claimed and maybe an insurance claim."

"Some itinerant orderly, you're thinking? Worked both places—Detroit or Birmingham and Atlanta?"

"If you spend time in a mental hospital you pick up the drill. You could pass as an orderly, get a job doing it when you got out," Graham said.

"Want some dinner?"

"I'll wait till later. I get dumb after I eat."

Leaving, Crawford looked back at Graham from the gloom of the doorway. He didn't care for what he saw. The hanging lights deepened the hollows in Graham's face as he studied with the victims staring at him from the photographs. The room smelled of desperation.

Would it be better for the case to put Graham back on the street? Crawford couldn't afford to let him burn himself out in here for nothing. But for something?

Crawford's excellent administrative instincts were not tempered by mercy. They told him to leave Graham alone.

CHAPTER 33

BY TEN P.M. Dolarhyde had worked out to near-exhaustion with the weights, had watched his films and tried to satisfy himself. Still he was restless.

Excitement bumped his chest like a cold medallion when he thought of Reba McClane. He should not think of Reba McClane.

Stretched out in his recliner, his torso pumped up and reddened by the workout, he watched the television news to see how the police were coming along with Freddy Lounds.

There was Will Graham standing near the casket with the choir howling away. Graham was slender. It would be easy to break his back. Better than killing him. Break his back and twist it just to be sure. They could roll him to the next investigation.

There was no hurry. Let Graham dread it.

Dolarhyde felt a quiet sense of power all the time now.

The Chicago police department made some noise at a news conference. Behind the racket about how hard they were working, the essence was: no progress on Freddy. Jack Crawford was in the group behind the microphones. Dolarhyde recognized him from a *Tattler* picture.

A spokesman from the *Tattler*, flanked by two bodyguards, said, "This savage and senseless act will only make the *Tattler's* voice ring louder."

Dolarhyde snorted. Maybe so. It had certainly shut Freddy up.

The news readers were calling him "the Dragon" now. His acts were "what the police *had* termed the 'Tooth Fairy murders.'"

Definite progress.

Nothing but local news left. Some prognathous lout was reporting from the zoo. Clearly they'd send him anywhere to keep him out of the office.

Dolarhyde had reached for his remote control when he saw on the screen someone he had talked with only hours ago on the telephone: Zoo Director Dr. Frank Warfield, who had been so pleased to have the film Dolarhyde offered.

Dr. Warfield and a dentist were working on a tiger with a broken tooth. Dolarhyde wanted to see the tiger, but the reporter was in the way. Finally the newsman moved.

Rocked back in his recliner, looking along his own powerful torso at the screen, Dolarhyde saw the great tiger stretched unconscious on a heavy work table.

Today they were preparing the tooth. In a few days they would cap it, the oaf reported.

Dolarhyde watched them calmly working between the jaws of the tiger's terrible striped face.

"May I touch your face?" said Miss Reba McClane.

He wanted to tell Reba McClane something. He wished she had one inkling of what she had almost done. He wished she had one flash of his Glory. But she could not have that and live. She must live: he had been seen with her and she was too close to home.

He had tried to share with Lecter, and Lecter had betrayed him.

Still, he would like to share. He would like to share with her a little, in a way she could survive.

CHAPTER 34

"*I* KNOW IT'S POLITICAL, *you* know it's political, but it's pretty much what you're doing anyway," Crawford told Graham. They were walking down the State Street Mall toward the federal office building in the late afternoon. "Do what you're doing, just write out the parallels and I'll do the rest."

The Chicago police department had asked the FBI's Behavioral Science section for a detailed victim profile. Police officials said they would use it in planning disposition of extra patrols during the period of the full moon.

"Covering their ass is what they're doing," Crawford said, waving his bag of Tater Tots. "The victims have been affluent people, they need to stack the patrols in affluent neighborhoods. They know there'll be a squawk about that—the ward bosses have been fighting over the extra manpower ever since Freddy lit off. If they patrol the upper-middle-class neighborhoods and he hits the South Side, God help the city fathers. But if it happens, they can point at the damned feds. I can hear it now—'They told us to do it that way. That's what *they* said do.'"

"I don't think he's any more likely to hit Chicago than anywhere else," Graham said. "There's no reason to think so. It's a jerkoff. Why can't Bloom do the profile? He's a consultant to Behavioral Science."

"They don't want it from Bloom, they want it from us. It wouldn't do them any good to blame Bloom. Besides, he's still in the hospital. I'm instructed to do this. Somebody on the Hill has been on the phone with Justice. Above says do it. Will you just do it?"

"I'll do it. It's what I'm doing anyway."

"That's what I know," Crawford said. "Just keep doing it."

"I'd rather go back to Birmingham."

"No," Crawford said. "Stay with me on this."

The last of Friday burned down the west.

Ten days to go.

CHAPTER 35

"READY TO TELL ME what kind of an 'outing' this is?" Reba McClane asked Dolarhyde on Saturday morning when they had ridden in silence for ten minutes. She hoped it was a picnic.

The van stopped. She heard Dolarhyde roll down his window.

"Dolarhyde," he said. "Dr. Warfield left my name."

"Yes, sir. Would you put this under your wiper when you leave the vehicle?"

They moved forward slowly. Reba felt a gentle curve in the road. Strange and heavy odors on the wind. An elephant trumpeted.

"The zoo," she said. "Terrific." She would have preferred a picnic. What the hell, this was okay. "Who's Dr. Warfield?"

"The zoo director."

"Is he a friend of yours?"

"No. We did the zoo a favor with the film. They're paying back."

"How?"

"You get to touch the tiger."

"Don't surprise me too much!"

"Did you ever look at a tiger?"

She was glad he could ask the question. "No. I remember a puma when I was little. That's all they had at the zoo in Red Deer. I think we better talk about this."

"They're working on the tiger's tooth. They have to put him to . . . sleep. If you want to, you can touch him."

"Will there be a crowd, people waiting?"

"No. No audience. Warfield, me, a couple of people. TV's coming in after we leave. Want to do it?" An odd urgency in the question.

"Hell fuzzy yes, I do! Thank you . . . that's a fine surprise."

The van stopped.

"Uh, how do I know he's sound asleep?"

"Tickle him. If he laughs, run for it."

The floor of the treatment room felt like linoleum under Reba's shoes. The room was cool with large echoes. Radiant heat was coming from the far side.

A rhythmic shuffling of burdened feet and Dolarhyde guided her to one side until she felt the forked pressure of a corner.

It was in here now, she could smell it.

A voice. "Up, now. Easy. Down. Can we leave the sling under him, Dr. Warfield?"

"Yeah, wrap that cushion in one of the green towels and put it under his head. I'll send John for you when we've finished."

Footsteps leaving.

She waited for Dolarhyde to tell her something. He didn't.

"It's in here," she said.

"Ten men carried it in on a sling. It's big. Ten feet. Dr. Warfield's listening to its heart. Now he's looking under one eyelid. Here he comes."

A body damped the noise in front of her.

"Dr. Warfield, Reba McClane," Dolarhyde said.

She held out her hand. A large, soft hand took it.

"Thanks for letting me come," she said. "It's a treat."

"Glad you *could* come. Enlivens my day. We appreciate the film, by the way."

Dr. Warfield's voice was middle-aged, deep, cultured, black. Virginia, she guessed.

"We're waiting to be sure his respiration and heartbeat are strong and steady before Dr. Hassler starts. Hassler's over there adjusting his head mirror. Just between us, he only wears it to hold down his toupee. Come meet him. Mr. Dolarhyde?"

"You go ahead."

She put out her hand to Dolarhyde. The pat was slow in coming, light when it came. His palm left sweat on her knuckles.

Dr. Warfield placed her hand on his arm and they walked forward slowly.

"He's sound asleep. Do you have a general impression . . . ? I'll describe as much as you like." He stopped, uncertain how to put it.

"I remember pictures in books when I was a child, and I saw a puma once in the zoo near home."

"This tiger is like a super puma," he said. "Deeper chest, more massive head, and a heavier frame and musculature. He's a four-year-old male Bengal. He's about ten feet long, from his nose to the tip of his tail, and he weighs eight hundred and fifteen pounds. He's lying on his right side under bright lights."

"I can feel the lights."

"He's striking, orange and black stripes, the orange is so bright it seems almost to bleed into the air around him." Suddenly Dr. Warfield feared that it was cruel to talk of colors. A glance at her face reassured him.

"He's six feet away, can you smell him?"

"Yes."

"Mr. Dolarhyde may have told you, some dimwit poked at him through the barrier with one of our gardener's spades. He snapped off the long fang on the upper left side on the blade. Okay, Dr. Hassler?"

"He's fine. We'll give it another minute or two."

Warfield introduced the dentist to Reba.

"My dear, you're the first *pleasant* surprise I've ever had from Frank Warfield," Hassler said. "You might like to examine this. It's a gold tooth, fang actually." He put it in her hand. "Heavy, isn't it? I cleaned up the broken tooth and took an impression several days ago, and today I'll cap it with this one. I could have done it in white of course, but I thought this would be more fun. Dr. Warfield will tell you I never pass up an opportunity to show off. He's too inconsiderate to let me put an advertisement on the cage."

She felt the taper, curve, and point with her sensitive battered fingers. "What a nice piece of work!" She heard deep, slow breathing nearby.

"It'll give the kids a start when he yawns," Hassler said. "And I don't think it'll tempt any thieves. Now for the fun. You're not apprehensive, are you? Your muscular gentleman over there is watching us like a ferret. He's not making you do this?"

"No! No, I want to."

"We're facing his back," Dr. Warfield said. "He's just sleeping away about two and a half feet from you, waist-high on a work table. Tell you what: I'll put your left hand—you're right-handed aren't you?—I'll put your left hand on the edge of the table and you can explore with your right. Take your time. I'll be right here beside you."

"So will I," Dr. Hassler said. They were enjoying this. Under the hot lights her hair smelled like fresh sawdust in the sun.

Reba could feel the heat on the top of her head. It made her scalp tingle. She could smell her warm hair, Warfield's soap, alcohol and disinfectant, and the cat. She felt a touch of faintness, quickly over.

She gripped the edge of the table and reached out tentatively until her fingers touched tips of fur, warm from the lights, a cooler layer and then a deep steady warmth from below. She flattened her hand on the thick coat and moved it gently, feeling the fur slide across her palm, with and against the lay, felt the hide slide over the wide ribs as they rose and fell.

She gripped the pelt and fur sprang between her fingers. In the very presence of the tiger her face grew pink and she lapsed into blindisms, inappropriate facial movements she had schooled herself against.

Warfield and Hassler saw her forget herself and were glad. They saw her through a wavy window, a pane of new sensation she pressed her face against.

As he watched from the shadows, the great muscles in Dolarhyde's back quivered. A drop of sweat bounced down his ribs.

"The other side's all business," Dr. Warfield said close to her ear.

He led her around the table, her hand trailing down the tail.

A sudden constriction in Dolarhyde's chest as her fingers trailed over the furry testicles. She cupped them and moved on.

Warfield lifted a great paw and put it in her hand. She felt the roughness of the pads and smelled faintly the cage floor. He pressed a toe to make the claw slide out. The heavy, supple muscles of the shoulders filled her hands.

She felt the tiger's ears, the width of its head and, carefully, the veterinarian guiding her, touched the roughness of its tongue. Hot breath stirred the hair on her forearms.

Last, Dr. Warfield put the stethoscope in her ears. Her hands on the rhythmic chest, her face upturned, she was filled with the tiger heart's bright thunder.

➤

Reba McClane was quiet, flushed, elated as they drove away. She turned to Dolarhyde once and said slowly, "Thank you . . . very much. If you don't mind, I would dearly love a martini."

➤

"Wait here a minute," Dolarhyde said as he parked in his yard.

She was glad they hadn't gone back to her apartment. It was stale and safe. "Don't tidy up. Take me in and tell me it's neat."

"Wait here."

He carried in the sack from the liquor store and made a fast inspection tour. He stopped in the kitchen and stood for a moment with his hands over his face. He wasn't sure what he was doing. He felt danger, but not from the woman. He couldn't look up the stairs. He had to do something and he didn't know how. He should take her back home.

Before his Becoming, he would not have dared any of this.

Now he realized he could do anything. Anything. Anything.

He came outside, into the sunset, into the long blue shadow of the van. Reba McClane held on to his shoulders until her foot touched the ground.

She felt the loom of the house. She sensed its height in the echo of the van door closing.

"Four steps on the grass. Then there's a ramp," he said.

She took his arm. A tremor through him. Clean perspiration in cotton.

"You *do* have a ramp. What for?"

"Old people were here."

"Not now, though."

"No."

"It feels cool and tall," she said in the parlor. Museum air. And was that incense? A clock ticked far away. "It's a big house, isn't it? How many rooms?"

"Fourteen."

"It's old. The things in here are old." She brushed against a fringed lampshade and touched it with her fingers.

Shy Mr. Dolarhyde. She was perfectly aware that it had excited him to see her with the tiger; he had shuddered like a horse when she took his arm leaving the treatment room.

An elegant gesture, his arranging that. Maybe eloquent as well, she wasn't sure.

"Martini?"

"Let me go with you and do it," she said, taking off her shoes.

She flicked vermouth from her finger into the glass. Two and a half ounces of gin on top, and two olives. She picked up points of reference quickly in the house—the ticking clock, the hum of a window air conditioner. There was a warm place on the floor near the kitchen door where the sunlight had fallen through the afternoon.

He took her to his big chair. He sat on the couch.

There was a charge in the air. Like fluorescence in the sea, it limned movement; she found a place for her drink on the stand beside her, he put on music.

To Dolarhyde the room seemed changed. She was the first voluntary company he ever had in the house, and now the room was divided into her part and his.

There was the music, Debussy as the light failed.

He asked her about Denver and she told him a little, absently, as though she thought of something else. He described the house and the big hedged yard. There wasn't much need to talk.

In the silence while he changed records, she said, "That wonderful tiger, this house, you're just full of surprises, D. I don't think anybody knows you at all."

"Did you ask them?"

"Who?"

"Anybody."

"No."

"Then how do you know that nobody knows me?" His concentration on the tongue-twister kept the tone of the question neutral.

"Oh, some of the women from Gateway saw us getting into your van the other day. Boy, were they curious. All of a sudden I have company at the Coke machine."

"What do they want to know?"

"They just wanted some juicy gossip. When they found out there isn't any, they went away. They were just fishing."

"And what did they say?"

She had meant to make the women's avid curiosity into humor directed at herself. It was not working out that way.

"They wonder about everything," she said. "They find you very mysterious and interesting. Come on, it's a compliment."

"Did they tell you how I look?"

The question was spoken lightly, very well done, but Reba knew that nobody is ever kidding. She met it head-on.

"I didn't ask them. But, yes, they told me how they think you look. Want to hear it? Verbatim? Don't ask if you don't." She was sure he would ask.

No reply.

Suddenly Reba felt that she was alone in the room, that the place where he had stood was emptier than empty, a black hole swallowing everything and emanating nothing. She knew he could not have left without her hearing him.

"I think I'll tell you," she said. "You have a kind of hard clean neatness that they like. They said you have a remarkable body." Clearly she couldn't leave it at that. "They say you're very sensitive about your face and that you shouldn't be. Okay, here's the dippy one with the Dentine, is it Eileen?"

"Eileen."

Ah, a return signal. She felt like a radio astronomer.

Reba was an excellent mimic. She could have reproduced Eileen's speech with startling fidelity, but she was too wise to mimic anyone's speech for Dolarhyde. She quoted Eileen as though she read from a transcript.

"'He's not a bad-looking guy. Honest to God I've gone out with lots of guys didn't look that good. I went out with a hockey player one time—played for the Blues?—had a little dip in his lip where his gum shrank back from his bridge? They all have that, hockey players. It's kind of, you know, *macho*, I think. Mr. D.'s got the nicest skin, and what I wouldn't give for his hair.' Satisfied? Oh, and she asked me if you're as strong as you look."

"And?"

"I said I didn't know." She drained her glass and got up. "Where the hell are you anyway, D.?" She knew when he moved between her and a stereo speaker. "Aha. Here you are. Do you want to know what I think about it?"

She found his mouth with her fingers and kissed it, lightly pressing his lips against his clenched teeth. She registered instantly that it was shyness and not distaste that held him rigid.

He was astonished.

"Now, would you show me where the bathroom is?"

She took his arm and went with him down the hall.

"I can find my own way back."

In the bathroom she patted her hair and ran her fingers along the top of the basin, hunting toothpaste or mouthwash. She tried to find the door of the medicine cabinet and found there was no door, only hinges and exposed shelves. She touched the objects on them carefully, leery of a razor, until she found a bottle. She took off the cap, smelled to verify mouthwash, and swished some around.

When she returned to the parlor, she heard a familiar sound—the whir of a projector rewinding.

"I have to do a little homework," Dolarhyde said, handing her a fresh martini.

"Sure," she said. She didn't know how to take it. "If I'm keeping you from working, I'll go. Will a cab come up here?"

"No. I want you to be here. I do. It's just some film I need to check. It won't take long."

He started to take her to the big chair. She knew where the couch was. She went to it instead.

"Does it have a soundtrack?"

"No."

"May I keep the music?"

"Um-hmmm."

She felt his attention. He wanted her to stay, he was just frightened. He shouldn't be. All right. She sat down.

The martini was wonderfully cold and crisp.

He sat on the other end of the couch, his weight clinking the ice in her glass. The projector was still rewinding.

"I think I'll stretch out for a few minutes if you don't mind," she said. "No, don't move, I have plenty of room. Wake me up if I drop off, okay?"

She lay on the couch, holding the glass on her stomach; the tips of her hair just touched his hand beside his thigh.

He flicked the remote switch and the film began.

Dolarhyde had wanted to watch his Leeds film or his Jacobi film with this woman in the room. He wanted to look back and forth from the screen to Reba. He knew she would never survive that. The women saw her getting into his van. Don't even think about that. The women saw her getting into his van.

He would watch his film of the Shermans, the people he would visit next. He would see the promise of relief to come, and do it in Reba's presence, looking at her all he liked.

On the screen, *The New House* spelled in pennies on a shirt cardboard. A long shot of Mrs. Sherman and the children. Fun in the pool. Mrs. Sherman holds to the ladder and looks up at the camera, bosom swelling shining wet above her suit, pale legs scissoring.

Dolarhyde was proud of his self-control. He would think of this film, not the other one. But in his mind he began to speak to Mrs. Sherman as he had spoken to Valerie Leeds in Atlanta.

You see me now, yes

That's how you feel to see me, yes

Fun with old clothes. Mrs. Sherman has the wide hat on. She is before the mirror. She turns with an arch smile and strikes a pose for the camera, her hand at the back of her neck. There is a cameo at her throat.

Reba McClane stirs on the couch. She sets her glass on the floor. Dolarhyde feels a weight and warmth. She has rested her head on his thigh. The nape of her neck is pale and the movie light plays on it.

He sits very still, moves only his thumb to stop the film, back it up. On the screen, Mrs. Sherman poses before the mirror in the hat. She turns to the camera and smiles.

You see me now, yes

That's how you feel to see me, yes

Do you feel me now? yes

Dolarhyde is trembling. His trousers are mashing him so hard. He feels heat. He feels warm breath through the cloth. Reba has made a discovery.

Convulsively his thumb works the switch.

You see me now, yes

That's how you feel to see me, yes

Do you feel this? yes

Reba has unzipped his trousers.

A stab of fear in him; he has never been erect before in the presence of a living woman. He is the Dragon, he doesn't have to be afraid.

Busy fingers spring him free.

OH.

Do you feel me now? yes

Do you feel this yes

You do I know it yes

Your heart is loud yes

He must keep his hands off Reba's neck. Keep them off. The women saw them in the van. His hand is squeezing the arm of the couch. His fingers pop through the upholstery.

Your heart is loud yes

And fluttering now

It's fluttering now

It's trying to get out yes

And now it's quick and light and quicker and light and . . .

Gone.

Oh, gone.

Reba rests her head on his thigh and turns her gleaming cheek to him. She runs her hand inside his shirt and rests it warm on his chest.

"I hope I didn't shock you," she said.

It was the sound of her living voice that shocked him, and he felt to see if her heart was going and it was. She held his hand there gently.

"My goodness, you're not through yet, are you?"

A living woman. How bizarre. Filled with power, the Dragon's or his own, he lifted her from the couch easily. She weighed nothing, so much easier to carry because she wasn't limp. Not upstairs. Not upstairs. Hurrying now. Somewhere. Quick. Grandmother's bed, the satin comforter sliding under them.

"Oh, wait, I'll get them off. Oh, now it's torn. I don't care. Come on. My God, man. That's so sweeeet. Don't please hold me down, let me come up to you and take it."

➤

With Reba, his only living woman, held with her in this one bubbleskin of time, he felt for the first time that it was all right: it was his life he was releasing, himself past all mortality that he was sending into her starry darkness, away from this pain planet, ringing harmonic distances away to peace and the promise of rest.

Beside her in the dark, he put his hand on her and pressed her together gently to seal the way back. As she slept, Dolarhyde, damned murderer of eleven, listened time and again to her heart.

Images. Baroque pearls flying through the friendly dark. A Very pistol he had fired at the moon. A great firework he saw in Hong Kong called "The Dragon Sows His Pearls."

The Dragon.

He felt stunned, cloven. And all the long night beside her he listened, fearful, for himself coming down the stairs in the kimono.

She stirred once in the night, searching sleepily until she found the bedside glass. Grandmother's teeth rattled in it.

Dolarhyde brought her water. She held him in the dark. When she slept again, he took her hand off his great tattoo and put it on his face.

➤

He slept hard at dawn.

Reba McClane woke at nine and heard his steady breathing. She stretched lazily in the big bed. He didn't stir. She reviewed the layout of the house, the order of rugs and floor, the direction of the ticking clock. When she had it straight, she rose quietly and found the bathroom.

After her long shower, he was still asleep. Her torn underclothes were on the floor. She found them with her feet and stuffed them in her purse. She pulled her cotton dress on over her head, picked up her cane and walked outside.

He had told her the yard was large and level, bounded by hedges grown wild, but she was cautious at first.

The morning breeze was cool, the sun warm. She stood in the yard and let the wind toss the seed heads of the elderberry through her hands. The wind found the creases of her body, fresh from the shower. She raised her arms to it and the wind blew cool beneath her breasts and arms and between her legs. Bees went by. She was not afraid of them and they left her alone.

Dolarhyde woke, puzzled for an instant because he was not in his room upstairs. His yellow eyes grew wide as he remembered. An owlish turn of his head to the other pillow. Empty.

Was she wandering around the house? What might she find? Or had something happened in the night? Something to clean up. He would be suspected. He might have to run.

He looked in the bathroom, in the kitchen. Down in the basement where his other wheelchair stood. The upper floor. He didn't want to go upstairs. He had to look. His tattoo flexed as he climbed the stairs. The Dragon glowed at him from the picture in his bedroom. He could not stay in the room with the Dragon.

From an upstairs window he spotted her in the yard.

"FRANCIS." He knew the voice came from his room. He knew it was the voice of the Dragon. This new twoness with the Dragon disoriented him. He first felt it when he put his hand on Reba's heart.

The Dragon had never spoken *to* him before. It was frightening.

"FRANCIS, COME HERE."

He tried to shut out the voice calling him, calling him as he hurried down the stairs.

What could she have found? Grandmother's teeth had rattled in the glass, but he put them away when he brought her water. She couldn't see anything.

Freddy's tape. It was in a cassette recorder in the parlor. He checked it. The cassette was rewound to the beginning. He couldn't remember if he had rewound it after he played it on the telephone to the *Tattler*.

She must not come back in the house. He didn't know what might happen in the house. She might get a surprise. The Dragon might come down. He knew how easily she would tear.

The women saw her getting in his van. Warfield would remember them together. Hurriedly he dressed.

Reba McClane felt the cool bar of a tree trunk's shadow, and then the sun again as she wandered across the yard. She could always tell where she was by the heat of the sun and the hum of the window air conditioner. Navigation, her life's discipline, was easy here. She turned around and around, trailing her hands on the shrubs and overgrown flowers.

A cloud blocked the sun and she stopped, not knowing in which direction she faced. She listened for the air conditioner. It was off. She felt a moment of uneasiness, then clapped her hands and heard the reassuring echo from the house. Reba flipped up her watch crystal and felt the time. She'd have to wake D. soon. She needed to go home.

The screen door slammed.

"Good morning," she said.

His keys tinkled as he came across the grass.

He approached her cautiously, as though the wind of his coming might blow her down, and saw that she was not afraid of him.

She didn't seem embarrassed or ashamed of what they had done in the night. She didn't seem angry. She didn't run from him or threaten him. He wondered if it was because she had not seen his private parts.

Reba put her arms around him and laid her head on his hard chest. His heart was going fast.

He managed to say good morning.

"I've had a really terrific time, D."

Really? What would someone say back? "Good. Me too." *That seemed all right. Get her away from here.*

"But I need to go home now," she was saying. "My sister's coming by to pick me up for lunch. You could come too if you like."

"I have to go to the plant," he said, modifying the lie he had ready.

"I'll get my purse."

Oh no. "I'll get it."

Almost blind to his own true feelings, no more able to express them than a scar can blush, Dolarhyde did not know what had happened to him with Reba McClane, or why. He was confused, spiked with new fright at being Two.

She threatened him, she did not threaten him.

There was the matter of her startling live movements of acceptance in Grandmother's bed.

Often Dolarhyde did not find out what he felt until he acted. He didn't know how he felt toward Reba McClane.

An ugly incident as he drove her home enlightened him a little.

Just past the Lindbergh Boulevard exit off Interstate 70, Dolarhyde pulled into a Servco Supreme station to fill his van.

The attendant was a heavyset, sullen man with muscatel on his breath. He made a face when Dolarhyde asked him to check the oil.

The van was a quart low. The attendant jammed the oil spout into the can and stuck the spout into the engine.

Dolarhyde climbed out to pay.

The attendant seemed enthusiastic about wiping the windshield; the passenger side of the windshield. He wiped and wiped.

Reba McClane sat in the high bucket seat, her legs crossed, her skirt riding up over her knee. Her white cane lay between the seats.

The attendant started over on the windshield. He was looking up her dress.

Dolarhyde glanced up from his wallet and caught him. He reached in through the window of the van and turned the wipers on high speed, batting the attendant's fingers.

"Hey, watch that." The attendant got busy removing the oil can from the engine compartment. He knew he was caught and he wore a sly grin until Dolarhyde came around the van to him.

"You son of a bitch." Fast over the /s/.

"What the hell's the matter with you?" The attendant was about Dolarhyde's height and weight, but he had nowhere near the muscle. He was young to have dentures, and he didn't take care of them.

Their greenness disgusted Dolarhyde. "What happened to your teeth?" he asked softly.

"What's it to you?"

"Did you pull them for your boyfriend, you rotten prick?" Dolarhyde stood too close.

"Get the hell away from me."

Quietly, "Pig. Idiot. Trash. Fool."

With a one-hand shove Dolarhyde sent him flying back to slam against the van. The oil can and spout clattered on the asphalt.

Dolarhyde picked it up.

"Don't run. I can catch you." He pulled the spout from the can and looked at its sharp end.

The attendant was pale. There was something in Dolarhyde's face that he had never seen before, anywhere.

For a red instant Dolarhyde saw the spout jammed in the man's chest, draining his heart. He saw Reba's face through the windshield. She was shaking her head, saying something. She was trying to find the handle to roll her window down.

"Ever had anything broken, ass-eyes?"

The attendant shook his head fast. "I didn't mean no offense, now. Honest to God."

Dolarhyde held the curved metal spout in front of the man's face.

He held it in both hands and his chest muscles bunched as he bent it double. He pulled out the man's waistband and dropped the spout down the front of his pants.

"Keep your pig eyes to yourself." He stuffed money for the gas in the man's shirt pocket. "You can run now," he said. "But I could catch you anytime."

CHAPTER 36

THE TAPE CAME ON SATURDAY in a small package addressed to Will Graham, c/o FBI Headquarters, Washington. It had been mailed in Chicago on the day Lounds was killed.

The laboratory and Latent Prints found nothing useful on the cassette case or the wrapper.

A copy of the tape went to Chicago in the afternoon pouch. Special Agent Chester brought it to Graham in the jury room at midafternoon. A memo from Lloyd Bowman was attached:

> Voiceprints verify this is Lounds. Obviously he was repeating dictation. It's a new tape, manufactured in the last three months and never used before. Behavioral Science is picking at the content. Dr. Bloom should hear it when he's well enough—you decide about that.
>
> Clearly the killer's trying to rattle you.
> He'll do that once too often, I think.

A dry vote of confidence, much appreciated.

Graham knew he had to listen to the tape. He waited until Chester left.

He didn't want to be closed up in the jury room with it. The empty courtroom was better—some sun came in the tall windows. The cleaning women had been in and dust still hung in the sunlight.

The tape recorder was small and gray. Graham put it on a counsel table and pushed the button.

A technician's monotone: "Case number 426238, item 814, tagged and logged, a tape cassette. This is a rerecording."

A shift in the quality of the sound.

Graham held on to the railing of the jury box with both hands.

Freddy Lounds sounded tired and frightened.

"I have had a great privilege. I have seen . . . I have seen with wonder . . . wonder and awe . . . awe . . . the strength of the Great Red Dragon."

The original recording had been interrupted frequently as it was made. The machine caught the clack of the stop key each time. Graham saw the finger on the key. Dragon finger.

"I lied about Him. All I wrote was lies from Will Graham. He made me write them. I have . . . I have blasphemed against the Dragon. Even so . . . the Dragon is merciful. Now I want to serve Him. He . . . has helped me understand . . . His Splendor and I will praise Him. Newspapers, when you print this, always capitalize the H in 'Him.'

"He knows you made me lie, Will Graham. Because I was forced to lie, He will be more . . . more merciful to me than to you, Will Graham.

"Reach behind you, Will Graham . . . and feel for the small . . . knobs on the top of your pelvis. Feel your spine between them . . . that is the precise spot . . . where the Dragon will snap your spine."

Graham kept his hands on the railing. Damn if I'll feel. Did the Dragon not know the nomenclature of the iliac spine, or did he choose not to use it?

"There's much . . . for you to dread. From . . . from my own lips you'll learn a little more to dread."

A pause before the awful screaming. Worse, the blubbering lipless cry, "You goddanned astard you romised."

Graham put his head between his knees until the bright spots stopped dancing in front of his eyes. He opened his mouth and breathed deep.

An hour passed before he could listen to it again.

He took the recorder into the jury room and tried to listen there.

Too close. He left the tape recorder turning and went back into the courtroom. He could hear through the open door.

"I have had a great privilege . . ."

Someone was at the courtroom door. Graham recognized the young clerk from the Chicago FBI office and motioned for him to come in.

"A letter came for you," the clerk said. "Mr. Chester sent me with it. He told me to be sure and say the postal inspector fluoroscoped it."

The clerk pulled the letter out of his breast pocket. Heavy mauve stationery. Graham hoped it was from Molly.

"It's stamped, see?"

"Thank you."

"Also it's payday." The clerk handed him his check.

On the tape, Freddy screamed.

The young man flinched.

"Sorry," Graham said.

"I don't see how you stand it," the young man said.

"Go home," Graham said.

He sat in the jury box to read his letter. He wanted some relief. The letter was from Dr. Hannibal Lecter.

Dear Will,

A brief note of congratulations for the job you did on Mr. Lounds. I admired it enormously. What a cunning boy you are!

Mr. Lounds often offended me with his ignorant drivel, but he did enlighten me on one thing—your confinement in the mental hospital. My inept attorney should have brought that out in court, but never mind.

You know, Will, you worry too much. You'd be so much more comfortable if you relaxed with yourself.

We don't invent our natures, Will; they're issued to us along with our lungs and pancreas and everything else. Why fight it?

I want to help you, Will, and I'd like to start by asking you this: When you were so depressed after you shot Mr. Garrett Jacob Hobbs to death, it wasn't the *act* that got you down, was it? Really, didn't you feel so bad *because killing him felt so good?*

Think about it, but don't worry about it. Why shouldn't it feel good? It must feel good to God—He does it all the time, and are we not made in His image?

You may have noticed in the paper yesterday, God dropped a church roof on thirty-four of His worshipers in Texas Wednesday night—just as they were groveling through a hymn. Don't you think that felt good?

Thirty-four. He'd let you have Hobbs.

He got 160 Filipinos in one plane crash last week—He'll let you have measly Hobbs. He won't begrudge you one measly murder. Two now. That's all right.

Watch the papers. God always stays ahead.

> Best,
> Hannibal Lecter, M.D.

Graham knew that Lecter was dead wrong about Hobbs, but for a half-second he wondered if Lecter might be a little bit right in the case of Freddy Lounds. The enemy inside Graham agreed with any accusation.

He had put his hand on Freddy's shoulder in the *Tattler* photograph to establish that he really had told Freddy those insulting things about the Dragon. Or had he wanted to put Freddy at risk, just a little? He wondered.

The certain knowledge that he would not knowingly miss a chance at the Dragon reprieved him.

"I'm just about worn out with you crazy sons of bitches," Graham said aloud.

He wanted a break. He called Molly, but no one answered the telephone at Willy's grandparents' house. "Probably out in their damned motorhome," he mumbled.

He went out for coffee, partly to assure himself that he was not hiding in the jury room.

In the window of a jewelry store he saw a delicate antique gold bracelet. It cost him most of his paycheck. He had it wrapped and stamped for mailing. Only when he was sure he was alone at the mail drop did he address it to Molly in Oregon. Graham did not realize, as Molly did, that he gave presents when he was angry.

He didn't want to go back to his jury room and work, but he had to. The thought of Valerie Leeds spurred him.

I'm sorry I can't come to the phone right now, Valerie Leeds had said.

He wished that he had known her. He wished . . . Useless, childish thought.

Graham was tired, selfish, resentful, fatigued to a child-minded state in which his standards of measurement were the first ones he learned; where the direction "north" was Highway 61 and "six feet" was forever the length of his father.

He made himself settle down to the minutely detailed victim profile he was putting together from a fan of reports and his own observations.

Affluence. That was one parallel. Both families were affluent. Odd that Valerie Leeds saved money on panty hose.

Graham wondered if she had been a poor child. He thought so; her own children were a little too well turned out.

Graham had been a poor child, following his father from the boatyards in Biloxi and Greenville to the lake boats on Erie. Always the new boy at school, always the stranger. He had a half-buried grudge against the rich.

Valerie Leeds might have been a poor child. He was tempted to watch his film of her again. He could do it in the courtroom. No. The Leedses were not his immediate problem. He knew the Leedses. He did not know the Jacobis.

His lack of intimate knowledge about the Jacobis plagued him. The house fire in Detroit had taken everything—family albums, probably diaries too.

Graham tried to know them through the objects they wanted, bought and used. That was all he had.

The Jacobi probate file was three inches thick, and a lot of it was lists of possessions—a new household outfitted since the move to Birmingham. *Look at all this shit.* It was all insured, listed with serial numbers as the insurance companies required. Trust a man who has been burned out to buy plenty of insurance for the next time.

The attorney, Byron Metcalf, had sent him carbons instead of Xerox copies of the insurance declarations. The carbons were fuzzy and hard to read.

Jacobi had a ski boat, Leeds had a ski boat. Jacobi had a three-wheeler, Leeds had a trail bike. Graham licked his thumb and turned the page.

The fourth item on the second page was a Chinon Pacific movie projector.

Graham stopped. How had he missed it? He had looked through every crate on every pallet in the Birmingham warehouse, alert for anything that would give him an intimate view of the Jacobis.

Where was the projector? He could cross-check this insurance declaration against the inventory Byron Metcalf had prepared as executor when he stored the Jacobis' things. The items had been checked off by the warehouse supervisor who signed the storage contract.

It took fifteen minutes to go down the list of stored items. No projector, no camera, no film.

Graham leaned back in his chair and stared at the Jacobis smiling from the picture propped before him.

What the hell did you do with it?

Was it stolen?

Did the killer steal it?

If the killer stole it, did he fence it?

Dear God, give me a traceable fence.

Graham wasn't tired anymore. He wanted to know if anything else was missing. He looked for an hour, comparing the warehouse storage inventory with the insurance declarations. Everything was accounted for except the small precious items. They should all be on Byron Metcalf's own lockbox list of things he had put in the bank vault in Birmingham.

All of them were on the list. Except two.

"Crystal oddment box, 4" × 3", sterling silver lid" appeared on the insurance declaration, but was not in the lockbox. "Sterling picture frame, 9 × 11 inches, worked with vines and flowers" wasn't in the vault either.

Stolen? Mislaid? They were small items, easily concealed. Usually fenced silver is melted down immediately. It would be hard to trace. But movie equipment had serial numbers inside and out. It could be traced.

Was the killer the thief?

As he stared at his stained photograph of the Jacobis, Graham felt the sweet jolt of a new connection. But when he saw the answer whole it was seedy and disappointing and small.

There was a telephone in the jury room. Graham called Birmingham Homicide. He got the three-to-eleven watch commander.

"In the Jacobi case I noticed you kept an in-and-out log at the house after it was sealed off, right?"

"Let me get somebody to look," the watch commander said.

Graham knew they kept one. It was good procedure to record every person entering or leaving a murder scene, and Graham had been pleased to see that Birmingham did it. He waited five minutes before a clerk picked up the telephone.

"Okay, in-and-out, what do you want to know?"

"Is Niles Jacobi, son of the deceased—is he on it?"

"Umm-hmmm, yep. July 2, seven P.M. He had permission to get personal items."

"Did he have a suitcase, does it say?"

"Nope. Sorry."

Byron Metcalf's voice was husky and his breathing heavy when he answered the telephone. Graham wondered what he was doing.

"Hope I didn't disturb you."

"What can I do for you, Will?"

"I need a little help with Niles Jacobi."

"What's he done now?"

"I think he lifted a few things out of the Jacobi house after they were killed."

"Ummm."

"There's a sterling picture frame missing from your lockbox inventory. When I was in Birmingham I picked up a loose photograph of the family in Niles's dormitory room. It used to be in a frame—I can see the impression the mat left on it."

"The little bastard. I gave permission for him to get his clothes and some books he needed," Metcalf said.

"Niles has expensive friendships. This is mainly what I'm after, though—a movie projector and a movie camera are missing too. I want to know if he got them. Probably he did, but if he *didn't,* maybe the killer got them. In that case we need to get the serial numbers out to the hock shops. We need to put 'em on the national hot sheet. The frame's probably melted down by now."

"He'll think 'frame' when I get through with him."

"One thing—if Niles took the projector, he might have kept the film. He couldn't get anything for it. I want the film. I need to see it. If you come at him from the front, he'll deny everything and flush the film if he has any."

"Okay," Metcalf said. "His car title reverted to the estate. I'm executor, so I can search it without a warrant. My friend the judge won't mind papering his room for me. I'll call you."

Graham went back to work.

Affluence. Put affluence in the profile the police would use.

Graham wondered if Mrs. Leeds and Mrs. Jacobi ever did their marketing in tennis clothes. That was a fashionable thing to do in some areas. It was a dumb thing to do in some areas because it was doubly provocative—arousing class resentment and lust at the same time.

Graham imagined them pushing grocery carts, short pleated skirts brushing the brown thighs, the little balls on their sweat socks winking—passing the husky man with the barracuda eyes who was buying cold lunch meat to gnaw in his car.

How many families were there with three children and a pet, and only common locks between them and the Dragon as they slept?

When Graham pictured possible victims, he saw clever, successful people in graceful houses.

But the next person to confront the Dragon did not have children or a pet, and there was no grace in his house. The next person to confront the Dragon was Francis Dolarhyde.

CHAPTER 37

THE THUMP OF WEIGHTS on the attic floor carried through the old house.

Dolarhyde was lifting, straining, pumping more weight than he had ever lifted. His costume was different; sweatpants covered his tattoo. The sweatshirt hung over *The Great Red Dragon and the Woman Clothed with the Sun*. The kimono hung on the wall like the shed skin of a tree snake. It covered the mirror.

Dolarhyde wore no mask.

Up. Two hundred and eighty pounds from the floor to his chest in one heave. Now over his head.

"WHOM ARE YOU THINKING ABOUT?"

Startled by the voice, he nearly dropped the weight, swayed beneath it. Down. The plates thudded and clanked on the floor.

He turned, his great arms hanging, and stared in the direction of the voice.

"WHOM ARE YOU THINKING ABOUT?"

It seemed to come from behind the sweatshirt, but its rasp and volume hurt his throat.

"WHOM ARE YOU THINKING ABOUT?"

He knew who spoke and he was frightened. From the beginning, he and the Dragon had been one. He was Becoming and the Dragon was his higher self. Their bodies, voices, wills were one.

272

Not now. Not since Reba. Don't think Reba.

"WHO IS ACCEPTABLE?" the Dragon asked.

"Mrs. . . . erhman—Sherman." It was hard for Dolarhyde to say.

"SPEAK UP. I CAN'T UNDERSTAND YOU. WHOM ARE YOU THINKING ABOUT?"

Dolarhyde, his face set, turned to the barbell. Up. Over his head. Much harder this time.

"Mrs. . . . erhman wet in the water."

"YOU THINK ABOUT YOUR LITTLE BUDDY, DON'T YOU? YOU WANT HER TO BE YOUR LITTLE BUDDY, DON'T YOU?"

The weight came down with a thud.

"I on't have a li'l . . . huddy." With the fear his speech was failing. He had to occlude his nostrils with his upper lip.

"A STUPID LIE." The Dragon's voice was strong and clear. He said the /s/ without effort. "YOU FORGET THE BECOMING. PREPARE FOR THE SHERMANS. LIFT THE WEIGHT."

Dolarhyde seized the barbell and strained. His mind strained with his body. Desperately he tried to think of the Shermans. He forced himself to think of the weight of Mrs. Sherman in his arms. Mrs. Sherman was next. It was Mrs. Sherman. He was fighting Mr. Sherman in the dark. Holding him down until loss of blood made Sherman's heart quiver like a bird. It was the only heart he heard. He didn't hear Reba's heart. He didn't.

Fear leeched his strength. He got the weight up to his thighs, could not make the turn up to his chest. He thought of the Shermans ranged around him, eyes wide, as he took the Dragon's due. It was no good. It was hollow, empty. The weight thudded down.

"NOT ACCEPTABLE."

"Mrs. . . ."

"YOU CAN'T EVEN SAY 'MRS. SHERMAN.' YOU NEVER INTEND TO TAKE THE SHERMANS. YOU WANT REBA MCCLANE. YOU WANT HER TO BE YOUR LITTLE BUDDY, DON'T YOU? YOU WANT TO BE 'FRIENDS.'"

"No."

"LIE!"

"Nyus mhor a niddow wyow."

"JUST FOR A LITTLE WHILE? YOU SNIVELING HARELIP, WHO WOULD BE FRIENDS WITH YOU? COME HERE. I'LL SHOW YOU WHAT YOU ARE."

Dolarhyde did not move.

"I'VE NEVER SEEN A CHILD AS DISGUSTING AND DIRTY AS YOU. COME HERE."

He went.

"TAKE DOWN THE SWEATSHIRT."

He took it down.

"LOOK AT ME."

The Dragon glowed from the wall.

"TAKE DOWN THE KIMONO. LOOK IN THE MIRROR."

He looked. He could not help himself or turn his face from the scalding light. He saw himself drool.

"LOOK AT YOURSELF. I'M GOING TO GIVE YOU A SURPRISE FOR YOUR LITTLE BUDDY. TAKE OFF THAT RAG."

Dolarhyde's hands fought each other at the waistband of the sweatpants. The sweatpants tore. He stripped them away from him with his right hand, held the rags to him with his left.

His right hand snatched the rags away from his trembling, failing left. He threw them into the corner and fell back on the mat, curling on himself like a lobster split live. He hugged himself and groaned, breathing hard, his tattoo brilliant in the harsh gym lights.

"I'VE NEVER SEEN A CHILD AS DISGUSTING AND DIRTY AS YOU. GO GET THEM."

"aaaymah."

"GET THEM."

He padded from the room and returned with the Dragon's teeth.

"PUT THEM IN YOUR PALMS. LOCK YOUR FINGERS AND SQUEEZE MY TEETH TOGETHER."

Dolarhyde's pectoral muscles bunched.

"YOU KNOW HOW THEY CAN SNAP. NOW HOLD THEM UNDER YOUR BELLY. HOLD YOURSELF BETWEEN THE TEETH."

"no."

"DO IT. . . . NOW LOOK."

The teeth were beginning to hurt him. Spit and tears fell on his chest.

"mleadse."

"YOU ARE OFFAL LEFT BEHIND IN THE BECOMING. YOU ARE OFFAL AND I WILL NAME YOU. YOU ARE CUNT FACE. SAY IT."

"i am cunt face." He occluded his nostrils with his lip to say the words.

"SOON I WILL BE CLEANSED OF YOU," the Dragon said effortlessly. "WILL THAT BE GOOD?"

"good."

"WHO WILL BE NEXT WHEN IT IS TIME?"

"mrs. . . . ehrman . . ."

Sharp pain shot through Dolarhyde, pain and terrible fear.

"I'LL TEAR IT OFF."

"reba. reba. i'll give you reba." Already his speech was improving.

"YOU'LL GIVE ME NOTHING. SHE IS MINE. THEY ARE ALL MINE. REBA MCCLANE AND THEN THE SHERMANS."

"reba and then the shermans. the law will know."

"I HAVE PROVIDED FOR THAT DAY. DO YOU DOUBT IT?"

"no."

"WHO ARE YOU?"

"cunt face."

"YOU MAY PUT AWAY MY TEETH. YOU PITIFUL WEAK HARELIP, YOU'D KEEP YOUR LITTLE BUDDY FROM ME, WOULD YOU? I'LL TEAR HER APART AND RUB THE PIECES IN YOUR UGLY FACE. I'LL HANG YOU WITH HER LARGE INTESTINE IF YOU OPPOSE ME. YOU KNOW I CAN. PUT THREE HUNDRED POUNDS ON THE BAR."

Dolarhyde added the plates to the bar. He had never lifted as much as 280 until today.

"LIFT IT."

If he were not as strong as the Dragon, Reba would die. He knew it. He strained until the room turned red before his bulging eyes.

"i can't."

"NO YOU CAN'T. BUT I CAN."

Dolarhyde gripped the bar. It bowed as the weight rose to his shoulders. UP. Above his head easily. "GOOD-BYE, CUNT FACE," he said, proud Dragon, quivering in the light.

CHAPTER 38

FRANCIS DOLARHYDE never got to work on Monday morning.

He started from his house exactly on time, as he always did. His appearance was impeccable, his driving precise. He put on his dark glasses when he made the turn at the Missouri River bridge and drove into the morning sun.

His Styrofoam cooler squeaked as it jiggled against the passenger seat. He leaned across and set it on the floor, remembering that he must pick up the dry ice and get the film from . . .

Crossing the Missouri channel now, moving water under him. He looked at the whitecaps on the sliding river and suddenly felt that he was sliding and the river was still. A strange, disjointed, collapsing feeling flooded him. He let up on the accelerator.

The van slowed in the outside lane and stopped. Traffic behind him was stacking up, honking. He didn't hear it.

He sat, sliding slowly northward over the still river, facing the morning sun. Tears leaked from beneath his sunglasses and fell hot on his forearms.

Someone was pecking on the window. A driver, face early-morning pale and puffed with sleep, had gotten out of a car behind him. The driver was yelling something through the window.

Dolarhyde looked at the man. Flashing blue lights were coming from the other end of the bridge. He knew he should drive. He asked his body to step on the gas, and it did. The man beside the van skipped backward to save his feet.

Dolarhyde pulled into the parking lot of a big motel near the U.S. 270 interchange. A school bus was parked in the lot, the bell of a tuba leaning against its back window.

Dolarhyde wondered if he was supposed to get on the bus with the old people.

No, that wasn't it. He looked around for his mother's Packard.

"Get in. Don't put your feet on the seat," his mother said.

That wasn't it either.

He was in a motel parking lot on the west side of St. Louis and he wanted to be able to Choose and he couldn't.

In six days, if he could wait that long, he would kill Reba McClane. He made a sudden high sound through his nose.

Maybe the Dragon would be willing to take the Shermans first and wait another moon.

No. He wouldn't.

Reba McClane didn't know about the Dragon. She thought she was with Francis Dolarhyde. She wanted to put her body on Francis Dolarhyde. She welcomed Francis Dolarhyde in Grandmother's bed.

"I've had a really terrific time, D.," Reba McClane said in the yard.

Maybe she liked Francis Dolarhyde. That was a perverted, despicable thing for a woman to do. He understood that he should despise her for it, but oh God it was good.

Reba McClane was guilty of liking Francis Dolarhyde. Demonstrably guilty.

If it weren't for the power of his Becoming, if it weren't for the Dragon, he could never have taken her to his house. He would not have been capable of sex. Or would he?

"My God, man. That's so sweeeet."

That's what she said. She said "man."

The breakfast crowd was coming out of the motel, passing his van. Their idle glances walked on him with many tiny feet.

He needed to think. He couldn't go home. He checked into the motel, called his office and reported himself sick. The room he got was bland and quiet. The only decorations were bad steamboat prints. Nothing glowed from the walls.

Dolarhyde lay down in his clothes. The ceiling had sparkling flecks in the plaster. Every few minutes he had to get up and urinate. He shivered, then he sweated. An hour passed.

He did not want to give Reba McClane to the Dragon. He thought about what the Dragon would do to him if he didn't serve her up.

Intense fear comes in waves; the body can't stand it for long at a time. In the heavy calm between the waves, Dolarhyde could think.

How could he keep from giving her to the Dragon? One way kept nudging him. He got up.

The light switch clacked loud in the tiled bathroom. Dolarhyde looked at the shower-curtain rod, a solid piece of one-inch pipe bolted to the bathroom walls. He took down the shower curtain and hung it over the mirror.

Grasping the pipe, he chinned himself with one arm, his toes dragging up the side of the bathtub. It was stout enough. His belt was stout enough too. He could make himself do it. He wasn't afraid of *that*.

He tied the end of his belt around the pipe in a bowline knot. The buckle end formed a noose. The thick belt didn't swing, it hung down in a stiff noose.

He sat on the toilet lid and looked at it. He wouldn't get any drop, but he could stand it. He could keep his hands off the noose until he was too weak to raise his arms.

But how could he be positive that his death would affect the Dragon, now that he and the Dragon were Two? Maybe it wouldn't. How could he be sure the Dragon then would leave her alone?

It might be days before they found his body. She would wonder where he was. In that time would she go to his house and feel around for him? Go upstairs and feel around for him and get a surprise?

The Great Red Dragon would take an hour spitting her down the stairs.

Should he call her and warn her? What could she do against Him, even warned? Nothing. She could hope to die quickly, hope that in His rage He would quickly bite deep enough.

Upstairs in Dolarhyde's house, the Dragon waited in pictures he had framed with his own hands. The Dragon waited in art books and magazines beyond number, reborn every time a photographer . . . did what?

Dolarhyde could hear in his mind the Dragon's powerful voice cursing Reba. He would curse her first, before he bit. He would curse Dolarhyde too—tell her he was nothing.

"Don't do that. Don't . . . do that," Dolarhyde said to the echoing tile. He listened to his voice, the voice of Francis Dolarhyde, the voice that Reba McClane understood easily, his own voice. He had been ashamed of it all his life, had said bitter and vicious things to others with it.

But he had never heard the voice of Francis Dolarhyde curse him. "Don't do that."

The voice he heard now had never, ever cursed him. It had repeated the Dragon's abuse. The memory shamed him.

He probably was not much of a man, he thought. It occurred to him that he had never really found out about that, and now he was curious.

He had one rag of pride that Reba McClane had given him. It told him dying in a bathroom was a sorry end.

What else? What other way was there?

There was a way and when it came to him it was blasphemy, he knew. But it was a way.

He paced the motel room, paced between the beds and from the door to the windows. As he walked he practiced speaking. The words came out all right if he breathed deep between the sentences and didn't hurry.

He could talk very well between the rushes of fear. Now he had a bad one, he had one that made him retch. A calm was coming after. He waited for it and when it came he hurried to the telephone and placed a call to Brooklyn.

➤

A junior high school band was getting on the bus in the motel parking lot. The children saw Dolarhyde coming. He had to go through them to get to his van.

A fat, round-faced boy with his Sam Browne belt all crooked put on a scowl, puffed up his chest and flexed his biceps after Dolarhyde passed. Two girls giggled. The tuba blatted out the bus window as Dolarhyde went by, and he never heard the laughter behind him.

In twenty minutes he stopped the van in the lane three hundred yards from Grandmother's house.

He mopped his face, inhaled deeply three or four times. He gripped his house key in his left hand, the steering wheel with his right.

A high keening sounded through his nose. And again, louder. Louder, louder again. Go.

Gravel showered behind the van as it shot forward, the house bouncing bigger in the windshield. The van slid sideways into the yard and Dolarhyde was out of it, running.

Inside, not looking left or right, pounding down the basement stairs, fumbling at the padlocked trunk in the basement, looking at his keys.

The trunk keys were upstairs. He didn't give himself time to think. A high humming through his nose as loud as he could to numb thought, drown out voices as he climbed the stairs at a run.

At the bureau now, fumbling in the drawer for the keys, not looking at the picture of the Dragon at the foot of the bed.

"WHAT ARE YOU DOING?"

Where were the keys, where were the keys?

"WHAT ARE YOU DOING? STOP. I'VE NEVER SEEN A CHILD AS DISGUSTING AND DIRTY AS YOU. STOP."

His searching hands slowed.

"LOOK . . . LOOK AT ME."

He gripped the edge of the bureau—tried not to turn to the wall. He cut his eyes painfully away as his head turned in spite of him.

"WHAT ARE YOU DOING?"

"nothing."

The telephone was ringing, telephone ringing, telephone ringing. He picked it up, his back to the picture.

"Hey, D., how are you feeling?" Reba McClane's voice.

He cleared his throat. "Okay"—hardly a whisper.

"I tried to call you down here. Your office said you were sick—you sound terrible."

"Talk to me."

"Of course I'll talk to you. What do you think I called you for? What's wrong?"

"Flu," he said.

"Are you going to the doctor? . . . Hello? I said, are you going to the doctor?"

"Talk loud." He scrabbled in the drawer, tried the drawer next to it.

"Have we got a bad connection? D., you shouldn't be there sick by yourself."

"TELL HER TO COME OVER TONIGHT AND TAKE CARE OF YOU."

Dolarhyde almost got his hand over the mouthpiece in time.

"My God, what was that? Is somebody with you?"

"The radio, I grabbed the wrong knob."

"Hey, D., do you want me to send somebody? You don't sound so hot. I'll come myself. I'll get Marcia to bring me at lunch."

"No." The keys were under a belt coiled in the drawer. He had them now. He backed into the hall, carrying the telephone. "I'm okay. I'll see you soon." The /s/s nearly foundered him. He ran down the stairs. The phone cord jerked out of the wall and the telephone tumbled down the stairs behind him.

A scream of savage rage. "COME HERE CUNT FACE."

Down to the basement. In the trunk beside his case of dynamite was a small valise packed with cash, credit cards and driver's licenses in various names, his pistol, knife, and blackjack.

He grabbed the valise and ran up to the ground floor, quickly past the stairs, ready to fight if the Dragon came down them. Into the van and driving hard, fishtailing in the gravel lane.

He slowed on the highway and pulled over to the shoulder to heave yellow bile. Some of the fear went away.

Proceeding at legal speed, using his flashers well ahead of turns, carefully he drove to the airport.

CHAPTER 39

DOLARHYDE PAID his taxi fare in front of an apartment house on Eastern Parkway two blocks from the Brooklyn Museum. He walked the rest of the way. Joggers passed him, heading for Prospect Park.

Standing on the traffic island near the IRT subway station, he got a good view of the Greek Revival building. He had never seen the Brooklyn Museum before, though he had read its guidebook—he had ordered the book when he first saw "Brooklyn Museum" in tiny letters beneath photographs of *The Great Red Dragon and the Woman Clothed with the Sun.*

The names of the great thinkers from Confucius to Demosthenes were carved in stone above the entrance. It was an imposing building with botanical gardens beside it, a fitting house for the Dragon.

The subway rumbled beneath the street, tingling the soles of his feet. Stale air puffed from the gratings and mixed with the smell of the dye in his mustache.

Only an hour left before closing time. He crossed the street and went inside. The checkroom attendant took his valise.

"Will the checkroom be open tomorrow?" he asked.

"The museum's closed tomorrow." The attendant was a wizened woman in a blue smock. She turned away from him.

"The people who come in tomorrow, do they use the checkroom?"

"No. The museum's closed, the checkroom's closed."

Good. "Thank you."

"Don't mention it."

Dolarhyde cruised among the great glass cases in the Oceanic Hall and the Hall of the Americas on the ground floor—Andes pottery, primitive edged weapons, artifacts and powerful masks from the Indians of the Northwest coast.

Now there were only forty minutes left before the museum closed. There was no more time to learn the ground floor. He knew where the exits and the public elevators were.

He rode up to the fifth floor. He could feel that he was closer to the Dragon now, but it was all right—he wouldn't turn a corner and run into Him.

The Dragon was not on public display; the painting had been locked away in the dark since its return from the Tate Gallery in London.

Dolarhyde had learned on the telephone that *The Great Red Dragon and the Woman Clothed with the Sun* was rarely displayed. It was almost two hundred years old and a watercolor—light would fade it.

Dolarhyde stopped in front of Albert Bierstadt's *A Storm in the Rocky Mountains—Mt. Rosalie 1866.* From there he could see the locked doors of the Painting Study and Storage Department. That's where the Dragon was. Not a copy, not a photograph: the Dragon. This is where he would come tomorrow when he had his appointment.

He walked around the perimeter of the fifth floor, past the corridor of portraits, seeing nothing of the paintings. The exits were what interested him. He found the fire exits and the main stairs, and marked the location of the public elevators.

The guards were polite middle-aged men in thick-soled shoes, years of standing in the set of their legs. None was armed, Dolarhyde noted; one of the guards in the lobby was armed. Maybe he was a moonlighting cop.

The announcement of closing time came over the public-address system.

Dolarhyde stood on the pavement under the allegorical figure of

Brooklyn and watched the crowd come out into the pleasant summer evening.

Joggers ran in place, waiting while the stream of people crossed the sidewalk toward the subway.

Dolarhyde spent a few minutes in the botanical gardens. Then he flagged a taxi and gave the driver the address of a store he had found in the Yellow Pages.

CHAPTER 40

AT NINE P.M. MONDAY Graham set his briefcase on the floor outside the Chicago apartment he was using and rooted in his pocket for the keys.

He had spent a long day in Detroit interviewing staff and checking employment records at a hospital where Mrs. Jacobi did volunteer work before the family moved to Birmingham. He was looking for a drifter, someone who might have worked in both Detroit and Atlanta or in Birmingham and Atlanta; someone with access to a van and a wheelchair who saw Mrs. Jacobi and Mrs. Leeds before he broke into their houses.

Crawford thought the trip was a waste of time, but humored him. Crawford had been right. Damn Crawford. He was right too much.

Graham could hear the telephone ringing in the apartment. The keys caught in the lining of his pocket. When he jerked them out, a long thread came with them. Change spilled down the inside of his trouser leg and scattered on the floor.

"Son of a bitch."

He made it halfway across the room before the phone stopped ringing. Maybe that was Molly trying to reach him.

He called her in Oregon.

Willy's grandfather answered the telephone with his mouth full. It was suppertime in Oregon.

"Just ask Molly to call me when she's finished," Graham told him.

He was in the shower with shampoo in his eyes when the telephone rang again. He sluiced his head and went dripping to grab the receiver. "Hello, Hotlips."

"You silver-tongued devil, this is Byron Metcalf in Birmingham."

"Sorry."

"I've got good news and bad news. You were right about Niles Jacobi. He took the stuff out of the house. He'd gotten rid of it, but I squeezed him with some hash that was in his room and he owned up. That's the bad news—I know you hoped the Tooth Fairy stole it and fenced it.

"The good news is there's some film. I don't have it yet. Niles says there are two reels stuffed under the seat in his car. You still want it, right?"

"Sure, sure I do."

"Well, his intimate friend Randy's using the car and we haven't caught up with him yet, but it won't be long. Want me to put the film on the first plane to Chicago and call you when it's coming?"

"Please do. That's good, Byron, thanks."

"Nothing to it."

Molly called just as Graham was drifting off to sleep. After they assured each other that they were all right, there didn't seem to be much to say.

Willy was having a real good time, Molly said. She let Willy say good night.

Willy had plenty more to say than just good night—he told Will the exciting news: Grandpa bought him a pony.

Molly hadn't mentioned it.

CHAPTER 41

THE BROOKLYN MUSEUM is closed to the general public on Tuesdays, but art classes and researchers are admitted.

The museum is an excellent facility for serious scholarship. The staff members are knowledgeable and accommodating; often they allow researchers to come by appointment on Tuesdays to see items not on public display.

Francis Dolarhyde came out of the IRT subway station shortly after 2 P.M. on Tuesday carrying his scholarly materials. He had a notebook, a Tate Gallery catalog, and a biography of William Blake under his arm.

He had a flat 9-mm pistol, a leather sap and his razor-edged fileting knife under his shirt. An elastic bandage held the weapons against his flat belly. His sport coat would button over them. A cloth soaked in chloroform and sealed in a plastic bag was in his coat pocket.

In his hand he carried a new guitar case.

Three pay telephones stand near the subway exit in the center of Eastern Parkway. One of the telephones has been ripped out. One of the others works.

Dolarhyde fed it quarters until Reba said, "Hello."

He could hear darkroom noises over her voice.

"Hello, Reba," he said.

"Hey, D. How're you feeling?"

Traffic passing on both sides made it hard for him to hear. "Okay."

"Sounds like you're at a pay phone. I thought you were home sick."

"I want to talk to you later."

"Okay. Call me late, all right?"

"I need to . . . see you."

"I want you to see me, but I can't tonight. I have to work. Will you call me?"

"Yeah. If nothing . . ."

"Excuse me?"

"I'll call."

"I do want you to come soon, D."

"Yeah. Good-bye . . . Reba."

All right. Fear trickled from his breastbone to his belly. He squeezed it and crossed the street.

Entrance to the Brooklyn Museum on Tuesdays is through a single door on the extreme right. Dolarhyde went in behind four art students. The students piled their knapsacks and satchels against the wall and got out their passes. The guard behind the desk checked them.

He came to Dolarhyde.

"Do you have an appointment?"

Dolarhyde nodded. "Painting Study, Miss Harper."

"Sign the register, please." The guard offered a pen.

Dolarhyde had his own pen ready. He signed "Paul Crane."

The guard dialed an upstairs extension. Dolarhyde turned his back to the desk and studied Robert Blum's *Vintage Festival* over the entrance while the guard confirmed his appointment. From the corner of his eye he could see one more security guard in the lobby. Yes, that was the one with the gun.

"Back of the lobby by the shop there's a bench next to the main elevators," the desk officer said. "Wait there. Miss Harper's coming down for you." He handed Dolarhyde a pink-on-white plastic badge.

"Okay if I leave my guitar here?"

"I'll keep an eye on it."

The museum was different with the lights turned down. There was twilight among the great glass cases.

Dolarhyde waited on the bench for three minutes before Miss Harper got off the public elevator.

"Mr. Crane? I'm Paula Harper."

She was younger than she had sounded on the telephone when he called from St. Louis; a sensible-looking woman, severely pretty. She wore her blouse and skirt like a uniform.

"You called about the Blake watercolor," she said. "Let's go upstairs and I'll show it to you. We'll take the staff elevator—this way."

She led him past the dark museum shop and through a small room lined with primitive weapons. He looked around fast to keep his bearings. In the corner of the Americas section was a corridor which led to the small elevator.

Miss Harper pushed the button. She hugged her elbows and waited. The clear blue eyes fell on the pass, pink on white, clipped to Dolarhyde's lapel.

"That's a sixth-floor pass he gave you," she said. "It doesn't matter—there aren't any guards on five today. What kind of research are you doing?"

Dolarhyde had made it on smiles and nods until now. "A paper on Butts," he said.

"On William Butts?"

He nodded.

"I've never read much on him. You only see him in footnotes as a patron of Blake's. Is he interesting?"

"I'm just beginning. I'll have to go to England."

"I think the National Gallery has two watercolors he did for Butts. Have you seen them yet?"

"Not yet."

"Better write ahead of time."

He nodded. The elevator came.

Fifth floor. He was tingling a little, but he had blood in his arms and legs. Soon it would be just yes or no. If it went wrong, he wouldn't let them take him.

She led him down the corridor of American portraits. This wasn't the way he came before. He could tell where he was. It was all right.

But something waited in the corridor for him, and when he saw it he stopped dead still.

Paula Harper realized he wasn't following and turned around.

He was rigid before a niche in the wall of portraits.

She came back to him and saw what he was staring at.

"That's a Gilbert Stuart portrait of George Washington," she said.
No it wasn't.

"You see a similar one on the dollar bill. They call it a Lansdowne
portrait because Stuart did one for the Marquis of Lansdowne to thank
him for his support in the American Revolution . . . Are you all
right, Mr. Crane?"

Dolarhyde was pale. This was worse than all the dollar bills he had
ever seen. Washington with his hooded eyes and bad false teeth stared
out of the frame. My God he looked like Grandmother. Dolarhyde
felt like a child with a rubber knife.

"Mr. Crane, are you okay?"

Answer or blow it all. Get past this. *My God, man, that's so
sweeeet.* YOU'RE THE DIRTIEST . . . No.

Say something.

"I'm taking cobalt," he said.

"Would you like to sit down for a few minutes?" There *was* a faint
medicinal smell about him.

"No. Go ahead. I'm coming."

And you are not going to cut me, Grandmother. God damn you,
I'd kill you if you weren't already dead. Already dead. Already dead.
Grandmother was already dead! Dead now, dead for always. My God,
man, that's so sweeeet.

The other wasn't dead though, and Dolarhyde knew it.

He followed Miss Harper through thickets of fear.

They went through double doors into the Painting Study and
Storage Department. Dolarhyde looked around quickly. It was a long,
peaceful room, well-lighted and filled with carousel racks of draped
paintings. A row of small office cubicles was partitioned off along the
wall. The door to the cubicle on the far end was ajar, and he heard
typing.

He saw no one but Paula Harper.

She took him to a counter-height work table and brought him a
stool.

"Wait here. I'll bring the painting to you."

She disappeared behind the racks.

Dolarhyde undid a button at his belly.

Miss Harper was coming. She carried a flat black case no bigger
than a briefcase. It was in there. How did she have the strength to
carry the picture? He had never thought of it as flat. He had seen the

dimensions in the catalogs—17⅛ by 13½ inches—but he had paid no attention to them. He expected it to be immense. But it was small. It was small and it was *here* in a quiet room. He had never realized how much strength the Dragon drew from the old house in the orchard.

Miss Harper was saying something ". . . have to keep it in this solander box because light will fade it. That's why it's not on display very often."

She put the case on the table and unclasped it. A noise at the double doors. "Excuse me, I have to get the door for Julio." She refastened the case and carried it with her to the glass doors. A man with a wheeled dolly waited outside. She held the doors open while he rolled it in.

"Over here okay?"

"Yes, thank you, Julio."

The man went out.

Here came Miss Harper with the solander box.

"I'm sorry, Mr. Crane. Julio's dusting today and getting the tarnish off some frames." She opened the case and took out a white cardboard folder. "You understand that you aren't allowed to touch it. I'll display it for you—that's the rule. Okay?"

Dolarhyde nodded. He couldn't speak.

She opened the folder and removed the covering plastic sheet and mat.

There it was. *The Great Red Dragon and the Woman Clothed with the Sun*—the Man-Dragon rampant over the prostrate pleading woman caught in a coil of his tail.

It was small all right, but it was powerful. Stunning. The best reproductions didn't do justice to the details and the colors.

Dolarhyde saw it clear, saw it all in an instant—Blake's handwriting on the borders, two brown spots at the right edge of the paper. It seized him hard. It was too much . . . the colors were so much stronger.

Look at the woman wrapped in the Dragon's tail. Look.

He saw that her hair was the exact color of Reba McClane's. He saw that he was twenty feet from the door. He held in voices.

I hope I didn't shock you, said Reba McClane.

"It appears that he used chalk as well as watercolor," Paula Harper was saying. She stood at an angle so that she could see what he was doing. Her eyes never left the painting.

Dolarhyde put his hand inside his shirt.

Somewhere a telephone was ringing. The typing stopped. A woman stuck her head out of the far cubicle.

"Paula, telephone for you. It's your mother."

Miss Harper did not turn her head. Her eyes never left Dolarhyde or the painting. "Would you take a message?" she said. "Tell her I'll call her back."

The woman disappeared into the office. In a moment the typing started again.

Dolarhyde couldn't hold it anymore. Play for it all, right now.

But the Dragon moved first. "I'VE NEVER SEEN—"

"What?" Miss Harper's eyes were wide.

"—a rat that big!" Dolarhyde said, pointing. "Climbing that frame!"

Miss Harper was turning. "Where?"

The blackjack slid out of his shirt. With his wrist more than his arm, he tapped the back of her skull. She sagged as Dolarhyde grabbed a handful of her blouse and clapped the chloroform rag over her face. She made a high sound once, not overloud, and went limp.

He eased her to the floor between the table and the racks of paintings, pulled the folder with the watercolor to the floor, and squatted over her. Rustling, wadding, hoarse breathing and a telephone ringing.

The woman came out of the far office.

"Paula?" She looked around the room. "It's your mother," she called. "She needs to talk to you *now.*"

She walked behind the table. "I'll take care of the visitor if you . . ." She saw them then. Paula Harper on the floor, her hair across her face, and squatting over her, his pistol in his hand, Dolarhyde stuffing the last bite of the watercolor in his mouth. Rising, chewing, running. Toward her.

She ran for her office, slammed the flimsy door, grabbed at the phone and knocked it to the floor, scrambled for it on her hands and knees and tried to dial on the busy line as her door caved in. The lighted dial burst in bright colors at the impact behind her ear. The receiver fell quacking to the floor.

Dolarhyde in the staff elevator watched the indicator lights blink down, his gun held flat across his stomach, covered by his books.

First floor.

Out into the deserted galleries. He walked fast, his running shoes whispering on the terrazzo. A wrong turn and he was passing the whale masks, the great mask of Sisuit, losing seconds, running now into the presence of the Haida high totems and lost. He ran to the totems, looked left, saw the primitive edged weapons and knew where he was.

He peered around the corner at the lobby.

The desk officer stood at the bulletin board, thirty feet from the reception desk.

The armed guard was closer to the door. His holster creaked as he bent to rub a spot on the toe of his shoe.

If they fight, drop him first. Dolarhyde put the gun under his belt and buttoned his coat over it. He walked across the lobby, unclipping his pass.

The desk officer turned when he heard the footsteps.

"Thank you," Dolarhyde said. He held up his pass by the edges, then dropped it on the desk.

The guard nodded. "Would you put it through the slot there, please?"

The reception desk telephone rang.

The pass was hard to pick up off the glass top.

The telephone rang again. Hurry.

Dolarhyde got hold of the pass, dropped it through the slot. He picked up his guitar case from the pile of knapsacks.

The guard was coming to the telephone.

Out the door now, walking fast for the botanical gardens, he was ready to turn and fire if he heard pursuit.

Inside the gardens and to the left, Dolarhyde ducked into a space between a small shed and a hedge. He opened the guitar case and dumped out a tennis racket, a tennis ball, a towel, a folded grocery sack and a big bunch of leafy celery.

Buttons flew as he tore off his coat and shirt in one move and stepped out of his trousers. Underneath he wore a Brooklyn College T-shirt and warm-up pants. He stuffed his books and clothing into the grocery bag, then the weapons. The celery stuck out the top. He wiped the handle and clasps of the case and shoved it under the hedge.

Cutting across the gardens now toward Prospect Park, the towel around his neck, he came out onto Empire Boulevard. Joggers were ahead of him. As he followed the joggers into the park, the first police cruisers screamed past. None of the joggers paid any attention to them. Neither did Dolarhyde.

He alternated jogging and walking, carrying his grocery bag and racket and bouncing his tennis ball, a man cooling off from a hard workout who had stopped by the store on the way home.

He made himself slow down; he shouldn't run on a full stomach. He could choose his pace now.

He could choose anything.

CHAPTER 42

CRAWFORD sat in the back row of the jury box eating Redskin peanuts while Graham closed the courtroom blinds.

"You'll have the profile for me later this afternoon, I take it," Crawford said. "You told me Tuesday; this is Tuesday."

"I'll finish it. I want to watch this first."

Graham opened the express envelope from Byron Metcalf and dumped out the contents—two dusty rolls of home-movie film, each in plastic sandwich bag.

"Is Metcalf pressing charges against Niles Jacobi?"

"Not for theft—he'll probably inherit anyway—he and Jacobi's brother," Graham said. "On the hash, I don't know. Birmingham DA's inclined to break his chops."

"Good," Crawford said.

The movie screen swung down from the courtroom ceiling to face the jury box, an arrangement which made it easy to show jurors filmed evidence.

Graham threaded the projector.

"On checking the newsstands where the Tooth Fairy could have gotten a *Tattler* so fast—I've had reports back from Cincinnati, Detroit, and a bunch from Chicago," Crawford said. "Various weirdos to run down."

Graham started the film. It was a fishing movie.

The Jacobi children hunkered on the bank of a pond with cane poles and bobbers.

Graham tried not to think of them in their small boxes in the ground. He tried to think of them just fishing.

The girl's cork bobbed and disappeared. She had a bite.

Crawford crackled his peanut sack. "Indianapolis is dragging ass on questioning newsies and checking the Servco Supreme stations," he said.

"Do you want to watch this or what?" Graham said.

Crawford was silent until the end of the two-minute film. "Terrific, she caught a perch," he said. "Now the profile—"

"Jack, you were in Birmingham right after it happened. I didn't get there for a month. You saw the house while it was still their house—I didn't. It was stripped and remodeled when I got there. Now, for Christ's sake let me look at these people and then I'll finish the profile."

He started the second film.

A birthday party appeared on the screen in the courtroom. The Jacobis were seated around a dining table. They were singing.

Graham lip-read "Haaappy Birth-day to you."

Eleven-year-old Donald Jacobi faced the camera. He was seated at the end of the table with the cake in front of him. The candles reflected in his glasses.

Around the corner of the table, his brother and sister were side by side watching him as he blew out the candles.

Graham shifted in his seat.

Mrs. Jacobi leaned over, her dark hair swinging, to catch the cat and dump it off the table.

Now Mrs. Jacobi brought a large envelope to her son. A long ribbon trailed from it. Donald Jacobi opened the envelope and took out a big birthday card. He looked up at the camera and turned the card around. It said "Happy Birthday—follow the ribbon."

Bouncing progress as the camera followed the procession to the kitchen. A door there, fastened with a hook. Down the basement stairs, Donald first, then the others, following the ribbon down the steps. The end of the ribbon was tied around the handlebars of a ten-speed bicycle.

Graham wondered why they hadn't given him the bike outdoors.

A jumpy cut to the next scene, and his question was answered.

Outdoors now, and clearly it had been raining hard. Water stood in the yard. The house looked different. Realtor Geehan had changed the color when he did it over after the murders. The outside basement door opened and Mr. Jacobi emerged carrying the bicycle. This was the first view of him in the movie. A breeze lifted the hair combed across his bald spot. He set the bicycle ceremoniously on the ground.

The film ended with Donald's cautious first ride.

"Sad damn thing," Crawford said, "but we already knew that."

Graham started the birthday film over.

Crawford shook his head and began to read something from his briefcase with the aid of a penlight.

On the screen Mr. Jacobi brought the bicycle out of the basement. The basement door swung closed behind him. A padlock hung from it.

Graham froze the frame.

"There. That's what he wanted the bolt cutter for, Jack—to cut that padlock and go in through the basement. Why didn't he go in that way?"

Crawford clicked off his penlight and looked over his glasses at the screen. "What's that?"

"I know he had a bolt cutter—he used it to trim that branch out of his way when he was watching from the woods. Why didn't he use it and go in through the basement door?"

"He couldn't." With a small crocodile smile, Crawford waited. He loved to catch people in assumptions.

"Did he try? Did he mark it up? I never even saw that door—Geehan had put in a steel one with deadbolts by the time I got there."

Crawford opened his jaws. "You *assume* Geehan put it in. Geehan didn't put it in. The steel door was there when they were killed. Jacobi must have put it in—he was a Detroit guy, he'd favor deadbolts."

"*When* did Jacobi put it in?"

"I don't know. Obviously it was after the kid's birthday—when was that? It'll be in the autopsy if you've got it here."

"His birthday was April 14, a Monday," Graham said, staring at the screen, his chin in his hand. "I want to know when Jacobi changed the door."

Crawford's scalp wrinkled. It smoothed out again as he saw the point. "You think the Tooth Fairy cased the Jacobi house while the old door with the padlock was still there," he said.

"He brought a bolt cutter, didn't he? How do you break in someplace with a bolt cutter?" Graham said. "You cut padlocks, bars, or chain. Jacobi didn't have any bars or chained gates, did he?"

"No."

"Then he went there expecting a padlock. A bolt cutter's fairly heavy and it's long. He was moving in daylight, and from where he parked he had to hike a long way to the Jacobi house. For all he knew, he might be coming back in one hell of a hurry if something went wrong. He wouldn't have carried a bolt cutter unless he knew he'd need it. He was expecting a padlock."

"You figure he cased the place *before* Jacobi changed the door. Then he shows up to kill them, waits in the woods—"

"You can't see this side of the house from the woods."

Crawford nodded. "He waits in the woods. They go to bed and he moves in with his bolt cutter and finds the new door with the deadbolts."

"Say he finds the new door. He had it all worked out, and now this," Graham said, throwing up his hands. "He's really pissed off, frustrated, he's hot to get in there. So he does a fast, loud pry job on the patio door. It was messy the way he went in—he woke Jacobi up and had to blow him away on the stairs. That's not like the Dragon. He's not messy that way. He's careful and he leaves nothing behind. He did a neat job at the Leedses' going in."

"Okay, all right," Crawford said. "If we find out when Jacobi changed his door, maybe we'll establish the interval between when he cased it and when he killed them. The *minimum* time that elapsed, anyway. That seems like a useful thing to know. Maybe it'll match some interval the Birmingham convention and visitors bureau could show us. We can check car rentals again. This time we'll do vans too. I'll have a word with the Birmingham field office."

Crawford's word must have been emphatic: in forty minutes flat a Birmingham FBI agent, with realtor Geehan in tow, was shouting to a carpenter working in the rafters of a new house. The carpenter's information was relayed in a radio patch to Chicago.

"Last week in April," Crawford said, putting down the telephone. "That's when they put in the new door. My God, that's two months before the Jacobis were hit. Why would he case it two months in advance?"

"I don't know, but I promise you he saw Mrs. Jacobi or saw the whole family before he checked out their house. Unless he followed them down there from Detroit, he spotted Mrs. Jacobi sometime between April 10, when they moved to Birmingham, and the end of April, when the door was changed. Sometime in that period he was in Birmingham. The bureau's going on with it down there?"

"Cops too," Crawford said. "Tell me this: how did he know there was an inside door from the basement into the house? You couldn't count on that—not in the South."

"He saw the inside of the house, no question."

"Has your buddy Metcalf got the Jacobi bank statements?"

"I'm sure he does."

"Let's see what service calls they paid for between April 10 and the end of the month. I know the service calls have been checked for a couple of weeks back from the killings, but maybe we aren't looking back far enough. Same for the Leedses."

"We always figured he looked around inside the *Leeds* house," Graham said. "From the alley he couldn't have seen the glass in the kitchen door. There's a latticed porch back there. But he was ready with his glass cutter. And they didn't have any service calls for three months before they were killed."

"If he's casing this far ahead, maybe we didn't check back far enough. We will now. At the Leedses' though—when he was in the alley reading meters behind the Leeds house two days before he killed them—maybe he saw them going in the house. He could have looked in there while the porch door was open."

"No, the doors don't line up—remember? Look here."

Graham threaded the projector with the Leeds home movie.

The Leedses' gray Scotty perked up his ears and ran to the kitchen door. Valerie Leeds and the children came in carrying groceries. Through the kitchen door nothing but lattice was visible.

"All right, you want to get Byron Metcalf busy on the bank statement for April? Any kind of service call or purchase that a door-to-door salesman might handle. No—I'll do that while you wind up the profile. Have you got Metcalf's number?"

Seeing the Leedses preoccupied Graham. Absently he told Crawford three numbers for Byron Metcalf.

He ran the films again while Crawford used the phone in the jury room.

The Leeds film first.

There was the Leedses' dog. It wore no collar, and the neighbor-hood was full of dogs, but the Dragon knew which dog was theirs.

Here was Valerie Leeds. The sight of her tugged at Graham. There was the door behind her, vulnerable with its big glass pane. Her children played on the courtroom screen.

Graham had never felt as close to the Jacobis as he did to the Leedses. Their movie disturbed him now. It bothered him that he had thought of the Jacobis as chalk marks on a bloody floor.

There were the Jacobi children, ranged around the corner of the table, the birthday candles flickering on their faces.

For a flash Graham saw the blob of candle wax on the Jacobis' bedside table, the bloodstains around the corner of the bedroom at the Leedses'. Something . . .

Crawford was coming back. "Metcalf said to ask you—"

"Don't talk to me!"

Crawford wasn't offended. He waited stock-still and his little eyes grew narrow and bright.

The film ran on, its light and shadows playing over Graham's face.

There was the Jacobis' cat. The Dragon knew it was the Jacobis' cat.

There was the inside basement door.

There was the outside basement door with its padlock. The Dragon had brought a bolt cutter.

The film ended. Finally it came off the reel and the end flapped around and around.

Everything the Dragon needed to know was on the two films.

They hadn't been shown in public, there wasn't any film club, film festi . . .

Graham looked at the familiar green box the Leeds movie came in. Their name and address were on it. And Gateway Film Laboratory, St. Louis, Mo. 63102.

His mind retrieved "St. Louis" just as it would retrieve any telephone number he had ever seen. What about St. Louis? It was one of the places where the *Tattler* was available on Monday night, the same day it was printed—the day before Lounds was abducted.

"Oh me," Graham said. "Oh Jesus."

He clamped his hands on the sides of his head to keep the thought from getting away.

"Do you still have Metcalf on the phone?"

Crawford handed him the receiver.

"Byron, it's Graham. Listen, did those reels of Jacobi film you sent—were they in any containers? . . . Sure, sure I know you would have sent 'em along. I need help bad on something. Do you have the Jacobi bank statements there? Okay, I want to know where they got movie film developed. Probably a store sent it off for them. If there're any checks to pharmacies or camera stores, we can find out where they did business. It's urgent, Byron. I'll tell you about it first chance. Birmingham FBI will start now checking the stores. If you find something, shoot it straight to them, then to us. Will you do that? Great. What? *No, I will not* introduce you to Hotlips."

Birmingham FBI agents checked four camera stores before they found the one where the Jacobis traded. The manager said all customers' film was sent to one place for processing.

Crawford had watched the films twelve times before Birmingham called back. He took the message.

Curiously formal, he held out his hand to Graham. "It's Gateway," he said.

CHAPTER 43

CRAWFORD was stirring an Alka-Seltzer in a plastic glass when the stewardess's voice came over the 727's public-address system.

"Passenger Crawford, please?"

When he waved from his aisle seat, she came aft to him. "Mr. Crawford, would you go to the cockpit, please?"

Crawford was gone for four minutes. He slid back into the seat beside Graham.

"Tooth Fairy was in New York today."

Graham winced and his teeth clicked together.

"No. He just tapped a couple of women on the head at the Brooklyn Museum and, listen to this, he *ate* a painting."

"Ate it?"

"Ate it. The Art Squad in New York snapped to it when they found out what he ate. They got two partial prints off the plastic pass he used and they flashed them down to Price a little while ago. When Price put 'em together on the screen, he rang the cherries. No ID, but it's the same thumb that was on the Leeds kid's eye."

"New York," Graham said.

"Means nothing, he was in New York today. He could still work at Gateway. If he does, he was off the job today. Makes it easier."

"What did he eat?"

"It was a thing called *The Great Red Dragon and the Woman Clothed with the Sun.* William Blake drew it, they said."

"What about the women?"

"He's got a sweet touch with the sap. Younger one's just at the hospital for observation. The older one had to have four stitches. Mild concussion."

"Could they give a description?"

"The younger one did. Quiet, husky, dark mustache and hair—a wig, I think. The guard at the door said the same thing. The older woman—he could've been in a rabbit suit for all she saw."

"But he didn't kill anybody."

"Odd," Crawford said. "He'd have been better off to wax 'em both—he could have been sure of his lead time leaving and saved himself a description or two. Behavioral Science called Bloom in the hospital about it. You know what he said? Bloom said maybe he's trying to stop."

CHAPTER 44

DOLARHYDE heard the flaps moan down. The lights of St. Louis wheeled slowly beneath the black wing. Under his feet the landing gear rumbled into a rush of air and locked down with a thud.

He rolled his head on his shoulders to ease the stiffness in his powerful neck.

Coming home.

He had taken a great risk, and the prize he brought back was the power to choose. He could choose to have Reba McClane alive. He could have her to talk to, and he could have her startling and harmless mobility in his bed.

He did not have to dread his house. He had the Dragon in his belly now. He could go into his house, walk up to a copy Dragon on the wall and wad him up if he wanted to.

He did not have to worry about feeling Love for Reba. If he felt Love for her, he could toss the Shermans to the Dragon and ease it that way, go back to Reba calm and easy, and treat her well.

From the terminal Dolarhyde telephoned her apartment. Not home yet. He tried Baeder Chemical. The night line was busy. He thought of Reba walking toward the bus stop after work, tapping along with her cane, her raincoat over her shoulders.

He drove to the film laboratory through the light evening traffic in less than fifteen minutes.

She wasn't at the bus stop. He parked on the street behind Baeder Chemical, near the entrance closest to the darkrooms. He'd tell her he was here, wait until she had finished working, and drive her home. He was proud of his new power to choose. He wanted to use it.

There were things he could catch up on in his office while he waited.

Only a few lights were on in Baeder Chemical.

Reba's darkroom was locked. The light above the door was neither red nor green. It was off. He pressed the buzzer. No response.

Maybe she had left a message in his office.

He heard footsteps in the corridor.

The Baeder supervisor, Dandridge, passed the darkroom area and never looked up. He was walking fast and carrying a thick bundle of buff personnel files under his arm.

A small crease appeared in Dolarhyde's forehead.

Dandridge was halfway across the parking lot, heading for the Gateway building, when Dolarhyde came out of Baeder behind him.

Two delivery vans and half a dozen cars were on the lot. That Buick belonged to Fisk, Gateway's personnel director. What were they doing?

There was no night shift at Gateway. Much of the building was dark. Dolarhyde could see by the red exit signs in the corridor as he went toward his office. The lights were on behind the frosted glass door of the personnel department. Dolarhyde heard voices in there, Dandridge's for one, and Fisk's.

A woman's footsteps coming. Fisk's secretary turned the corner into the corridor ahead of Dolarhyde. She had a scarf tied over her curlers and she carried ledgers from Accounting. She was in a hurry. The ledgers were heavy, a big armload. She pecked on Fisk's office door with her toe.

Will Graham opened it for her.

Dolarhyde froze in the dark hall. His gun was in his van.

The office door closed again.

Dolarhyde moved fast, his running shoes quiet on the smooth floor. He put his face close to the glass of the exit door and scanned the parking lot. Movement now under the floodlights. A man moving. He was beside one of the delivery vans and he had a flashlight. Flicking something. He was dusting the outside mirror for fingerprints.

Behind Dolarhyde, somewhere in the corridors, a man was walking. Get away from the door. He ducked around the corner and down the stairs to the basement and the furnace room on the opposite side of the building.

By standing on a workbench he could reach the high windows that opened at ground level behind the shrubbery. He rolled over the sill and came up on his hands and knees in the bushes, ready to run or fight.

Nothing moved on this side of the building. He stood up, put a hand in his pocket and strolled across the street. Running when the sidewalk was dark, walking as cars went by, he made a long loop around Gateway and Baeder Chemical.

His van stood at the curb behind Baeder. There was no place to hide close to it. All right. He sprinted across the street and leaped in, clawing at his valise.

Full clip in the automatic. He jacked a round into the chamber and laid the pistol on the console, covering it with a T-shirt.

Slowly he drove away—don't catch the light red—slowly around the corner and into the scattered traffic.

He had to think now and it was hard to think.

It had to be the films. Graham knew about the films somehow. Graham knew *where*. He didn't know *who*. If he knew who, he wouldn't need personnel records. Why accounting records too? Absences, that's why. Match absences against the dates when the Dragon struck. No, those were Saturdays, except for Lounds. Absences on the days before those Saturdays; he'd look for those. Fool him there—no workmen's compensation slips were kept for management.

Dolarhyde drove slowly up Lindbergh Boulevard, gesturing with his free hand as he ticked off the points.

They were looking for fingerprints. He'd given them no chance for fingerprints—except maybe on the plastic pass at Brooklyn Museum. He'd picked it up in a hurry, mostly by the edges.

They must have a print. Why fingerprint if they didn't have something to match it to?

They were checking that van for prints. No time to see if they were checking cars too.

Van. Carrying the wheelchair with Lounds in it—that tipped them. Or maybe somebody in Chicago saw the van. There were a lot of vans at Gateway, private vans, delivery vans.

No, Graham just knew he had a van. Graham knew because he knew. Graham knew. Graham knew. The son of a bitch was a monster.

They'd fingerprint everyone at Gateway and Baeder too. If they didn't spot him tonight, they'd do it tomorrow. He had to run forever with his *face* on every bulletin board in every post office and police station. It was all coming to pieces. He was puny and small before them.

"Reba," he said aloud. Reba couldn't save him now. They were closing in on him, and he was nothing but a puny hareli—

"ARE YOU SORRY NOW THAT YOU BETRAYED ME?"

The Dragon's voice rumbled from deep within him, deep as the shredded painting in his bowels.

"I didn't. I just wanted to choose. You called me—"

"GIVE ME WHAT I WANT AND I'LL SAVE YOU."

"No. I'll run."

"GIVE ME WHAT I WANT AND YOU'LL HEAR GRAHAM'S SPINE SNAP."

"No."

"NOW ADMIRE WHAT YOU DID TODAY. WE'RE CLOSE NOW. WE CAN BE ONE AGAIN. DO YOU FEEL ME INSIDE YOU? YOU DO, DON'T YOU?"

"Yes."

"AND YOU KNOW I CAN SAVE YOU. YOU KNOW THEY'LL SEND YOU TO A PLACE WORSE THAN BROTHER BUDDY'S. GIVE ME WHAT I WANT AND YOU'LL BE FREE."

"No."

"THEY'LL KILL YOU. YOU'LL JERK ON THE GROUND."

"No."

"WHEN YOU'RE GONE SHE'LL FUCK OTHER PEOPLE, SHE'LL—"

"No! Shut up."

"SHE'LL FUCK OTHER PEOPLE, PRETTY PEOPLE, SHE'LL PUT THEIR—"

"Stop it. Shut up."

"SLOW DOWN AND I WON'T SAY IT."

Dolarhyde's foot lifted on the accelerator.

"THAT'S GOOD. GIVE ME WHAT I WANT AND IT CAN'T HAPPEN. GIVE IT TO ME AND THEN I'LL ALWAYS LET YOU CHOOSE, YOU CAN ALWAYS CHOOSE, AND YOU'LL SPEAK WELL, I WANT YOU TO SPEAK WELL, SLOW DOWN, THAT'S RIGHT, SEE THE SERVICE STATION? PULL OVER THERE AND LET ME TALK TO YOU. . . ."

CHAPTER 45

GRAHAM came out of the office suite and rested his eyes for a moment in the dim hallway. He was restive, uneasy. This was taking too long.

Crawford was sifting the 380 Gateway and Baeder employees as fast and well as it could be done—the man was a marvel at this kind of job—but time was passing and secrecy could be maintained only so long.

Crawford had kept the working group at Gateway to a minimum. ("We want to find him, not spook him," Crawford had told them. "If we can spot him tonight, we can take him outside the plant, maybe at his house or on the lot.")

The St. Louis police department was cooperating. Lieutenant Fogel of St. Louis homicide and one sergeant came quietly in an unmarked car, bringing a Datafax.

Wired to a Gateway telephone, in minutes the Datafax was transmitting the employment roll simultaneously to the FBI identification section in Washington and the Missouri Department of Motor Vehicles.

In Washington, the names would be checked against both the civil and criminal fingerprint records. Names of Baeder employees with security clearances were flagged for faster handling.

The Department of Motor Vehicles would check for ownership of vans.

Only four employees were brought in—the personnel manager, Fisk; Fisk's secretary; Dandridge from Baeder Chemical; and Gateway's chief accountant.

No telephones were used to summon the employees to this late-night meeting at the plant. Agents called at their houses and stated their business privately. ("Look 'em over before you tell 'em why you want 'em," Crawford said. "And don't let them use the telephone after. This kind of news travels fast.")

They had hoped for a quick identification from the teeth. None of the four employees recognized them.

Graham looked down the long corridors lit with red exit signs. Damn it felt right.

What else could they do tonight?

Crawford had requested that the woman from the Brooklyn Museum—Miss Harper—be flown out as soon as she could travel. Probably that would be in the morning. The St. Louis police department had a good surveillance van. She could sit in it and watch the employees go in.

If they didn't hit it tonight, all traces of the operation would be removed from Gateway before work started in the morning. Graham didn't kid himself—they'd be lucky to have a whole day to work before the word got out at Gateway. The Dragon would be watching for anything suspicious. He would fly.

CHAPTER 46

A LATE SUPPER with Ralph Mandy had seemed all right. Reba McClane knew she had to tell him sometime, and she didn't believe in leaving things hanging.

Actually, she thought Mandy knew what was coming when she insisted on going dutch.

She told him in the car as he took her home; that it was no big deal, she'd had a lot of fun with him and wanted to be his friend, but she was involved with somebody now.

Maybe he was hurt a little, but she knew he was relieved a little too. He was pretty good about it, she thought.

At her door he didn't ask to come in. He did ask to kiss her good-bye, and she responded gladly. He opened her door and gave her the keys. He waited until she was inside and had closed the door and locked it.

When he turned around Dolarhyde shot him in the throat and twice in the chest. Three putts from the silenced pistol. A scooter is louder.

Dolarhyde lifted Mandy's body easily, laid him between the shrubs and the house and left him there.

Seeing Reba kiss Mandy had stabbed Dolarhyde deep. Then the pain left him for good.

He still looked and sounded like Francis Dolarhyde—the Dragon was a very good actor; he played Dolarhyde well.

Reba was washing her face when she heard the doorbell. It rang four times before she got there. She touched the chain, but didn't take it off.

"Who is it?"

"Francis Dolarhyde."

She eased the door open, still on the chain. "Tell me again."

"Dolarhyde. It's me."

She knew it was. She took off the chain.

Reba did not like surprises. "I thought you said you'd call me, D."

"I would have. But this is an emergency, really," he said, clapping the chloroformed cloth over her face as he stepped inside.

The street was empty. Most of the houses were dark. He carried her to the van. Ralph Mandy's feet stuck out of the shrubbery into the yard. Dolarhyde didn't bother with him anymore.

She woke on the ride. She was on her side, her cheek in the dusty carpet of the van, transmission whine loud in her ear.

She tried to bring her hands to her face. The movement mashed her bosom. Her forearms were stuck together.

She felt them with her face. They were bound together from her elbows to her wrists with what felt like soft strips of cloth. Her legs were tied the same way from knees to ankles. Something was across her mouth.

What . . . what . . . ? D. was at the door, and then . . . She remembered twisting her face away and the terrible strength of him. Oh Lord . . . what was it . . . ? D. was at the door and then she was choking something cold and she tried to twist her face away but there was a terrible grip on her head.

She was in D.'s van now. She recognized the resonances. The van was going. Fear ballooned in her. Her instinct said be quiet, but the fumes were in her throat, chloroform and gasoline. She retched against the gag.

D.'s voice. "It won't be long now."

She felt a turn and they were on gravel now, rocks pinging under the fenders and floorboard.

He's crazy. All right. That's it: Crazy.

"Crazy" is a fearsome word.

What was it? Ralph Mandy. He must have seen them at her house. It set him off.

Christ Jesus, get it all ready. A man had tried to slap her once at Reiker Institute. She was quiet and he couldn't find her—he couldn't see either. This one could fucking well see. Get it all ready. Get ready to talk. God he could kill me with this gag in my mouth. God he could be killing me and not understand what I was saying.

Be ready. Have it all ready and don't say "Huh?" Tell him he can back out, no damage. I won't tell. Be passive as long as you can. If you can't be passive, wait until you can find his eyes.

The van stopped. The van rocked as he got out. Side door sliding open. Grass and hot tires on the air. Crickets. He came in the van.

In spite of herself she squealed into the gag and twisted her face away from him when he touched her.

Soft pats on the shoulder didn't stop her writhing. A stinging slap across the face did.

She tried to talk into the gag. She was lifted, carried. His footsteps hollow on the ramp. She was sure where she was now. His house. Where in his house? Clock ticking to the right. Rug, then floor. The bedroom where they did it. She was sinking in his arms, felt the bed under her.

She tried to talk into the gag. He was leaving. Noise outside. Van door slammed. Here he comes. Setting something on the floor— metal cans.

She smelled gasoline.

"Reba." D.'s voice all right, but so calm. So terribly calm and strange. "Reba, I don't know what to . . . say to you. You felt so good, and you don't know what I did for you. And I was wrong, Reba. You made me weak and then you hurt me."

She tried to talk into the gag.

"If I untie you and let you sit up, will you be good? Don't try to run. I can catch you. Will you be good?"

She twisted her head toward the voice to nod.

A touch of cold steel against her skin, whisper of a knife through cloth and her arms were free. Now her legs. Her cheeks were wet where the gag came off.

Carefully and slowly she sat up in the bed. Take your best shot.

"D.," she said, "I didn't know you cared this much about me. I'm glad you feel that way but, see, you scared me with this."

No answer. She knew he was there.

"D., was it old dumb Ralph Mandy that made you mad? Did you see him at my house? That's it, isn't it? I was telling him I don't want to see him anymore. Because I want to see you. I'm never going to see Ralph again."

"Ralph died," Dolarhyde said. "I don't think he liked it very much."

Fantasy. He's making it up Jesus do I hope. "I've never hurt you, D. I never wanted to. Let's just be friends and fuck and have a good time and forget about this."

"Shut up," he said calmly. "I'll tell you something. The most important thing you'll ever hear. Sermon-on-the-Mount important. Ten-Commandments important. Got it?"

"Yes, D. I—"

"Shut up. Reba, some remarkable events have happened in Birmingham and Atlanta. Do you know what I'm talking about?"

She shook her head.

"It's been on the news a lot. Two groups of people were changed. Leeds. And Jacobi. The police think they were murdered. Do you know now?"

She started to shake her head. Then she did know and slowly she nodded.

"Do you know what they call the Being that visited those people? You can say."

"The Tooth—"

A hand gripped her face, shutting off the sound.

"Think carefully and answer correctly."

"It's Dragon something. Dragon . . . Red Dragon."

He was close to her. She could feel his breath on her face.

"I AM THE DRAGON."

Leaping back, driven by the volume and terrible timbre of the voice, she slammed against the headboard.

"The Dragon wants you, Reba. He always has. I didn't want to give you to Him. I did a thing for you today so He couldn't have you. And I was wrong."

This was D., she could talk to D. "Please. Please don't let him have me. You won't, please don't, you wouldn't—I'm for *you*. Keep me with you. You like me, I know you do."

"I haven't made up my mind yet. Maybe I can't help giving you to Him. I don't know. I'm going to see if you do as I tell you. Will you? Can I depend on you?"

"I'll try. I will try. Don't scare me too much or I can't."

"Get up, Reba. Stand by the bed. Do you know where you are in the room?"

She nodded.

"You know where you are in the house, don't you? You wandered around in the house while I was asleep, didn't you?"

"Asleep?"

"Don't be stupid. When we spent the night here. You went through the house, didn't you? Did you find something odd? Did you take it and show it to somebody? Did you do that, Reba?"

"I just went outside. You were asleep and I went outside. I promise."

"Then you know where the front door is, don't you?"

She nodded.

"Reba, feel on my chest. Bring your hands up slowly."

Try for his eyes?

His thumb and fingers touched lightly on each side of her windpipe. "Don't do what you're thinking, or I'll squeeze. Just feel on my chest. Just at my throat. Feel the key on the chain? Take it off over my head. Careful . . . that's right. Now I'm going to see if I can trust you. Go close the front door and lock it and bring me back the key. Go ahead. I'll wait right here. Don't try to run. I can catch you."

She held the key in her hand, the chain tapping against her thigh. It was harder navigating in her shoes, but she kept them on. The ticking clock helped.

Rug, then floor, rug again. Loom of the sofa. Go to the right.

What's my best shot? Which? Fool along with him or go for it? Did the others fool along with him? She felt dizzy from deep breathing. Don't be dizzy. Don't be dead.

It depends on whether the door is open. Find out where he is.

"Am I going right?" She knew she was.

"It's about five more steps." The voice was from the bedroom all right.

She felt air on her face. The door was half-open. She kept her body between the door and the voice behind her. She slipped the key in the keyhole below the knob. On the outside.

Now. Through the door fast making herself pull it to and turn the key. Down the ramp, no cane, trying to remember where the van was, running. Running. Into what—a bush—screaming now. Screaming "Help me. Help me. Help me, help me." On gravel running. A truck horn far away. Highway that way, a fast walk and trot and run, fast as she could, veering when she felt grass instead of gravel, zigging down the lane.

Behind her footsteps coming fast and hard, running in the gravel. She stooped and picked up a handful of rocks, waited until he was close and flung them, heard them thump on him.

A shove on the shoulder spun her, a big arm under her chin, around her neck, squeezing, squeezing, blood roared in her ears. She kicked backward, hit a shin as it

became   increasingly   quiet.

CHAPTER 47

IN TWO HOURS, the list of white male employees twenty to fifty years old who owned vans was completed. There were twenty-six names on it.

Missouri DMV provided hair color from driver's-license information, but it was not used as an exclusionary factor; the Dragon might wear a wig.

Fisk's secretary, Miss Trillman, made copies of the list and passed them around.

Lieutenant Fogel was going down the list of names when his beeper went off.

Fogel spoke to his headquarters briefly on the telephone, then put his hand over the receiver. "Mr. Crawford . . . Jack, one Ralph Mandy, white male, thirty-eight, was found shot to death a few minutes ago in University City—that's in the middle of town, close to Washington University—he was in the front yard of a house occupied by a woman named Reba McClane. The neighbors said she works for Baeder. Her door's unlocked, she's not home."

"Dandridge!" Crawford called. "Reba McClane, what about her?"

"She works in the darkroom. She's blind. She's from someplace in Colorado—"

"You know a Ralph Mandy?"

"Mandy?" Dandridge said. "Randy Mandy?"

"*Ralph* Mandy, he work here?"

A check of the roll showed he didn't.

"Coincidence maybe," Fogel said.

"Maybe," Crawford said.

"I hope nothing's happened to Reba," Miss Trillman said.

"You know her?" Graham said.

"I've talked with her several times."

"What about Mandy?"

"I don't know him. The only man I've seen her with, I saw her getting into Mr. Dolarhyde's van."

"Mr. Dolarhyde's van, Miss Trillman? What color is Mr. Dolarhyde's van?"

"Let's see. Dark brown, or maybe black."

"Where does Mr. Dolarhyde work?" Crawford asked.

"He's production supervisor," Fisk said.

"Where's his office?"

"Right down the hall."

Crawford turned to speak to Graham, but he was already moving.

Mr. Dolarhyde's office was locked. A passkey from Maintenance worked.

Graham reached in and flipped on the light. He stood still in the doorway while his eyes went over the room. It was extremely neat. No personal items were anywhere in sight. The bookshelf held only technical manuals.

The desk lamp was on the left side of the chair, so he was right-handed. Need a left thumbprint fast off a right-handed man.

"Let's toss it for a clipboard," he said to Crawford, behind him in the hall. "He'll use his left thumb on the clip."

They had started on the drawers when the desk appointment calendar caught Graham's eye. He flipped back through the scribbled pages to Saturday, June 28, the date of the Jacobi killings.

The calendar was unmarked on the Thursday and Friday before that weekend.

He flipped forward to the last week in July. The Thursday and Friday were blank. There was a note on Wednesday. It said: "Am 552 3:45–6:15."

Graham copied the entry. "I want to find out where this flight goes."

"Let me do it, you go ahead here," Crawford said. He went to a telephone across the hall.

Graham was looking at a tube of denture adhesive in the bottom desk drawer when Crawford called from the door.

"It goes to Atlanta, Will. Let's take him out."

CHAPTER 48

WATER COLD on Reba's face, running in her hair. Dizzy. Something hard under her, sloping. She turned her head. Wood under her. A cold wet towel wiped her face.

"Are you all right, Reba?" Dolarhyde's calm voice.

She shied from the sound. "Uhhhh."

"Breathe deeply."

A minute passed.

"Do you think you can stand up? Try to stand up."

She could stand with his arm around her. Her stomach heaved. He waited until the spasm passed.

"Up the ramp. Do you remember where you are?"

She nodded.

"Take the key out of the door, Reba. Come inside. Now lock it and put the key around my neck. Hang it around my neck. Good. Let's just be sure it's locked."

She heard the knob rattle.

"That's good. Now go in the bedroom, you know the way."

She stumbled and went down on her knees, her head bowed. He lifted her by the arms and supported her into the bedroom.

"Sit in this chair."

She sat.

"GIVE HER TO ME NOW."

She struggled to rise; big hands on her shoulders held her down.

"Sit still or I can't keep Him off you," Dolarhyde said.

Her mind was coming back. It didn't want to.

"Please try," she said.

"Reba, it's all over for me."

He was up, doing something. The odor of gasoline was very strong.

"Put out your hand. Feel this. Don't grab it, feel it."

She felt something like steel nostrils, slick inside. The muzzle of a gun.

"That's a shotgun, Reba. A twelve-gauge magnum. Do you know what it will do?"

She nodded.

"Take your hand down." The cold muzzle rested in the hollow of her throat.

"Reba, I wish I could have trusted you. I wanted to trust you."

He sounded like he was crying.

"You felt so good."

He *was* crying.

"So did you, D. I love it. Please don't hurt me now."

"It's all over for me. I can't leave you to Him. You know what He'll do?"

Bawling now.

"Do you know what He'll do? He'll bite you to death. Better you go with me."

She heard a match struck, smelled sulfur, heard a whoosh. Heat in the room. Smoke. Fire. The thing she feared most in the world. Fire. Anything was better than that. She hoped the first shot killed her. She tensed her legs to run.

Blubbering.

"Oh, Reba, I can't stand to watch you burn."

The muzzle left her throat.

Both barrels of the shotgun went off at once as she came to her feet.

Ears numbed, she thought she was shot, thought she was dead, felt the heavy thump on the floor more than she heard it.

Smoke now and the crackle of flames. Fire. Fire brought her to herself. She felt heat on her arms and face. Out. She stepped on legs, stumbled choking into the foot of the bed.

Stoop low, they said, under the smoke. Don't run, you'll bump into things and die.

She was locked in. Locked in. Walking, stooping low, fingers trailing on the floor, she found legs—other end—she found hair, a hairy flap, put her hand in something soft below the hair. Only pulp, sharp bone splinters and a loose eye in it.

Key around his neck . . . hurry. Both hands on the chain, legs under her, snatch. The chain broke and she fell backward, scrambling up again. Turned around, confused. Trying to feel, trying to listen with her numbed ears over the crackle of the flames. Side of the bed . . . which side? She stumbled on the body, tried to listen.

BONG, BONG, the clock striking. BONG, BONG, into the living room, BONG, BONG, take a right.

Throat seared with smoke. BONG BONG. Door here. Under the knob. Don't drop it. Click the lock. Snatch it open. Air. Down the ramp. Air. Collapsed in the grass. Up again on hands and knees, crawling.

She came up on her knees to clap, picked up the house echo and crawled away from it, breathing deep until she could stand, walk, run until she hit something, run again.

CHAPTER 49

LOCATING FRANCIS DOLARHYDE'S HOUSE was not so easy. The address listed at Gateway was a post-office box in St. Charles.

Even the St. Charles sheriff's department had to check a service map at the power-company office to be sure.

The sheriff's department welcomed St. Louis SWAT to the other side of the river, and the caravan moved quietly up State Highway 94. A deputy beside Graham in the lead car showed the way. Crawford leaned between them from the back seat and sucked at something in his teeth. They met light traffic at the north end of St. Charles, a pickup full of children, a Greyhound bus, a tow truck.

They saw the glow as they cleared the northern city limits.

"That's *it!*" the deputy said. "That's where it is!"

Graham put his foot down. The glow brightened and swelled as they roared up the highway.

Crawford snapped his fingers for the microphone.

"All units, that's his house burning. Watch it now. He may be coming out. Sheriff, let us have a roadblock here, if you will."

A thick column of sparks and smoke leaned southeast over the fields, hanging over them now.

"Here," the deputy said, "turn in on this gravel."

They saw the woman then, silhouetted black against the fire, saw her as she heard them and raised her arms to them.

And then the great fire blasted upward, outward, burning beams and window frames describing slow high arcs into the night sky, the blazing van rocked over on its side, orange tracery of the burning trees suddenly blown out and dark. The ground shuddered as the explosion whump rocked the police cars.

The woman was face down in the road. Crawford and Graham and the deputies out, running to her as fire rained in the road, some running past her with their weapons drawn.

Crawford took Reba from a deputy batting sparks from her hair.

He held her arms, face close to hers, red in the firelight.

"Francis Dolarhyde," he said. He shook her gently. "Francis Dolarhyde, where is he?"

"He's in there," she said, raising her stained hand toward the heat, letting it fall. "He's dead in there."

"You *know* that?" Crawford peered into her sightless eyes.

"I was with him."

"Tell me, please."

"He shot himself in the face. I put my hand in it. He set fire to the house. He shot himself. I put my hand in it. He was on the floor. I put my hand in it can I sit down?"

"Yes," Crawford said. He got into the back of a police car with her. He put his arms around her and let her cry into his jowl.

Graham stood in the road and watched the flames until his face was red and sore.

The winds aloft whipped smoke across the moon.

CHAPTER 50

THE WIND IN THE MORNING was warm and wet. It blew wisps of cloud over the blackened chimneys where Dolarhyde's house had stood. Thin smoke blew flat across the fields.

A few raindrops struck coals and exploded in tiny puffs of steam and ashes.

A fire truck stood by, its light revolving.

S. F. Aynesworth, FBI section chief, Explosives, stood with Graham upwind of the ruins, pouring coffee from a thermos.

Aynesworth winced as the local fire marshal reached into the ashes with a rake.

"Thank God it's still too hot for him in there," he said out of the side of his mouth. He had been carefully cordial to the local authorities. To Graham, he spoke his mind. "I got to wade it, hell. This place'll look like a fucking turkey farm soon as all the special deputies and constables finish their pancakes and take a crap. They'll be right on down to help."

Until Aynesworth's beloved bomb van arrived from Washington, he had to make do with what he could bring on the plane. He pulled a faded Marine Corps duffel bag out of the trunk of a patrol car and unpacked his Nomex underwear and asbestos boots and coveralls.

"What did it look like when it went up, Will?"

"A flash of intense light that died down. Then it looked darker at the base. A lot of stuff was going up, window frames, flat pieces of the roof, and chunks flying sideways, tumbling in the fields. There was a shock wave, and the wind after. It blew out and sucked back in again. It looked like it almost blew the fire out."

"The fire was going good when it blew?"

"Yeah, it was through the roof and out the windows upstairs and down. The trees were burning."

Aynesworth recruited two local firemen to stand by with a hose, and a third dressed in asbestos stood by with a winch line in case something fell on him.

He cleared the basement steps, now open to the sky, and went down into the tangle of black timbers. He could stay only a few minutes at a time. He made eight trips.

All he got for his effort was one flat piece of torn metal, but it seemed to make him happy.

Red-faced and wet with sweat, he stripped off his asbestos clothing and sat on the running board of the fire truck with a fireman's raincoat over his shoulders.

He laid the flat piece of metal on the ground and blew away a film of ash.

"Dynamite," he told Graham. "Look here, see the fern pattern in the metal? This stuff's the right gauge for a trunk or a footlocker. That's probably it. Dynamite in a footlocker. It didn't go off in the basement, though. Looks like the ground floor to me. See where the tree's cut there where that marble tabletop hit it? Blown out sideways. The dynamite was in something that kept the fire off of it for a while."

"How about remains?"

"There may not be a lot, but there's always something. We've got a lot of sifting to do. We'll find him. I'll give him to you in a small sack."

➤

A sedative had finally put Reba McClane to sleep at DePaul Hospital shortly after dawn. She wanted the policewoman to sit close beside her bed. Several times through the morning she woke and reached out for the officer's hand.

When she asked for breakfast, Graham brought it in.

Which way to go? Sometimes it was easier for them if you were impersonal. With Reba McClane, he didn't think so.

He told her who he was.

"Do you know him?" she asked the policewoman.

Graham passed the officer his credentials. She didn't need them.

"I know he's a federal officer, Miss McClane."

She told him everything, finally. All about her time with Francis Dolarhyde. Her throat was sore, and she stopped frequently to suck cracked ice.

He asked her the unpleasant questions and she took him through it, once waving him out the door while the policewoman held the basin to catch her breakfast.

She was pale and her face was scrubbed and shiny when he came back into the room.

He asked the last of it and closed his notebook.

"I won't put you through this again," he said, "but I'd like to come back by. Just to say hi and see how you're doing."

"How could you help it?—a charmer like me."

For the first time he saw tears and realized where it ate her.

"Would you excuse us for a minute, officer?" Graham said. He took Reba's hand.

"Look here. There was plenty wrong with Dolarhyde, but there's nothing wrong with you. You said he was kind and thoughtful to you. I believe it. That's what you brought out in him. At the end, he couldn't kill you and he couldn't watch you die. People who study this kind of thing say he was trying to stop. Why? Because you helped him. That probably saved some lives. You didn't draw a freak. You drew a man with a freak on his back. Nothing wrong with you, kid. If you let yourself believe there is, you're a sap. I'm coming back to see you in a day or so. I have to look at cops all the time, and I need relief—try to do something about your hair there."

She shook her head and waved him toward the door. Maybe she grinned a little, he couldn't be sure.

➤

Graham called Molly from the St. Louis FBI office. Willy's grandfather answered the telephone.

"It's Will Graham, Mama," he said. "Hello, Mr. Graham."

Willy's grandparents always called him "Mr. Graham."

"Mama said he killed himself. She was looking at Donahue and they broke in with it. Damn lucky thing. Saved you fellows a lot of trouble catching him. Saves us taxpayers footing any more bills for this thing too. Was he really white?"

"Yes sir. Blond. Looked Scandinavian."

Willy's grandparents were Scandinavian.

"May I speak to Molly, please?"

"Are you going back down to Florida now?"

"Soon. Is Molly there?"

"Mama, he wants to speak to Molly. She's in the bathroom, Mr. Graham. My grandboy's eating breakfast again. Been out riding in that good air. You ought to see that little booger eat. I bet he's gained ten pounds. Here she is."

"Hello."

"Hi, hotshot."

"Good news, huh?"

"Looks like it."

"I was out in the garden. Mamamma came out and told me when she saw it on TV. When did you find out?"

"Late last night."

"Why didn't you call me?"

"Mamamma was probably asleep."

"No, she was watching Johnny Carson. I can't tell you, Will. I'm so glad you didn't have to catch him."

"I'll be here a little longer."

"Four or five days?"

"I'm not sure. Maybe not that long. I want to see you, kid."

"I want to see you too, when you get through with everything you need to do."

"Today's Wednesday. By Friday I ought to—"

"Will, Mamamma has all Willy's uncles and aunts coming down from Seattle next week, and—"

"Fuck Mamamma. What is this 'Mamamma' anyway?"

"When Willy was real little, he couldn't say—"

"Come home with me."

"Will, *I've* waited for *you*. They never get to see Willy and a few more days—"

"Come yourself. Leave Willy there, and your ex-mother-in-law can stick him on a plane next week. Tell you what—let's stop in New Orleans. There's a place called—"

"I don't think so. I've been working—just part-time—at this western store in town, and I have to give them a little notice."

"What's wrong, Molly?"

"Nothing. Nothing's wrong. . . . I got so sad, Will. You know I came up here after Willy's father died." She always said "Willy's father" as though it were an office. She never used his name. "And we were all together—I got myself together, I got calm. I've gotten myself together now, too, and I—"

"Small difference: I'm not dead."

"Don't be that way."

"What way? Don't be what way?"

"You're mad."

Graham closed his eyes for a moment.

"Hello."

"I'm not mad, Molly. You do what you want to. I'll call you when things wind up here."

"You could come up here."

"I don't think so."

"Why not? There's plenty of room. Mamamma would—"

"Molly, they don't like me and you know why. Every time they look at me, I remind them."

"That's not fair and it's not true either."

Graham was very tired.

"Okay. They're full of shit and they make me sick—try that one."

"Don't say that."

"They want the boy. Maybe they like you all right, probably they do, if they ever think about it. But they want the boy and they'll take you. They don't want me and I could care less. *I* want *you*. In Florida. Willy too, when he gets tired of his pony."

"You'll feel better when you get some sleep."

"I doubt it. Look, I'll call you when I know something here."

"Sure." She hung up.

"*Ape* shit," Graham said. "*Ape* shit."

Crawford stuck his head in the door. "Did I hear you say 'ape shit'?"

"You did."

"Well, cheer up. Aynesworth called in from the site. He has something for you. He said we ought to come on out, he's got some static from the locals."

CHAPTER 51

AYNESWORTH was pouring ashes carefully into new paint cans when Graham and Crawford got to the black ruin where Dolarhyde's house had stood.

He was covered with soot and a large blister puffed under his ear. Special Agent Janowitz from Explosives was working down in the cellar.

A tall sack of a man fidgeted beside a dusty Oldsmobile in the drive. He intercepted Crawford and Graham as they crossed the yard.

"Are you Crawford?"

"That's right."

"I'm Robert L. Dulaney. I'm the coroner and this is my jurisdiction." He showed them his card. It said "Vote for Robert L. Dulaney."

Crawford waited.

"Your man here has some evidence that should have been turned over to me. He's kept me waiting for nearly an hour."

"Sorry for the inconvenience, Mr. Dulaney. He was following my instructions. Why don't you have a seat in your car and I'll clear this up."

Dulaney started after them.

Crawford turned around. "You'll excuse us, Mr. Dulaney. Have a seat in your car."

Section Chief Aynesworth was grinning, his teeth white in his sooty face. He had been sieving ashes all morning.

"As section chief, it gives me great pleasure—"

"To pull your prong, we all know that," Janowitz said, climbing from the black tangle of the cellar.

"Silence in the ranks, Indian Janowitz. Fetch the items of interest." He tossed Janowitz a set of car keys.

From the trunk of an FBI sedan Janowitz brought a long cardboard box. A shotgun, the stock burned off and barrels twisted by the heat, was wired to the bottom of the box. A smaller box contained a blackened automatic pistol.

"The pistol came out better," Aynesworth said. "Ballistics may be able to make a match with it. Come on, Janowitz, get to it."

Aynesworth took three plastic freezer bags from him.

"Front and center, Graham." For a moment the humor left Aynesworth's face. This was a hunter's ritual, like smearing Graham's forehead with blood.

"That was a real sly show, podna." Aynesworth put the bags in Graham's hands.

One bag contained five inches of a charred human femur and the ball of a hip. Another contained a wristwatch. The third held the teeth.

The plate was black and broken and only half was there, but that half contained the unmistakable pegged lateral incisor.

Graham supposed he should say something. "Thanks. Thanks a lot."

His head swam briefly and he relaxed all over.

". . . museum piece," Aynesworth was saying. "We have to turn it over to the turkey, don't we, Jack?"

"Yeah. But there're some pros in the St. Louis coroner's office. They'll come over and make good impressions. We'll have those."

Crawford and the others huddled with the coroner beside his car.

Graham was alone with the house. He listened to the wind in the chimneys. He hoped Bloom would come here when he was well. Probably he would.

Graham wanted to know about Dolarhyde. He wanted to know

what happened here, what bred the Dragon. But he had had enough for now.

A mockingbird lit on the top of a chimney and whistled.

Graham whistled back.

He was going home.

CHAPTER 52

GRAHAM smiled when he felt the jet's big push rocket him up and away from St. Louis, turning across the sun's path south and east at last toward home.

Molly and Willy would be there.

"Let's don't jack around about who's sorry for what. I'll pick you up in Marathon, kiddo," she said on the phone.

In time he hoped he would remember the few good moments—the satisfaction of seeing people at work who were deeply committed to their skills. He supposed you could find that anywhere if you knew enough about what you were watching.

It would have been presumptuous to thank Lloyd Bowman and Beverly Katz, so he just told them on the telephone that he was glad to have worked with them again.

One thing bothered him a little: the way he felt when Crawford turned from the telephone in Chicago and said, "It's Gateway."

Possibly that was the most intense and savage joy that had ever burst in him. It was unsettling to know that the happiest moment of his life had come then, in that stuffy jury room in the city of Chicago. *When even before he knew, he knew.*

He didn't tell Lloyd Bowman how it felt; he didn't have to.

"You know, when his theorem rang the cherries, Pythagoras gave one hundred oxen to the Muse," Bowman said. "Nothing sweeter, is there? Don't answer—it lasts better if you don't spend it talking."

Graham grew more impatient the closer he got to home and to Molly. In Miami he had to go out on the apron to board *Aunt Lula*, the old DC-3 that flew to Marathon.

He liked DC-3's. He liked everything today.

Aunt Lula was built when Graham was five years old and her wings were always dirty with a film of oil that blew back from the engines. He had great confidence in her. He ran to her as though she had landed in a jungle clearing to rescue him.

Islamorada's lights were coming on as the island passed under the wing. Graham could still see whitecaps on the Atlantic side. In minutes they were descending to Marathon.

It was like the first time he came to Marathon. He had come aboard *Aunt Lula* that time too, and often afterward he went to the airfield at dusk to watch her coming in, slow and steady, flaps down, fire flickering out her exhausts and all the passengers safe behind their lighted windows.

The takeoffs were good to watch as well, but when the old airplane made her great arc to the north it left him sad and empty and the air was acrid with good-byes. He learned to watch only the landings and hellos.

That was before Molly.

With a final grunt, the airplane swung onto the apron. Graham saw Molly and Willy standing behind the fence, under the floodlights.

Willy was solidly planted in front of her. He'd stay there until Graham joined them. Only then would he wander along, examining whatever interested him. Graham liked him for that.

Molly was the same height as Graham, five feet ten inches. A level kiss in public carries a pleasant jolt, possibly because level kisses usually are exchanged in bed.

Willy offered to carry his suitcase. Graham gave him the suit bag instead.

Riding home to Sugarloaf Key, Molly driving, Graham remembered the things picked out by the headlights, imagined the rest.

When he opened the car door in the yard, he could hear the sea.

Willy went into the house, holding the suit bag on top of his head, the bottom flapping against the backs of his legs.

Graham stood in the yard absently brushing mosquitoes away from his face.

Molly put her hand on his cheek. "What you ought to do is come on in the house before you get eaten up."

He nodded. His eyes were wet.

She waited a moment longer, tucked her head and peered up at him, wiggling her eyebrows. "Tanqueray martinis, steaks, hugging and stuff. Right this way . . . and the light bill and the water bill and lengthy conversations with my child," she added out of the side of her mouth.

CHAPTER 53

GRAHAM AND MOLLY wanted very much for it to be the same again between them, to go on as they had before.

When they saw that it was not the same, the unspoken knowledge lived with them like unwanted company in thc house. The mutual assurances they tried to exchange in the dark and in the day passcd through some refraction that made them miss the mark.

Molly had never looked better to him. From a painful distance, he admired her unconscious grace.

She tried to be good to him, but she had been to Oregon and she had raised the dead.

Willy felt it and he was cool to Graham, maddeningly polite.

A letter came from Crawford. Molly brought it in the mail and did not mention it.

It contained a picture of the Sherman family, printed from movie film. Not everything had burned, Crawford's note explained. A search of the fields around the house had turned this picture up, along with a few other things the explosion had blown far from the fire.

"These people were probably on his itinerary," Crawford wrote. "Safe now. Thought you'd like to know."

Graham showed it to Molly.

"See? That's why," he said. "That's why it was worth it."

"I know," she said. "I understand that, really I do."

The bluefish were running under the moon. Molly packed suppers and they fished and they built fires, and none of it was any good.

Grandpa and Mamamma sent Willy a picture of his pony and he tacked it to the wall in his room.

The fifth day home was the last day before Graham and Molly would go back to work in Marathon. They fished in the surf, walking a quarter-mile around the curving beach to a place where they had luck before.

Graham had decided to talk to both of them together.

The expedition did not begin well. Willy pointedly put aside the rod Graham had rigged for him and brought the new surf-casting rod his grandfather sent home with him.

They fished for three hours in silence. Graham opened his mouth to speak several times, but it didn't seem right.

He was tired of being disliked.

Graham caught four snappers, using sand fleas for bait. Willy caught nothing. He was casting a big Rapala with three treble hooks which his grandfather had given him. He was fishing too fast, casting again and again, retrieving too fast, until he was red-faced and his T-shirt stuck to him.

Graham waded into the water, scooped sand in the backwash of a wave, and came up with two sand fleas, their legs waving from their shells.

"How about one of these, partner?" He held out a sand flea to Willy.

"I'll use the Rapala. It was my father's, did you know that?"

"No," Graham said. He glanced at Molly.

She hugged her knees and looked far off at a frigate bird sailing high.

She got up and brushed off the sand. "I'll go fix some sandwiches," she said.

When Molly had gone, Graham was tempted to talk to the boy by himself. No. Willy would feel whatever his mother felt. He'd wait and get them both together when she came back. He'd do it this time.

She wasn't gone long and she came back without the sandwiches, walking swiftly on the packed sand above the surf.

"Jack Crawford's on the phone. I told him you'd call him back, but he said it's urgent," she said, examining a fingernail. "Better hurry."

Graham blushed. He stuck the butt of his rod in the sand and trotted toward the dunes. It was quicker than going around the beach if you carried nothing to catch in the brush.

He heard a low whirring sound carried on the wind and, wary of a rattler, he scanned the ground as he went into the scrub cedar.

He saw boots beneath the brush, the glint of a lens and a flash of khaki rising.

He looked into the yellow eyes of Francis Dolarhyde and fear raised the hammers of his heart.

Snick of a pistol action working, an automatic coming up and Graham kicked at it, struck it as the muzzle bloomed pale yellow in the sun, and the pistol flew into the brush. Graham on his back, something burning in the left side of his chest, slid headfirst down the dune onto the beach.

Dolarhyde leaped high to land on Graham's stomach with both feet and he had the knife out now and never looked up at the thin screaming from the water's edge. He pinned Graham with his knees, raised the knife high and grunted as he brought it down. The blade missed Graham's eye and crunched deep into his cheek.

Dolarhyde rocked forward and put his weight on the handle of the knife to shove it through Graham's head.

The rod whistled as Molly swung it hard at Dolarhyde's face. The big Rapala's hooks sank solidly in his cheek and the reel screamed, paying out line as she drew back to strike again.

He growled, grabbed at his face as she hit him, and the treble hooks jammed into his hand as well. One hand free, one hand hooked to his face, he tugged the knife out and started after her.

Graham rolled over, got to his knees, then his feet, eyes wild and choking blood he ran, ran from Dolarhyde, ran until he collapsed.

Molly ran for the dunes, Willy ahead of her. Dolarhyde was coming, dragging the rod. It caught on a bush and pulled him howling to a stop before he thought to cut the line.

"Run baby, run baby, run baby! Don't look back," she gasped. Her legs were long and she shoved the boy ahead of her, the crashing ever closer in the brush behind them.

They had one hundred yards on him when they left the dunes, seventy yards when they reached the house. Scrambling up the stairs. Clawing in Will's closet.

To Willy, "Stay here."

Down again to meet him. Down to the kitchen, not ready, fumbling with the speedloader.

She forgot the stance and she forgot the front sight but she got a good two-handed grip on the pistol and as the door exploded inward she blew a rat hole through his thigh—"Muhner!"—and she shot him in the face as he slid down the door facing and she shot him in the face as he sat on the floor and she ran to him and shot him twice in the face as he sprawled against the wall, scalp down to his chin and his hair on fire.

➤

Willy tore up a sheet and went to look for Will. His legs were shaking and he fell several times crossing the yard.

The sheriff's deputies and ambulances came before Molly ever thought to call them. She was taking a shower when they came in the house behind their pistols. She was scrubbing hard at the flecks of blood and bone on her face and hair and she couldn't answer when a deputy tried to talk to her through the shower curtain.

One of the deputies finally picked up the dangling telephone receiver and talked to Crawford in Washington, who had heard the shots and summoned them.

"I don't know, they're bringing him in now," the deputy said. He looked out the window as the litter passed. "It don't look good to me," he said.

CHAPTER 54

ON THE WALL at the foot of the bed there was a clock with numbers large enough to read through the drugs and the pain.

When Will Graham could open his right eye, he saw the clock and knew where he was—an intensive-care unit. He knew to watch the clock. Its movement assured him that this was passing, would pass.

That's what it was there for.

It said four o'clock. He had no idea which four o'clock and he didn't care, as long as the hands were moving. He drifted away.

The clock said eight when he opened his eye again.

Someone was to the side of him. Cautiously he turned his eye. It was Molly, looking out the window. She was thin. He tried to speak, but a great ache filled the left side of his head when he moved his jaw. His head and his chest did not throb together. It was more of a syncopation. He made a noise as she left the room.

The window was light when they pulled and tugged at him and did things that made the cords in his neck stand out.

Yellow light when he saw Crawford's face over him.

Graham managed to wink. When Crawford grinned, Graham could see a piece of spinach between his teeth.

Odd. Crawford eschewed most vegetables.

Graham made writing motions on the sheet beneath his hand.

Crawford slid his notebook under Graham's hand and put a pen between his fingers.

"Willy OK," he wrote.

"Yeah, he's fine," Crawford said. "Molly too. She's been in here while you were asleep. Dolarhyde's dead, Will. I promise you, he's dead. I took the prints myself and had Price match them. There's no question. He's dead."

Graham drew a question mark on the pad.

"We'll get into it. I'll be here, I can tell you the whole thing when you feel good. They only give me five minutes."

"Now," Graham wrote.

"Has the doctor talked to you? No? About you first—you'll be okay. Your eye's just swollen shut from a deep stab wound in the face. They've got it fixed, but it'll take time. They took out your spleen. But who needs a spleen? Price left his in Burma in '41."

A nurse pecked on the glass.

"I've got to go. They don't respect credentials, nothing, around here. They just throw you out when the time's up. See you later."

Molly was in the ICU waiting room. A lot of tired people were.

Crawford went to her. "Molly . . ."

"Hello, Jack," she said. "*You're* looking really well. Want to give him a face transplant?"

"Don't, Molly."

"Did you look at him?"

"Yes."

"I didn't think I could look at him, but I did."

"They'll fix him up. The doctor told me. They can do it. You want somebody to stay with you, Molly? I brought Phyllis down, she—"

"No. Don't do anything else for me."

She turned away, fumbling for a tissue. He saw the letter when she opened her purse: expensive mauve stationery that he had seen before.

Crawford hated this. He had to do it.

"Molly."

"What is it?"

"Will got a letter?"

"Yes."

"Did the nurse give it to you?"

"Yes, she *gave* it to me. They're holding some flowers from all his *friends* in Washington, too."

"May I see the letter?"

"I'll give it to him when he feels like it."

"Please let me see it."

"Why?"

"Because he doesn't need to hear from . . . that particular person."

Something was wrong with the expression on his face and she looked down at the letter and dropped it, purse and all. A lipstick rolled across the floor.

Stooping to pick up Molly's things, Crawford heard her heels tap fast as she left him, abandoning her purse.

He gave the purse to the charge nurse.

Crawford knew it would be nearly impossible for Lecter to get what he would need, but with Lecter he took no chances.

He had an intern fluoroscope the letter in the X-ray department. Crawford slit the envelope on all sides with a penknife and examined its inside surface and the note for any stain or dust—they would have lye for scrubbing at Chesapeake Hospital, and there was a pharmacy.

Satisfied at last, he read it:

Dear Will,

Here we are, you and I, languishing in our hospitals. You have your pain and I am without my books—the learned Dr. Chilton has seen to that.

We live in a primitive time—don't we, Will?—neither savage nor wise. Half measures are the curse of it. Any rational society would either kill me or give me my books.

I wish you a speedy convalescence and hope you won't be very ugly.

I think of you often.

Hannibal Lecter

The intern looked at his watch, "Do you need me anymore?"

"No," Crawford said. "Where's the incinerator?"

When Crawford returned in four hours for the next visiting period, Molly wasn't in the waiting room and she wasn't in the intensive-care unit.

Graham was awake. He drew a question mark on the pad at once. "D. dead how?" he wrote under it.

Crawford told him. Graham lay still for a full minute. Then he wrote, "Lammed how?"

"Okay," Crawford said. "St. Louis. Dolarhyde must have been looking for Reba McClane. He came in the lab while we were there and spotted us. His prints were on an open furnace-room window—it wasn't reported until yesterday."

Graham tapped the pad. "Body?"

"We think it was a guy named Arnold Lang—he's missing. His car was found in Memphis. It had been wiped down. They'll run me out in a minute. Let me give it to you in order.

"Dolarhyde knew we were there. He gave us the slip at the plant and drove to a Servco Supreme station at Lindbergh and U.S. 270. Arnold Lang worked there.

"Reba McClane said Dolarhyde had a tiff with a service-station attendant on Saturday before last. We think it was Lang.

"He snuffed Lang and took his body to the house. Then he went by Reba McClane's. She was in a clinch with Ralph Mandy at the door. He shot Mandy and dragged him into the hedge."

The nurse came in.

"For God's sake, it's police business," Crawford said. He talked fast as she pulled him by the coat sleeve to the door. "He chloroformed Reba McClane and took her to the house. The body was there," Crawford said from the hall.

Graham had to wait four hours to find out the rest.

"He gave her this and that, you know, 'Will I kill you or not?'" Crawford said as he came in the door.

"You know the routine about the key hanging around his neck—that was to make sure she felt the body. So she could tell *us* she certainly did feel a body. All right, it's this way and that way. 'I can't stand to see you burn,' he says, and blows Lang's head off with a twelve-gauge.

"Lang was perfect. He didn't have any teeth anyway. Maybe Dolarhyde knew the maxillary arch survives fires a lot of times—who knows what he knew? Anyway, Lang didn't have any maxillary arch after Dolarhyde got through with him. He shot the head off Lang's body and he must have tipped a chair or something for the thud of the body falling. He'd hung the key around Lang's neck.

"Now Reba's scrambling around looking for the key. Dolarhyde's in the corner watching. Her ears are ringing from the shotgun. She won't hear his little noises.

"He's started a fire, but he hasn't put the gas to it yet. He's got gas in the room. She got out of the house okay. If she had panicked too much, run into a wall or something or frozen, I guess he'd have sapped her and dragged her outside. She wouldn't have known how she got out. But she had to get out for it to work. Oh hell, here comes that nurse."

Graham wrote fast. "How vehicle?"

"You have to admire this," Crawford said. "He knew he'd have to leave his van at the house. He couldn't drive two vehicles out there, and he needed a getaway piece.

"This is what he did: he made *Lang* hook up the service-station tow truck to his van. He snuffed Lang, locked the station, and towed his van out to his house. Then he left the tow truck on a dirt road back in the fields behind the house, got back in his van and went after Reba. When she got out of the house all right, he dragged out his dynamite, put the gasoline around the fire, and lammed out the back. He drove the tow truck *back* to the service station, left it and got Lang's car. No loose ends.

"It drove me crazy until we figured it out. I know it's right because he left a couple of prints on the tow bar.

"We probably met him in the road when we were going up there to the house . . . Yes, ma'am. I'm coming. Yes, ma'am."

Graham wanted to ask a question, but it was too late.

Molly took the next five-minute visit.

Graham wrote "I love you" on Crawford's pad.

She nodded and held his hand.

A minute later he wrote again. "Willy okay?"

She nodded.

"Here?"

She looked up at him too quickly from the pad. She made a kiss with her mouth and pointed to the approaching nurse.

He tugged her thumb.

"*Where?*" he insisted, underlining twice.

"Oregon," she said.

Crawford came a final time.

Graham was ready with his note. It said, "Teeth?"

"His grandmother's," Crawford said. "The ones we found in the house were his grandmother's. St. Louis PD located one Ned Vogt—Dolarhyde's mother was Vogt's stepmother. Vogt saw Mrs. Dolarhyde when he was a kid, and he never forgot the teeth.

"That's what I was calling you about when you ran into Dolarhyde. The Smithsonian had just called me. They finally had gotten the teeth from the Missouri authorities, just to examine for their own satisfaction. They noticed the upper part was made of vulcanite instead of acrylic like they use now. Nobody's made vulcanite plates in thirty-five years.

"Dolarhyde had a new acrylic pair just like them made to fit him. The new ones were on his body. Smithsonian looked at some features on them—the fluting, they said, and rugae. Chinese manufacture. The old ones were Swiss.

"He had a key on him too, for a locker in Miami. Big book in there. Kind of a diary—hell of a thing. I'll have it when you want to see it.

"Look, sport, I have to go back to Washington. I'll get back down here the weekend, if I can. You gonna be okay?"

Graham drew a question mark, then scratched it out and wrote "sure."

The nurse came after Crawford left. She shot some Demerol into his intravenous line and the clock grew fuzzy. He couldn't keep up with the second hand.

He wondered if Demerol would work on your feelings. He could hold Molly a while with his face. Until they finished fixing it anyway. That would be a cheap shot. Hold her for what? He was drifting off and he hoped he wouldn't dream.

He did drift between memory and dream, but it wasn't so bad. He didn't dream of Molly leaving, or of Dolarhyde. It was a long memory-dream of Shiloh, interrupted by lights shone in his face and the gasp and hiss of the blood-pressure cuff. . . .

It was spring, soon after he shot Garrett Jacob Hobbs, when Graham visited Shiloh.

On a soft April day he walked across the asphalt road to Bloody Pond. The new grass, still light green, grew down the slope to the water. The clear water had risen into the grass, and the grass was visible in the water, growing down, down, as though it covered the bottom of the pond.

Graham knew what had happened there in April 1862.

He sat down in the grass, felt the damp ground through his trousers.

A tourist's automobile went by and after it had passed, Graham saw movement behind it in the road. The car had broken a chicken snake's back. It slid in endless figure eights across itself in the center of the asphalt road, sometimes showing its black back, sometimes its pale belly.

Shiloh's awesome presence hooded him with cold, though he was sweating in the mild spring sun.

Graham got up off the grass, his trousers damp behind. He was light-headed.

The snake looped on itself. He stood over it, picked it up by the end of its smooth dry tail, and with a long fluid motion cracked it like a whip.

Its brains zinged into the pond. A bream rose to them.

He had thought Shiloh haunted, its beauty sinister like flags.

Now, drifting between memory and narcotic sleep, he saw that Shiloh was not sinister; it was indifferent. Beautiful Shiloh could witness anything. Its unforgivable beauty simply underscored the indifference of nature, the Green Machine. The loveliness of Shiloh mocked our plight.

He roused and watched the mindless clock, but he couldn't stop thinking:

In the Green Machine there is no mercy; we make mercy, manufacture it in the parts that have overgrown our basic reptile brain.

There is no murder. We make murder, and it matters only to us.

Graham knew too well that he contained all the elements to make murder; perhaps mercy too.

He understood murder uncomfortably well, though.

He wondered if, in the great body of humankind, in the minds of men set on civilization, the vicious urges we control in ourselves and the dark instinctive knowledge of those urges function like the crippled virus the body arms against.

He wondered if old, awful urges are the virus that makes vaccine.

Yes, he had been wrong about Shiloh. Shiloh isn't haunted—men are haunted.

Shiloh doesn't care.

And I gave my heart to know wisdom, and to know madness and folly: I perceived that this also is vexation of spirit.

—ECCLESIASTES